Interpreting European History

THE DORSEY SERIES IN EUROPEAN HISTORY

EDITOR THEODORE S. HAMEROW *University of Wisconsin*

STROMBERG *A History of Western Civilization*

BLACK *Posture of Europe, 1815–1940: Readings in European Intellectual History*

WHITE *Medieval History: A Source Book*

SENN *Readings in Russian Political and Diplomatic History,* Volumes I and II

GOOCH *Interpreting European History,* Volumes I and II

Interpreting

European History

Volume I

From the Renaissance to Napoleon

Edited by

BRISON D. GOOCH

University of Oklahoma

1967

THE DORSEY PRESS

Homewood, Illinois

© THE DORSEY PRESS, 1967

First Printing, April, 1967

Library of Congress Catalog Card No. 67–17039

Printed in the United States of America

Preface

IN STUDYING the history of Europe before 1815, a student comes in contact
with a varied and interesting array of men and issues. How these relate
to one another and to later developments, extending even into our own
day, has been the object of much careful thought by acute and dis-
criminating minds. Beyond the elementary level of the factual narrative
lies a world of fascinating interpretation and shades of opinion, an area
where certainty is much more elusive. To introduce some of these aspects
of historical study is an objective of *Interpreting European History.*

Various personalities or aspects of the period before 1815 are here considered in a series of careful evaluations. Every section has been devised
by a prominent historian who has himself contributed substantially to the
study of the topic he is presenting. Each is uniquely qualified to select
the materials and to point out for the reader any special problems attending the investigation of the particular topic.

The relationships beween the particular selections vary considerably.
In some cases different aspects of the subject are presented, as in the
first topic where one meets a number of the characteristics of modern
society already well developed during the Middle Ages. In other topics
the reader encounters very nearly contradictory judgments. Here the
student must consider and weigh the subject, asking whether or not the
materials he has read are all equally sound. He may find himself driven
back to the factual narrative for more data. On the other hand, he may
find that he would like to read more widely among interpretive materials.
In either case he will have a deeper understanding and a greater appreciation for the complexities and importance of European history.

While all the topics in this volume clearly concern the period before
1815, some of the materials in the second volume, *From Metternich to the
Present,* also are relevant to the earlier period. This is particularly true
with the topic on "Nationalism" by Professor Boyd C. Shafer. Also of
special interest is the topic prepared by Professor W. Warren Wagar
dealing with "The Idea of Progress." Those desiring more evaluations of
Napoleon will find them in Professor Enno Kraehe's presentation of
Metternich and Napoleon as rivals in 1813. Professor Vernon J. Puryear

begins his consideration of Turkey's role in international affairs with 1798. Some of the materials in this first volume are similarly relevant to topics in the second.

The two volumes of *Interpreting European History* divide roughly at at the career of Napoleon, mainly as a matter of convenience since many college courses use 1815 as a point of reference. Thus the volumes may be used separately in semester courses or together in year courses in European history or Western civilization. The intent is to lend an awareness of varying perspectives to what may be acquired from an orthodox text and from classroom lectures and discussions. In most cases the footnotes denoting the locations of documentary materials have been deleted in order to make the selections less cumbersome. However some discursive notes of considerable value have been included so that a student may meet this aspect of historical writing.

While other topics could as readily have been selected, all presented here are of special significance. In the materials on Danton and Robespierre, Professor John Hall Stewart introduces us to a controversy of long-standing importance in historical writing. Louis XIV is presented by Professor John B. Wolf as he has appeared in the writing of several scholars with quite different views of the nature of their craft, samples coming from the 18th century (Voltaire), the 19th century (Guizot), a Ranke Adherent (Lavisse), and scholars with the perspectives of today. Professor Robert Holtman presents Napoleon in the context of the question of war guilt and the renewal of hostilities after the Peace of Amiens. This presentation is of special interest when considered with topics in the second volume on the origins of World War I (Professor Joseph O. Baylen) and World War II (Professor Keith Eubank).

Special mention should also be made of the materials prepared by Professor Chester V. Easum on Frederick the Great. In addition to presenting the Prussian monarch as seen by both critics and admirers, he shows us how the Nazis presented Frederick. Further, the student will find it of some interest to compare how Frederick and Louis XIV have been treated by historians through the ages.

While the topics may all be studied separately, many are mutually relevant and there is a cumulative impact for the student who progresses through the volume. Among the results should be an appreciation for the value of different perspectives on a given subject and a realization of how difficult real objectivity is. True understanding of a subject, as Herbert Butterfield reminds us, requires an awareness of its historiography. *Interpreting European History* makes it possible for this aspect of historical study to be a part of a student's early study of history. While the problems approach is now well established, all too often the student comes belatedly to this aspect of the discipline. The premise of the designers of this volume is that such delay is neither necesary nor even desirable. It is also believed that it is important to see many different problems and that this, for beginning students, must be accomplished within the confines of no more than two moderately sized volumes. All of the topics could have been far more extended presentations but within the present format the student is able to discern the possibilities for conflict arising from differing perspectives. At the end of each volume he will have learned more about the history of Europe, and he will have had occasion to ponder many broad and intriguing aspects of the study of history itself. To wonder about the writing and meaning of history is to acquire a dimension of learning and sophistication which is the mark of a civilized man.

April, 1967   BRISON D. GOOCH

Table of Contents

VOLUME I

William M. Bowsky, Professor of History at the University of Nebraska, was born in New York City in 1930. A graduate of New York University, he received his M.A. and Ph.D. degrees from Princeton. He has taught history at Princeton University and the University of Oregon. In the fall of 1967 Dr. Bowsky will take the post of Professor of History at the University of California, Davis. He is the founder and editor of the annual series *Studies in Medieval and Renaissance History* and is the author of the book *Henvy VII in Italy: The Conflict of Empire and City-State, 1310–1313* (Lincoln, Nebr., 1960) and of numerous articles in the fields of medieval and early renaissance history. His most recent book is *Siena under the Nine (1287–1355).* He is a member of the American Historical Association and of the Medieval Academy of America.

CHAPTER ONE

WILLIAM M. BOWSKY
University of Nebraska

Medieval Roots

"MEDIEVAL ROOTS": origins and beginnings of modern problems, interests, and values; medieval anticipations of the modern world. Many are to be found in the Middle Ages, a somewhat arbitary but convenient periodization within the course of Western history that can be defined variously depending upon one's viewpoint and emphasis. Generally speaking, we may view it as beginning no later than the fifth century, when the unity of the Mediterranean world—cultural as well as economic and political—already was disintegrating in the West in what has come to be called "the decline and fall of the Roman Empire," while one province after another fell beneath the sway of barbarian kinglets. The Middle Ages did not markedly wane, in Western Europe at least, until, at the earliest, the mid-14th century—that chaotic time of the Black Death, the Hundred Years War, economic and social disorganization, and the moral and religious crises that led to the Great Schism and, later, the Reformation. But even in the early 16th century many medieval values, patterns, and institutions remained; not without reason do some scholars refuse to usher out the Middle Ages until as late as the age of Newton and the Scientific Revolution.

Almost everywhere we find medieval roots of modern concerns and ways of thought and action. Nowhere is this clearer than in an area of great interest in our own times, that of government, politics, and political theory. The incredibly intricate and delicate problem of defining and achieving a correct relationship between church and state, for example, made its appearance with the arrival on the scene of the first Christian emperor, Constantine, in the first half of the fourth century; but this prob-

3

lem was only confronted directly and met squarely in the Middle Ages, as churchmen and lay rulers worked—at times in harmony and at times in opposition—to hammer out an answer. The issue was joined most clearly in what a modern historian has described as no less than a "world revolution," the Investiture Controversy in the second half of the 11th century, that pitted against each other champions of medieval theocratic monarchy and of the supremacy of the church as headed by the bishop of Rome, in the persons of the "Holy Roman Emperor," Henry IV, and Pope Gregory VII [Selection 1].

Of modern political interests, values, and institutions that originated in the Middle Ages none is more significant than the national state, which now holds an enormously—and perhaps dangerously—large share of the basic allegiance of peoples throughout the world [Selection 2]. But important as are problems of church-state relations, or the rise of nationalism and national states, they are just two among a host of examples to which we might point within only the area of politics and government. Medieval, too, are the bases of our representative institutions. It is a truism that the roots of our U.S. Congress may be sought in representative assemblies common to most of Western Europe by the 14th century—in particular in the English parliament, of which the germ already existed in the 13th century, and in the even earlier obligations of lord and vassal contained within what we label as the "Feudal System." Similarly, our own precious jury system, now challenged, is a direct descendant of medieval inquests.

Nor should we illuminate only the bright spots: in the Middle Ages, too, are roots of negative aspects of modern Western political life and, in particular, of political disunity. The contention, for example, that so long has marked Franco-German relations concerning their borderlands, especially Alsace-Lorraine, can be traced to the disintegration of that ill-conceived Carolingian "Middle Kingdom" of Lotharingia in the ninth century. And, sadly, political disunity marked the Middle Ages far more sharply than did the glimmerings of a possible solution to the problem, such as the stillborn "federation" of peoples apparently envisioned by the young Emperor Otto III and his collaborator, Pope Sylvester II, at the end of the 10th century.

Medieval also are numerous other roots of the modern world, both ideal and institutional. From the revival of industry, commerce, and town life, visible by the 10th century at the latest, were to emerge the cities of the high Middle Ages, with their economic specialization and social divisions—the progenitors of modern urban civilization. The same medieval growth of industry and international exchange gave birth to a nascent capitalism, in Italy at least, by the 13th century [Selection 3]. Even some of the technological and scientific interests that were so to dominate a later age have their foreshadowings in a 13th century Grosseteste or Roger Bacon.

That modern European religious interests and developments stem from medieval roots is obvious but nonetheless of crucial importance. The ideals and institutions of Latin Christendom were hammered out during the so-called Dark Ages that followed the disintegration of the Roman Empire. Tested in the forge of the Investiture Controversy, they received new impetus and direction; retested by heresy and schism, they were the direct antecedents of the world of the Reformation. Sixteenth-century reformer, revolutionary, and defender of orthodoxy—all drew upon the thought and practices of their medieval forebears, whether of anti-sacerdotal Waldensian heretic, conciliar theorist, or canon lawyer.

Lest the apparently ubiquitous religiosity of the medieval West create an unbalanced picture, let us recall that many origins of modern lay culture lie deep in the heart of the Middle Ages. In medieval Europe do we find the beginnings of a culture that is vernacular and even secular, the origins, for example, of Italian, French, and German literature. The greatest of all Italian poets, Dante Alighieri, wrote his *Comedy* early in the 14th century—the same century in which Geoffrey Chaucer composed the *Canterbury Tales*.

In the Middle Ages did there first arise great and serious interest in the ancient world of Greece and Rome, in classical literature, thought, and art, in those outbursts of intellectual activity labeled "renaissances"—Irish and Anglo-Saxon, Carolingian and Ottonian, and, of course, the "Renaissance of the Twelfth Century." Concern with the ancient world and its culture waxed and waned, changed in nature and intensity; but in a very real sense the greatest Renaissance of all—the Italian Renaissance of the 14th to 16th centuries—stemmed from these medieval roots.

The Renaissance itself is the subject of intense historical debate and controversy, as scholars question not only its nature and chronology but its very existence. How, if at all, did the "Age of the Renaissance" differ in its values and interests from the preceding Middle Ages? When did it begin? Some scholars have pushed the Middle Ages forward, deep into the so-called Renaissance period, finding medieval attitudes and institutions still vital in the 14th and 15th centuries; others push the origins of renaissance modes and interests so far back into the Middle Ages as to make useless the very term "Renaissance Age." The individualism of a St. Francis in the early 13th century has been seen as a herald of the renaissance spirit, and contrasted with medieval corporatism and a hierarchical society. (Interested students should read the seminal essay, first published in 1860, from which all modern debate concerning the Renaissance springs, Jacob Burckhardt's *Civilization of the Renaissance in Italy*.)

Of all the cultural and institutional medieval origins of our own age one of immediate concern to the readers of this book should not pass unmentioned: the roots of our modern system of higher education lie in the Middle Ages, and the university itself emerged from the cathedral schools of the 12th century and gained formal recognition in the 13th. Even the 20th-century undergraduate will experience a feeling of kinship with his counterpart of more than a half millenium ago [Selection 4].

These few examples of medieval roots could be multiplied manyfold, but it is our intention only to hint at the general phenomenon and to pique the reader's curiosity and interest. Hopefully, he will delve into these matters more deeply for himself, and examine their development and changing roles in the history of the modern world.

1. A STRUGGLE BETWEEN CHURCH AND STATE

In this passage from the most important historical work treating the Investiture Controversy, an eminent medieval historian and director of the German Historical Institute in Rome summarizes his exciting interpretation of a complex and crucial phenomenon in European religiopolitical history.

GERD TELLENBACH[*]

The age of the Investiture Controversy may rightly be regarded as the culmination of medieval history; it was a turning point, a time both of completion and of beginning. It was the fulfillment of the early Middle Ages, because in it the blending of the Western European peoples with Christian spirituality reached a decisive stage. On the other hand, the later Middle Ages grew directly out of the events and thoughts of the decades immediately before and after the year 1100; as early as this the general lines, the characteristic religious, spiritual, and political views

---

[*] Gerd Tellenbach, *Church, State and Christian Society at the Time of the Investiture Controversy*, trans. R. F. Bennett (Oxford, Basil Blackwell, 1940), pp. 162–68.

of later times had been laid down, and the chief impulses for subsequent development given.

The great struggle had a threefold theme. On the basis of a deeper understanding of the nature of the Catholic Church, an attempt was made to remodel three things: first, the relations of clergy and laity with each other; secondly, the internal constitution of the church, through the imposition of papal primacy; and thirdly, the relations of church and world. The first of these disputed questions in which lay investiture played the most important part has given its name to the whole period. The old state-controlled constitution of the church and the proprietary church system, both of them factors of the first importance in the conversion of the Western European peoples and in the building up of church organization, had originated in pre-Christian times and were at bottom foreign to the church's real nature. Only after long and wearisome struggles did the church succeed in restricting them or incorporating them in the structure of the canon law. Lay investiture and the whole proprietary system were, however, burning questions only for a few centuries during the earlier part of the Middle Ages; but the battle between episcopalism and papalism has, in spite of periodic interruptions, intermittently disturbed the church from the earliest Christian era down to the present time, and the relationship between Christianity and the secular state is, for Catholics and Protestants alike, still a deeply moving and not yet completely solved question. The best-known and most violent conflict to which it ever gave rise, the struggle in which church and state met each other in the pride of their strength and fully armed with their natural weapons, was the Investiture Controversy.

It will never be quite possible to discover what were the real causes of the great 11th-century crisis in Christian history; many factors in the political life of the times which did in fact coalesce to form a developing situation the main lines of which are clear, might, it seems to us now, have operated very differently. It is just as difficult to explain why it was that men who were capable of great things came together in Rome at that particular time, and above all, why at the critical moment the demonic figure of the greatest of the popes occupied the throne of the Prince of the Apostles. Only a very wide-ranging view can make clear, even in part the concurrence of events out of which the new age was born, for only thus will due influence be assigned to the advanced stage which the christianization of the world had then reached. Ecclesiastical organization had spread far and wide, monastic religion had taken a strong hold on men and made them more concerned for their souls' health, had spurred them on to greater conscientiousness and made them more anx-

ious for the purity and right order of the church. Thus a new and victorious strength was lent to the old belief in the saving grace of the
sacraments and to the hierarchical conceptions based on their administration. Out of this arose the conviction that the Christian peoples of the
West formed the true City of God, and as a result the leaders of the
church were able to abandon their ancient aversion from the wickedness
of worldly men and to feel themselves called upon to reorder earthly life
in accordance with divine precept. In the 11th century the position had
not yet been reached where the pope, the imperial Lord of the Church,
appointed and confirmed the kings of the earth and watched over and
judged their actions, but the enormous advance made by Gregory VII
had opened the way for this, and he himself had already realized more
of it in practice than any single one of his successors was able to do.
Gregory stands at the greatest—from the spiritual point of view perhaps
the only—turning point in the history of Catholic Christendom; in his
time the policy of converting the world gained once and for all the upper
hand over the policy of withdrawing from it: the world was drawn into
the church, and the leading spirits of the new age made it their aim to
establish the "right order" in this united Christian world. In their eyes,
however, the most immediate task seemed to be that of successfully
asserting the supremacy of the "Servant of the servants of God" over the
kings of the earth.

Gregory VII was not particularly notable for his faithfulness to tradition. He was at heart a revolutionary; reform in the ordinary sense of the
word, which implies little more than the modification and improvement
of existing forms, could not really satisfy him. He desired a drastic change
and could be content with nothing short of the effective realization on
earth of justice, of the "right order," and of "that which ought to be."
"The Lord hath not said 'I am Tradition,'" he once wrote, "but 'I am
the Truth.'" And yet, in spite of this reaction against the merely traditional, Gregory himself embodied the essence of Catholic tradition in a
peculiarly characteristic manner; this fact shows, therefore, how instinctive and unreasoning—in a sense, how primitive—his faith was. Catholicism was to him the directive principle of life itself. For him the age-old
Catholic ideas of righteousness (*justitia*), a Christian hierarchy (*ordo*),
and a proper standing for everyone before God and man (*libertas*) were
the core of religious experience, and their realization the purpose of life
here on earth. It would be incorrect to treat these and related ideas as the
personal discoveries of St. Augustine or any other particular individual
among the early Fathers, or to attempt to trace out exactly the stages by
which Gregory is supposed to have inherited them; they are in reality an

inseparable part of the Catholic faith and can only be understood on that
assumption. It is just as wide of the mark to suggest that ideas such as
these were discovered for the first time by Gregory and his contemporaries, or that they were in any significant way remolded during the
Gregorian period; Gregory's real service was to leaven the earthly lump
with the principles of Catholicism and to make the latter, in a manner
hitherto undreamed of, a really decisive force in politics. His aim was to
bring the Kingdom of God on earth, as he saw it in his mind, nearer to
realization, and to serve the cause of order, justice, and "freedom." "He
was indeed," writes Bernold of St. Blasien, "a most zealous propagator
(*institutor*) of the Catholic religion and a most determined defender of
the freedom of the Church. For he did not wish the clergy to be subject
to the power of the laity, but desired them to excel all laymen by their
holiness and by the dignity of their order."

The unity of the Christian world, as Gregory and his contemporaries
wished to see it, could never quite be established in practice; nevertheless, unity has always remained an idea of the greatest historical influence,
though neither before nor after Gregory's time was it ever completely
realized. Before the 11th century, the principle of unity was represented
by the kingship; but the persistence of the old Christian feeling of indifference toward the world, together with the remains of paganism,
robbed the monarchy of full cooperation and hampered its action. Later
on, the clerical claim to leadership was advanced with such intensity that
it provoked resistance of another kind: belief in the divine right of kings
and princes immediately made itself more strongly felt and was never
quite overcome wherever monarchy was the prevailing form of the state.
But as divine right was no longer fully accepted by the church, tension
and some impairment of the principle of unity was often the result. The
assertion of their own direct responsibility to God—put forward so forcefully by Henry IV—still remained for the kings of Europe their strongest
argument against excessive claims on the part of the papacy, for the
conception that the rule of one man over others can only be justified
and made holy by direct divine intervention must always retain a certain
moral value. It is further probable, as has often been pointed out recently,
that the papacy's attacks on the divine right of kings led directly to later
attempts to set the state on new, and this time secular, foundations. Conclusions such as this, the truth of which is difficult to demonstrate, must
however be handled with great caution. The "order" which Gregory introduced remained dominant for centuries and showed an astounding
ability to overcome all opposing forces or to turn them to its own service.
A similar picture is presented by Gothic art, which combined numberless

powerful elements fundamentally at variance with each other, and yet
was able to create out of them a stylistic unity in spite of the resultant
stress and strain.

The enormous strength of the ecclesiastical claim to world domination
is only to be explained if we recognize how profoundly religious were its
roots; it grew directly out of the fundamental tenets of the Catholic
faith, and failure to realize this is the reason why many earlier attempts
at explanation must be rejected as mistaken or insufficient. To derive a
demand for worldwide power from asceticism and the flight from the
earthly life, as some historians have done, is to ascribe an improbable
religious perversity to the church; and there is equally little logic in the
connected theory that the church wished to reduce the world to subjec-
tion in order to be free from it. Nor is it possible to suppose that the
emperor was deprived of the right of investiture simply in order that the
clergy alone should represent the unity of the church. Further, it is
scarcely a half-truth to assert, as is sometimes done, that Gregory VII
combated lay influence in order to increase his opportunities of carrying
out moral reform and the internal reorganization of the church. This was
only part of his purpose; as we have seen, the real reason for the action
he took lies deeper: his moral principles were outraged by the mere fact
that the laity were occupying a position which, according to the sacra-
mental conception of the hierarchy, was not really theirs at all. A true
understanding of the ideas of Gregory VII and of post-Gregorian Catholicism about the relation of the spiritual power to the world, and of the
origins of these ideas themselves, can only be reached by going right back
to the belief in the incarnation of God in Christ. This is the most fundamental of the church's beliefs, for in the church the saving grace of the
incarnation has become an ever-present reality, and all the church's institutions find in this belief their *raison d'être* and their ultimate justification. Mystical and hierarchical trains of thought arise naturally from the
belief that God comes down from heaven to man, and that the multitude
of His priests serves as the steps by which He descends. If, therefore, the
church and the hierarchy of its servants have a part in the mediating
office of Christ, if they exist in order to link heaven and earth, then it is
only just that the world should meekly accept their guidance and be
subject to them. This demand forms a principle the validity of which
Catholicism is always bound to assert; it is this principle which must
ultimately decide its attitude toward the state, although in recent centuries it has been applied less in the purely political field than during the
Middle Ages, and more as a claim to the care of souls and to moral
leadership.

The superiority of the church over the state derives, therefore, from Catholic belief in the church and its vocation: nobody can admit the superiority if he does not share the belief. Hence Protestant Christianity immediately reoriented its attitude toward the state. Protestantism recognizes no visible institution on earth which is infallibly entitled to speak in the name of God, or which possesses an unqualified claim to represent Him. For the Protestant there is consequently no authority which can issue commands to the state, since the dignity of the state is in his eyes second to that of no other community on earth. On the other hand, much as he may respect authority as a gift from heaven, he is forced to draw as sharp a distinction between earthly kingdoms and the Kingdom of God as has been drawn at any other time in Christian history. Protestant and Catholic Christianity are therefore at one, though for totally different reasons, in the firm conviction that the problem of man's existence can never find its ultimate explanation in those sterile territories which are all that a purely human understanding can ever penetrate and all that a purely human activity can ever subdue.

2. LAICIZATION OF FRENCH AND ENGLISH SOCIETY[1]

In this provocative essay a leading American medievalist and professor of history at Princeton University offers an individualistic analysis of the political aspect of secularization as he examines the origins of the national state and incipient nationalism.

JOSEPH R. STRAYER[*]

Students of medieval society have long been aware of a sharp change in attitudes and values which took place in the 13th century. During that period, while Europe remained sincerely and completely Catholic, the

---

[1] This paper was read, in a somewhat abbreviated form, at the 1938 meeting of the American Historical Association. An excellent discussion of the topic, from a somewhat different point of view, may be found in G. de Lagarde, *La naissance de l'esprit laïque* (Saint-Paul-Trois Châteaux et Vienne, 1934).

[*] Joseph R. Strayer, "The Laicization of French and English Society in the Thirteenth Century," *Speculum* (Mediaeval Academy of America), Vol. XV (1940), pp. 76–86.

church lost much of its influence. Though it perfected its organization and carried on its religious activities with great energy, the standards which it had set for secular activities were increasingly disregarded. The forces released by the great revival of civilization in the 12th century could no longer be controlled by the church. They broke out of the old channels and either found new courses for themselves or dissipated their energy in the swamps and backwaters of uncoordinated endeavor. This secularization of European society is apparent in every field of human activity, in art and literature as well as in politics and economics. But while the fact of secularization is undisputed, the reasons for this great change in European opinion and the way in which the change was brought about are not clear. It is a problem which is well worth studying, not only because it is the key to much of the later history of the Middle Ages, but also because it is an interesting example of the ways in which public opinion are changed.

This paper is an attempt to study one aspect of secularization, the laicization of French and English society in the 13th century. Laicization may be defined as the development of a society in which primary allegiance is given to lay governments, in which final decisions regarding social objectives are made by lay governments, in which the church is merely a private society with no public powers or duties. When society has been laicized leadership has passed from the church to the state. In the modern period this assumption of leadership by the state is usually manifested in attempts to control social services, such as education, to regulate family relationships, and to confiscate all or part of the church's property. These particular manifestations of the idea of laicization should not be confused with the idea itself. There was no demand for government regulation of marriage and divorce in the 13th century and very little protest against church control of education. There were efforts to limit the church's acquisition of new property, but only a few fanatics advocated confiscation of what the church already possessed. Yet during the 13th century leadership passed from the church to lay governments, and when the test came under Boniface VIII it was apparent that lay rulers, rather than the pope, could count on the primary allegiance of the people.

Laicization is the political aspect of secularization. As such, it cannot be wholly explained by purely economic factors. I am quite willing to accept the conventional view that the economic changes of the 12th and 13th centuries made society more worldly, but worldliness is not the same thing as laicization. One is negative, the other positive. Worldliness made the leadership of the church less effective but it did not necessarily create a new leadership to supplant that of the church. Gothic art, for example, did not express religious ideas as well in 1300 as it did in 1200, yet it was still an art dominated by the church. Society was more worldly everywhere in 1300 than in 1200, yet the church did not lose political power to the same extent everywhere. Germany was fully as worldly as England, yet England was far more independent of the papacy. It took strong lay governments to challenge the leadership of the church, and economic change by itself does not explain the development of such governments. For example, throughout Europe the new economic forces were concentrated in the towns, but outside of Italy the towns were not the dominant factor in creating the new leadership. In England and France the royal officials who were most active in pursuing the policy of laicization were not exclusively, or even primarily, bourgeois. In short, while economic changes created an atmosphere in which it was easier for lay governments to assume leadership, they did not ensure the creation of lay governments which could make the most of the opportunity.

A discussion of laicization really should be prefaced by a discussion of the way in which the church had obtained the leadership of society. For the church's leadership was not unquestioned in the earliest centuries of the Middle Ages. It may even be argued that the complete predominance of the church was attained only as a result of the great revival of civilization which began in the latter part of the 11th century. Limitations of space forbid the discussion of this problem; at least we can assume that in the 12th century the church's control of society reached its highest point. Disregarding the endless variations of a pattern which was everywhere fundamentally the same, we can say that political units of the 12th century fell into three classes. First, there were the local units, the feudal baronies and the towns. Then there were the intermediate units, the kingdoms, and the great feudal states which were practically independent. Finally there was the great unit of Christendom, headed nominally by the emperor and the pope, but which, as an effective political force, was almost wholly controlled by the pope. All men were subject to at least three governments, which represented these three types of political organization. No government had a monopoly of power, each had its own work to do and each was supposed to give the other governments a free hand to do their work. In practice there were endless quarrels, especially among the local and intermediate units, but for a long time these quarrels led to no decisive changes. This was a situation which, from a political point of view, was wholly favorable to the church. Loyalty to lay governments was divided between the local and intermediate units. In many cases the greater loyalty was to the small local unit, for it was the local unit which controlled economic and social status. Far more important than this divided allegiance to lay governments was the loyalty to the great undivided unit of Christendom. The scale of allegiance of most men would have gone something like this: I am first of all a Christian, second a Burgundian, and only third a Frenchman. The emphasis on Christianity as the most important bond between men meant that there was a real European patriotism, expressed in the armies of the Crusade. It means that there was such a thing as European citizenship or nationality, shown by the fact that a well-trained clerk or knight could find employment anywhere in Christendom, regardless of his origin. And the pope controlled the citizens of Europe, and through this control he could exercise decisive influence on all aspects of European society.

From a political point of view this situation was satisfactory to the church. From the point of view of morality there was less reason for complacency. The division of responsibility between governments meant that none of them did their work very well. The quarrels between lay governments created a chronic state of warfare. This was intolerable to a church which had been preaching the ideals of peace and justice for centuries. The church was bound to support, or at least to look favorably on any reforms which would make lay governments more capable of enforcing peace and dispensing justice. Here the contrast between political and economic change is most apparent. From the very beginning the church was suspicious of the increase in business activities, and did nothing to aid it. On the other hand the church wanted more efficient lay governments, and was of great assistance in the development of such governments. Yet stronger lay governments proved to be at least as dangerous to the church as the increase in trade and the growth of urban settlements.

Efficient lay governments were dangerous to the church because they could become efficient only by obtaining a practical monopoly of political power in the districts which they controlled. Then the mere exercise of this power, even without a deliberate plan, would tend to transfer primary allegiance from the church to the state. Finally, as lay officials became aware of what was happening they could make deliberate efforts to secure the allegiance of the people. These three tendencies led to the laicization of society.

During the latter part of the 12th and the first half of the 13th centuries the old medieval hierarchy of governments broke down in many regions. The old division of responsibility and power ended. In each region affected by these changes one government became dominant, and gained control of political activities. The dominant government was not always that of a king—in Italy, for example, it was that of the town—but whether king, count, or commune came out on top the result was the same. Only one government was left which was strong enough to inspire loyalty.

The monopoly of power secured by the dominant government was, of course, not complete. It was a *de facto* monopoly, which would not meet the tests of later political theorists any more than our present economic monopolies meet the tests of the lawyer or the economist. The political monopolies of the 13th century worked very much as our economic monopolies work today. Other units were tolerated, and were allowed a certain share of the business of government, as long as they recognized that they held this share only by grace of the dominant power. This is the policy of Edward I in the *Quo Warranto* proceedings, and of Philip the Fair in his *pariages* with the semi-independent feudal lords of southern France.[2] Only admit that you hold your power from us, that you exercise it subject to our correction, and we will let you retain a large degree of jurisdiction. It was a policy which could be applied to the church fully as much as it was applied to competing lay governments. A direct attack on all ecclesiastical jurisdiction would have been futile and dangerous. Minor officials who were tactless enough to make such attacks were always disavowed by their superiors. The inner circle of royal advisers wanted to weaken the church courts, but they knew that a head-on collision of authorities was not the best way of securing this result. They never denied that the church courts should have a certain amount of power. But they were going to define that power; ecclesiastical courts were to retain only the jurisdiction recognized by the royal council. The first example of this policy is found in the reign of Henry II of England, and while his attempt at definition was not completely successful, the precedent was not forgotten. By the end of the 13th century royal governments in both France and England were regularly defining the powers of church courts. The excesses of minor officials were a useful weapon in establishing this power of the central government. When the church was annoyed by such officials its only recourse was to beg the royal government to define and defend ecclesiastical jurisdiction.[3] As Professor Graves has shown, this is the story behind *Circumspecte Agatis* in Eng-

---

[2] *Ordonnances*, VII, 7, in a compromise with the bishop of Viviers the king insists only on recognition of his "superioritas," his right to hear appeals from the bishop's court, and his power to punish temporal officials of the bishopric. 1308.

[3] *Ibid.*, XVII, 221. The monastery of St. Saturnin surrenders many of its rights in a *pariage* after being harassed by local officials, 1302; *Gallia Christiana*, I, *Instr.* 33, the bishop of Cahors made a *pariage* for the same reason in 1307; *Archives Nationales*, JJ 45 nos 88 and 90, similar transactions with the chapter of Rodez and St Papoul, 1309 and 1310.

land.[4] In France, even so powerful a prelate as the bishop of Toulouse had to seek the intervention of the royal council almost every year in order to preserve the most elementary rights.[5] The effects of this policy on public opinion are obvious. If the church's rights of government were dependent on the goodwill of lay rulers, if the church could maintain its jurisdiction only through the aid of the state, lay governments must be more powerful and important than the church.

Then, as certain governments obtained a *de facto* monopoly of political power they began to do more work. Their courts met more frequently, they heard more cases, they welcomed appeals from subordinate jurisdictions. These governments began to tax and to legislate, even though taxation was at first considered little better than robbery and legislation was felt to be sacrilegious tinkering with the sacred and unchangeable law. In order to perform this increased amount of work they multiplied the number of their officials. All this meant that they had more contacts with the mass of the people, that they touched at some point on the life of every man. No one could be ignorant of the fact that he was subject to one of these dominant governments. No one could fail to realize that the activities of his government were important, perhaps more important than the activities of the church. This sense of the increasing importance of lay governments was not the same thing as loyalty to those governments, but the first sentiment could very easily lead to the second. Men respect what is powerful and they can easily become loyal to what they respect.

The multiplication of the number of lay officials is one of the most striking phenomena of the 13th century. In every country the conservatives protested again and again that there were too many officials, and in every country the number of officials went right on increasing in spite of the protests. This increase had important effects on public opinion. It was not only that officials, with their friends and families, formed a large group which would support any action of the government. More important was the fact that every official, consciously or unconsciously, was a propagandist for his government. He had to spread the government's explanation of its policies; he had to enforce decisions which showed the government's power. Many officials, especially those of lower rank who were in direct contact with the people, were openly anticlerical. The fact that such men could brutally disregard the church's rights and still keep their positions must have convinced many people that lay gov-

---

[4] *English Historical Review*, XLIII (1928), 1.
[5] Ad. Baudouin, *Lettres inédites de Philippe le Bel* (Paris, 1887), nos. 1, 6, 10, 11, 12, 13, 14, 22, 24, and *passim*.

ernments were going to be supreme. Finally, with the steady increase in the number of government jobs a new career was open up for able men of all classes. The church could no longer count on securing the services of the great majority of educated and intelligent men. Many laymen who might have entered the church chose to serve the king instead. Many churchmen entered the service of lay governments and became so absorbed in that service that they forgot their duty to the church. And as the church lost exclusive control of the educated class it lost much of its ability to control public opinion.

Fully as important as the increase in the number of permanent lay officials was the increase in the number of men who were not officials, but who were forced to aid the government in its work from time to time. Professor A. B. White has shown how much of the work of local government in England was performed by juries, or selected knights of the shire.[6] France had a much larger paid bureaucracy, but even in France the royal government could not function without requiring the services of its subjects. In France, as in England, local notables were associated with royal officials in administrative investigations or judicial inquests.[7] In France, as in England, thousands of men were forced to aid the government in the wearisome work of assessing and collecting taxes. For example, when the aid for knighting Louis of Navarre was collected in 1314, there were 322 collectors in the viscounty of Paris alone, excluding the city proper and the castellany of Poissy.[8] It seems unlikely that many people enjoyed dropping their own work in order to spend days and weeks in serving the government for little or no pay. Yet the men who performed these expensive and burdensome tasks did not become disloyal to the government which imposed them. Rather they became increasingly conscious of the dignity and power of secular government. They acquired the habit of obedience to lay authorities, they accepted the point of view of the permanent officials with whom they had frequent contacts. A modern parallel to this process would be found in the results of military conscription. Most men who are drafted into an army regard military service as a burden. Yet compulsory military service has proved one of the most successful means for building up fanatical loyalty to the

---

[6] A. B. White, *Self-Government at the King's Command* (Minneapolis, 1933).

[7] P. Guilhiermoz, *Enquêtes et procès* (Paris, 1892), p. 605, ordinance for Parlement of 1278. In order to obtain auditors to hold inquests "baille chascuns des bailliz les nons en escrit jusques a .x. personnes aus clers des arrè, lesquiex personnes soient souffisables a faire ce que l'en leur commandera en droit . . ." *Archives Nationales*, J 237 no. 120, J 208 no. 6, J 292 no. 9[10], examples of the use of local notables in appraising and assigning land.

[8] *Bibliothèque nationale*, Clairembault 228, pp. 929 ff.

state. Just so the compulsory civil service of the 13th century created loyalty to the governments which imposed it.

The processes discussed so far worked indirectly, and almost automatically, to build up loyalty to lay governments. It was natural for any ruler to try to increase his power in a given area. As he gained a virtual monopoly of power it was necessary for him to add new functions to his government and to increase the number of men who assisted him in governing. There was little theorizing behind these developments, merely the desire to gain power and to use that power effectively. But the result of this drive for power was the creation of something very like a sovereign state. There was no place for such an entity in the old medieval system; it was absolutely opposed to the belief in the unity of Christendom and the hierarchy of political organizations. It had to be justified, explained, sold to the people. As a result, toward the end of the 13th century a definite theory to justify laicization appears.

This theory, like so many other things in the 13th century, was the work of lawyers. This new class of men, produced by the increased activity of 12th-century governments, set the tone of the 13th century even more than the new class produced by increased business activity. The 13th century was a legalistic century, a century in which men sought exact definitions of all human relationships, a century in which men wanted to work out the logical implications of all general ideas and projects, a century in which men wanted to complete and to justify the work of their predecessors. And because the 13th century was legalistic, because it was a period of definitions and detailed explanations, it was a much less tolerant century than the 12th. It was no longer possible to harmonize divergent views by thinking of them as merely different aspects of universal truth. Thus definition of the doctrines of the church forced many reformers into heresy. Definition of the rights of the state forced many men to choose between loyalty to the state and loyalty to the church. It was only when a choice had to be made that laicization was possible.

The definition of the powers of the ruler worked out by 13th-century lawyers developed into something which was almost a theory of the sovereign state. Such a theory could not be reconciled with the old medieval system; it forced a choice between loyalties. Briefly, it ran something like this. First, there are definite boundaries to all states. The 12th century had known spheres of influence rather than boundaries; power decreased in proportion to the distance from the ruler until a region was reached in which his authority was counterbalanced by that of another lord. In the 13th-century theory the power of the dominant government was to extend, undiminished, to a precise frontier. This idea may be seen especially clearly in the South of France, where royal officials worked

steadily to fix an exact boundary with Aragon;[9] where they insisted again
and again that the eastern boundary of the realm was the Rhone; where
they flatly denied that there could be a no man's land of independent
bishoprics,[10] in which the king's authority was neutralized by that of the
emperor. Then, within these precise boundaries there is to be a definite
superior, who can supervise and correct the work of all subordinate
governments. This idea may be found in England earlier than in France,[11]
but it was most clearly expressed by Beaumanoir: "The king is sovereign
over all, and has as his right the general guardianship of all the realm . . .
There is none so great beneath him that he cannot be haled to his court
for default of justice or for false judgment."[12] Moreover, this definite superior, if he observes certain formalities, may issue orders which are
binding on all men in the realm. As the *dictum de Kenilworth* says: "The
king, and his legitimate orders and instructions, must be fully obeyed
by each and every man, great and small, in the realm."[13] Guillaume de
Plaisian is even more emphatic: "All those in the realm are ruled by the
king's authority; even prelates and clerks, in temporal matters, are bound
by the laws, edicts, and constitutions of the king."[14] The central government may state the law, or make special rulings where the laws fail to
give a solution to a problem. This was recognized in England as early as
Glanvill's time, when it was said that laws for the entire kingdom might

---

[9] *Archives nationales*, J 1029 no. 9; JJ 42 A no. 110. Cf. F. Kern, *Die Anfänge der
französischen Ausdehnungspolitik* (Tübingen, 1910), p. 17 ff. for similar efforts on the
eastern frontier.

[10] *Ordonnances*, VII, 7; *Bulletin de la Société d'Agriculture, Industrie, Sciences et
Arts du Département da la Lozère* 1896–97, 'Mémoire relatif au Paréage de 1307,' p.
520. Guillaume de Plaisian argued that 'fines Francie usque ad flumen Rodani ex-
tenduntur' and that 'omnia que sunt infra fines regni sui sint domini regis, saltim quoad
protectionem et altam jurisdictionem et dominationem . . .' The bishop of Mende stated
the older point of view when he replied 'non sequitur quod infra fines regni non possit
aliquid esse liberum a jurisdictione regali . . .' It is unfortunate that this important document, which contains the fullest summary of the theories of Philip's officials, is available only in this rare and incomplete edition.

[11] Glanvill (ed. Woodbine), pp. 149 ff.; Bracton, *de legibus*, II, 24, all justice is
held of the king, and power of supervising it remains with him.

[12] Beaumanoir (ed. Salmon), XXXIV, 1043. 'Voirs est que li rois est souverains par
dessus tous, et a de son droit la general garde de tout son roiaume . . . Et si n'i a nul
si grant dessous li qui ne puist estre tres en sa court pour defaute de droit ou pour faus
jugement. . . .'

[13] *Statutes of the Realm*, I, 12. '. . . atque ab universis et singulis majoribus et
minoribus ipsius regni hominibus, ipsi domino Regi et mandatis ac preceptis suis licitis
plene obediatur et humiliter intendatur.' Edward I's lawyers said that the king's orders
could override even the common law. *Rotuli Parliamentorum*, I, 71, 'dominus Rex, . . .
pro communi utilitate, per prerogativam suam in multis casibus est supra leges et con-
suetudines in regno suo usitatas.' 1292.

[14] 'Mémoire relatif au paréage,' p. 521. 'Item, quod dominus Rex sit imperator in
regno suo, et imperare possit terre et mari, et omnes populi regni sui regantur im-
perio, et omnes etiam prelati et clerici quoad temporalia legibus et edictis et con-
stitutionibus suis ligentur. . . .'

be made "in doubtful cases by the authority of the prince with the advice of the magnates."[15] It took somewhat longer for this power to be recognized in France, but by the end of the 13th century Beaumanoir could say: "The king may make such establishments as please him for the common good, and that which he establishes must be obeyed."[16] For the common good taxes may be imposed on all property in the kingdom. The most extreme statement of this right was made by Guillaume de Plaisian: "Everything within the boundaries of his realm is the lord king's, at least as to protection, superior jurisdiction, and lordship. Even as property it is the king's, for he can give, receive, and use any property, movable and immovable, in his realm for the public good and defense of the kingdom."[17] An English lawyer would not have said this, but the English government did insist that all property could be taxed for defense of the realm."[18] Finally, while no lesser political authority can be exempt from, or control, the decisions of the king, there is no higher political authority which can interfere with the king's powers of government. Here English and French lawyers are equally emphatic. Bracton's "the king has no equal, much less a superior"[19] is matched in a letter sent by the French government to the Emperor Henry VII: "Since the time of Christ the realm of France has had only its own king, who never recognized nor had a temporal superior."[20]

---

[15] Glanvill (ed. Woodbine), p. 24. English laws are 'eas quas super dubiis in consilio definiendis procerum quidem consilio, et principis accedente auctoritate, constat esse promulgatas.' By the time of Edward I general laws were made by the central government without hesitation. For our purposes, the question as to who controlled the central government is unimportant. The barons claimed the right to be consulted, but they did not deny that the central government could make law.

[16] Beaumanior (ed. Salmon), XXXIV, 1043, '... il [li rois] puet fere teus establissemens comme il li plest pour le commun pourfit, et ce qu'il establist doit estre tenu.'

[17] 'Mémoire relatif au paréage,' p. 521, '... omnia que sunt infra fines regni sui sint domini Regis, saltim quoad protectionem et altam jurisdictionem et dominationem et etiam quantum ad proprietatem omnium singularum rerum mobilium et immobilium regni sui, quas idem dominus Rex donare, recipere et consumere potest, ex causa publice utilitatis et deffensionis regni sui ...' This doctrine was repeated in a letter to the clergy of Tours in 1305, cf. Archives Nationales, J 350 no. 5.

[18] Bartholomaeus Cotton, Historia Anglicana (Rolls Series 16), p. 317, in asking the clergy for a grant in 1296, after the pope had forbidden taxation of the Church, Hugh le Despenser said: 'Ego ex parte domini regis, comitum, baronum, militum et aliorum domini regis fidelium vobis dico, quod de tali subsidio per quod terra defendatur de bonis ecclesiae provideatis, ne dominus rex, comites et barones de rebus vestris ecclesiasticis ordinent et disponant pro suae libito voluntatis.' Parliamentary Writs (London, 1827), I, 393, the clergy were outlawed until they paid.

[19] Bracton III, 9. 3 '[Rex] parem autem habere non debet, nec multo fortius superiorem...'

[20] K. Wenck, Philipp der Schöne (Marburg, 1905), p. 72, '... quod a tempore Christi citra regnum Francie solum regem suum sub ipso Jhesu Christo ... habuit, nullum temporalem superiorem cognoscens aut habens...'

These ideas add up to something very like the theory of sovereignty. Within fixed boundaries there is a definite superior who has the final decision regarding all political activities. It is not quite the theory of sovereignty, not only because the word is lacking, but also because it is a theory of comparative rather than absolute power. The words which the French lawyers use show this: the king has "superioritas," he has "majus dominium," he has "altior dominatio." His power is greater than that of any subject, but it is not a different power; he makes the final decisions, but he does not make all the decisions. But, sovereignty or not, this theory clearly conflicts with earlier medieval ideas. It sets up the kingdom as the most important unit of government and demands that all subjects give their primary allegiance to the kingdom.

Moreover, these ideas were not the work of isolated theorists. Every quotation which has been given was written by a high royal official. Most of them were taken from official documents—laws, pleas in royal courts, or letters written in the king's name. Innumerable statements of a similar sort could be found in official records. This means that everyone who attended a royal court, everyone who did business with the government, was exposed to the new theories. This must have done a great deal to spread the idea of the supremacy of royal government, and, hence, to make laicization easier. Even this was not enough, and at the end of the century deliberate propaganda in favor of the new theories was begun in both France and England. Local and national assemblies were called, at which royal officials could expound their new doctrine. It has long been apparent that the Estates-General and local assemblies held in France at the time of the quarrel with Boniface were called solely for purposes of propaganda. In a book recently published, Professor C. H. Taylor of Harvard has given strong reasons for believing that the French Assemblies which met to consider taxation were called primarily to create a public opinion favorable to taxation. They did not consent to taxation; in 1314, for example, the tax was already ordered before the assembly met.[21] But they could be impressed by arguments showing the necessity for taxation, and they would report those arguments to their constituents. I feel that the same thing is true of the English Parliament, as far as the knights and burgesses were concerned. True, they were asked to assent to taxation, but their assent was, at first, a matter of form. Much more important was the fact that they could be harangued by royal officials, that they could be used to spread propaganda which would make the work of the tax collector easier.

[21] J. R. Strayer and C. H. Taylor, *Studies in Early French Taxation* (Cambridge, 1939), p. 151.

At the same time the governments of France and England began to encourage nationalism in order to gain support for their policies. There had always been a certain amount of latent nationalism in Europe; the French had sneered at the drunken English and the Italians had despised the boorish Germans. But this early nationalism had not been very strong in comparison with provincial loyalties and it had been frowned on by lay and ecclesiastical rulers alike. It was contrary to the basic principles of Christianity and it was dangerous to lay rulers whose territories seldom coincided with national units and whose policies were not always nationalistic. The concentration of political authority in France and England encouraged the growth of nationalism by decreasing the differences between provinces and increasing the differences between countries. But even in the middle of the 13th century nationalism was not yet respectable. Nationalism was associated with rebellion against constituted authority, with such movements as the protests of the English clergy against papal exactions, or the opposition of the English baronage to Henry III. Men like St. Louis and Henry III, who believed sincerely in the old international ideals, could not follow a nationalistic policy. In fact, many of Henry's troubles were caused by his unwillingness to accept the nationalistic ideas of his selfish and narrow-minded barons. About 1300, however, the governments of France and England began to see that nationalism could be useful to them, and once the idea was supported by a recognized authority it grew rapidly. At one point in the war over Gascony, Edward I accused the French of wishing to annihilate the English race[22] and the anticlerical legislation of his reign shows a tacit acceptance of nationalistic ideas. In France, the government appealed even more openly to nationalism. During the struggle against Boniface VIII repeated efforts were made to convince the country that the pope was anti-French, and that he was threatening the independence of France.[23] In the same way when the French clergy were asked for money to carry on the war with Flanders, they were reminded of the preeminence of France as a Christian country and were told that it was their duty as Frenchmen to defend their native land.[24] In 1305 the king wrote to the clergy of the province of Tours: "You should realize that all the clergy

---

[22] *Parliamentary Writs*, I, 30. The king of France, 'praedictis fraude et nequitia non contentus . . . linguam Anglicam . . . omnino de terra delere proponit.'

[23] G. Picot, *Documents relatifs aux Etats Généraux* (Paris, 1901), p. 37, Boniface was accused of saying 'se magis velle esse canem vel asinum . . . quam Gallicum,' that 'ad deprimendum regem et Gallicos, si aliter non posset fieri, precipitaret se, et totum mundum et totam Ecclesiam,' and that no scandal was too great 'dum tamen Gallici et eorum superbia destruantur.'

[24] *Archives Nationales*, J 1035 nos. 36, 37, 39; J 259 Cluny 3.

and laity of our kingdom, like members of one body . . . are bound to give each other spiritual and temporal aid to preserve, defend, and protect the unity of this realm."[25] The extremes to which French nationalism could go appear in the ingenious schemes of Pierre Dubois for subjecting all Europe to French rule. It is true that Dubois was only a minor official and was never promoted, but that does not mean that his views were not in harmony with those of the central administration. Generally speaking, minor officials spoke more bluntly and acted more brutally than the immediate advisers of the king, but the basic ideas of the two groups were the same. A tactless minor official, such as Dubois, might not be promoted, but neither would he be discharged. And the views of such a man, since they were never expressly repudiated, might be very influential with certain groups.

When Boniface VIII, alarmed by the growing power of lay governments, tried to limit their authority, he found that he was too late. The people of France and England remained loyal to their kings; there was not even a halfhearted rebellion in favor of the pope. In France the government had such control of public opinion that it was able to seize the church's own weapon of a charge of heresy and turn it against Boniface. A few years later it succeeded in ruining the Templars by the same method. This perhaps marks the extreme limit of medieval laicization— a secular ruler determines the policy of the church and uses the church for his own ends. This feat was not immediately repeated, but from the time of Boniface on there was no doubt that lay rulers had the primary allegiance of their people. Society was controlled, as far as it was controlled at all, by lay governments and not by the church. It is true that during the 14th and 15th centuries this lay control was not always very intelligent, or very effective. During these years there was a reaction against central governments; a reaction caused, at least in part, by the fact that they had gained power by a mixture of blackmail, chicanery, and bullying and that a generation educated in these techniques began to use them against their rulers. But this very period of weak lay government showed how effective the work of laicization had been. The church could not regain its old power in spite of the opportunity afforded by a new period of anarchy. There was no substitute for centralized, lay government in France or England, however weak that government might be.

The reaction against central governments after 1300 may explain why

---

[25] *Ibid.*, J 350 no. 5. 'Novistis plenius qualiter omnes et singuli clerici et laici regni nostri tanquam membra simul in uno corpore vere vivancia sibi debent ad invicem compati, mutuumque sibi prestare teneretur auxilium spiritualiter et temporaliter ad conservationem, deffensionem, et custodiam unitatis ipsius regni . . . ' 1305.

laicization went no further; why education, and care of the sick and poor remained in the province of the church. But it should also be remembered that medieval governments were satisfied with relative, rather than absolute, power. Totalitarianism was foreign to their ways of thinking—it would also have been too expensive. Police work cost money—so there was no objection to letting the barons do much of it. Education was expensive— so there was no objection to letting the church do it. Some townspeople in England and France did object to church control of education and tried to set up their own schools, but as far as I know the Count of Flanders was the only lay ruler who gave any support to this movement.[26] As for social service work, the whole tendency was to make the church do more of it, rather than less. Anyone who has studied grants to the church must have been struck by the great increase in the number of gifts made specifically to hospitals, poorhouses, and university colleges after the middle of the 13th century.[27] The old unlimited grant for the general purposes of the church almost disappears in the 14th century. This may be, indirectly, a form of laicization; the church is to be made to do "useful" work instead of spending its money on purely religious purposes. But there is no hesitation in allowing the church to perform these services; rather it is encouraged to do so. Not until the next great wave of laicization in the 16th century is there an attempt to deprive the church of its educational and philanthropic functions. Once the leadership, the "superiority" of medieval lay governments was recognized, they had no further quarrel with the church.

3. ECONOMIC REVIVAL AND URBANISM

In these pages a major Italian economic historian of our own century illustrates with vivid and specific historical examples some aspects of the industrial, commercial, and urban revival from the late 9th to the 11th

---

[26] H. Pirenne, 'L'Instruction des marchands au moyen âge,' *Annales d'histoire economique et sociale*, I, 24–26; C. Stallaert and P. Van Der Haeghen; *De l'instruction publique au moyen âge* (Brussels (1850), extract from vol. XXIII of *Mémoires couronnés et mémoires des savants étrangers publiés par l'académie royale de Belgique*), pp. 101, 107–108, 109.

[27] Powerful communes, such as those of the Rhineland and the Low Countries, did place certain hospitals under lay control, cf. *Hist. littéraire*, XXXV, 120, and de Lagarde, *op. cit.*, I, 220. But while there are no statistics on the subject, my impression is that the church gained more hospitals through new foundations than it lost through such acts of secularization.

century. While this Italian revival was precocious and especially vigorous it presaged a general development in much of medieval Western Europe.

GINO LUZZATTO[*]

At Genoa, before the second half of the 10th century, there was little to recall the flourishing city of Roman times. Even the walls, destroyed by Rothari, were left to lie for centuries in ruins; while the site, never large, of the former Roman town was invaded by cultivated plots and fields and by pieces of waste interspersed with makeshift houses of wood. Because of neglect or Saracen attacks, the two Roman roads which at one time met at Genoa had both been abandoned for a different highway further to the east, the so-called Via Francigena, which crossed from Piacenza on the Po by way of the Cisa pass to Luni, near Sarzana, and in this manner avoided entirely the Arab-infested coast of eastern Liguria. The decay of Genoa is also reflected in the fact that it never became the seat of any high official of the realm. The only authorities to reside in or near the town were the bishops and the viscounts; and it was under their rule that Genoa started to revive with astonishing rapidity toward the middle of the 10th century, just when Arab power was on the wane. The city walls were now rebuilt and the cathedral church established inside their perimeter. About the same period, in 987, feudal forces from Provence overcame the dreaded Arab stronghold at Fraxinetum and finally removed the threat of Muslim attack by land. This enabled Genoa to join Pisa and counterattack by sea, with the result that in less than 30 years the northern Tyrrhenian was cleared of the Arabs for good.

This rapid rise to naval power encouraged the Pisans and Genoese to open commercial dealings with the maritime communities of the south: Gaeta, Naples, and Amalfi. They also traded with the Arabs, in the frequent periods of truce with the Saracen world, interrupting their regular pirate raids and visiting the ports of Sicily, Spain, and Africa in the peaceful character of merchants. But throughout the course of the 11th century there is scarcely any sign of commercial relations with the East. Only after the Norman conquest of Sicily, which freed the Straits of Messina, and more particularly after the First Crusade, in which the Pisan and Genoese fleets played a dominant part, were the two cities able to challenge the power of Venice along the Syrian coast and eventually all over the Levant. In the meantime, during the century before the First Crusade, the measure

_____
[*] Gino Luzzatto, *An Economic History of Italy from the Fall of the Roman Empire to the Beginning of the Sixteenth Century*, trans. Philip Jones (New York: Barnes and Noble, Inc.; and London: Routledge and Kegan Paul, Ltd., 1961), pp. 54–60.

and intensity of Pisan and Genoese trade, restricted though it was to the western Mediterranean, is revealed in the rapid progress of new building, in the growth of a mercantile middle class, in the evolution of a code of maritime custom, and in the lively concourse of visiting merchants who came from all the coastal cities between Barcelona and Salerno, from the inland parts of Lombardy and Tuscany, and from the countries beyond the Alps.

Not only on the coasts of Byzantine and Lombard Italy but also in the interior of the Italian kingdom the greater vigor of urban life continued to distinguish Italy from the northern countries of post-Carolingian Europe where feudalism had obtained a firmer hold. By the later ninth century we already find several causes combining to increase the importance of many inland towns, especially those along the rivers: the development of trade between the coastal cities and the Byzantine and Arab world, which inevitably affected the hinterland; the needs of defense, which compelled townspeople to build or reconstruct the city walls; and the influx of numerous country folk seeking protection. No doubt the towns of the interior preserved little of the Roman past beyond their names; indeed, with few exceptions, they can hardly be considered towns at all, in the economic sense of densely settled communities engaged in every kind of business other than agriculture. As we have seen at Genoa, fields and meadows covered the greater part of many towns, and the landlords who dwelt there—the bishop, the count, and other officials, together with certain feudal vassals great and small—all had food rents delivered by their tenants in the country. If we remember also that the towns possessed rights of common in the neighboring woods and meadows, we can only conclude that land and the income from farming and forests, pasture and hunting, remained the principal support of part, and possibly a large part, of the urban population.

At the same time it is obvious that, however unpretentious their life might be, the great officeholders of church and state who resided with their retinues in the city were quite unable to supply all their needs from local sources. This is why whatever glimpses we get of urban life from the casual names, phrases, and professional titles preserved in the few surviving records and inscriptions of the time always reveal a complex society, consisting not merely of magnates and clergy, peasants and slaves, but of other groups of people as well, who can only be described as precursors of the later bourgeoisie. We have seen that the laws of Aistulf, published in the last years of the Lombard kingdom, already treat the *negotiantes* as a separate class, divided into three grades, of whom the highest were placed on the same level as the middle class of landowners.

There is some doubt whether the term *negotiantes* was used, as in Roman times, to denote persons whose main business was moneylending, or was meant to describe professional merchants. But in view of the limited opportunity presented for credit operations in the small depopulated inland towns of that period, it is much more likely that Aistulf's legislation was addressed to genuine merchants, some of whom no doubt were still itinerant traders, while others, and perhaps the greater number, were permanently resident in the city. So much may be inferred from the numerous licenses granted by the Italian kings, and still more by the Ottonian emperors, to open markets in the towns or beneath their walls, and also from the names of certain taxes such as *buticaticum, curatura,* and *portaticum,* which clearly refer to a periodic or continuous urban trade. Similarly the places appointed for the payment of river tolls (*ripaticum* and *palefictura*), though sometimes located on the borders of some great landed estates, were normally sited near the towns, particularly the towns which lay along the Po and other navigable rivers or along the highways leading from the Alps to Pavia and Rome. It should be added that the development of markets also encouraged the rise of a class of free artisans, most of whom we find mentioned in market towns. There was one industry, it is true, the cloth industry, in which down to the 12th century artisans of free condition probably found it hard to compete with the slaverun workshops of the great monasteries; but in other industries they were quite independent of any manorial controls, and indeed were placed under the direct protection of the king. Artisans of this type were the workers in the building trades, the soapmakers and the metal workers (especially those engaged in arms manufacture), the jewelers, moneyers, and skinners.

The most detailed evidence of progress in urban industry and trade, apart from scattered hints in documents and inscriptions, is contained in the *Honorantiae civitatis Papiae,* which were a sort of tract or memorial (*Memoratorium*) written to vindicate the fiscal claims of the crown on merchandise crossing the frontiers and on monopolies granted by the state to certain trades. Particularly valuable, for the proof they provide that international trade was also carried on by land and across the Alps, are the rules mentioned in the *Memoratorium* regarding the customs stations (*clusae*) of the realm. With the sole exception of three stations situated on the eastern frontier, which was moved toward the lowlands during the Ottonian period, the *clusae* were all located at the foot of the principal Alpine valleys: at Susa and Bard, Bellinzona and Chiavenna, Bolzano and then Valorgne (near the *clusa* of Rivoli). They were fixed, that is, in places which were easily reached from the plain and at the same time opened the way to central Lombardy and thence across the Po, at Cremona, Piacenza, or Pavia, to Tuscany and Rome. All pilgrims and merchants from north and central Europe passed through the customs. The pilgrims paid no duty on their personal effects, but like the merchants they had to pay 10 percent on all goods brought in for purpose of trade, such as horses, slaves, and swords, and woolen, linen, and hempen cloth. The Anglo-Saxons, for the most part pilgrims, objected to having their baggage inspected by the customs officials, and eventually, after long dispute, a special agreement was arranged between the English king and the king of Lombard Italy which freed them from molestation at the customs, in return for the payment of a lump sum every three years to the palace at Pavia of 50 pounds of silver and some gifts in kind.

The geographical position of the customs stations explains the rise to prosperity after the ninth century of certain towns along the roads which they commanded, in particular Asti and Vercelli, Milan and Pavia, Verona, Cremona, Piacenza, and (just beyond the Apennines) Lucca. The last two towns were especially fortunate in being situated at vital points on the road from France and the British Isles to Rome. Piacenza stands where the Via Francesca crossed the river Po, and as early as the ninth century it was the meeting place of four annual markets each lasting 8 days; then in 896 a yearly fair was also instituted, of 17 days. Lucca lies at the southern end of the Garfagnana, not far from the Magra valley and Pisa. It had been a center of considerable economic and political importance ever since the later Lombard period. It possessed a mint and issued coins which circulated all over Italy as far as Rome, alongside the money of Pavia; it manufactured luxury cloth; and its merchants were rich and numerous enough to secure from the Emperor Henry IV complete exemption from duty (*curatura*) on all their sales and acquisitions in the markets from Pavia to Rome.

The *Memoratorium* then, in agreement with other records, clearly shows that the road system retained some importance for traffic and trade even during the early Middle Ages; but it also leaves us in no doubt that much the most favored means of inland transport, at least in the valley of the Po, were the waterways. This was so already in the eighth century, when people traveled regularly up the Po from Venice and Comacchio to Pavia and Milan, putting in at Ferrara, Cremona, and Piacenza. Their way was slow and embarrassed by numerous customs duties, for the rivers were considered public property to be exploited as a source of revenue or granted out on feudal terms to royal officials, religious corporations, and private subjects. And so at every step travelers were held up by agents of the crown or the feudatories, demanding payments in money or part of the cargo. On goods simply passing through these charges were mostly trifling, but they rose substantially whenever boats were brought in and moored for loading and unloading. We learn from documents that the rivers were used by great landlords who kept simple flat-bottomed boats for moving produce from outlying estates to the central manor, or made their tenants ship from nearby markets the few goods they needed from outside. But this was small-scale transport over fairly short distances. Most river traffic was organized by merchants, some of whom traveled anything up to 200 miles or more, with their shiploads of salt and salted fish, slaves, precious fabrics, spices and drugs, medicines, perfumes, ornaments, and other rare and valuable merchandise. In course of time the Venetians were joined by merchants from other riverside towns such as Ferrara, Mantua, Cremona, Piacenza, and Milan. All of them used the rivers, so that the Po and its tributaries rapidly became flourishing highways of commerce, of which the records of Cremona in the 10th and 11th centuries give especially rich and lively evidence.

However, the most important commercial center of the Po valley, for at least three centuries, was certainly Pavia, which only started to decline in favor of Milan after the year 1000. Pavia was the seat of government and financial administration. It was also situated at the junction of the Po and the main roads from the Alps and Apennines; and it was the terminus for most ships coming up river. So the city had every right to be considered the economic as well as the political capital of the kingdom. Down to the late 11th century the coinage of Pavia prevailed throughout Lombard Italy. At Pavia the richest monasteries and churches of Lombardy and other regions all had houses or hostels or manorial centers, often with a shop or two, which they rented out to merchants, and with the right to make use of the ports on the Ticino and the Po. So notable a center of exchange was not frequented only by merchants from other towns, Venice, Amalfi, or Gaeta; the *Memoratorium* informs us that Pavia had its own merchants, "men of great worth and wealth" (*magni honorabiles et multum divites*), who were organized in "mysteries" (*ministeria*) or guilds under royal tutelage and had the special privilege of preemption in all the markets they attended by land or water; by this concession they avoided competition from local traders in whatever business they transacted. Beside the merchants, we find the members of many other Pavian trades and professions joined together in guilds under their own masters; such were the moneyers (*monetarii*), who farmed the mint, the fishermen and boatmen, the soapmakers, and the curriers, who were limited to 12 in all with a like number of apprentices. At Pavia therefore, and probably also at Piacenza, the evidence of the *Memora-*

torium makes it certain that toward the end of the 10th century there existed a group of professional and trade associations, controlled and taxed by the crown, which in return invested them with rights of monopoly.

4. THE BEGINNINGS OF UNIVERSITIES

This selection is from the book in which an American historian first championed the existence of a major intellectual and cultural revival in 12th-century Western Europe and attempted to describe its basic nature and outstanding characteristics, in part, to demonstrate that "the great [Italian] Renaissance was not so unique or so decisive as has been supposed."

CHARLES HOMER HASKINS[*]

The 12th century was not only an age of revival in the field of learning, it was an age of new creation in the field of institutions, most of all in the institutions of higher education. It begins with the monastic and cathedral schools; it ends with the earliest universities. We may say that it institutionalized higher learning or at least determined that process. In 1100 "the school followed the teacher"; by 1200 the teacher followed the school. At the same time these intervening years created a more advanced type of school by the very fact of the revival of learning. At the close of the 11th century learning was almost entirely confined to the seven liberal arts of the traditional curriculum; the 12th century filled out the *trivium* and *quadrivium* with the new logic, the new mathematics, and the new astronomy, while it brought into existence the professional faculties of law, medicine, and theology. Universities had not existed hitherto because there was not enough learning in Western Europe to justify their existence; they came into being naturally with the expansion of knowledge in this period. The intellectual revolution and the institutional revolution went hand in hand.

Besides producing the earliest universities, the 12th century also fixed their form of organization for succeeding ages. This was not a revival of

[*] Reprinted by permission of the publishers from Charles Homer Haskins' *The Renaissance of the Twelfth Century*. Cambridge, Massachusetts, Harvard University Press, Copyright 1927 by the President and Fellows of Harvard College, and 1955, by Clare Allen Haskins.

some ancient model, for the Greco-Roman world had no universities in the modern sense of the term. It had higher education, it is true, really superior instruction in law, rhetoric, and philosophy, but this was not organized into faculties and colleges with the mechanism of fixed curricula and academic degrees. Even when the state took on the responsibility of advanced instruction in the state-paid teachers and public law schools of the later Roman Empire, it did not establish universities. These arise first in the 12th century, and the modern university is derived in its fundamental features from them, from Salerno, Bologna, Paris, Montpellier, and Oxford. From these the continuity is direct to our own day, and there was no other source. The university is a medieval contribution to civilization, and more specifically a contribution of the 12th century.

The word university originally meant a corporation or guild in general, and the Middle Ages had many such forms of corporate life. Only gradually did the term become narrowed so as to denote exclusively a learned corporation or society of masters and scholars, *universitas societas magistrorum discipulorumque*, as it is expressed in the earliest and still the best definition of a university. In this general sense there might be several universities in the same town, just as there were several craft guilds, and these separate universities of law or of medicine were each jealous of their corporate life and were slow to coalesce into a single university with its special faculties. Speaking broadly, the nucleus of the new development was in northern Europe a guild of masters and in the south a guild of students, but in both cases the point of chief importance centers about admission to the guild of masters or professors. Without such admission there could be no license to teach; until then one could be only a student, thereafter one was a master, in rank if not by occupation, and had passed out of the journeyman stage. In order to guard against favoritism and monopoly, such admission was determined by an examination, and ability to pass this examination was the natural test of academic attainment in the several subjects of study. This license to teach (*licentia docendi*) was thus the earliest form of academic degree. Historically, all degrees are in their origin teachers' certificates, as the names doctor and master still show us; a Master of Arts was a qualified teacher of arts, a Doctor of Laws or Medicine was a certified teacher of these subjects. Moreover the candidate regularly gave a specimen lecture, or, as it was said, incepted, and this inception is the origin of the modern commencement, which means commencing to teach. An examination presupposes a body of material upon which the candidate is examined, usually a set of standard textbooks, and this in turn implies systematic teaching and a minimum period of study. Curriculum, examinations, commencement, degrees are all part of the same system; they are all inherited from the Middle Ages, and in some form they go back to the 12th century....

By the 13th century Paris has become the mother of universities as well as the mother of the sciences, counting the first of that numerous progeny which was to comprise all the medieval universities of northern Europe, in Great Britain and in Germany as well as in northern France and the Low Countries. An even wider field is suggested in a letter of 1205, in which the new Latin emperor of Constantinople asks for aid from Paris to reform the study of letters in Greece. The eldest daughter of this large family was Oxford, mother in turn of English universities....

Bologna, too, was a mother of universities, parent of the institutions of higher learning in southern Europe as Paris was in the north, although, with the exception of whatever influence Bologna had upon Montpellier, it is not clear that any of these daughters came into being in the 12th century. The first quarter of the 13th century, however, sees the foundation of Bologna's neighboring rival Padua in 1222 by a secession from Bologna, not to mention the less important though somewhat earlier examples of Modena, Reggio, and Vicenza; of Frederick II's university at Naples in 1224, created with Bolognese masters for the purpose of keeping at home the students of his Sicilian kingdom; and of the earliest Spanish universities at Palencia and, probably by this time, at Salamanca. In northern Italy this propagation was usually by fission, as in the case of Oxford from Paris, and in any event the Bolognese type of organization was followed. To a large extent also these later universities were universities of law....

The letters of the students depict them in all aspects, from the naïve chalk and lambskins of the Chartres letterbook to the polished love letters of the Orleanese *dictatores*. They show the scholars set upon by the townsmen of Paris and Oxford, praising the medicine and the climate of Montpellier, begging their way through the mud of Bologna, penning ingenious and ingenuous missives home for money and necessaries, turning the left cheek to paternal reproof, appealing artfully to a mother's affection, borrowing a Priscian from a comrade, exalting their special master and their special subject of study. One example from Oxford *ca.* 1220 must suffice:

B. to his venerable master A., greeting. This is to inform you that I am studying at Oxford with the greatest diligence, but the matter of money stands greatly in the way of my promotion, as it is now two months since I spent the last of what you sent me. The city is expensive and makes many demands; I have to rent lodgings, buy necessaries, and provide for many other things which I cannot now specify. Wherefore I respectfully beg your paternity that by the promptings of divine pity you may assist me, so that I may be able to complete what I have well begun. For you must know that without Ceres and Bacchus Apollo grows cold. . . .

The student of all subsequent time is here, sure proof of the existence of the new university life.

This student class is singularly mobile and singularly international, if we may use this term in an age when nations were only in process of formation. Bologna has its English archdeacons and German civilians, Paris its clerks from Sweden and Hungary, as well as from England, Germany, and Italy. Even the cathedral schools drew from beyond the Alps and across the narrow seas. Moreover the same student might attend more than one university. Adalbert of Mainz early in the century and Guy de Bazoches toward its close visit both northern Paris and southern Montpellier; one of John of Salisbury's masters went from Paris to Bologna where he unlearned what he had taught and then came back and untaught it. Brunellus the Ass was doubtless not the only English student who moved from Salerno to Paris. The international student of the *studium generale* is the natural accompaniment of the international language and the international culture of the 12th century.

Edward J. Goodman, Professor of History and Director of the Institute of Hispanic Studies at Xavier University in Cincinnati, Ohio, was born in Dubuque, Iowa, in 1916. A graduate of Loras College, he received his M.A. and Ph.D. degrees from Columbia University. He has taught history, government, and international law at Notre Dame College (Staten Island), Seton Hall University, and the U.S. Naval Academy, and was a visiting professor at the University of Illinois. He is the editor of *The United States and Latin America Look at Each Other* (Cincinnati, 1958) and *Colombia, Ecuador, and Venezuela: Their Peoples and Economies Today and Tomorrow* (Cincinnati, 1961). He has also been a contributor to the *Hispanic American Historical Review,* the *Review of Politics,* and *Thought,* as well as to the *New Catholic Encyclopedia* and the *Catholic Encyclopedia for School and Home.* He is a member of the American Historical Association, the Association for Latin American Studies, and Phi Alpha Theta.

CHAPTER TWO

EDWARD J. GOODMAN

Xavier University

Explorations

UNTIL THE FIRST CRUSADE, European geographical knowledge had made scant progress since the days of Claudius Ptolemy. Little was known of Africa beyond the Mediterranean coast, and knowledge of Asia beyond the bounds of the Hellenistic East was extremely limited, and was in many instances largely a matter of fable. Medieval map making was largely confined to the T-in-O maps, more theological than geographical, which placed Jerusalem in the center, with the Mediterranean, Nile, and Don forming the T (east was at the top), and an all-encircling ocean forming the O. In the absence of reliable charts to guide them, navigators did not venture beyond sight of land.

The Crusades were to bring the Near East back into focus, and the 13th century witnessed a considerable expansion of geographical knowledge through overland expeditions into farthest Asia. Best known of these were the travels of the Polos to the court of Kublai Khan at Peking; the account of one of them, the *Book of Ser Marco Polo*, was one of the most influential books of the age and appeared in many copies, one of which was owned by Christopher Columbus. The demand for the riches of the East, and for spices in particular, stimulated by the Crusades and Marco Polo's work, resulted in the establishment of a lively trade with Asia. The Venetians and Genoese were particularly active, and after the fall of Constantinople to the Ottoman Turks, the Venetians secured a near monopoly of the trade.

Meanwhile, inventions and developments in ship construction and map making greatly facilitated travel by sea. The compass, astrolabe, and quadrant made it possible for medieval navigators to ascertain their direction and position with a fair degree of certitude. The T-in-O maps gave way to navigational charts of surprising accuracy; chief among these was the *Catalan Atlas* of 1375, which incorporated all of the existing geographical knowledge, including the far reaches of Asia. The maps in this atlas were of the portolan type, which originated in Genoa; they showed coastlines only, in considerable detail. They were laced with loxodromes (or rhumb lines), but, lacking lines of latitude and longitude, were not useful far out at sea. Later Portuguese maps made use of this refinement; a prime meridian was indicated (usually through Cape São Vicente), which was marked off in degrees of latitude. The latter could be determined at sea by sighting the polestar, but longitude remained a vexing problem; the ship's hourglass was not very dependable, nor was the method of measuring speed by dropping chips alongside the ship. Amerigo Vespucci, by careful astronomical observations and the use of an almanac, was able to determine longitude with some degree of accuracy, but only the invention of the chronometer provided a complete solution to the problem. Ship construction also changed. After 1400 vessels began to be square-rigged for greater ease of handling; the Portuguese *naus* were so rigged, but the lateen-rigged caravel continued to be widely used.

The great breakthrough in exploration, which took Europeans out of the Mediterranean and the coastal waters of Europe to the uttermost parts of the earth, came in the 15th century under the aegis of Portugal. This small kingdom, already a unified national state, was forced by its size to seek its future in trade, and was uniquely situated for this purpose. Furthermore, its dynasty was blessed with a gifted prince, Henry the Navigator (1394–1460), whose navigation school at Sagres gave a tremendous impetus to discovery and exploration. Two motives dominated Portuguese enterprise: a desire to spread the faith and outflank Islam and a desire for the wealth of the East. Prince Henry, Grand Master of the Order of Christ, devoutly hoped to put his country in the fore in missionary enterprise; part of his grand design was to halt the progress of Islam by a flanking movement, to be accomplished by an alliance with the legendary powerful Christian ruler in Africa, Prester John. If the continent of Africa could be rounded, of course, the Venetian monopoly would be broken and the wealth of the Indies would pass through Lisbon.

The first fruit of Prince Henry's enthusiasm was the rounding of Cape Bojador in Morocco in 1434, beyond which Europeans had long feared to sail. Considerable progress was made along the African coast to Sierra Leone before Prince Henry's death, but exploration languished somewhat thereafter until taken up in earnest by Dom João II (1481–95), under whom Diogo Cão discovered the Congo River, and Bartolomeu Dias successfully rounded the Cape of Good Hope, opening the way to India. Under Dom João's successor, Manuel I, "the Fortunate," Vasco da Gama sailed boldly into the middle of the Atlantic Ocean and thence direct to the Cape of Good Hope, proceeding on, with the aid of an Arab pilot, to Calicut in India. A little later, Albuquerque was to establish at Goa the foundation of a powerful Portuguese empire in the Indies.

Beyond all question, the greatest single event in the whole history of discovery and exploration was the discovery of America, and the credit for it belongs unreservedly to Christopher Columbus. There is no doubt that the Norsemen preceded Columbus by centuries, and Portuguese historians have been diligent in attempting to prove a Portuguese priority. But whatever was accomplished before 1492 left no permanent result, while the work of Columbus was enduring. Seeking a direct route to the Indies by sailing west, unaware of the existence of the Western continents and hence underestimating the size of the earth, the Genoese admiral believed he had indeed reached his goal, but searched in vain for a passage to the Indian Ocean. It remained for the Florentine Amerigo Vespucci to realize that this was a new world, and for the Portuguese Magellan, sailing in the service of Spain, to find the passage and reach the Indies. After his untimely death in the Philippines, his ship, the *Victoria,* completed the first circumnavigation of the globe.

Exploration of the New World proceeded rapidly in the 16th century. Lured by gold, motivated by a desire to Christianize the Indians, or driven by the sheer love of adventure, men left the Iberian peninsula to subdue a continent. *Conquistadores* from Spain overturned the extensive Aztec and Inca empires and explored the interior of South America and the southern portions of the United States; missionaries followed them, penetrating deep into the interior in their search for souls to save. In the far north, English and Dutch navigators entered the Arctic in a futile search for a northwest passage to the Orient.

The lead in exploration in the 17th and 18th centuries was taken by the English and the Dutch (and, to a lesser extent, the French), and great commercial companies were organized to exploit the areas they visited. To mention only a few, Schouten and Le Maire proved Tierra del Fuego to be an island, thus dispelling the myth of an enormous southern continent; the Scot Mackenzie first crossed North America at its broadest part; Abel Tasman accomplished the singular feat of sailing completely around Australia without seeing it, while Captain James Cook explored the far reaches of the Pacific Ocean. Meanwhile the British sent several expeditions to explore south Asia, the Russians began and completed the conquest of Siberia, and Italian Jesuit missionaries explored the interior of China and Tibet.

In the New World, Jacques Cartier had sailed up the St. Lawrence River in 1534, and subsequently La Salle, Marquette, and Jolliet, and numerous unremembered French *voyageurs* penetrated the Great Lakes region and the Mississippi valley. Meanwhile, hardy Brazilian *bandeirantes* explored the interior of Brazil, and Pedro Teixeira and Father Samuel Fritz explored the upper reaches of the Amazon to Quito. In the 18th century a new type of explorer was to appear—the scientist: La Condamine, Juan, and Ulloa set out to measure an arc of the meridian at the equator near Quito and subsequently explored the Amazon valley and the highlands of the cordillera; naturalists explored the valley of the Orinoco.

By 1800, only comparatively remote areas of the world remained largely unexplored. Much of Arctic and sub-Arctic North America still remained unknown, and only a hardy few penetrated into Patagonia and Tierra del Fuego. New Zealand was but slightly known, and Australia had been discovered but remained largely an unknown quantity. Africa was still the "dark continent" and European settlements—mainly Portuguese, Dutch, and British—clung precariously to the coast. The existence of the Antarctic continent was unknown.

The following selections have been chosen from some of the outstanding literature in the field of exploration, and will present certain problems of fact and interpretation, motivation and accomplishment, the rise of colonial empires and the extent of discovery and exploration down to the end of the 18th century.

1. THE PORTUGUESE POLICY OF
SECRECY—A PORTUGUESE VIEW

Jaime Cortesão has written extensively on the question of Portuguese priority in the discovery of America. In the following excerpt from his article he asserts that the prior Portuguese discovery was kept secret as a matter of policy to protect the new trade routes, and summons Columbus himself in witness to the Portuguese achievements, a theory which he develops more extensively in the remainder of the article.

JAIME CORTESÃO:
THE PRE-COLUMBIAN DISCOVERY OF AMERICA*

I propose to confine myself to the discussion of some new documents and to show their importance in order to arrive at a solution of the problem of the pre-Columbian discovery of America, in connection with the voyages of Christopher Columbus. I omit all references to the Norse discovery of America, which I consider a historic fact, as well as the hypothesis of the discovery by the Mandingo Negroes, studied by the American historian Leo Wiener, and by the Basques, which has also been frequently discussed by French and Spanish historians, and intend to deal only with the hypothesis of the pre-Columbian discovery of America by the Portuguese. I say the hypothesis, but it is convenient to add that it has become a historic fact for the majority of Portuguese historians and for many foreigners, of whom I will quote only Prestage, Zechlin, Biggar, Babcock, and Oliveira Lima, who at least accept it as very probable. For my part I have endeavored, in successive works, to establish a method for the study of the problem.

In my opinion, although I have to consider new sources, it was not owing to the lack of documents, but to want of method in their study, that some events of the past have remained obscure. The problem with which I deal becomes much clearer when we study it in the light of the two following considerations: first, the geographical environment systematically connecting the facts with the circumstances in which they have been produced; and second, the preponderant role played by economic factors in the evolution of the knowledge of the earth. This allows us to establish a new scale of values for the whole of the known texts and documents. Two errors have obscured this chapter in the history of geography: (1) the supposition that transoceanic voyages were more difficult than those along the coasts; (2) the neglect of the consideration that the economic objectives, pursued by the state, mght prevent the divulgation of geographical discoveries from reasons of high policy. When we study the three Atlantic continents together, from the point of view of the duration of the voyages between them, we reach the conclusion that, in a general manner, America is rather nearer Europe than is West Africa. A sailing ship takes the same time to come from Newfoundland to the English Channel as from the Straits of Gibraltar; and the same time from Cape

* From Jaime Cortesão, "The Pre-Columbian Discovery of America," *Geographical Journal,* Vol. LXXXIX, pp. 29–32, January, 1937. Reprinted by permission of the Royal Geographical Society and Dr. Armando Cortesão.

Horn, the farthest point of South America, to the Channel, as from Lagos, in the Gulf of Guinea. A glance at the map is enough to make us realize the big difference between these several distances. With regard to the voyages from Europe to America or Africa, the disparity, though less noticeable, remains. Furthermore, the crossing from one continent to another, making use of the northeast trade winds and the equatorial stream from the north—which in the 16th century the Spaniards called the Ladies' Gulf—was as nothing compared with the voyage from Europe to the Gulf of Guinea or to the Cape of Good Hope, in which the zone of the equatorial calms or that of the storms in the South Atlantic had to be crossed.

Another error is to suppose that all the truth about the geographical discoveries of the Portuguese must be found in their official chroniclers; this is what an eminent Italian historian, Carlo Errera, treating of this subject, called "the insuperable argument of the silence." But we must remember that the Portuguese monarchs of the 15th and 16th centuries were merchant kings, who pursued economic objectives through their navigations—that is, to establish commerce in tropical products, mainly those of the Orient, in order to become the intermediaries between the countries of production and Europe.

It has been forgotten that all nations which have discovered new routes toward countries of rich products and secured their commerce have sought to act as follows: to transform the trade into a monopoly; to close the routes by means of treaties and prohibitory fables, or by persecution of all transgressors; to conceal their policies and commercial activities, as well as the facts connected with them; to keep an eye on foreigners abroad and at home and to exclude them from their social circle. This was typical of the Carthaginians, who having discovered the countries producing tin, a product indispensable to the industries of that time, concealed the routes leading to the Cassiterides, closed the Straits of Gibraltar, and prohibited access thither by the most cunning and ruthless means; it was so with the Hanseatic League of the Middle Ages; and the Dutch in more modern times. This policy of monopoly and secrecy was the stricter in proportion to the weakness of their defensive means, the number of potential competitors, and the extent of the maritime routes and of the newly discovered lands. Portugal, a country of a very limited population during the 15th century—it had no more than 1,200,000 inhabitants—which had discovered immense and very rich lands, of which she had seen a part invaded and ravaged during the war of the Succession to the Spanish throne (1475–79), was a typical state fitted to be the organizer of the "Mare Clausum" and the monopoly of trade beyond the seas. The gold and the spices which the Portuguese looked for so eagerly were not less coveted in Europe than tin at the time of the Carthaginians, and their role as intermediaries also required monopoly and secrecy.

Prince Henry the Navigator began by organizing in 1443 the monopoly of the trade and navigation of the newly discovered lands. In 1454 the pope ratified this monopoly, forbidding all Christians to navigate toward the discovered lands without permission of the king of Portugal. Other prohibitive decrees followed, and, in 1480, the king ordered that the crews of foreign ships found in the Portuguese zone of navigation should be thrown into the sea.

Thus it is necessary to consider the policy of secrecy of the Portuguese princes, and other means of concealing from foreigners the knowledge of the sea routes toward the new countries. Having analyzed the context of the Portuguese chronicles I have arrived at the following conclusions: The *Chronicle of Guinea*, of Zurara, the existence of which was discovered only in the last century, from the copy in the Bibliothèque Nationale at Paris, is a résumé of a previous chronicle only, and has been truncated and mutilated in those passages which could better enlighten foreigners on the intentions of Prince Henry, or the commercial geography of the newly discovered lands and perhaps other unknown objectives. Thus, for instance, Zurara quotes the chapters of his work, where he referred to the division of the Oriental countries, in connection with the reasons which impelled him to undertake the discoveries. All these chapters have disappeared from the chronicles. On the other hand, a series of chronicles of Fernão Lopes, Cerveira, and Zurara, which is known to have existed formerly, and which might contain the history of the discoveries, has also disappeared. One of the official chroniclers, Rui de Pina, has summarized these chronicles and it is clear that he suppressed some information about the discoveries which were recorded there. Finally in the chronicles of Rui de Pina these voyages of discovery toward the west are not mentioned, although today we have no doubt about such voyages. However, this is not astonishing, because in the chronicle of King John II there is no word about such important events as the voyage of Bartolomeu Dias, during which he doubled the Cape of Good Hope, or the voyage of Pero da Covilhã to Calicut and from there to Sofala, which together contain the secret of the true sea route to the Indies. Taking these facts together, one may conclude that policy treated these discoveries as a state secret and forbade mention of them.

As a last proof, I have already recalled the following forgotten fact: in the *Côrtes* of 1481, that is to say in the first year of the reign of King John II, the people asked him in future to forbid foreigners to settle in his kingdoms and dominions, pointing out that the Genoese and the Florentines became too dangerous because they revealed his secrets of the Mina and the Atlantic Islands. It was no longer a political plan of the rulers alone: the whole nation demanded severe measures for maintaining the secret of the discovered lands. The documents were sequestered; to record new lands on the maps was forbidden; the nautical works became secret books; prohibitory tales were spread; and the navigators forced to keep the oath of silence. This is why João de Barros, historian of the discoveries of the time of Afonso V, after mentioning the coasts and islands of Africa discovered, adds: "other trades and islands have been discovered, of which we will not speak in particular, because we do not know when and by which captains they have been discovered. However everybody knows that at the time of this king many more things happened and were discovered than we have written. . . ."

The argument of silence cannot therefore be invoked about the Portuguese chroniclers. Official historians were silent, either from ignorance or for reason of state, about many facts connected with the secret policy of the nation. Once these two fundamental points are established—that America, as regards the voyages of sailing vessels, was nearer to Europe than was West Africa; and that the Portuguese chroniclers hid or ignored many of the principal facts of the history of the navigations—we may proceed to examine the sources in which we can find indications of the concealed voyages.

The following supposition seems reasonable. Since Christopher Columbus lived for some years in Portugal, where he matured his projects, we might expect to find in his notes some information about the voyages of the Portuguese toward the West, if such voyages had been made. Unfortunately many of his notes are known only through the transcription of his son Ferdinand in the *Historie della vite e dei fatti di Cristoforo Colombo,* and it is known that he endeavored to hide or to distort all that could diminish his father's glory. Even so, we find plenty of rather conclusive evidence in the *Historie* of Ferdinand Columbus, the *Historia de las Indias* of Las Casas, and the ship's journal of Columbus' third voyage.

In his *Histoire critique de la grande entreprise de Christophe Colomb,* H. Vignaud had already called attention to some of these notes, and the fact that during his sojourn at the monastery of La Rábida, the navigator had spoken with some sailors from Palos, a village near the convent. "Columbus himself," writes Vignaud, "reports that a pilot called Pedro de Velasco who dwelt in Palos told him, at the convent of Santa María de La Rábida, that with a certain Diego Detiene he had navigated 150 leagues towards the southwest of the island of Fayal (one of the Azores) seeking for the island of the Seven Cities, and that, as they did not find any land on that side, they came back and after discovering the island of Flores, they continued towards the northeast where they made some observations which led them to think that there existed some land to the West." In his notes Columbus dated this voyage from 1452. From Portuguese documents we know that this Diego de Tiene, that is to say Diogo de Teive, a navigator in the service of Prince Henry, had discovered the Island of Flores by that time, and that at the end of the same year the Prince granted him the monopoly of the sugar production in the Island of Madeira—which might represent the reward for very important services.

2. THE PORTUGUESE POLICY OF
SECRECY—AN AMERICAN DISSENT

Professor Morison has serious reservations concerning pre-Columbian Portuguese voyages to America, and views the assertion of a "policy of secrecy" as a device to cover the absence of any evidence of important discoveries resulting from them, if indeed they were made at all.

SAMUEL ELIOT MORISON
THE POLICY OF SECRECY*

Before proceeding to the southern voyages, let us consider what the Portuguese call a *política de sigilo* or *de mistério*—"the policy of secrecy" or "of mystery," with regard to maritime discoveries. According to the canon of certain historians of Portugal, this presumed policy of their crown fills all inconvenient holes in the record. It does not matter, we are told, that there is no evidence of de Teive and Velasco, João Vaz, Teles, Dulmo, and the rest finding anything; since the Portuguese kings always kept such matters under their hats, lest Spain or some other country jump the claim. Portuguese navigators do not, we are reminded, come home empty-handed; consequently there must have been *some* result from so many voyages to the west and northwest; it must be owing to royal

---

* Reprinted by permission of the publishers from Samuel Eliot Morison, *Portuguese Voyages to America in the Fifteenth Century*, Ch. II. Cambridge, Mass.: Harvard University Press, Copyright 1940 by the President and Fellows of Harvard College.

mystification and our imperfect knowledge, that we have no direct evidence of discoveries.

Yet what evidence have we of this 20th-century discovery, unknown to all earlier historians, the "policy of secrecy"? Its leading exponent, Dr. Jaime Cortesão, adduces one undoubted fact and a mountain of inferences. Here is the fact: in 1504 D. Manuel forbade the construction of globes or the reproduction of charts of Africa beyond the Rio Manicongo. But what of the period down to 1500, and of discoveries outside Africa? The Portuguese Cortes of 1481 petitioned D. João II to exclude foreigners, especially Genoese and Florentines, from settling in his dominions, alleging that they were good for nothing except to steal precious metals, and the royal "secrets as to Africa and the islands." But there seems to be no evidence that the King took action. A young man from Genoa named Cristoforo Colombo accompanied Diogo d'Azambuja when he built São Jorge da Mina in 1482. Fernão Dulmo, who received royal letters patent for discovery in 1486, was a Fleming. At the same time Martin Behaim of Nuremberg was not only welcomed to Portugal but made a member of the royal *junta dos matemáticos* and knight of the Order of Christ; and Martin revealed all the Portuguese secrets that we knew (and some that he made up) on his globe of 1492.

Other evidences of the "policy of secrecy" adduced by recent historians are these. The existing manuscript copy of the Azurara *Chronicle of Guinea* appears to be incomplete. Maps and sketches have disappeared from the *Esmeraldo de Situ Orbis*. João de Barros in the prologue to his "Decades of Asia" bewails the carelessness of the chroniclers in recording great deeds of discovery. De Góis, in his chronicle of D. João II, insinuates low work on the part of Rui de Pina, who does not even mention the important voyage of Bartolomeu Dias in his own chronicle of the King's reign. Barros further declares, after mentioning the discovery of islands in the Gulf of Guinea in the reign of Afonso V,

and other trades and islands have been discovered, of which we will not speak in particular, because we know not when or by what captains they were discovered; yet we know by common report that more things happened and were discovered in the time of this king than whereof we have written: such as an island, today unknown to us, which was found in 1438.

On the basis of these hints, and what is *not* found in the contemporary chronicles, Dr. Cortesão concludes: "the documents were sequestered; to record new lands on the maps was forbidden; the nautical works became secret books; prohibitory tales were spread; and the navigators forced to keep the oath of silence."

Is there anything more here than the natural disappointment that historical investigators feel at the slight attention paid by chroniclers and other contemporaries to what particularly interests them? Was Barros really any worse off than Richard Hakluyt, who bewailed the same careless recording of early English voyages overseas? Perhaps a little more, respecting Africa; and it was to African voyages alone that the complaints of Barros and Góis referred. In the early days, Prince Henry had been eager to employ Italians in voyages of discovery, as he had used Majorcans to teach navigation. Cadamosto, for instance, tells the story of his ship being detained by weather at Sagres, and Prince Henry sending an agent aboard offering to equip a ship for any of the Venetian officers who would make an African voyage for him, and to share the profits. Later, when the Portuguese had developed an immensely valuable trade in slaves and pepper, ivory and gold—the Lagos Company made a profit of 500 percent in 1485—they naturally became more exclusive. And although Portugal's monopoly in West Africa was recognized by a series of papal bulls, her rights were challenged by other countries, and her profits threatened by interlopers from England, the Netherlands, Genoa, and especially from Spain. Castile did not recognize the Portuguese overlordship of the Guinea Coast until after a short war, concluded by the Treaty of Alcáçovas in 1479; and the Spanish sovereigns were never eager to do their duty by restraining their subjects from private interloping. Undoubtedly D. João II, who was secretive by nature, did everything in his power to keep dark the immense sums he was making from the West African trade, and to conceal details of the African coast and islands.

This trait in his character, and line of his policy, are illustrated by the following anecdote. In order to discourage African interlopers, D. João II gave it out that only lateen-rigged caravels were capable of making the return passage from São Jorge da Mina, the fort that he had built in 1482. Building materials were laden thither in big-bellied, square-rigged ships called *hurcas*, which the King caused to be broken up after their cargoes were delivered, in order to maintain this fiction. Actually, *hurcas* could return well enough, since the Portuguese had discovered the trick of dropping down to the Line from Guinea in order to avoid the easterly setting current; but a master pilot who asserted as much at the king's table was roundly rebuked by him. Afterward D. João apologized, saying that he knew the pilot was right, but he wished nobody to suspect the truth.

Nevertheless, there was no secrecy about the *fact* of Portugal having discovered the West African coast below Cape Bojador. Her overlordship there was recognized by Spain and by the papacy. Yet we are asked to infer from D. João's and D. Manuel's national policy of African exclusiveness that they and their predecessors not only made secret discoveries of North America and Brazil but kept these discoveries so secret that they allowed Spain to obtain them rather than betray the secrecy; so secret that the Portuguese kings even concealed their prior discovery of America in negotiations partitioning the New World! In other words, we are asked to believe that the kings of Portugal were secret for secrecy's sake, that they pushed mystery to the point of idiocy.

Even of Africa, much knowledge did leak out. D. Afonso V presented a copy of Azurara's *Chronicle of Guinea* to the King of Naples in 1453; D. João II sent samples of Benin pepper to Flanders and elsewhere in 1486; and several Italian maps of the 1460's keep pace with the Portuguese African discoveries. The Henricus Martellus Germanus Atlas of 1489 (or at latest 1490) records the voyage of Bartolomeu Dias, who only returned in the last month of 1488; and the Cantino Map of 1502, prepared by a Portuguese cartographer in Lisbon for the agent of an Italian prince, is surprisingly accurate about the Portuguese discoveries in Africa, Asia, and Newfoundland. Consequently it is not very likely that the government could have kept dark so astounding a discovery as a new world beyond the seas, even had they been so stupid as to attempt it.

In a sense, it is true to say that a Portuguese policy of secrecy did exist with regard to Africa; yet this policy differed only in degree from the exclusive colonial policies of other countries. Philip II did not advertise the sailing dates of his treasure galleons, nor did Queen Elizabeth notify her royal cousin of Spain that Sir Walter Raleigh was about to found an English colony in Virginia. But the only evidence of a Portuguese policy of secrecy with regard to the discovery of America is *lack of evidence of a Portuguese discovery of America!*

In order to infer such a policy, we must show that it made sense. It was natural for the Portuguese monarchs to try to keep details of West Africa to themselves. But what would have been the sense in keeping an American discovery dark, and allowing Spain to get away with *mundus novus?* Fidelino de Figueiredo makes the surprising statement that D. João II declined the services of Columbus because he had "information concerning the western lands more positive than the visions" of the Admiral. Why, then, did he not do something about it? And the King's attitude toward Columbus, when he returned to Lisbon triumphant after his First Voyage, strongly suggests that D. João then knew nothing positive about transatlantic lands. "He believed," reports the chronicler Rui de Pina, "that this discovery was made within the seas and bounds of his dominion of Guinea which was prohibited" by the Treaty of Alcáçovas.

It is regrettable that we know no more of this conversation between Columbus and his royal host; but from the brief account of the official court chronicler, it is evident that the Admiral's story that he had discovered Antillia and Cipangu (Marco Polo's Japan) did not greatly impress the King. D. João believed that his Genoese guest had merely been poaching somewhere off the Guinea Coast. Now, if the Portuguese had already made transatlantic discoveries, this was the occasion for their king to assert it. Secrecy would have been most inappropriate.

The pro-Spanish bulls of Pope Alexander VI left very little of the Atlantic open to future discoveries of the Portuguese, and even failed to safeguard their southern route to the Indies. D. João II made prompt protest, which resulted in the famous Hispano-Portuguese Treaty of Tordesillas (1494) establishing a line of demarcation 370 leagues west of the Cape Verde Islands. This treaty also has been seized upon by the mystery school of thought to prove that D. João II had found something east of the demarcation line, and was saving it up, as it were. On the contrary, both Spain and Portugal were concerned therein to reserve hemispheres for future discovery; and in the Compact of 1495, which supplements the treaty, D. João consented to postpone marking the line until some island or mainland was discovered in the Portuguese section of the Atlantic as well as the Spanish. Even this does not stump the mystery boys; they will have it that D. João was still keeping his discovery of Brazil secret. In other words, they are asking us to believe that the King, who was nobody's fool, had pushed secrecy to such a degree that he was even secret about his discoveries in a treaty partitioning discoveries. Secrecy in such circumstances would have been no policy, but sheer imbecility.

No "policy of secrecy" hindered a good deal being known and published abroad about the voyages of Gaspar Corte-Real to Newfoundland in 1500 and 1501. The Cantino, Canerio, King and Oliveriana Maps of 1502–3, all Portuguese or derived from Portuguese sources, have considerable information about them, both in graphic form and in the legends; and the official chronicle of that reign describes Corte-Real's discoveries in some detail. None of the contemporary authorities mention any earlier Portuguese discovery in that region, despite the fact that the Cabot voyage of 1497 gave England good ground to contest the Portuguese title. A policy of secrecy under such circumstances would have been very bad policy indeed.

Actually, we know more about the Corte-Real voyages than we do about the English voyages to Newfoundland in the same decade. Consideration of these parallel sets of voyages, the Portuguese and the English, may explain the disappointing paucity of information about Portuguese attempts to discover Western lands, on grounds other than mystery.

Despite the great interest in the Cabot voyages from the time of Richard Hakluyt, their significance for English, Canadian, and United States history, and after a century of intensive research, very little is known about them from English sources. The bulk of our information still comes from letters of foreigners, and from the Juan de la Cosa Map. A Venetian merchant in London wrote home that "Zuam Talbot," whom the English called "the great admiral," after returning from his first voyage, went dressed in silk, and was "run after ... like mad"; yet from the very slight mention of him by contemporary English chroniclers we might infer a Tudor "policy of secrecy." No letter or even signature of John Cabot has survived; we do not even know when or where he died. His second voyage, in 1498, can only be reconstructed by hypotheses, in which no two historians agree. And of the voyages made by the Anglo-Portuguese syndicate of Bristol between 1501 and 1505, we have no record except trifling presents to the king from the "newe founde lande," and royal pensions to the surviving adventurers. Richard Hakluyt found the same difficulty in tracking down these early English "traffiques and discoueries," as did the Portuguese historian Barros in obtaining information on early *gesta Lusitanorum.*

The reasons for this paucity of evidence are doubtless the same in the one country as in the other: lack of interest on the part of chroniclers and other literary contemporaries; failure to preserve letters, receipts, and legal documents that might help us to reconstruct the story. It is fantastic to infer from absence of evidence that important discoveries must have been made, and that royal officials went about silencing seamen, expurgating chronicles, and destroying sections of the crown archives, in order to conceal from the Old World what the Portuguese had discovered in the New. There was reason for doing that sort of thing about the sources of Guinea gold and slaves, to which Portugal had a publicly admitted exclusive right; but to suppose that the Portuguese deliberately concealed discoveries in the New World, and based their titles to those lands on voyages made in the year 1500, when they were actually discovered years before, would be as reasonable as for the English to have suppressed all knowledge of John Cabot, and to have based the English title to North America on the voyages of Frobisher and Gilbert.

3. INTERPRETING COLUMBUS' DISCOVERY

The Mexican historian Edmundo O'Gorman is concerned in his writings on the discovery of America less with the fact of Columbus' discovery than an interpretation of the fact. After a consideration of Columbus' belief that he had found Asia in 1492, Professor O'Gorman suggests three different ways of interpreting the discovery in the light of the historical evidence.

EDMUNDO O'GORMAN*

Since we now intend to subject an interpretation to a test, it is well to have a clear idea of just what an interpretation is.

Any act considered in itself is a mere happening that lacks meaning; we cannot say what it *is;* it has no particular being. In order that it may possess a being, that we may be able to say just what it is, it is necessary to assign to it some intention or purpose. The moment we do this, the act takes on a meaning and we can then state what it is; we endow it with a specific being chosen from various possibilities. This operation is what is known as an interpretation. To interpret an act is to endow it with a specific being by granting it a particular intention.

Let us take an example. We see a man leave his house and walk toward a nearby forest. The acts considered in itself, is a pure happening, a *factum.* But what is the act? Obviously it can be any one of many different things: a stroll, an escape, a survey aimed at lucrative ends, a scientific exploration, the beginning of a long journey, or as many other things as imagination can provide, always depending on the intention which the man may be supposed to entertain.

Our capacity for granting a specific being to an act by interpreting it is, however, subject to limits. Whatever intention is assumed, it must be attributed to an agent not necessarily capable of carrying it out, since he may use another agent for that purpose, but capable of having intentions, since otherwise we should have an absurdity. There are all sorts of entities which can be and have been conceived as capable of volition and of

* From Emundo O'Gorman, *The Invention of America* (Bloomington: Indiana University Press, 1961), pp. 35–40. Used by permission of the publisher.

carrying out their intentions, such as God, the angels, man, spirits from the outer world, and even animals, whereas others are capable of volition, but not of action, such as certain metaphysical entities, Nature, or Universal History, depending on the way in which some philosophical doctrines understand them. But what may not be conceived in such a way are all inanimate entities, such as geometric figures, numbers, or material things: a triangle, the number two, a table, the sun, or the sea. Should we conceive of them as capable of having intentions, it is in a metaphorical sense only; otherwise we go beyond the bounds of reason and arrive at a logical absurdity.

Thus an interpretation of an act can be admissible even though the agent carrying it out may be incapable of having intentions, provided that the purpose which gives the act its significance derives from an entity capable of having them. The opposite case, though, would be absurd, even if we assume that the agent carrying out the act has this capacity.

In the light of these considerations, let us examine the historical evolution of the idea of the discovery of America as we know it. We are dealing with three different ways of interpreting the same act, namely Columbus' voyage of 1492.

In the first stage, the interpretation consists in affirming that Columbus showed that the lands which he found in 1492 were an unknown continent, since it was with that intention that he undertook the voyage. Here we have an admissible interpretation, since the intention which endows the act under interpretation with the meaning of being a venture of discovery is placed on a person, that is, on someone capable of having intentions and of carrying them out. We know, however, that this interpretation had to be discarded, because documentary evidence rendered its empirical basis untenable.

In the second stage, the interpretation consists in affirming that Columbus showed that the lands which he found in 1492 were an unknown continent for, although this was not the intention with which he undertook the voyage, and although he had no idea of what he had accomplished, in carrying out this act he fulfilled the designs of history, which required that humanity be made aware of the existence and being of that continent.

In this second case the interpretation is still admissible, since the intention which gives the act under interpretation the meaning of a venture of discovery is placed on the act itself; that is, it is conceived as immanent in history, an entity previously understood as capable of embracing intentions, though without the capacity of carrying them out, so that it makes use of Columbus as an instrument for that purpose. We know, however, that this interpretation also had to be discarded, not through the failure of its empirical basis, but because the theoretical premise became untenable.

In the third stage, the interpretation consists in affirming that Columbus showed that the lands which he found in 1492 were an unknown continent purely by chance, that is, with no intention whatever being involved in the process.

In this case it is clear that, from the point of view of the requisites of any interpretation, the thesis offers a serious difficulty, because in spite of its denying the intention, the act is endowed with the same meaning as in the previous cases. Since this is impossible, because without that requisite the act could not assume the meaning which is assigned to it, it is necessary to assume that the intention exists in spite of its having been denied. The problem therefore appears in a twofold aspect: first, how to reconcile that contradiction, and second, to find out the whereabouts of the intention which must be assumed in order that the act may have the meaning which it has been given.

The contradiction can be got around if we bear in mind that it is not necessary for the agent who is carrying out the act to have the intention which gives it its meaning, since we know that he may be acting as a mere instrument of some design that is not his own. In this way Columbus could have revealed the being of the lands which he found without having the intention of doing so, so that from Columbus' point of view it would be legitimate to assert that the act was not intentional. Only by assuming that Columbus acted as an instrument of a design which was not his own can we avoid the contradiction that we have pointed out. On this score the thesis under consideration may be salvaged.

But where are we to find this concealed and mysterious intention which gives the 1492 voyage its meaning as a "discovery"? The answer leaves no room for doubt. Since any act can in this respect offer only three possibilities, namely, (1) the agent or subject of the act, (2) the act itself, and (3) the thing or object of the act, and since in this case the first two have already been tested and discarded, we can only conclude that in this third stage the intention is placed on the object which is said to have been discovered as something immanent in it. But it then seems obvious that the thesis ends in an absurdity, since the continent which we call America is clearly one of those inanimate entities incapable of conceiving intentions.

Thus we have disclosed the basic logical absurdity of this thesis and have arrived, at long last, at an explanation of what seemed to us so very suspicious from the beginning, that is, to have held a man historically responsible for something that it is known he did not do. When it is affirmed that Columbus discovered the American continent by chance when he hit upon some lands which he believed were part of Asia, that is, when we are told that Columbus revealed the being of an object entirely different from the one with which he had endowed it, we are actually being asked to believe that that object itself revealed its secret and hidden being at the moment when Columbus perceived it and by virtue only of that perception, for otherwise there is no other possible way to explain the revelation which we are told took place.

The logical absurdity in this thesis becomes even more patent as soon as we draw the inevitable consequences, for it is now clear that the idea of a chance discovery of the American continent not only cancels Columbus' personal purposes and opinions as inoperative, but also turns him into a docile and blind instrument, no longer of some assumed designs of historical progress, but of some intentions absurdly supposed to be immanent in a mere physical object. When we admit this, however, we have turned history upside down and deprived man of even the questionable liberty which was granted to him by philosophical idealism. Instead of conceiving history as the result of decisions taken by men and carried out by men, it is now conceived as the result of designs that are immanent in objects, blindly and inexorably fulfilled by men. Thus man is no longer the serf of historical development, conceived as a rational process according to idealism—which in itself was bad enough; he is now the slave of nobody knows what mechanical blind process pertaining to inanimate material objects.

4. SEVENTEENTH- AND

EIGHTEENTH-CENTURY DISCOVERIES

The onetime librarian of the Royal Geographical Society outlines the vast extent of exploration down to 1800, both on land and by sea. During these centuries, leadership passed from Spain and Portugal to the English and the Dutch (and, to a lesser extent in terms of permanent results, to the French), and much attention was given to Asia and the Pacific area.

EDWARD HEAWOOD*

The closing years of the 16th century formed an important turning point in the history of the world, and, as a natural consequence, in the more special field of geographical discovery also. A hundred years had elapsed since the great events which gave to the latter end of the 15th century its unique influence on the story of the nations—the discovery of America, and the first voyage to India round the Cape of Good Hope. During that interval Spain and Portugal, the pioneers in the new movement toward worldwide empire and commerce, had attained a degree of expansion unknown since the days of the Roman Empire, and, in virtue of the famous bull of Pope Alexander VI, had practically divided the extra-European world between them. Fleet after fleet had been despatched from their shores, straining to the utmost the too scanty resources of the two nations, reinforced though they were by the riches of Peru, and the spices and other valuable commodities of the East. Meanwhile, other nations were standing forth as possible rivals, and the arrogant claims of Spain and Portugal to exclude all others from the world's commerce did but hasten the downfall of their supremacy.

In the hope of securing a share in the East Indian trade the English long expended their energies on fruitless efforts to open a route by the frozen North, though the bold exploits of Drake and others brought them into actual collision with Spain on the ground claimed by her as her exclusive property. Private adventurers also made their way to the East, but it was not until the nautical supremacy of Spain had been broken in 1588 by the defeat of the "Invincible Armada," that the equal rights of all to the use of the maritime highways were vindicated.

It was, however, not the English, but the Dutch who were the first to avail themselves of the new opportunities. After the voyages of the Portuguese had made Lisbon the chief entrepôt of the valuable Indian trade, Antwerp and Amsterdam rose to importance as centers of distribution of Indian goods over Northern Europe. Rendered desperate by Spanish oppression, the seven northern provinces of the Netherlands in 1580 declared their independence, and in retaliation Philip II, under whom the whole dominions of Spain and Portugal were then united, took the shortsighted step of forbidding the Amsterdam merchants to trade

---

* From Edward Heawood, *A History of Geographical Discovery in the Seventeenth and Eighteenth Centuries* (Cambridge: The University Press, 1912), pp. 1–11. Used by permission of the Cambridge University Press.

with Lisbon. Threatened with ruin, they were of necessity driven to more determined efforts to obtain an independent trade with the East, and though they too, for a time, made the mistake of searching for a northern route, they soon boldly resolved to enter into open competition with the Portuguese, and in 1595–96 the first Dutch fleet sailed for India. An English expedition had, it is true, made its way to the East in 1591, but it proved unsuccessful, and it was not until 1599 that systematic steps for a direct trade with India were taken by the formation of the English East India Company.

With the change thus brought about in the distribution of material power among the nations of Europe, it was natural that geographical discovery should also in future follow a different course. Whereas the great discoveries of the 15th and 16th centuries had been almost entirely the work of Spain and Portugal, with the beginning of the 17th the energies of both nations became suddenly paralyzed, and after the first decade of the new century no more great navigators set sail from their shores. Their place was taken by the Dutch, French, and English; the Dutch especially—who, as already stated, had gained a start on the English in the matter of Eastern trade—leading the way, during the early part of the new period, in the path of maritime discovery. But although the French lagged somewhat behind, as compared with the Dutch and English, in the prosecution of Eastern enterprises, they were destined to play an important part in the exploration of the New World, especially in North America, to which their view had been directed from an early period, even in the 16th century. By a curious coincidence the Russians were simultaneously entering upon a new period of activity in the broad regions of northern Asia. It was to these four nations therefore that the principal work in completing the geographical picture of the world in its broad outlines was now to fall. . . .

The *extensive* exploration of Europe may be said to have been completed by the close of the 16th century. Such fantastic forms as had been given to the northern parts of the continent, including the British Islands, in maps of the early part of the century, and even in the famous map of Olaus Magnus of 1539 (though this showed a great improvement on its predecessors), had given place to more correct outlines, thanks principally to the English voyages of Willoughby, Chancellor, Burroughs, and others, and the Dutch voyages of Nai, Tetgales, and Barents in 1594–96. The copies of Barents' own map, published at Amsterdam in 1599 and 1611, show well the advance that had been made in the previous half century. Russia too, though still imperfectly known to the rest of Europe, had been rescued from the obscurity hitherto enveloping it by the work of

Von Herberstein (1549), as well as by the travels of Giles Fletcher, Queen Elizabeth's ambasador to the Czar (1588), and of Anthony Jenkinson and other agents of the British Muscovy Company.

The knowledge of Asia attained before the end of the 16th century may be considered under three heads. First, that acquired by medieval travelers before the voyage of Vasco da Gama; second, that due to the voyages of the Portuguese and others by the sea route to India; and third, the somewhat vague information respecting northern Asia acquired by Russian and Finnish merchants and voyagers during the course of the century. The first of these sources had supplied more or less detailed information respecting the whole of Asia south of Siberia, but the absence of accurate maps or scientific description caused much confusion of ideas with respect to it. For the southern and southeastern countries, especially the coastlines, this information was now superseded by the results of recent voyages, though, as we have seen, the statements of the early travelers continued to exercise a powerful influence with map makers and cosmographers in Europe, if not with the voyagers themselves. For the whole of Central Asia, however, as well as the interior of China, the writings of Friar Odoric, Willem de Rubruk, Marco Polo, and the early missionary friars remained the only sources of knowledge, and could at best present a most imperfect picture of those vast regions. In the south and east the Portuguese voyages (recorded in the history of De Barros and the poems of Camoens) had before the close of the 16th century reopened to the world a knowledge of the whole coastline as far as the North of China and the Japanese islands. The greater part of the Malay Archipelago had become well known, including the northern coasts of New Guinea; but whether the southern coast of the great island had been explored is uncertain, the statement by Wytfliet that a strait existed between it and a land to the south being possibly based only on Mercator's theoretical representation. Some information had also been supplied regarding the various kingdoms of India and Indo-China by the travels of Duarte Barbosa, Caesar Frederik, Gasparo Balbi, Ralph Fitch, Jan Huyghen van Linschoten, and others, some of these having reached India overland, and thus contributed to a better knowledge of the countries of western Asia. The extensive travels of Fernão Mendes Pinto, though not published till the beginning of the next century, were carried out during the 16th, and, in spite of much exaggeration on the part of the traveler, threw considerable light on the state of the East in his time. Lastly, in northern Asia, the newly awakened enterprise of Russian and other merchants had begun to make known the western parts of Siberia, including the coasts of the Arctic Ocean as far as the mouth of the Yenesei.

The state of knowledge of this region at the beginning of the new century is shown by the map by Isaac Massa published in Holland in 1612. But the great advance of fur hunters and of others across the wilds of Siberia was only just beginning, and the discovery and conquest of that vast region belongs almost entirely to the period dealt with in the following pages.

In Africa, the end of the 16th century marks the close of a period of activity, to be followed by nearly two centuries of stagnation, so far as geographical discovery is concerned. The entire coasts were of course known, and in places, such as Benin, the acquaintance with the lands immediately in their rear was closer than was the case in our own times until quite recent years. There is no doubt, too, that some knowledge of the interior was possessed by the Portuguese at the time we are treating of, though to determine exactly the extent of that knowledge is a task of great difficulty, if it is not impossible, with the limited material we now possess. From the fact that maps of the 15th and 16th centuries show the African interior filled in with lakes and rivers such as are now known to exist there, it has even been imagined that the Portuguese of those days possessed an intimate knowledge of Central African geography, rivaling that due to the explorers of the 19th century....

In other quarters the knowledge of the Portuguese was probably confined to the districts closely adjoining their colonies of Angola, Mozambique, and Sofala. Behind the two last named, expeditions had been pushed to a considerable distance, and Portuguese envoys had reached the country of the celebrated chief known as the Monomotapa, south of the central Zambezi. The power of this potentate became greatly exaggerated and he was supposed to rule over an empire equal to those of Asiatic monarchs. The Portuguese writers were acquainted with the famous ruins at Zimbabwe, which place the Jesuit priests are even supposed to have visited; but this appears doubtful, as the name Zimbabwe was then applied to the residence of any important chief. The gold-producing region of Manica had certainly been visited before the end of the 16th century, and ruined forts now existing prove that the Portuguese occupation extended to the Inyaga country, a little further north, and was not confined to the Zambezi valley. On that river itself their knowledge seems to have extended about to the site of the present post of Zumbo, at the confluence of the Loangwa.

In South America, discovery had made vast strides during the century following the first arrival of white men. Within the first 50 years the whole contour of the coasts had been brought to light, though as the passage round Cape Horn had not been made before the close of the century it was still supposed by some that Tierra del Fuego formed part of a great southern continent. Before the new century began, the range of the Andes, with the important empires occupying its broad uplands, had been made known by the conquests of the great Spanish captains, while explorers of the same nation had also traced the general courses of the three largest rivers of the continent. By the voyage of Orellana in 1540–41, followed 20 years later by that of the tyrant Aguirre, almost the whole of the course of the Amazon had been laid down. In the system of the Plata the Spanish governors Mendoza and Alvar Núñez had ascended the Paraguay, penetrating almost to the frontiers of Peru, besides forcing a way from the coast to the upper Paraná. Of the Orinoco, the shortest of the three, less had been explored, as the cataract of Atures had turned back more than one adventurous voyager. Its western tributary, the Meta, had, however, been ascended for some distance, and the wide plains at the eastern foot of the Andes of New Granada, about which our information is even at the present day far from perfect, had been traversed again and again by searchers after the fabulous city of "El Dorado"—the Golden Monarch. These included German adventurers like Georg von Speier, Nicholas Federmann, and Philip von Hutten, as well as Spanish captains like Hernán Pérez de Quesada and Antonio de Berrio. Under the latter the site of the city changed its locality, and the southern tributary of the Orinoco, the Caroni, became the imagined channel of access to its fabled lake; but little success attended his efforts to penetrate in this direction. Nor did much increase of knowledge result from the voyages of Raleigh and other Englishmen to the same regions. In spite of all this activity vast tracts of forest, especially in the Amazon basin, remained unexplored, and the whole southern extremity of the continent was entirely neglected while, even where travelers had penetrated, the geographical knowledge obtained was often of the vaguest, and imaginary delineations of lakes and rivers long filled the maps.

In North America much less progress had been made in the work of discovery. While the coasts facing the Atlantic up to the threshold of the Arctic regions had gradually been surveyed by voyagers of various nations, and a few had pushed up the remote Pacific coasts as far as Lat. 42° N., the whole of the northern and northwestern shores—the former by reason of their icy barrier, the latter because of their distance from Europe—still remained unknown, though, as already stated, ideas of the existence of a strait separating northwest America from Asia began to be current about this time. The whole of the northern and central interior, too, remained a blank on the map, and only on the confines of the Spanish viceroyalty of Mexico had any progress in land exploration been made.

The example of the wealth of Mexico had led adventurers to roam the wide plains of the southern United States in search of fortune, and the expeditions of De Soto, Coronado, and others had made known something of the lower Mississippi and its tributaries, and of the more western regions up to the Grand Canyon of the Colorado. But the absence of rich empires in this direction soon caused these efforts to be abandoned. In Florida, unsuccessful attempts at a settlement had been made by French Protestants, and further north, in Virginia, the first beginnings of the English settlements destined to grow in time to such vast proportions were in existence. Still further north, off the coasts of Newfoundland, French, Spanish, Portuguese, and English ships frequented the banks in large numbers for the sake of the fishery, and the French under Cartier had already led the way in discovery by the ascent of the St. Lawrence beyond the present site of Quebec, soon to be the scene of colonizing efforts on the part of their countrymen. A wide field for discovery was thus open in eastern North America, and the coming century was to witness a well-sustained activity, leading to a great enlargement of the bounds of geographical knowledge.

In the wide domain of the Pacific Ocean much remained to be done, though fairly correct ideas as to its nature and extent had become current. Since the voyage of Magellan many Spanish navigators had crossed from the coast of America to the islands of the Eastern Archipelago, to which this was their regular route, owing to the division of the world between Spain and Portugal, the return voyage being made across the North Pacific in fairly high latitudes. From Callao in Peru Mendaña had twice crossed the ocean in about 10° S., discovering the Solomon and Santa Cruz groups and supplying apparent confirmation of the ideas then current as to the existence of a southern continent. On the second voyage he had been accompanied by the celebrated navigator Quiros, whose own chief work fell within the new century, and will be dealt with in the following pages. Other Spanish navigators had crossed the ocean north of the equator from Mexico to the Philippines, and it has been supposed that Gaetano—the pilot who accompanied one of these, Villalobos, in 1542 —afterward made a voyage to the Sandwich Islands. But this discovery, if made, was carefully kept secret, and had no influence on the subsequent history of Pacific exploration. The Englishmen Drake and Cavendish had likewise crossed the northern Pacific, and just at the close of the century the Dutch expedition under Van Noort had followed in the tracks of Magellan and for the fourth time effected the circumnavigation of the globe—but this belongs rather to the new than to the old period. In most of these voyages certain definite routes had been followed, which missed many of the most important groups of islands. The information brought home with respect to those seen was very vague and fragmentary, and for the most part they can with difficulty be now identified. Both in the north and south, vast expanses of ocean remained untraversed, and the exploration of these, especially in the south, was one of the principal tasks of the coming century.

5. EXPLORING THE FAR NORTH

The importance of the discovery and exploration of the New World tends to obscure the purpose of the early voyages of discovery—to find a new route to the wealth of the Indies. The search for a northern passage —the beginning of Arctic exploration—in competition with the southern routes controlled by Spain and Portugal is discussed in the following selection.

PERCY SYKES:
EXPLORERS IN NORTHERN LATITUDES DURING THE
16TH AND 17TH CENTURIES*

"Learned men and painefull travellers have affirmed with one consent and voice, that America was an Island: and that there lyeth a great Sea between it, Cathaia and Grondland, by the which any man of our countrey, that will give the attempt, may with small danger passe to Cathaia, the Moluccae and India."

Discourse of Sir Humphrey Gilbert.

It is not generally realized that the early exploration of the Arctic regions, which was mainly undertaken by English navigators, was due to the desire to reach Cathay and the Spice Islands. It was hoped to sell broadcloth, the chief manufacture at that period, to the Chinese and to Cape of Good Hope and the Straits of Magellan were monopolized by the Portuguese and Spaniards respectively, albeit this monopoly was being challenged, as we have already seen. But, should a northern route to the Moluccas be discovered, it would avoid the risk of death, capture, or imprisonment, if not of becoming the victim of an auto da fé, and, so far as Cathay was concerned, it would be a much shorter route.

---

* From Percy Sykes, *A History of Exploration* (New York: Harper and Row, 1961), chap. XVI. Reprinted by permission of the publishers.

In the first instance a search was made for a northeast passage to Cathay by the merchant adventurer of the Muscovy Company, on whose behalf Sebastian Cabot drew up the instructions for the first voyage, which enjoined that "You use all wayes and meanes possible to learne how men by the merchant adventurers of the Muscovy Company, on whose behalf may passe from Russia either by land or by sea to Cathaia." Its leaders were Sir Hugh Willoughby and Richard Chancelor, who sailed in command of three ships from Deptford in 1553. Before striking the coast of Norway, Willoughby disappeared in a great storm, and both he and his crew died of cold in the bay of Arzina, on the coast of Lapland. The third ship was also lost, but Chancelor had better fortune, for "he held on his course towards that unknown part of the world, and sailed so farre, that he came at last to the place where he found no night at all, and it pleased God to bring them into a certaine great Bay." This was the White Sea, and the voyage led to the discovery of Russia by the English. On landing, Chancelor was well received, and proceeded to Moscow, "a troublesome journey, wherein he had the use of certaine sleds." The Grand Duke Ivan entertained the Englishman most hospitably, and thus was inaugurated a valuable trade with Russia, regarding which country Chancelor collected much valuable information, the earliest to be received in England. It was speedily utilized, and in 1555 Chancelor returned to Russia, and secured from Ivan a monopoly of trade in the White Sea for the Muscovy Company.

From the standpoint of Arctic exploration, Stephen Burrough led a more successful expedition, which sailed in April, 1556. He was off the North Cape a month later, and, meeting some friendly Russian fishermen, he accompanied them across the Cronian Sea, as Pliny called it, to the Kola River. In July he "went in over the dangerous barre of Pechora," and sailed as far east as the island of Vaigaich, where he found Samoyeds who "for their carriages have no beasts to serve them, but Deer only."

We learn from Purchas that Antony Marsh, a Chief Factor of the Muscovy Company, not only gained detailed information about the Ob, but despatched some members of his Russian staff, who reached it by land in 1584. He refers to an English vessel which had reached Ob, where it had been shipwrecked and its crew murdered by the natives. This was the eastern limit of the English.

The Dutch, who had watched the voyages of the English explorers with deep interest, now began to take part in expeditions to the Arctic. The object of Jan van Linschoten's expedition, consisting of four ships, two of which were commanded by William Barents, was "to saile into the North seas, to discover the kingdoms of Cathaia and China." Starting in June, 1594, Novaya Zemlya was reached a month later. Barents sailed up its west coast, in spite of much difficulty owing to the ice, and reached its north part, which is called after its discoverer.

A second voyage in 1595 was not so successful, but in the following year a third expedition was made under Heemskerck with Barents as pilot and was notable for the discovery of Northwest Spitsbergen. Later the explorers attempted to sail round Novaya Zemlya, but were unable to do so. The unfortunate crew were forced to winter in great misery—the first time an Arctic winter had been faced. The heroic Barents, who died during the homeward voyage, certainly ranks among the great Arctic explorers.

In 1607, Henry Hudson sailed from England in an attempt to reach Japan by the North Pole. In this expedition he explored the east coast of Greenland, but bore away to Spitsbergen when a very high latitude was reached. He found his way barred by ice, and returned to England. It is interesting to note that in the map of Ortelius published in 1570, and indeed in other maps of the period, a clear passage is shown running due east across the northern coast of Asia. Actually the strenuous efforts made by the brave and experienced navigators barely succeeded in traversing one quarter of the enormous distance which separated North Cape from Bering Strait. To quote Milton:

> As when two polar winds, blowing adverse
> Upon the Cronian sea, together drive
> Mountains of ice, that stop the imagin'd way,
> Beyond Petsora eastward, to the rich
> Cathaian coast.

The search for a northeast passage had failed, but attempts continued to the northwest. Sir Humphrey Gilbert wrote a learned work "to prove a Passage by the North-west to Cathaia and the East Indies." His thesis was that America was undoubtedly the lost Atlantis of the classical geographers, and while relying on "Plato, Aristotle and other phylosophers," he argued that symmetry demanded a strait in the north of America to balance the Straits of Magellan in the south. Martin Frobisher, who was undoubtedly encouraged by such views as these, led an expedition to find a northwest passage in 1576. Rounding the south of Greenland (which he thought was the fictitious Frisland), he found what he hoped was the sought-for strait; but it was merely a bay, which is called after the explorer. He described the Eskimos as "like Tartars, with long blacke haire, broad faces, and flatte noses, and tawnie in colour, wearing Seale skinnes.... The women are marked in the face with blewe streekes down the cheekes, and round about the eyes." His experience of these "salvages" was not happy, as they carried off five of his men, who were never seen again. He, in return, kidnapped a male Eskimo to show in England.

After Frobisher came John Davis, who, in 1585, sailed along the western shores of Greenland, naming it the Land of Desolation, and crossing Davis Strait discovered the vast Cumberland Sound which he believed would prove to be the elusive Strait. In a third voyage, undertaken in 1587, Davis reached latitude 72° 41′ N. on the west coast of Greenland.

We now return to Hudson, who started on his fourth and last voyage in 1610. From Greenland he entered the Strait which had been accidentally discovered by Frobisher on a third voyage which he had made in search of gold. Following it up in the hope that it would lead to the passage, the ill-fated Hudson reached the vast bay which, like the Strait, was destined to be called after him. The last entry of Hudson runs: "The third day we put through the narrow passage.... After wee had sailed ten leagues, the land fell away to the southward, and the other iles, and land left us to the westward. Then I observed and found the ship at noone in 61 degrees, 20 minutes, and a sea to the westward." Hudson explored the east side of the vast bay, the ship "being haled aground" on November 1, and, 10 days later, it was frozen in. The following summer the crew mutinied, and Hudson with his son, Philip Staffe the carpenter, and the sick men were forced into the shallop and were never heard of again. It is satisfactory to read in the report of the not altogether blameless Abacuk Prickett, that the leaders of the mutiny all come to a miserable end.

We next come to William Baffin, who was one of the greatest of the splendid line of English navigators and explorers. The discovery of Hudson Bay had naturally excited high hopes, but further examination by Baffin proved that the quest must be continued farther north.

Under Bylot as captain he explored Hudson Strait in 1615. In the following year they sailed again much farther north than any of their predecessors up the coast of Greenland, naming the various peninsulas, and discovering Smith Sound and then Jones Sound and Lancaster Sound to the west, all three leading out of Baffin Bay as it is fittingly called. Baffin came to the conclusion that he had failed in his quest, whereas he had in reality marked out the route which, followed by his successors, led to final achievement, though not until two centuries later.

William Baffin ended his splendid career in the Persian Gulf. He had surveyed its coast, for which received a gratuity from the East India Company, and in 1622 he took part in the attack by the English on the fort of Kishm, held by the Portuguese. To quote *Purchas his Pilgrimes*, "Master Baffin went on shoare with his Geometricall Instruments, for the taking the height and distance of the castle wall; but as he was about the same, he received a small shot from the Castle into his belly, wherewith he gave three leapes, by report, and died immediately." I have visited Kishm fort, where I was shown the Portuguese guns and cannonballs.

The search for the Northwest Passage was unsuccessful at this period, but as in the case of the earlier quest it yielded invaluable results to the successors of these great navigators, while the training in navigation in the Arctic was of inestimable value to the seamen.

Hitherto in this chapter we have dealt with sea voyages. We must now turn to the discovery of Canada by Jacques Cartier, who, like other explorers, was searching for a new route to the Spice Islands. The cod fisheries discovered by Cabot were regularly visited by French, Spanish, Portuguese, and English vessels. The French fishing fleet sailed from Saint Malo, where its departure and return are still the chief subjects of interest in that picturesque port.

No attempt at serious exploration had been attempted since the voyages of Cabot until Cartier appeared on the scene off Cape Bonavista, Newfoundland, which is situated in the same latitude as Saint-Malo, in 1534. Coasting Newfoundland he sailed through the Belle Isle Strait, and examined the coast of Labrador, the sterile appearance of which caused him to write that "I am rather inclined to believe that this is the land God gave to Cain." The inhabitants he described as "wild and savage folk clothed with furs and painted with tan colours."

Sailing along the west coast of Newfoundland, he crossed Cabot Strait to the fertile Magdalen Islands, "the best land we have seen; for two acres of it are worth more than the whole of Newfoundland." He admired Prince Edward Island but could not land owing to the absence of a good harbor, and after reaching the mainland of Canada he crossed the mouth of the St. Lawrence to Anticosti Island. He attempted to explore the great river, but the "tides ran so strong that the vessels only lost way," and so it was decided to return to Saint-Malo.

In the following year Cartier started exploration at the point where he had left off, and after examining the northern shore for the hoped-for strait, he ascended the Hochelaga, as he called what is now the St. Lawrence. Friendly relations with the Indians were established through the agency of two natives, who had been taken to France and well treated, and, in spite of the strong current, good progress was made as far as Stadacona, the Indian village in the Charles River, of which he writes: "The region is as fine land as it is possible to see, being very fertile and covered with magnificent trees."

Continuing up the river with a bark and two longboats, the grapes and the wonderful bird life delighted Cartier, who reached Hochelaga in the longboats, to be received with dances and other signs of joy, the women bringing their babies to be touched by the strangers. He found Hochelaga to be a village of 50 large houses circular in shape and defended by a wooden palisade. Climbing an adjacent mountain, which he named Mount Royal, the French explorers enjoyed a marvelous view, ranging over plains with mountain ranges to the north and south, while following up the course of the great river they sighted "the most violent rapid it is possible to see." Thus was discovered the celebrated Lachine rapid.

Cartier had been remarkably successful. Not only had he discovered the fertile lower valley of the St. Lawrence and gained much valuable information as to the reaches above Hochelaga, which country was shortly destined to be colonized by France, but his discovery of the Strait of Cabot and of other islands bordering on the Gulf of St. Lawrence justify the high honor in which his name is held as an explorer.

6. THE EARLY COLONIAL EMPIRES

The centuries following the discovery of America and the eastern route to the Indies saw the establishment of five major colonial empires—Spanish, Portuguese, English, Dutch, and French—and the less important or less successful efforts of Denmark, Sweden, Scotland, and Prussia. By 1800 this first and perhaps most successful period of imperialism was nearing its end. In the following selection, Professor Nowell discusses the motivation behind this colonial activity, and the results.

CHARLES E. NOWELL[*]

An early 18th-century map compared with one made three centuries before would reveal at a glance how much man had learned about his earth. In 1400, a few years before Prince Henry's captains started sailing, the accepted picture of the world had not changed much from the one held by Seneca at the beginning of the Christian era. By 1700 the outlines of all the continents, except Australia, were known, and the seacoasts of the New World had been almost entirely explored. Circumnavigation of

---
[*] From Charles E. Nowell, *The Great Discoveries and the First Colonial Empires* (Ithaca, N.Y.: Cornell University Press, 1954), pp. 135–40. Copyright 1964, Cornell University. Used by permission of Cornell University Press.

the globe, first accomplished by El Cano's *Victoria* in 1522, had grown so commonplace a century later as to call for no comment at all.

True, a great deal remained to be learned. The interior of Africa was mysterious, and many dark spots existed in giant Asia. The Antarctic continent, to the best of our knowledge, had never been seen by a human being and more needed to be known about Australasia. Vitus Bering would soon find the strait parting America from Asia, and even later Captain Cook would banish the concept of *Terra Australis*. Though these and other details of unfinished geographical business remained and though some would not be wholly cleared up by the mid-20th century, no future discoveries could possibly equal those already made. By 1700 the great unknown, the world of Prester Johns, Antilias, and Fountains of Youth, had vanished. Seneca might have reveled in the new knowledge, but he might also have regretted the passing of something that could not be recaptured; the belief in a wonderful world, populated by the more preposterous hopes and fears of the human mind.

Thus Europe had already gone a long way toward preempting the vast lands and populations made available by the white man's discoveries. Imperial powers, working amid distractions and at differing speeds, had persevered. The two original ones, Spain and Portugal, simply because they were the first, had built their empires in comparative leisure; but France, the Netherlands, and England had struggled to build theirs in an era of colonial rivalry and bitter international jealousy. During the first century of imperialism the Iberian nations had the outside world almost entirely to themselves. Then, around 1600, Frenchmen, Hollanders, and Englishmen surged forth to seize what they could of the prized Iberian possessions and to grasp at any new places that seemed worth the taking. Minor efforts at colonizing were made by Sweden, Scotland, and Denmark, but these were either brief or insignificant. And while Western Europe reached beyond the ocean for empire, Russia stalked across Siberia to the Pacific and even temporarily beyond to Alaska. This Russian *drang nach osten* looms today as one of the decisive movements of history, but certainly it did not originate in the same background as the voyages of discovery and imperialism nor did it develop as a part of that movement.

Though the term "colonial empires" is loosely used here to designate all overseas dominions, conquest and colonization were not the same. Into such empty places as South Africa, Brazil, and North America, Europeans could freely move as settlers. In the Far East, Portuguese, Dutch, and English remained to the last a corporal's guard of palefaces, living and ruling amid the teeming native millions, whose essential way of life remained very little changed. In Spanish America both situations existed.

There were the lonely pampas of Argentina offering opportunities to colonists, and there were also the rich and heavily populated regions of Peru and Mexico, ripe for the swords of the conquistadors.

Europe's far-flung dominions were the product of many different needs and motives. Individuals pushed to the farthest corners of the Old World and the New to seek gold, adventure, freedom from tyranny, or escape from justice. They went to spread the true faith, or sometimes to escape the toils of what others considered the true faith. Or else they went merely to trade, to farm free land, to grow rich, or to live in the hope of growing free and rich.

The rulers and governments that fostered and regulated all these efforts were motivated largely by a hope of profits, a hope conceived in mercantilistic theories and developed along mercantilistic lines. The different European powers formed their companies and built their empires in different ways, but across the gap of several hundred years it is the similarities in their methods that now stand out most clearly.

European governments felt always more interest in the quick profits promised by trade or treasure troves than in the more solid investment of colonies. For this same reason they liked to avoid the burden of colonization wherever possible. Taking a page from the feudal past, they often escaped the expense of colonies by throwing the responsibility of pioneering and development upon private individuals. The Portuguese called these entrepreneurs donataries, the Spaniards called them adelantados or encomenderos. To the French they were seigneurs, to the Dutch patroons, and to the English proprietors. These territorial lords at times stimulated colonization, yet often blocked it either by failing to understand the needs of the colonists or by insisting on terms that prospective colonists were unable to meet. One after another, with very few exceptions, these proprietarial dignitaries were removed by their governments and were replaced by varying combinations of local and royal administrators.

The early empires failed strikingly to live up to the economic hopes and visions that had presided over their founding. Although their impact upon the economy and culture of Europe was tremendous, the impact came in ways not foreseen or planned. The empires had all been started on the mercantile theory, in the expectation that they would enrich the mother countries by causing gold and silver to pour in. Gold and silver did of course enter Europe through Spain from Spanish America, but this could not make mercantilism a sound doctrine. Since real wealth consists of goods, and since silver and gold are but convenient measuring sticks for determining value, the arrival of all this bullion created no wealth but merely brought a rise in prices and a dislocation of European economy.

Yet for centuries the governments of Europe stuck to mercantilism, each one trying, by colonial trade monopolies, to restrict commerce so as to pour cash into its own treasury and cut competitors out. The result was to keep trade from flourishing as it might have flourished and to force it into restricted, artificial channels. Europe, to be sure, was enormously richer by 1700 than in 1500, and the overseas world had contributed greatly to the increased prosperity. This, however, was in spite of mercantilism, not because of it. The true wealth consisted of the goods the outside world had sent to Europe, a flow that no mercantilistic regulations could altogether stop. Mercantilism had slowed the process of trade and wealth production; it could not stifle it entirely.

The colonists, in the meantime, failed to play passively the cut-and-dried role assigned to them. They were expected to buy the products of the mother country, to produce nothing that competed with those products, and to ship home raw stuffs priced much lower than the European goods they imported. The balance they were supposed to make up in cash. Insofar as they were able, the colonists declined to do as they were told. When opportunity offered they bought goods, from whatever source, at the lowest price. Likewise, they sold when they could in the best market, wherever it might be. This uncontrollable tendency on the part of their colonial subjects added to the mercantilists' difficulties by making law enforcement very costly, since it required fleets of ships patrolling the seas, revenue cutters patrolling the shores, and many vigilant officials on land. In the contest between the law and the law evader, colonial public opinions tended to be with the evader, and rightly. The smuggler who brought cheap goods into a colony and the local merchant who dealt sub rosa with him were unintentionally greater fomenters of world prosperity than were the sage European statesmen who spent their time planning ways and means of enforcing the laws.

Before the end of the 18th century Europeans were realizing, even without Adam Smith, that mercantilism somehow did not pay. This realization came at about the time the old colonial empires were starting to disintegrate. The French empire all but vanished in the smoke of the Seven Years' War, and 20 years later the American Revolution deprived England of her best colonies. The Dutch empire dwindled under the impact of the French Revolution and the Napoleonic Wars; and by 1825 Spain and Portugal had lost most of their possessions through the revolutions in Latin America. Imperialism now reached its lowest ebb, as European statesmen doubted for a time that colonial empires were worth the having. Gladstone, the noted English Liberal, would cheerfully have disposed of Canada as late as the American Civil War. Not until near the end of the 19th century, as a product of the Industrial Revolution, was a new, vigorous concept of empire to seize the minds and inflame the imaginations of Europe's leading statesmen.

Although the old empires brought economic disappointment, it is not enough to assess their value in immediate monetary terms. More important than the profits the long-dead merchants failed to amass are the tremendous legacies of human alteration they left. Millions of Latin Americans today speak with the accents of the conquistadors, and the English language was first carried abroad by the sea dogs of the virgin queen. The United States sprang from roots struck in New World soil by chartered companies and proprietary grants. Alongside the failures and faults of early imperialism must be placed the story of millions converted to Christianity, the spread of European civilization to the ends of the earth, and the complete revision of European economy, scientific thought, and moral values. Neither the dark man who was conquered nor the white man who did the conquering survived the process unchanged. Seneca, the Roman philosopher who speculated so wisely on the secrets of the world, would have marveled at all this, but then, as he himself makes clear, he would have expected to be surprised.

John M. Headley, Associate Professor of History at the University of North Carolina, was born in New York City in 1929. A graduate of Princeton University, he received his Ph.D. from Yale University. He formerly taught history at the University of Massachusetts and the University of British Columbia. He is the author of *Luther's View of Church History* (New Haven, Conn., and London, 1963) and of articles in the field of the Renaissance and Reformation. Present Chairman of the Southeastern Institute of Medieval and Renaissance Studies, he is a member of the American Historical Association, the Society for Reformation Research, and the Renaissance Society of America.

CHAPTER THREE

JOHN M. HEADLEY
University of North Carolina

Martin Luther—The Measure of the Man

FEW MEN in history have written so much and had so much written about them as Martin Luther. Rarely has a single man so effectively incorporated within his own mind and purpose the forces of an age and redirected the course of history as did Luther. In the case of the German reformer we are dealing with a man of colossal dimensions whose religious profundity and insight rank him among the first of Christian thinkers, whose rich and powerful personality never failed to provoke definite reactions and whose boundless energy found outstanding expression in the fields of pastor and theologian, biblical translator and reformer. The exceptional range and intensity of his thought inevitably promoted in the period of the Reformation and ever since a myriad of responses, often bewildering in their violence and number.

In the 400 years following Luther's death, each period has had its own understanding of the man; the image of Luther has been altered according to the mind and predisposition of that period. Indeed the historiography of Luther is in a very real sense a reflection of the intellectual history of the West. In the immediately subsequent period of Lutheran orthodoxy, Luther was transfigured into a prophet of superhuman dimensions, a herald of divine truth, a Moses of the Germans, and a new St. Michael whose written works expressed pure doctrine. Luther himself would have been the first to deplore this apotheosis and the hardening of his life's work into right doctrine. In the 17th and the 18th century Pietism preferred the young Luther who discovered faith as a trust in God's gracious mercy, to the Luther of passionate struggle and heroic determination for right doctrine. More interested in the spirituality than in the theology of Luther, Pietism found in him a living and intimate religion of the heart. In the subsequent eras of the Enlightenment and of German Idealism Luther became the great liberator, the man who expelled authoritarian dogmas and emancipated men's minds. In the course of the 19th century the presentation of Luther as a liberator had the detrimental effect of ignoring the religious focus in all his endeavors. The most important corrective to this tendency was given by the great German historian Leopold von Ranke, who in his history of the Reformation was the first to rediscover the historic Luther and to reestablish the polarity of politics and religion. For the Protestant masses, nevertheless, Luther still remained a sort of demigod or archangel. And with the nationalism and Pan-Germanism of William II and Hitler the public understanding of Luther suffered new and distinctive distortions.

The basis for a more exact knowledge of Luther had to await the careful editing of the reformer's writings. The beginning of the monumental Weimar Edition of Luther in 1883, which has now reached almost 100 volumes and is still not quite completed, advanced Luther research inestimably and continues to provide the basis for what is now called the "Luther Renaissance." While the new investigation of the primary sources promoted greater accuracy in the understanding of Luther and the recognition of relevant problems and issues, it did not, and of course could not, release Luther from the subjective judgments of scholars.

The quest for the true Luther, a Luther credibly accurate both theologically and historically, began at the turn of the century when the Protestant Johannes Ficker and the Catholic Heinrich Denifle almost simultaneously discovered different manuscripts of the reformer's 1515–16 lectures on the *Epistle to the Romans*. The controversy which spearheaded the revival of Luther studies and which placed the emphasis at the outset upon his formative years burst upon the scene with the publication of the first volume of *Luther und Luthertum* by the Vatican archivist Denifle. Ostensibly based upon the sources, the work shocked even German Catholics who had succumbed to a less hostile and relatively indifferent attitude toward Protestants. A student of monasticism in its late medieval decadence, Denifle portrayed Luther as the product of this decay. Luther appeared as a proud, lustful monk who invented his doctrine in order to provide a cover for his own failures and weaknesses. From the pages of the Dominican's study Luther emerged a liar, an imposter, and one whose licentiousness went beyond any discipline.

Modern scholarship has tempered the extreme position taken by Denifle in his theses. But at the time his accusations promoted certain traditions of interpretation and compelled Protestant scholars to examine more carefully the object of their admiration. Subsequent Catholic scholarship, striving for greater sympathy, gradually moderated Denifle's position while ultimately passing an unfavorable judgment upon Luther. Since Denifle, Catholic historians have come to abandon the thesis of the reformer's moral corruption, but they have moved the accent to the nervous and psychic weaknesses of Luther. One speaks of his abnormal character and morbid temperament; another sees in him an extremely complex psychological case. Even Joseph Lortz, in whom the Catholic interpretation of Luther attains its most distinguished and authoritative expression, advances doubts as to Luther's psychic health and finds him a subject of intellectual strain and of a hereditary inclination to melancholy.

Similar to the direction of Catholic interpretation is the professionally psychoanalytical approach to Luther. It is true that the intensity of his life, the violent abuse which he directed against the papacy, his depressions, fears, and apparent fixations expose Luther to psychoanalytic investigation. His father's alcoholism, his early years in an atmosphere of fear, his tendency to melancholy, and what some have seen as sexual obsessions are "sublimated" in a powerful intellectual activity. For psychoanalysis, in its efforts to disclose the mental unhealth of the patient, must still face the fact that in his lifetime Luther accomplished an enormous amount of work, much of unsurpassed quality. The most balanced and at the same time most provocative psychoanalytic study is Erik H. Erikson's, *Young Man Luther,* which manages to bring the insights of modern psychology to bear upon a late medieval subject and still preserve the historical context. No matter with how much humility and restraint the problem is approached, the use of psychoanalysis nevertheless inevitably encounters a number of difficulties. Professor Roland H. Bainton has astutely noted that the psychiatrist supports his case on a few scraps of evidence given by the old Luther concerning his infancy—evidence that has been transmitted second hand through the *Table Talk.* The weakness of the psychiatrist's efforts is that he reconstitutes the internal life of the reformer on the basis of often uncertain and ambiguous material. Another difficulty arises from the questionable effort to reduce theology to psychology.

The Protestant response to the challenge presented by the Catholic scholars really began with Karl Holl and his reexamination of Luther's theology in the first decades of the 20th century. Holl emphasized the actual ethical content of Luther's thought which broke with the previous epoch and its spiritual malaise, discovering joy and consolation in the

God whose wrath is His mercy. The wealth of scholars, particularly in Germany and Sweden, studying aspects and themes of Luther's theology has its counterpart in the biographers and students of Luther's actions. The reinterpretation of Luther the man, in accordance with the initial impetus given by Denifle's accusations, has led to an intensive examination of the reformer's early life and of the formative years of his theology prior to 1517. In fact this emphasis has gone so far that a study of Luther after 1530 is needed. Of scholarly biographies the most outstanding and best known to English-speaking readers is that of Bainton, *Here I Stand*. Less well known but equally fine are the biographical studies of Luther by the English Gordon Rupp and the German Gerhard Ritter. Each manifests the two prerequisites to any treatment of Luther's life and work: a sensitivity to and mastery of both the theology and the historical context.

Since Luther was so voluble, so candid and unguarded in expressing himself, it is hardly surprising that many misunderstandings of his thought have arisen. Much has been too easily attributed to him that has its sources elsewhere. The cataclysm of the Third Reich has tempted political analysts of the 20th century to find in Luther the source for a hyper-German nationalism, for German anti-Semitism, and for an absolute obedience to political authority. The last attribution is particularly persistent, although it ignores the most essential facts: that no man was so disrespectful of princes as was Luther, whenever the issue involved religion; that a right of resistance to rulers first emerged in the camp of Luther, and not that of the French reformer John Calvin; and that the existing political context in Germany seriously affected the reception of Luther's beliefs. Because Luther never wrote a systematic presentation of his doctrine but always addressed himself to immediate and pressing problems, his interpreter must read the man's own works widely and judge him in context.

The presence of conflicting interpretations should not lead one to a scepticism concerning historical materials, nor to the attitude that one opinion is as good as another. Each is an approximation to the truth and must be weighed according to its special perspective, its instruments of vision, and its focus. Some are better approximations than others, partly because of a greater command of the primary sources, partly because of an attitude which in being both impartial and sympathetic can recognize and treat with understanding the important problems. In this respect the mid-20th century is singularly blessed for the study of Luther. First, the reformer's own works are readily available in critical editions. Second, the new ecumenical spirit between Catholics and Protestants has displaced the old partisan polemical approach and allows more dispassionate examination at that point where the rift first occurred.

The following selections are representative of the best in recent Luther scholarship. The student will recognize that, despite important disagreements that reflect the perspectives of the authors, there are significant areas of agreement.

1. THE CATHOLIC APPROACH

Joseph Lortz (1887–   ), German historian, is professor of ecclesiastical history, the author of several scholarly works, and since 1950 the chief director of the Institut für europäischer Geschichte at Mainz. His most notable study is his two-volume Die Reformation in Deutschland, *which first appeared in 1939–40 and has gone through four editions. Lortz here saw Luther as a sea of forces, intensely subjective and shaped by direct experience. If Luther misconstrued revelation, it was not from laxness or superficiality but from excess of earnestness. The following selection is taken from* Die Reformation als religiöses Anligen (1948) *which appeared in English as* The Reformation: A Problem for Today (*New York, Newman Press, 1964*).

JOSEPH LORTZ*

Two characteristics strike us immediately: Luther was an amazingly rich and complex personality, and an extremely original one. He is a mine of inexhaustible wealth, amazingly productive in his writings and sermons. In a brief time he had a large number of books on the market. Luther is one of those men whose books simply cannot be reduced to a limited outline; any time a section is abstracted and then compared with its original context, it is surprising to see how ineffective the detached section is, how completely out of its own element. Luther is, in the ultimate sense of the word, an individual. It is true that all of his vast work is based on a small number of basic principles to which he recurs again and again. The presence of these fundamental themes in all his work is part of the mystery of Luther and the effectiveness of his work. These motifs are not merely repeated; Luther is always expressing them in new forms and connections. Driven by faith and the needs of preach-

---

* Reprinted from *The Reformation: A Problem for Today* by Joseph Lortz, translated by John C. Dwyer, S.J., copyright 1964, The Missionary Society of St. Paul the Apostle in the State of New York, pp. 104–29, 135, 143–45, 148, 151.

ing he is ceaselessly trying to get to the heart of them. He is always the master of his basic principles, expanding and deepening their field of application.

This is first of all true of Luther's work up to the year 1525. The great struggle that had so essential an influence on his formation and had stamped his character once and for all was aimed at liberating him from an oppressive burden; a specific bond that chained him had to be broken. It is quite understandable that after this goal was reached internally and then externally manifested, Luther's own struggle lost much of its momentum. The result was that some of Luther's characteristics, given above, do not really apply to him after 1525. On the other hand, his marriage and the completion of his significant systematic work *Vom geknechteten Willen* did not make him a lazy man. He never stopped learning and it is noteworthy that even as an old man he was ready to approach the "Our Father" again and seek to penetrate its depths, to "learn" it. This amazing drive was, of course, partially inspired by the necessity of defending his life and work time and time again. . . .

It is true that Luther was essentially independent of his Ockhamist background and that the latter had no influence on Luther's most distinctive characteristics. The real sources of Luther's development are all within him, in the dynamic factors at the very core of his personality. His struggle was a lonely one, inaccessible to others, and it is impossible to follow the course of his development step by step. In spite of Luther's dependence on the tradition in which he was educated, it is true in a deeper sense that absolutely no one had a part in Luther's formation.

Moreover, from his earliest days, he manifests great independence of the authorities of tradition to a dangerous degree—he rejects Aristotle, as he had been taught by his Ockhamist teachers, but also extends this attitude to Thomas Aquinas and even Augustine. One can easily see what an advantage this independence in regard to the tradition was for the professor who was later to organize the new University of Wittenberg. He was quite unrestricted and free to indulge his penchant for innovation. However, there is an obvious danger here in the intellectual as well as the religious sphere that became acute in the case of a man like Luther, with his absolutely unique character, his lack of balance, and his tendency to see only one side of any question, all of which made calm and balanced judgment so difficult. This attitude was dangerous in the intellectual sphere because tradition is one of the indispensable factors in intellectual life, which can exist only as a continuum. No one can attain truth by working alone; no one can reject the intellectual achievements of past generations without paying a penalty—too many truly valuable acquisitions will be lost. . . .

Essentially, however, the difficulty stems from the peculiarities of Luther's own mental makeup, which can be briefly formulated in the following way: Luther's inspiration was not primarily intellectual, nor was his work careful and systematic; emotion had a dominant role in his work. This is not to underestimate the intellectual value of Luther's work; its scope was wide and penetrating, but the distinctive note responsible for the originality in Luther's message is personal involvement and commitment.

His capacity for personal involvement in a situation was joined with great strength of will. He is relentless in hammering out solutions to the problems that faced him, and so deeply involved in the inner struggle that at times he has eyes for nothing but the pressing and immediate problems of the day, even of the moment. The solution to *this* difficulty, here and now, alone can give him inner peace. This most unique characteristic shows how far Luther was from the spirit of calm and objective reflection that makes a synthesis possible. His dialectic was essentially exclusive. . . .

Another fact worthy of note is that Luther was endowed with unusual gifts of expression which he could place at the disposal of his genius. He was able to give perfectly apt expression to the intertwined and violent forces at the depths of his personality. The man who reads Luther's writings is present on most intimate terms to his inner experience. Luther's words overwhelm and almost overpower the reader. Packed with meaning, coming directly to the point, filled with suggestive images, rhythmically phrased, with real ear appeal, his writing employs all the variations appropriate to the profound appeals he is making. . . .

Luther's character manifested an unusually excessive introversion. He was absolutely convinced that he alone was right, that he was his own pope, speaking ex cathedra. He had a reckless kind of boldness that knew no bounds. The demagogic force that moved him would at times indulge in the wildest arguments, holding on to its own opinion through thick and thin. Consequently, in thinking and speaking paradoxically, Luther was often in danger of contradicting himself by one and the same formula, which he actually did on a number of different matters. This tendency of Luther, together with the impetuous way his judgments and demands were put, constitutes one of the greatest stumbling blocks in our dialogue concerning the Reformation, for even the Protestants of today are heirs of this type of theological thought. The influence of Luther's own tremendous vitality has prevailed here, and in so doing has shown its most dangerous side. . . .

Above all, we have to remember that Luther's development was unlike anything any of us have experienced; with him it was practically a substantial change, involving the interplay of deep and violent forces in a gifted personality. It was hardly possible that in later years, after the long process of development was over and his thought had crystallized once and for all, he would be able to recognize and describe for us just what his exact situation had been at any given moment. . . .

Luther was fundamentally a religious man; some have acted as though this is rather insignificant, but in my opinion it is a real honor to be characterized as such, particularly if one has as clear-cut a title to it as does Luther. . . .

Luther's whole interior life was dominated by the tension between his obligations and his power to discharge them. Because of his background of popular Catholic teaching, a certain scrupulosity of disposition and Ockhamist theology, he was obsessed with the notion of becoming reconciled to God through his own powers, of being obliged to attain sanctity by his own actions; in this all-important matter, he experienced failure again and again.

This tension and Luther's own attitude were responsible for the great struggles of soul which led to the outbreak of the Reformation. They depend essentially first on Luther's life in the monastery and his struggle for perfection in the framework of a particular religious and ascetical system and secondly, on the theology of the Bible, particularly of the New Testament. . . .

We have to be quite clear about this unintentional process of development which was so dependent on his inner struggles and carried on almost in isolation. Then we can understand what a shock it must have been for Luther when in the dispute over indulgences he came up against the popular Catholic mind, or when in his dispute with Cardinal Cajetan and Eck he came into conflict with a type of theology utterly foreign to his own highly personal experience and views. . . .

The Bible was the source of Luther's inspirations; from it he drew a wealth of religious content for himself and others.

But Luther's development, nourished by the Bible, resulted in his leaving the church. How was that possible? Did Luther see the fundamental facts about the church which his monastic training and theology offered in the right light and did he make the right use of them? Or was he one-sided in his outlook? Furthermore, did his theology really give Brother Martin a thoroughly Catholic foundation? This is the point we wish to investigate. . . .

Luther's experience shows us first of all that he was a religious man, forced to his knees as it were by the tremendous reality of God. We see in his experience something which cannot without some restrictions be called healthy. Does this entitle us to speak of mental illness in his case? We see that he was often profoundly moved, subject to strong depressions, restless at intervals, and, later in life, subject to violent changes of temper. All of this is quite apparent and shows that Luther had a tempestuous character, and that in his soul raged forces that were beyond his power to control. It tells us, too, that we are dealing with a soul obsessed with anxiety in the face of sin and the divine judgment and caught in the net of scrupulosity. But scrupulosity is a weakness proper to a tender conscience; thus there is no reason to speak of mental illness in the proper sense of the word, at least at the time of his First Mass. This possibility is further excluded when we realize the tremendous amount and the fine quality of the works that Luther produced unceasingly.... At any rate we should be quite clear about the meaning of "mentally ill." It seems that the rather loosely used schema "manic-depressive" (when it is not used in the sense of insanity) can be quite easily verified in the average mentally healthy individual if that individual is unusually sensitive. It is quite easy to say what Luther was not: he was not balanced, moderate or prudent, not restrained; one might say that he was quite uninhibited, that in a typically Germanic way he escapes classification and categorization. His lack of restraint is shown by all sorts of exaggerations; they indicate a violent impulsiveness which extends even to the falsification of objective facts in such impossible forms that the reader is utterly amazed. What Christian conscience will, for example, be able to accept his statement that he preferred Christ to all the devils, because he stood in such deadly terror of Him? ...

The one conclusion we can come to now from Luther's experience at his First Mass is that he was entirely preoccupied with the anxiety that he felt as, with all his sins, he stood alone before the sovereign majesty of God. It is true that in the Canon, the living and true God is directly addressed, and that the Canon is preceded by the solemn, threefold *Sanctus* addressed to the divine majesty, but that is not the whole story....

He was so deeply involved in those ideas which he had from his early days, the preaching he had heard, the Ockhamist theology he had learned, and above all his own peculiar disposition and correspondingly unique experiences, that he was simply blind to the solution for which he was striving so violently and which was given to him here, word by word.

This was so characteristic of Luther. He could not accept anyone else's solution. He was so individualistic and in a sense so narrow that only solutions of his own appeared valid. Luther was capable of assimilating only those things which were adapted to the peculiarities of his personality. He was an individual in the strictest sense of the word and this influenced his every act; it was the source of both his greatness and his limitations. . . .

From the psychological point of view, we have before us a man who was extremely troubled by a serious type of scrupulosity. He had developed a real talent for disputing with himself, bringing forward arguments and counterarguments, and by so doing, tortured himself by running around in circles. . . .

Again and again we see the same picture: Luther stands alone; he is the lone warrior. He made everything his own. He was never able calmly and patiently to listen in the real sense of the word, in which the heart and soul are receptive to a message and ready to receive it in its fullness. He is a stranger to the attitude which would patiently permit even mysterious and disturbing influences to work on him without reacting at the inopportune moment.

Luther had no understanding for synthesis, the mutual interaction of more than one element, and thus he could not achieve a synthesis for himself. Forcefully and even violently he strove to simplify everything, to see it only in one light, in a one-sided way. It was obvious that for him the objective multiplicity of the real world would be given too little attention and the personal element would receive too much. All our investigations so far converge on one point: Luther is in the fullest sense of the word an individual. . . .

Luther himself thought that his point of departure was Catholic and that in leaving it behind he was abandoning Catholic doctrine. He was wrong. In starting the Reformation Luther was struggling against a Catholicism that was no longer Catholic in the full sense of the word. In this regard it is essential to remember what we saw in the first three chapters about the lack of theological clarity at the end of the 15th century and the role played by Ockhamist theology. This will shed some interesting light on the problem of the causes of the Reformation: Luther became a reformer because of the theological confusion of his day. . . .

A third consideration shows how wanting was the Catholicism against which Luther rebelled. The church was not a vital element in Luther's thought (and this was true of much of the theology of the day). Luther was essentially a lone worker, even in the cloister.

Thus, our conclusion is this: Luther rebelled against a Catholicism that was no longer fully Catholic. We can sum up everything that we have said about Luther by saying that he was not attentive to the voice of the church. We may now ask a further question: Was Luther attentive to the voice of the Bible? . . .

In what sense can we say that Luther was attentive to the spirit of the Bible? We have already seen how unfavorable Luther's whole mental and spiritual outlook was to accept theological knowledge from outside sources without warping it in the process, changing its key and reducing its content by limiting its scope to his personal experience, even when this knowledge lay along the course of development of his own thought and corresponded well to the very end for which he was striving. Remember how the reality of grace as it appeared in the various monastic prayers completely escaped Luther and that he never really achieved a personal appropriation of the great prayers of the Missal.

We find the same deficiency in Luther in regard to the New Testament during the period of the important developments of his life in the monastery. Above all, Luther, as is abundantly clear by now, did not see the Gospel as the good news of the fact that God is our Father. This was evident from the experience he had at the time of his First Mass. All of his struggles in religious life came from the same source. . . .

If we consider all the elements of the New Testament that are left out of Luther's doctrine (both at the time of the definitive break with the church and later on) and if we keep in mind that he revolted against a church which alone had been looked on by all Western Christendom as the source of eternal salvation, we would have reason to say that Luther's claim to be guided entirely and solely by Scripture was utterly unfounded. We are thus forced to the conclusion that Luther was not receptive to the full message of Scripture.

Luther's understanding of the full message of Scripture was defective not only because of his failure to incorporate all of Scripture into his teaching, insofar as certain sections of Scripture are strangely lacking, but also because of an oversimplification in which some of the essential aspects of the message are left out. More of this, however, later. . . .

The weakest aspect of Luther's doctrine was his exaggerated tendency to see justification as the sole content of revelation. Christianity is salvation, but it contains a number of elements beyond an anthropocentrically conceived process of justification: adoration of the Father; the prayer, "Thy Kingdom come"; the revelation of the divine life which our Lord shares with His elect—all of these are essential elements of Christianity. . . .

Luther was quite emphatic about considering himself God's Evangelist, and he referred to his own concerns as God's concern. But when he does this, it is often in matters which he felt to be a binding matter of conscience. This is important because all of Luther's work bears the stamp of profound humility. He never tired of repeating that the doctrine was not his, and his doctrine certainly did not tend to ennoble or flatter man; it rather demands and asserts a negation of human powers.

When Luther died they found on his desk a tablet that contained probably the last words written by the Reformer. Uniting his thoughts with those of the Psalmist, he had written: "It is true that we are beggars. . . ." Coming as they do at the conclusion of such a violent life, these words do not point in the direction of pride. . . .

This summary of Luther's objective attitude and the problems of the relation of his will to the real order lead us to some final conclusions on Luther. We have sufficiently seen that Luther's actions were extremely violent and unrestrained and that he relied too much on himself alone. Then, surveying his whole life and seeking for the ultimate causes, we come again and again to the same grave deficiency in Luther's intellectual and spiritual outlook: overdevelopment of the subjective and personal elements that tended toward real subjectivism. (Incidentally we have in Luther a prototype of the subjectivism that has been such a threat in our modern age and has wrought such havoc in Germany. More of this later.) . . .

I feel that I should interpose a warning here. Since we began to speak of Luther as a religious man, we discussed many of the man's deficiencies and weaknesses; we were forced to deny that his basic decisions were justified. But now we must take to heart what I said at the beginning: we must be willing to look at both sides of the picture. Despite all that we have said, Luther was a great and fervent believer, filled with the faith that moves mountains. He burned with love for the Lord Jesus and his zeal for preaching the Gospel was unquenchable. . . .

We conclude with a brief summary. During the period preceding the Reformation the church, particularly the higher clergy, and much of the contemporary theology, were in dire need of radical criticism; this made the Reformation a historical necessity. This is quite evident from the fact that the struggle of the Church against the Reformation was in large measure carried on in a manner and with means that were not religious. Thus the Reformation becomes a Catholic concern insofar as Catholics must share responsibility and guilt for bringing it about.

Martin Luther, the immediate cause of the Reformation, in the process of resolving his profound struggles of conscience, left the church although he had not previously intended to do so. For this action the Catholic theology of the day must bear a great deal of the blame. Throughout these events Luther appears as a thoroughly religious man who drew great inspiration from the Bible and shared this with others.

Luther's theology of confidence in God and of man's certitude of salvation has, in the sense in which Luther intended them, nothing to do with superficial indifference. Luther's whole doctrine on this point is characterized by an absolute seriousness proper to the Christian in such matters. . . .

2. THE PSYCHOANALYTIC APPROACH

Erik H. Erikson (1902–   ) American psychoanalyst, has been since 1960, Professor of Human Development and Lecturer on Psychiatry at Harvard University. In his first major work, Childhood and Society *(1950), he proved himself to be a leading figure in relating psychoanalysis to the social sciences. In his second work,* Young Man Luther *(1958), he continued this same endeavor by bringing the findings of psychoanalysis to bear upon history. His study of Luther is a pioneer work in trying to relate the two disciplines.*

ERIK H. ERIKSON*

The limitations of my knowledge and of the space at my disposal for this inquiry preclude any attempt to present a new Luther or to remodel an old one. I can only bring some newer psychological considerations to bear on the existing material pertaining to one period of Luther's life. As I indicated in Chapter I, the young monk interests me particularly as a young man in the process of becoming a great one.

It must have occurred to the reader that the story of the fit in the choir attracted me originally because I suspected that the words "I am *not!*" revealed the fit to be part of a most severe identity crisis—a crisis in which the young monk felt obliged to protest what he was *not* (possessed, sick, sinful) perhaps in order to break through to what he was or was to be. I will now state what remains of my suspicion, and what I intend to make of it.

Judging from an undisputed series of extreme mental states which attacked Luther throughout his life, leading to weeping, sweating, and fainting, the fit in the choir could well have happened; and it could have happened in the specific form reported, under the specific conditions of Martin's monastery years. If some of it is legend, so be it; the making of legend is as much part of the scholarly rewriting of history as it is part

---

* Reprinted from *Young Man Luther* by Erik H. Erikson, by permission of W. W. Norton & Company, Inc. Copyright © 1958 by Erik H. Erikson.

of the original facts used in the work of scholars. We are thus obliged to accept half-legend as half-history, provided only that a reported episode does not contradict other well-established facts; persists in having a ring of truth; and yields a meaning consistent with psychological theory.

Luther himself never mentioned this episode, although in his voluble later years he was extraordinarily free with references to physical and mental suffering. It seems that he always remembered most vividly those states in which he struggled through to an insight, but not those in which he was knocked out. Thus, in his old age, he remembers well having been seized at the age of 35 by terror, sweat, and the fear of fainting when he marched in the Corpus Christi procession behind his superior, Dr. Staupitz, who carried the holy of holies. (This Dr. Staupitz, as we will see, was the best father figure Luther ever encountered and acknowledged; he was a man who recognized a true *homo religiosus* in his subaltern and treated him with therapeutic wisdom.) But Staupitz did not let Luther get away with his assertion that it was Christ who had frightened him. He said, *"Non est Christus, quia Christus non terret, sed consolatur."* (It couldn't have been Christ who terrified you, for Christ consoles.) This was a therapeutic as well as a theological revelation to Luther, and he remembered it. However, for the fit in the choir, he may well have had an amnesia.

Assuming then that something like this episode happened, it could be considered as one of a series of seemingly senseless pathological explosions; as a meaningful symptom in a psychiatric case history; or as one of a series of religiously relevant experiences. It certainly has, as even Scheel suggests, *some* marks of a "religious attack," such as St. Paul, St. Augustine, and many lesser aspirants to saintliness have had. However, the inventory of a total revelation always includes an overwhelming illumination and a sudden insight. The fit in the choir presents only the symptomatic, the more pathological and defensive, aspects of a total revelation: partial loss of consciousness, loss of motor coordination, and automatic exclamations which the afflicted does not know he utters.

In a truly religious experience such automatic exclamations would sound as if they were dictated by divine inspiration; they would be positively illuminating and luminous, and be intensely remembered. In Luther's fit, his words obviously expressed an overwhelming inner need to deny an accusation. In a full religious attack the positive conscience of faith would reign and determine the words uttered; here negation and rebellion reign: "I am *not* what my father said I was and what my conscience, in bad moments, tends to confirm I am." The raving and roaring suggest a strong element of otherwise suppressed rage. And, indeed, this young man, who

later became a voice heard around the world, lived under monastic conditions of silence and meditation; at this time he was submissively subdued, painfully sad, and compulsively self-inspective—too much so even
for his stern superiors' religious taste. All in all, however, the paroxysm
occurred in a holy spot and was suggested by a biblical story, which places
the whole matter at least on the borderline between psychiatry and
religion.

If we approach the episode from the psychiatric viewpoint, we can
recognize in the described attack (and also in a variety of symptomatic
scruples and anxieties to which Martin was subject at the time) an
intrinsic ambivalence, an inner two-facedness, such as we find in all
neurotic symptoms. The attack could be said to deny in its verbal part
("I am not") what Martin's father had said, namely, that his son was
perhaps possessed rather than holy; but it also proves the father's point
by its very occurrence in front of the same congregation who had previously heard the father express his anger and apprehension. The fit, then,
is both unconscious obedience to the father and implied rebellion against
the monastery; the words uttered both deny the father's assertion, and
confirm the vow which Martin had made in that first known anxiety
attack during a thunderstorm at the age of 21, when he had exclaimed,
"I want to be a monk." We find the young monk, then, at the crossroads
of obedience to his father—an obedience of extraordinary tenacity and
deviousness—and to the monastic vows which at the time he was straining
to obey almost to the point of absurdity.

We may also view his position as being at the crossroads of mental
disease and religious creativity and we could speculate that perhaps
Luther received in three (or more) distinct and fragmentary experiences
those elements of a total revelation which other men are said to have
acquired in one explosive event. Let me list the elements again: physical
paroxysm; a degree of unconsciousness; an automatic verbal utterance; a
command to change the overall direction of effort and aspiration; and a
spiritual revelation, a flash of enlightenment, decisive and pervasive as a
rebirth. The thunderstorm had provided him with a change in the overall
direction of his life, a change toward the anonymous, the silent, and the
obedient. In fits such as the one in the choir, he experienced the epileptoid
paroxysm of ego loss, the rage of denial of the identity which was to be
discarded. And later in the experience in the tower, which we will discuss
in Chapter V, he perceived the light of a new spiritual formula.

The fact that Luther experienced these clearly separate stages of religious revelation might make it possible to establish a psychological
rationale for the conversion of other outstanding religionists, where tradi-

tion has come to insist on the transmission of a total event appealing to popular faith. Nothing, to my mind, makes Luther more a man of the future—the future which is our psychological present—than his utter integrity in reporting the steps which marked the emergence of his identity as a genuine *homo religiosus*. I emphasize this by no means only because it makes him a better case (although I admit it helps), but because it makes his total experience a historical event far beyond its immediate sectarian significance, namely, a decisive step in human awareness and responsibility. To indicate this step in its psychological coordinates is the burden of this book. . . .

This general discussion of the qualities of that critical area between neurosis and creativity will introduce the state of mind which engulfed Martin at the time of the fit in the choir. Even the possibly legendary aspects of this fit reflect an unconscious understanding on the part of the legend-makers, here Martin's monastic brothers, as to what was going on inside him. In the next chapter we will analyze what little is known of Martin's childhood. Then we will trace the subsequent personality change which made it possible for the young man who in the choir was literally felled by the power of the need to negate to stand before his emperor and before the pope's emissary at the Diet of Worms 12 years later and affirm human integrity in new terms: "My conscience is bound by God's words. Retract anything whatsoever I neither can nor will. For to act against one's conscience is neither saft nor honorable."

God's words: he had, by then, become God's "spokesman," preacher, teacher, orator, and pamphleteer. This had become the working part of his identity. The eventual liberation of Luther's voice made him creative. The one matter on which professor and priest, psychiatrist and sociologist, agree is Luther's immense gift for language: his receptivity for the written word; his memory for the significant phrase; and his range of verbal expression (lyrical, biblical, satirical, and vulgar) which in English is paralleled only by Shakespeare.

The development of this gift is implicit in the dramatic outcry in the choir of Erfurt: for was it not a "dumb" spirit which beset the patient before Jesus? And was it not muteness, also, which the monk had to deny by thus roaring "like an ox"? The theme of the Voice and of the Word, then, is intertwined with the theme of Luther's identity and with his influence on the ideology of his time.

We will therefore concentrate on this process: how young Martin, at the end of a somber and harsh childhood, was precipitated into a severe identity crisis for which he sought delay and cure in the silence of the monastery; how being silent, he became "possessed"; how being possessed, he gradually learned to speak a new language, *his* language; how being able to speak, he not only talked himself out of the monastery, and much of his country out of the Roman Church, but also formulated for himself and for all of mankind a new kind of ethical and psychological awareness: and how, at the end, this awareness, too, was marred by a return of the demons, whoever they may have been. . . .

I have so far mentioned two trends in the relationship between Hans and Martin: (1) the father's driving economic ambition, which was threatened by something (maybe even murder) done in the past, and by a feeling close to murder which he always carried inside; and (2) the concentration of the father's ambition on his oldest son, whom he treated with alternate periods of violent harshness and of habituating the son to himself in a manner which may well have been somewhat sentimental—a deadly combination.

I would add to these trends the father's display of righteousness. Hans seems to have considered himself the very conception, the *Inbegriff*, of justice. After all, he did not spare himself, and fought his own nature as ruthlessly as those of his children. But parents are dangerous who thus take revenge on their child for what circumstances and inner compulsion have done to them; who misuse one of the strongest forces in life—true indignation in the service of vital values—to justify their own small selves. Martin, however, seems to have sensed on more than one occasion that the father, behind his disciplined public identity, was possessed by an angry, and often alcoholic, impulsiveness which he loosed against his family (and would dare loose *only* against his family) under the pretense of being a hard taskmaster and righteous judge.

The fear of the father's anger, described as constant by some biographers, included the absolute injunction against any back talk, any *Widerrede*. Here again the fact that only much later, and only after an attempt to screw down the lid with the rules of monastic silence, did Martin become one of the biggest and most effective back talkers in history, forces us to ask what kept him silent for so long. But this was Martin: in Latin school he was caned for using the German language—and later he used that language with a vengeance! We can deduce from what burst forth later that which must have been forced to lie dormant in childhood; this may well have included some communality of experience with the mother, whose spontaneity and imagination are said to have suffered at the side of Hans Luder.

This much, I think, one can say about the paternal side of Martin's childhood dilemma. Faced with a father who made questionable use of his brute superiority; a father who had at his disposal the techniques of making others feel morally inferior without being quite able to justify his own moral superiority; a father to whom he could not get close and from whom he could not get away—faced with such a father, how was he going to submit without being emasculated, or rebel without emasculating the father?

Millions of boys face these problems and solve them in some way or another—they live, as Captain Ahab says, with half of their heart and with only one of their lungs, and the world is the worse for it. Now and again, however, an individual is called upon (called by *whom*, only the theologians claim to know, and by *what*, only bad psychologists) to lift his individual patienthood to the level of a universal one and to try to solve for all what he could not solve for himself alone. . . .

No doubt when Martin learned to speak up, much that he had to say to the devil was fueled by a highly compressed store of defiance consisting of what he had been unable to say to his father and to his teachers; in due time he said it all, with a vengeance, to the pope.

The Luder family, while traditional in structure, offered an extreme degree of moralistic paternalism, and, quite probably, a minimum degree of that compensatory free-for-all of small and highly satisfying delinquencies which barnyard, street, or park can provide for lucky children. The father's prohibitory presence, and the anticipation of his punishment seem to have pervaded the family milieu, which thus became an ideal breeding ground for the most pervasive form of the Oedipus complex—the ambivalent interplay of rivalry with the father, admiration for him, and fear of him which puts such a heavy burden of guilt and inferiority on all spontaneous initiative and on all phantasy. Where rebellion and deviousness are thus successfully undercut, and where, on the other hand, the father's alcoholic, sexual, and cruel self-indulgence obviously break through his moralistic mask, a child can only develop a precocious conscience, a precocious self-steering, and eventually an obsessive mixture of obedience and rebelliousness. Hans Luder was a "jealous God," one who probably interfered early with the mother's attempt to teach her children how to be before he taught them how to strive. It was probably his father's challenging injunction against the little boy's bond with his mother which made it impossible for Martin to accept the intercession of the holy Mary. But when a father usurps motherhood, he puts an additional and unbearable burden on that second of man's great nostalgias, which cannot be described better than it was by Thomas Wolfe:

From the beginning . . . the idea, the central legend that I wished my book to express—had not changed. And this central idea was this: the deepest search in life, it seemed to me, the thing that in one way or another was central to all living was man's search to find a father, not merely the father of his flesh, not merely the lost father of his youth, but the image of a strength and wisdom external to his need and superior to his hunger, to which the belief and power of his own life could be united.

. . . . .

We have quoted Luther's statement that as he celebrated his first Mass he was overcome by the feeling that he had to face God directly without a mediator. We must now discuss his other impending encounter: the one with his earthly father. Is it not astonishing that the biographers who have tried to account for Luther's anxiety have not considered it worth emphasizing that he had not seen his father since his impulsive visit home; and that he had not, as yet, faced him to see—yes, in his face—the result of that extracted permission? Could not Martin foresee that his father would be essentially unreconstructed and ready to remind Martin of the obedience due him, knowing, in turn, quite well that the son had never wholly relinquished his filial obedience—and that he never would, never could? In Martin's first Mass the paradox of paternal obediences was fully propounded. Martin, who had sought the identity of a monk, had been ordered to become a priest, a dispenser as well as a partaker of the Eucharist. There is no use saying he should have been glad: like other great young men, Martin never felt worthy of the next step in his career. Later he thought and said he would surely die when he was ordered to become a professor; and still later, after his unexpectedly triumphant entrance into Worms, when it was clear that he could not escape being the people's reformer, he stood most meekly before the emperor and was hardly audible. As always, he first had to grow into the role which he had usurped without meaning to. And this first and anxious anchorage of his future identity as a responsible churchman had to be witnessed by the father, who cursed it (and said so presently) as his son's final escape from the identity of being most of all Hans's son. The attempt of the biographers to separate the mystic presence of the Eucharist and the oppressive presence of the father is invalid in view of what happened later that day, and forever after.

It cannot be denied that Martin asked for it—he could not let his father go any more than the father could let him go. Martin knew that he had not won his father's *gantzen Willen*, his whole will. But during the meeting which they had after the ceremony, "as we sat at the table, I started to talk with him with a childish good comportment, wanting to put him in the wrong and myself in the right, by saying: 'Dear father, why did you resist so hard and become so angry because you did not want to let me be a monk, and maybe even now you do not like too much to see me here, although it is a sweet and godly life, full of peace?' But there [the father] carried on, in front of all the doctors, magisters and other gentle-men: 'You scholars, have you not read in the scriptures that one should honor father and mother?' " And as others started to argue with him, Hans Luder said what was as good as a curse: "God give that it wasn't a devil's spook" (*Satanae praestigium, Teuffel's Gespenst*)—referring, of course, to the thunderstorm on the road to Erfurt, Martin's "road to Damascus." As Luther wrote to his father publicly when he had become a great man: "You again hit me so cleverly and fittingly that in my whole life I have hardly heard a word that resounded in me more forcefully and stuck in me more firmly. But," he added—putting the father in his place more than a decade after the event—"but I, secure in my justice, listened to you as to a human being and felt deep contempt for you; yet belittle your word in my soul, I could not."

What would not some of us give if, in certain decisive moments, we could have felt clearly and said calmly to a parent what the great man could write only after many years: "I listened to you as to a human being" (*Te velut hominem audivi et fortiter contempsi*)? But at the time, Martin, too, fell silent. As he confessed later, he heard God's voice in his father's words, which helped to make the fusion of presences fatefully permanent. His father, he felt, had not given his benediction "as to a betrothal," and God had denied him the experience of the Eucharist. But for less, Martin (Hans's son) could not settle and remain whole; he would yet find the right word "to speak to God directly." . . .

Martin the son, who on a personal level had suffered deeply because he could not coerce his father into approving his religiosity as genuine, and who had borne with him the words of this father with an unduly pro-longed filial obedience, assumes now on a religious level a volitional role toward filial obedience, perhaps making out of his protracted sonhood the victory of his Christlikeness. In his first Mass, facing the altar—the Father in heaven—and at the same time waiting to face his angry earthly father, Martin had "overlooked" a passage concerning Christ's mediatorship. Yet now, in finding Christ in himself, he establishes an inner position which goes beyond that of a neurotic compromise identification. He finds the core of a praying man's identity, and advances Christian ideology by an important step. It is clear that Luther abandoned the appreciation of Christ as a substitute who has died "for"—in the sense of "instead of"—us; he also abandoned the concept of Christ as an ideal figure to be imitated, or abjectly venerated, or ceremonially remembered as an event in the past. Christ now becomes the core of the Christian's identity: *quotidianus Christi adventus*, Christ is today here, in me. The affirmed passivity of suffering becomes the daily Passion and the Passion is the substitution of the primitive sacrifice of others with a most active, most masterly, affirmation of man's nothingness—which, by his own masterly choice, becomes his existential identity.

The men revered by mankind as saviors face and describe in lasting words insights which the ordinary man must avoid with all possible self-deception and exploitation of others. These men prove their point by the magic of their voices which radiate to the farthest corner of their world and out into the millennia. Their passion contains elements of choice, mastery, and victory, and sooner or later earns them the name of King of Kings; their crown of thorns later becomes their successor's tiara. For a little while Luther, this first revolutionary individualist, saved the Savior from the tiaras and the ceremonies, the hierarchies and the thought police, and put him back where he arose: in each man's soul.

Is this not the counterpart, on the level of conscience, to Renaissance anthropocentrism? Luther left the heavens to science and restricted himself to what he could know of his own suffering and faith, that is, to what he could mean. He who had sought to dispel the angry cloud that darkened the face of the fathers and of The Father now said that Christ's life *is* God's face: *qui est facies patris.* The Passion is all that man can know of God: his conflicts, duly faced, are all that he can know of himself. The last judgment is the always present self-judgment. Christ did not live and die in order to make man poorer in the fear of his future judgment, but in order to make him abundant today: *nam judicia sunt ipsae passiones Christi quae in nobis abundant.* Look, Luther said at one point in these lectures, (IV, 87) how everywhere painters depict Christ's passion as if they agreed with St. Paul that we know nothing but Christ crucified. The artist closest to Luther in spirit was Dürer, who etched his own face into Christ's countenance. . . .

Luther (like any individual recovering from an oppressive mental state) had recourse to massive totalisms from which he derived the foundation stones for a new wholeness. The whole person includes certain total states in his balances: we are, Luther proclaimed, totally sinners (*totus homo peccator*) and totally just (*totus homo justus*), always both damned and blessed, both alive and dead. . . .

Luther's restatements about the total sinfulness and the total salvation which are in man at any given time can easily be shown to be alogical. With sufficient ill will they can be construed as contrived to save Martin's particular skin, which held together upswings of spiritual elations and cursing gloominess, not to speak of lusts for power and revenge, women, food, and beer. But the coexistence of all these contradictions has its psychologic—as has also the fury of their incompatibility. Martin's theological reformations imply a psychological fact, namely, that the ego gains strength *in practice,* and *in affectu* to the degree to which it can accept at the same time the total power of the drives and the total power of conscience—*provided* that it can nourish what Luther called *opera manum dei,* that particular combination of work and love which alone verifies our identity and confirms it. . . .

Luther's redefinitions of work have probably been more misunderstood than any other of his formulations, except, naturally, those pertaining to sex. In both these sensitive areas, theory and practice have become completely separated. In trying to decide what a great man meant by his original formulations, it is always good to find out what he was talking *against* at the time, or what previous overstatement he was trying to correct, for greatness is based on an excessive restatement of some previous overstatement, usually made by others, often by the master himself. . . .

When Luther spoke about works and work, he was speaking against a climate of opinion which, in matters of religion, asked a man how much he had done of what there was in him (or in his pocketbook) to do. When Luther spoke against works, he spoke against holy busywork which has nothing whatsoever to do with the nature or the quality of devoted craftsmanship. . . .

Against this inner psychic sequence Luther, in accord with his whole new space-time configuration, reemphasized the spirit in which a thing is done from the start for its own sake. Nobody is just, he said, because he does just works; the works are just *if* the man is just: *quia justus, opera justa.* . . .

Luther's theology contains an unsolved personal problem which is more accessible to psychoanalysis than is the theology itself. This unsolved personal problem becomes obvious later, when the suddenly changed course of his life endangers the identity which he had won as a lecturer and preacher; and even more obvious when the crisis of middle age brings to the fore again that inner store of self-hate, and that murderous intolerance of disobedience which in the lectures on the Psalms had been relatively balanced—within Luther's identity as a lecturer. . . .

The study of Luther's earliest lectures shows that in his self-cure from deep obsessive struggles he came, almost innocently, to express principles basic to the mastery of existence by religious and introspective means. As he stated in his notes for the lectures on Romans, in which he came much closer to perfection as a professor and to clarity as a dogmatist: "Perfect self-insight is perfect humility; perfect humility is perfect knowledge; perfect knowledge is perfect spirituality." At the same time Luther crowns his attempt to cure the wounds of this wrath by changing God's attributes: instead of being like an earthly father whose mood swings are incomprehensible to his small son, God is given the attribute of *ira misericordiae*—a wrath which is really compassion. With this concept, Luther was at last able to forgive God for being a Father, and grant Him justification. . . .

3. THE PROTESTANT APPROACH

A.

Gerhard Ritter (1888–) German Lutheran, professor of modern history at the University of Freiburg im Breisgau 1925–56 has written outstanding studies on many aspects of Germany's past from late medieval scholasticism to Hitler. His biography of Luther first appeared in 1925 and has passed through successive editions that reveal a gradual shift in the author's perspective. After 1943 he began to reduce the emphasis upon Luther the German and to see him as a universal rather than a distinctively national figure. The following selection is from the first English rendering of the sixth German edition.

GERHARD RITTER*

In the later Middle Ages, the growing emphasis on the spiritual life began to upset the harmony between reason and revelation, and between the human and spiritual way of life which had been everywhere dominant in the Western church in its best days. It was then that the hidden contradiction between the spiritual needs of the devout soul and the seemingly inflexible ordinances of the church began to assume the character of a spiritual dilemma. It was at this point that religious life in Germany began to be subjected to an extreme tension which already gave signs of its presence in the strange conflict between the increased devotion to the church and the simultaneously growing criticisms of her internal and external weaknesses. Only in Germany did this conflict

---

* From *Luther: His Life and Work* by Gerhard Ritter. Copyright © in English translation by William Collins and Co., Ltd., London, and Harper & Row, Inc., New York. Pp. 20–21, 22, 29–31, 32, 33, 34, 35, 37, 39, 43, 210, 211. Reprinted by permission of Harper & Row, Publishers.

become a decisive mark of ecclesiastical development. The Spanish church drew new vigor through its spiritual roots which stretched back into the 13th century, and this produced a new flowering of the old ideals of Roman Catholic piety. On the other hand, in Italy, cultural life began to grow out of the bonds of ecclesiastical tradition as the world of Christian ideas began to lose its completely exclusive hold on the minds of men. It was only in Germany that the growing religious needs of men, that Christian piety in its most intense form, came into conflict with the traditions of the church because of its own deep spiritual failings. There can be no other explanation: the distinction between the history of the German spirit and the general development of European culture first becomes clear at the point at which the religious needs of the German soul came into conflict with the spirit of the Roman Church; and if the 15th century has been called the most German century of our history, this can only be maintained, if indeed it can be, by pointing to the increasing fervor and sincerity with which the Germans of that period tried to make the spiritual treasures of the Christian inheritance their own. Whatever the art and literature of this century may have produced (including the so-called Folk-Books) outside this circle of ideas, in no way bears the unequivocal marks of the true German spirit.

Seen from this standpoint Luther's lifework might well appear as the final crowning point of a development which had started centuries before. He found the decisive word, for which others had searched in vain; he it was who helped their vague longing to its fulfillment. Indeed without these spiritual antecedents it would be quite impossible to explain the success of the great revolution which attacked the very foundations of the political and spiritual life of the West among a people separated by numerous geographical divisions and noted for its political inertia. Yet it is not possible to speak of a specific development of the reformation idea without completely distorting the course of events. When Luther set in motion the revolution which broke the spell of a tradition which had lasted for more than a thousand years, he was able to do this because he based this revolution in the very depths of his religious consciousness. This decisive element in his action which is completely new, completely unprecedented, completely unexpected. This one startling fact brought the Germans, who till then had been regarded by the other nations more as enjoying, than helping to create, Western culture, for a few (admittedly short) decades to the forefront of the spiritual development of Europe.

Yet we must be careful, for it is not in this way that we shall find the true meaning of these events. Not as a German, but as a Christian, as a living witness to the reality of God, Martin Luther became the Reformer of the Western church. There is no real precedent for his work, for his rediscovery of the mystery of primitive Christianity. It can only be understood when we see it relived in the spiritual life of the man himself. . . .

People have often tried to produce a psychological or rather medical explanation for his case, and it does suggest itself very readily for a young man of heated temperament. If one reads how Luther portrays the power of original sin, the evil desire which rages like a devouring fire in our veins and destroys all free will, then it is difficult, even if one is without prejudice on the subject, to avoid the impression that it is the sensual passions in a sexual sense which he is describing. But it is unlikely that temptations of this kind played a particularly important part in the life of the young monk. The testimony of all the sources, even when subjected to the most searching inquiry by bitter opponents, speaks against this. It is no mere chance that the vow of celibacy was the last of all the Catholic vows which the reformer renounced. The internal trials which tormented him most of all were set on a much higher plane. They disturbed him as profoundly in old age as in his youth; the only difference was that as he grew older the outward occasion of these trials changed and that above all he had meanwhile achieved an incomparably greater insight into the means of overcoming them. He was never seriously concerned with temptations of a worldly nature, with the struggle of the natural man with the strict monastic vows. All this lies far beneath him, and one can make no more radical misjudgment of him than if one sees his soul as the scene of a battle in which the natural desire for happiness of the earthly man struggled against the ascetic's longing for salvation. It was not that the asceticism of the monastery seemed to him too strict and too impossibly hard to fulfill, but that it seemed totally inadequate in face of the infinite demands of the divine commandment. Nor was it longing for heaven or fear of hell which rent his soul; his own personal well-being fades into total insignificance by comparison with the terrible force with which his spirit was torn by the question of an ethical religion as such.

A more accurate interpretation of his distress of soul may be found not in a "natural" but in a theological explanation, which takes as its starting point the internal tensions of late medieval piety. These sprang from the difficulty of reconciling man's free will in his own actions with the ideas of predestination forged by men like William of Ockham, that is from the internal contradiction between the idea of the retributive justice of God and his irrational and arbitrary election of men. On the one side stood the ability and duty of man in his free will to make himself worthy to receive grace by preparatory works, the ability particularly to produce in himself by means of self-abasement a complete hatred of evil and an infinite love of God; on, the other hand the dependence of all moral achievement, of all worth in the eyes of God, on the mysterious cooperation of the grace of God poured into the sacraments, which grace (unaccountably only present in the sacrament through the mediation of a priest) immediately disappears as soon as a mortal sin gains a foothold in a man's heart. Against both these there is God's arbitrary decision either to reject or to accept the works of the man which have been produced in this state of grace; to destine the sinner for eternal salvation or eternal damnation as an act of grace apparently without rhyme or reason. . . .

Whence comes this new conscience which made him feel this dilemma so deeply and directly—to such an infinitely greater extent than the rest of the world around him and in fact than any other theologian since the days of Augustine? Only now do we arrive at the secret of his greatness: that he was infinitely more than a theologian, that in a strange way for a man in the 16th century after 1500 years of Christianity he was able in spite of his scholastic heritage and upbringing to remain ultimately independent of all doctrinal traditions; that he was able to grasp anew the eternal mysteries of the divine in an utterly original manner. It is only when one passes beyond all rational concepts and the questions of doubt which they raise that the primary religious phenomenon becomes visible. It cannot be compassed in words, but at least an echo remains here and there struggling for expression.

Such things could only be related in the third person:

I knew a man, who told me that he had often borne these torments, although admittedly only for a short while. They were so great and hellish that no speech can tell of them, no pen write of them, indeed that no one can believe in them, who has not himself experienced them. . . . Then the soul is stretched out on the cross with Christ, so that one could number all her bones. And there is no corner in her which is not filled with the most terrible bitterness, with terror, fear, anguish—but all this eternal, infinite. . . .

But it is precisely this which is the mark of great men of history: that they do not comply with our standards and ideals but bring their own standards and ideals into the world. Whoever wishes to understand the fullness of the historical achievement of Luther, the warrior of God, must become fully acquainted with this dark mysterious force underlying his piety. Only then does the boldness of his decision of faith become really clear, the unheard-of strength of this soul which struggled constantly in extreme despair, even against God himself, to achieve a childlike trust in this Old Testament God of terror, to see him as "our dear Father," and to make this trust the central core of his life. For it is by no means true to say that these struggles belong only to the period of his monastic life or to the early years of his life there, and that they then died away thanks to a new knowledge of the salvation of the Gospel. ...

His life was always a fearful walk with God where every moment could bring new storms in his soul. The real secret of his prophecy is the highly paradoxical fact (perhaps because it is a religious fact) that it was precisely this domination of the natural man by fear which became for him a never-failing source of strength, of that freely flowing strength which overwhelms the world because there is nothing left in the world which can terrify it. It was precisely at the time when the storms in his soul were at their fiercest that the confidence of the prophet in his mission was as its greatest. For it was then that he was most confident in the holy purifying flame which burnt in his soul. ...

The spiritual content of Luther's life's work is predetermined by the ethical rather than by the mystical element of his religious experience. What distinguished his temptations from the dull fear of the primitive levels of religion was not his overcoming of a sense of despair by a concept of the absolute which embraces God and man in a perfect unity, but their ethical character. For him the infinite distance between God and man found expression in his consciousness of sin. All the concepts of late medieval Christianity are inextricably bound up with this idea. The peculiarly personal element in Luther's piety is first seen in the strange sensitivity of his conscience, in the scrupulous excess of the moral and religious impositions which he laid on himself. Only one must be careful not to imagine that one has exhausted the significance of the matter by emphasizing the ethical element in his piety, its origin in his feeling of guilt, and his constant concern with the central problems of sin, grace and salvation. Beneath this ethical element there is an even more radical, purely religious element, behind the fear of the damned lies the completely primitive fear of the creature confronted by the sight of the Eternal and Almighty. ...

For what he himself felt as the original and inherited sin of his humanity could in no way be grasped by the moral sensitivity of the average man—it was basically nothing other than the purely spiritual self-affirmation of the creature in the face of the Almighty, it was the despairing self-defense of the natural man in his terror of being enveloped in the infinite will of God. He carried this struggle through with that uncompromising honesty against himself which characterizes only the strong in spirit; he carried it through to the complete self-destruction of his own will. ...

In these experiences and in their interpretation (which for him was only the rediscovery of divine truths which had been revealed long before) lies hidden the true genius of Martin Luther. . . .

Only Luther penetrated to the heart of the matter; his mission was not to reestablish the forms of early Christian life and doctrine but to reveal the religious strength of the Christian tradition in a way which was closely related to the spirit of the earliest beginnings. In so doing he in fact discovered what was at the same time the oldest heritage in the Christian tradition. It was the all-dominating central idea of God's holiness and majesty, casting aside all men's claims to self-sufficiency, unconditional and unlimited in its moral demands, and yet at the same time God who is the Father who has pity on the fallen son, on the sinful creature in all his inadequacy. . . .

The most general and permanent achievement of his life lies in his own personal secret: in his life with God and in the direct relationship of all his thinking and willing with him—in this particular respect, that with Luther everything which is external springs as it were automatically from a faith which bursts the bonds of the human imagination. It is in his simple religious insights that we find the true meaning of the man. The key to his ethics is his proclamation of the supremacy of the eternal, the law of God, over all human action, and his consequent rejection of ecclesiastical authority or of any considerations of man's own happiness. He strove constantly to establish the idea of man's direct, personal, and inescapable responsibility to God firmly in men's consciousness until it completely dominated men's lives, so that they might experience again the release from the intolerable tensions which had been set up by casuistry and teleological ethics. . . .

The development of this religious message was the true fruit of his literary work, and it owed its power to the fact that Luther's message did not derive from any personal opinion, but from the depths of his fundamental religious experience: from an experience which was indeed of a highly personal nature, but which was intended in no way to be individual, original, or in any sense new, but rather a reliving, a faithful acceptance of the earliest Christian revelation.

B.

Ernest Gordon Rupp (1910–   ), English Methodist, has been professor in ecclesiastical history at the University of Manchester since 1956. Rupp combines an admirable mastery of Luther's theology with a biblical

majesty of expresion. His most notable work is The Righteousness of God
(1953), from which this selection is taken.

ERNEST GORDON RUPP*

It is no accident that Luther's doctrine of the Devil really develops
after the Diet of Worms. In the loneliness of the Wartburg there was
the inevitable reaction of a mind held taut for long, now relaxed, and
of a soul flung back upon itself. Luther's Devil is by no means to be
disposed of in terms of superstition, catarrh, noises in the head, and what
are now fashionably described as "poltergeist phenomena." The theologians have described the importance for Luther of the theme of conflict,
and of the dynamism and objectivity of evil. Here we remember the continuing significance for him of "Anfechtung." It is here that Luther
reminds us again and again of the great English writer with whom he
had most in common (far more than with John Wesley), John Bunyan.
As Bunyan found his own heart written out in Luther's Galatians, so
there is much of Luther in "Grace Abounding" and in the "Pilgrim's
Progress." Here is Luther, thinking of the Christian man as a St. George
against the dragon—and coming very close indeed to the immortal conference between Christian and Apollyon. In this case the Christian faces
Sin personified, sin which entices the Christian to "lust or avarice or
despair of hatred of God. . . ."

It is now when, for the first time, he had begun to put on weight, and
when bearded like the pard, as "Junker Georg" he looked really fierce,
that we get a glimpse of that unexpected gentleness which was a genuine
deep element in his character, and was evidenced much more in personal
contact than can be gauged from his writings. In search of needful
exercise he joined a hunting party "to get a taste of the pleasures which
fine gentlemen love." He was disgusted when the chase turned out to be,
not after some animal of prey, but after hares, and when one of the terrified creatures ran his way, "With great pains I saved one of them—and
let the live hare take refuge in the sleeves of my cloak." Luther let it stay
there, and began to edge away from the group of huntsmen, but was
soon the center of the group of baying, leaping hounds who had scented
"Poor Puss"—and when Luther uncovered his reddening sleeve he found
that the silly hare's leg and throat had been bitten through the cloth. As
he stared and shuddered, he saw the parable of his own situation and

his own possible fate, and he had done for a lifetime with the hunting of innocent things.

While Luther grappled in his Patmos with great literary tasks, and with sharp physical illness, and with spiritual "Anfechtungen," he had to meet a crisis in Wittenberg, provoked by Karlstadt and a handful of extremists, the premonition of a century of baneful Puritan iconoclasm. Luther paid a secret visit to the town, and in defiance of the express order of the Elector that if he valued his life, he must at all costs remain in hiding, he entered the city. On Sunday, March 6, 1522, he reentered his pulpit—his beard shaved off, his disguise put away and (the whole of his Reformation is in this touch) carefully habited as an Augustinian monk.

"Let us beware lest Wittenberg become a Capernaum . . . dear friends, a man must not insist on his rights, but must see what is useful and help-ful to his brother. . . . I would not have gone as far as you have done if I had been there. What you did was good, but you have gone too fast, for there are brothers and sisters on the other side who belong to us, and must still be won. . . .

"Faith never yields, but Love is guided according as our neighbours can grasp or follow it. There are some who can run, others must walk, and still others who can hardly creep. Therefore we must not look on our own, but on our brother's powers, so that he that is weak in faith . . . may not be destroyed . . . let us therefore cast ourselves at one an-other's feet, join hands and help one another. . . . I will do my part, for I love you even as I love my own soul. . . .

"We must first win the hearts of the people. And that is done when I teach only the Word of God, preach only the Word of God, for if you win the heart, you win the whole man."

Thus Luther began his war on two fronts, against the legalism of the papists on the one hand, and the legalism of the fanatics on the other. The new movements on the left had their own pedigree: the writings of Conrad Grebel and of Thomas Müntzer include a mystical terminology and an apocalyptic emphasis which did not derive at all from Luther's movement. That there were Anabaptists in that time of simple piety and gentle mien is undoubted, but we can hardly wonder if their still, small voice was swallowed in the fire and earthquake of the Peasant War and the Munster debacle. The great themes "Word—Spirit" were strained through the new tension, and as the radicals emphasized the voice of the Spirit within, so the conservatives stressed more and more the objective and written Word and prepared for the later uncompromising biblicism. Thomas Müntzer repaid every hard word he received from Luther with interest: he was "a blind archdevil," "a poisonous worm with your dirty humility that you got out of Augustine" . . . "sleep softly, Mr. Soft Life . . . Asses' Flesh . . . Dr. Martin Liar . . . Mr. Sit on the Fence . . . His Holiness the Pope of Wittenberg . . . Mr. Cleverstick. . . ."

Luther's intolerance may have hardened in later years, and his original insistence that heresy can only be fought by the Word was reluctantly and halfheartedly compromised by the pressure of his friends and patrons and his concern lest the Reformation movement go completely astray. But there is about him little of the unlovely rigidity of some forms of modern Lutheranism in this matter, and he maintained as few in that age or since two convictions: first, that as he said, "one point in doctrine is more important than heaven and earth"—and second, a conviction that the Word of God, not force, is only able to conquer in matters of truth. It was not simply obstinacy or fundamentalism which led him to write on the table the words which divided him and Zwingli, in the great matter of the Eucharist—"Hoc EST corpus meum." It was the conviction that to turn that "EST" into "significat" was to turn the religion of incarnation into that docetism and subjectivism which has haunted and impoverished Protestant eucharistic life for four centuries over the greater part of Protestantism. He warned his generation as he warns the Ecumenical movement in our time that the most urgent practical, political reasons of expediency cannot justify a reunion which involves the weakening of obedience to the truth as God gives men to believe it.

By 1525 Luther was ceasing to stand out with the clear isolation of a Perugino painting. He becomes part of a crowded canvas. The Reformation was afoot, not so much a movement as a series of ever-multiplying, ever-divided persons, events, causes. As earlier on, the tides of history supported him, and his resistance in 1517–21 was, as Müntzer gibed, made possible by the support of German national anticlericalism, so now he had the less pleasant experience of having to stand against the stream of public opinion, not only in the learned and public world, but among the common people.

His consistency in the matter of the Peasants can be fully demonstrated, from a succession of writings in the preceding years. He had warned the rulers, he had warned the cities, he had warned the peasants, and, above all, he had raised his voice against the fanaticism of the parsons who provided the heady ideological leadership among them. The brutality of his terrible broadsheet against the Peasants springs from his alarmed apprehension that the whole Reformation might now be swallowed up in bloodshed and anarchy. But he wrote at a time when the Peasants were carrying all before them and when he had reason to expect that he might pay for his plain speaking with his life.

Moreover, it seems that the writing appeared originally at the end of an edition of his moderate appeal to both sides, as a kind of appendix added when negotiations had broken down and the insurrections were in full spate. When it was over, and the dreadful reprisals were in swing, his words sounded harsh and provocative, and alarmed his friends, and enraged the defeated. His own obstinacy prevented him from retracting, though he made some bold comments against the Junkers and made personal intercession for some of the sufferers. But it was not all obstinacy. It was his own doctrine of obedience, conscientiously sustained, and it was his special count against the rebel leaders that as their movement swept along with blood and fire they conscripted innocent men and women into what Luther regarded as a damnable cause.

Our immediate point is not to make special pleading on his behalf but to point out that he deliberately refused to play to a very considerable gallery, as his friends urged him to do, and that his loyalty to the truth as he saw it lost him a public support which affected his whole later life, and turned important currents of the Reformation into other channels.

At the height of the Peasant war he married, deliberately, partly to show that his conscience was clear. Marriage in the 16th century was a marvelously commonsense affair. Luther's wooing was not romantic, but it turned out very well indeed. Those who dismiss it in terms of runaway nun and apostate monk beg one of the biggest of 16th-century questions. But certainly Luther needed looking after.

"Before I was married the bed was not made up for a whole year and became foul with sweat. But I worked all day and was so tired at night that I fell into bed without knowing that anything was amiss."

In the event his home life can stand comparison even with the home life of Sir Thomas More, and was, in respect of the relations between husband and wife, a good deal happier. We have a vivid picture of their relations together in the letters with their roughly gentle banter, and Luther could ask no more effective testimony than the letter which his Kate wrote her sister, full two months after his death:

"Who would not be sorrowful and mourn for so noble a man as was my dear lord? Truly I am so distressed I cannot tell the deep sorrow of my heart to anybody and I hardly know what to think or how I feel. I cannot eat or drink nor can I sleep. If I had a principality and an empire it would never have cost me so much pain to lose them as I have now that our Lord God has taken from me this dear and precious man. God knows that for sorrow and weeping I can neither speak nor dictate this letter. . . ."

We are all familiar with the portraits of Luther. The early engraving which shows him as a monk, and much as Mosellanus described him at the Leipzig disputation:

"Of middle height, with slender body worn out both by study and care, so that you can almost count his bones. He is in the vigour of manhood. His voice is sharp and clear."

There is the fine profile, which shows how very tough, and how very German Luther looked at the time when he was hailed as the "Hero of the German nation."

There are the series of Cranach portraits which show that, like Jabez in the Scriptures, Luther's coasts were continually being enlarged until he attained (let us admit it—since polemic has made so much of it) a Chestertonian girth almost as great as that of St. Thomas Aquinas, and from which Luther stares at us, with moody benevolence, or in one of his own favorite phrases, "like a cow staring at a new gate." That is a pity, for his eyes, flashing, quick, twinkling in fun or flaming in anger, were what all his contemporaries, friend and foe, remembered of him. The whole man was in them: the obstinacy and occasional malice, the unabating anger against those he believed to be the enemies of God, the humor and the gentleness and the unexpected timidities, and the charm which he could exercise, to melt even hostile, critical visitors.

But the fight never stopped and the strain was constant. And in the later years he had to watch the growing division among his friends, the growing power of his enemies, the evident and even growing strength of his papal foes. There is the story of how, in 1535, when the English delegates were with him, he received a visit from the papal nuncio, and took Robert Barnes along with him to dinner, no doubt with long spoons used all around. And Luther put on his best clothes, and brushed his hair, carefully hiding all traces (he was 52) of his age, lest it be whispered in the streets of Askelon that his strength was failing.

One of the legends of modern polemic has been of a great decline in Luther's last years. It is true that some of his fiercest polemic against the papacy (but it was the edge of the Council of Trent) and against the Jews was written at this time. But there is nothing which cannot be paralleled from his earlier writings, and a great weight of fine, edifying, constructive writing to set against it. He came to be racked with chronic illness, and knew few hours without physical pain. He suffered much from stone. Ebstein's list of his illnesses includes:

"Calculi, constipation, catarrh of the middle ear, piles, periostitis, stomach affections, weak heart, dysentery, cataract and rheumatism."

Whether he suffered from serious heart trouble, or whether his swoons and fainting periods from 1527 onward are what are now described, but hardly explained, as "psychophysical" cannot be accurately determined. He was prematurely aged. There were times when he thought of death as a coming blessing and longed for rest—the famous "volo esse miles emeritus"—and the half-joking:

"I am an old, tired, chilled, frozen man and now, to crown all, one-eyed, and now that I am already dead, so to speak, I might be allowed some peace . . . but no, I must be writing and talking as though I have never written a word."

When at last he brought his great course of Lectures on Genesis to a close, in November, 1545, it was with the same sense of burdened relief, "May our Lord God grant to somebody else to make a better job of it. I can no more, I am too weak—pray to God for me that he will give me a good, blessed end (*stündlein*)."

Here was no old reprobate, snarling in his cups, of polemical legend. But there were times when he had his tantrums and when his friends dreaded to bring him bad news (but always about the good cause of Reformation). It was at this very time that, disgusted and disheartened at the moral laxity of Wittenberg, he shook its dust from his feet and declared that rather than live in such a place he would wander round Germany begging the bread of charity, until a scared deputation of town and gown came after him, begging him to return.

Then in January, 1546, he was asked to mediate in a dispute between the two young lords of Mansfeld. He had every reason for not going, and he left his wife stiff with anxiety. But they were his "Obrigkeit" and Mansfeld was his home town. With two sons and with Justus Jonas he adventured the long 80 miles. He had taken pains that his wife should not be left destitute, and now he wrote her a series of frequent, homely, teasing, cheerful letters which are among his finest writings. They were halted by the flooded River Saale.

"We met a huge She-Anabaptist with great waves and huge blocks of ice, threatening to re-baptize us . . . we have had to wait."

The negotiations were long and difficult, not least because of the implacable arrogance of the gentry, of whom Luther wrote bitingly to his wife. He found committees always a trial, and for him it was always the hard thing to sit and watch. The Diet of Augsburg in 1530 had been for him a fidgeting torment when he had to wait outside in the Castle Coburg, leaving the care of the churches to God and to Philip Melanchthon. But he did not forget his wife and her worries, and did what he could to tease her out of them.

"My Dear Wife, Doctoress, Director of the Wittenberg Pig Market. Dear Kate, read St. John and that little Catechism of which you once told me, 'Why there's all about me in this book'. . . you seem to have taken on God's own worries, as though God couldn't create ten Doctor Martins if the old one gets choked in the River Saale. . . . I have a better protector. He it was who lay in a manger and was nursed at a maiden's breast and sits at the right hand of God the Father Almighty—so be at peace."

And again, three days later:

"Most holy Doctoress. We thank you most gratefully for your worry about us, which is so great that you can't sleep. . . . Say your prayers, my dear, and let God worry about me, for you and I are not commanded to worry, but as Ps. 55 says, Cast thy burden on the Lord for he cares for you, etc.' "

There was one more letter, happy, serene, telling of a difficult mission wonderfully accomplished, of a reconciliation made and confirmed in a meal at Luther's table. His last words of his last letter to her echo the constant refrain of all his correspondence from first to last, "we will wait and see what God will do." But now he was deathly tired. Afterward his friends noticed a special solemnity about those prayers of his, which, after his wont, he made audibly by an open upper window. Then, a few hours later, he halted before a chill river more dreadful than the flooded Saale.

Like so many "last words" his recorded final utterances are conventional. But years before he had written:

"If we believe the waters below us depart and . . . harm us not but flee from us. . . . And those above us stand up high as though they would overwhelm us: these are the horrors and apparitions of the other world, which at the hour of death terrify us. If, however, we pay no heed to them and pass on with a firm faith, we shall enter into eternal life dry shod and unharmed."

It seems to be the fact that for him those last terrors, that final temptation so often anticipated, were wonderfully abated.

He passed over, as one seeking a strong City.

Lacey Baldwin Smith, Professor of History at Northwestern University, was born in Princeton, N.J., in 1922. A graduate of Bowdoin College, he received his M.A. and Ph.D. degrees from Princeton. He formerly taught history at Princeton University and Massachusetts Institute of Technology and was a Guggenheim fellow and senior Fulbright scholar at London University. He has written numerous articles and reviews, and his books include *Tudor Prelates and Politics* (Princeton, N.J., 1953); *A Tudor Tragedy: The Life and Times of Catherine Howard* (London, 1961); *This Realm of England, 1399–1689* (Boston, 1966), and *The Elizabethan Epic* (London, 1966). He is a member of the Board of Editors of the *American Historical Review* and of the Advisory Board of *Studies in British History and Culture*.

CHAPTER FOUR

LACEY BALDWIN SMITH

Northwestern University

The Reformation in England

IT HAS NOW been almost 30 years since Lucien Febvre described the
origins of the Protestant Reformation as "une question mal posée." Today the problem remains just as complex as ever—especially the English
experience, where spiritual and ecclesiastical matters were befuddled
and bedeviled by motives of sex and state. In fact the religious debate
is pretty much what it was 400 years ago. Catholics still maintain that the
break with Rome was a deplorable and wicked act, and that Henry VIII
was an evil king and a worse man; Protestants, though they admit that
Henry left something to be desired, both as a monarch and as a husband,
continued to view the Reformation as a unique, vital, and "ordained"
event which helped to shape English character and determine the destiny
of the British Isles.

A stand on the Reformation is not merely a matter of theological
preference; religious prejudice is confounded by conflicting theories of
historical causation and by emotional reactions to such central figures as
Henry VIII, Cromwell, Luther, Cranmer, and Wolsey. If you insist that
Henry VIII was a silly brute of a sovereign, better suited to the locker
room than to the conference table, and at the same time look upon the
triumph of Protestantism in an unfavorable light, then it is easy enough
to blame the monarch; but you cannot drive your bias too far. Your
critics will ask: if Henry was so incompetent, then how and why did he
get away with what he did? Conversely, if you approve of the Reformation but still believe that Henry was a despicable sovereign, then it
obviously behooves you to find a man of proper heroic proportions to explain the King's success—in other words, a man behind the throne.

107

Finally, if you present the Reformation in terms of such modern phrases as group dynamics, intersocietal movements, and economic determinism, then it is dangerous to be too lavish with accolades or condemnations; there may be no one at all to blame or acclaim. The permutations and combinations are almost endless; suffice it to say that, over and above the religious division, the controversy has tended to divide into two schools—those who view the Reformation as an act of human will in which motives of lust and dynastic policy prevail, and those who see it as a part of the process of historical change in which men and leaders merely reflect the underlying intellectual, economic, institutional, and psychological forces of the day.

Very early in the 16th century Henry VIII was singled out as the will behind the Reformation; the only debate was the question of motive: Was the decision to divorce Catherine of Aragon really a matter of religious scruple or did "inordinate carnal love" or overwhelming need for a male heir lurk behind the mask of conscience? George Cavendish (whose hero and patron was Cardinal Wolsey) was outspoken on the subject: Is it not a wonder to "consider the desire of willful princes when they be fully bent and inclined to fulfill their voluptuous appetites," and ever since, historians have echoed the Shakespearean quip, "His conscience has crept too near another lady." A. F. Pollard, on the other hand, writing in the tradition of 19th-century self-confidence, presented Henry as the hero of the English nation, a man who opened the floodgates of religious change to save his kingdom from the threat of civil war. Presumably, the King had determined to sacrifice an outmoded medieval church, which still clung to the archaic concept of a universal Christendom and subservience to a foreign and Italianate papacy, upon the altar of our modern idol—the nation-state. In Pollard's hands Henry became the captain of the ship of state, a vessel blown by the winds of historic destiny; the only difficulty is that it is never absolutely clear whether the course was charted by the King or was mapped out for him by his biographer.

For those who find Henry deficient as a hero, there is the Cromwellian school of Reformation history, in which the King's great minister, Thomas Cromwell, is seen as the brains behind the sovereign. Hilaire Belloc, largely because he had little respect for the King, paints Thomas Cromwell as the evil genius who transformed the "accident" of the divorce into the "tragedy" of the break with Rome. G. R. Elton prefers the reverse argument. He agrees that there was nothing inevitable about the Reformation but uses this fact to praise his hero. Thomas Cromwell's original and foresighted mind produced the bold and imaginative plan which overcame the inertia of tradition and alleviated Henry's matrimonial frustration.

Tightly woven into the fabric of history is the age-old riddle of what produces change: the clamor of strong men exercising power or the silent and imperceptible course of events. Even the most fervent hero-worshiper cannot escape some delimiting and environmental influence upon his favorite character. For Pollard, the Reformation was not merely the work of a single man but the fulfillment of an inner historic necessity —the coming of age of the state. For G. R. Elton it was the triumph of the secular, categorical, and calculating mind over medieval confusion and ecclesiastical tutelage. Conversely, even the most convinced social, psychological, economic, and institutional determinist must make reference to a few select individuals, thereby indicating who is to be immortalized and who forgotten.

The historians who see the Reformation as part of the larger drama of Western European history and not as the act of willful men are best divided into four rather untidy camps. First there are the economic determinists who relate and explain spiritual controversy and transformation in terms of such basic economic factors as shifting patterns of land ownership, changing means of production, and new methods of business organization. (It is rather surprising that there has been no full-dress Marxist study of either the continental or the English Reformation.) Second are the institutional historians, who see the Reformation as the breakdown of the totality of medieval-Christian civilization and as the growth of divergent loyalties which forced men to choose between church and state, king and pope. From such a perspective the Reformation represents the culmination of a struggle which began even before Henry II clashed with Thomas á Becket; the eighth Henry, it is said, achieved what the second failed to accomplish—the transformation of an independent and international church into a department of state. The institutional camp also includes a cluster of scholars who have little in common with their state-oriented colleagues but who still explain the crisis in institutional terms: the corruption and worldliness of the church which antagonized the ruling elite and educated opinion of late medieval society.

Many historians feel that abnormalcies within the ecclessia were not causes but merely symptoms of a more basic metamorphosis of mind and soul. Thus there is a third interpretation which argues that Renaissance impulses such as secularism and humanism were at work, weakening ancient loyalties, corroding traditional habits of thought, and setting up fresh and rival standards by which to judge God and man. Fourth and finally there is the spiritual school, which emphasizes the failure of the old church to fulfill the spiritual needs of a civilization deeply disturbed by the widening gulf between the realities of late 15th-century life and the ideals which the church continued to mouth but made little effort to achieve.

One more element should be noted: the thorny issue of accident in history as opposed to design, etched either by the divine will of God or by the blind hand of historic determinism. Contemporaries saw the manifest hand of the deity; some perceived a wrathful God punishing Tudor society by inflicting upon it the scourge of heresy, others a merciful godhead leading his chosen people into a new and greater light by casting out that apostle of darkness, the bishop of Rome. Moderns are usually more cautious about God's role in history, but they can be almost as doctrinaire about inevitability. The Reformation, they say, would have come (or—a more difficult proposition—it would have succeeded) even without the divorce and the accident of Henry's domestic difficulties. But there are those who hold to the opposite position: the whole thing was a freak occurrence in which trifling events perversely produced monumental consequences.

If the reader of these selections finds himself in a labyrinth of conflicting interpretations, let him take heart in the knowledge that what he reads are mere words, "unable to completely reflect or exhaust the complexities of reality."

1. HENRY VIII

A. F. Pollard was the dean of Tudor studies, and most modern scholarship on Henry VIII has been revisionistic largely in terms of disproving his interpretation. He presented the Reformation as a necessary act of state, perpetrated by a determined and courageous sovereign who was one of history's giants and the master "pilot who weathered the storm."

A. F. POLLARD[*]

A philosopher has said that "to popularise philosophy is at once to debase it." That, no doubt, is true of every kind of truth, but history runs

[*] From A. F. Pollard, "Henry VIII," in Katharine Garvin (ed.), *The Great Tudors* (New York, 1935), pp. 23–27. Reprinted by permission of the publishers, E. P. Dutton & Co., Inc., New York.

a greater risk than most. Philosophy, like physical science, is the per-
quisite of experts; but history is the happy hunting ground of the novelist,
the playwright, the film producer, and the correspondent who writes to
the press about things he admits he did not even learn at school. The
"taste for Tudors" is less a taste for history or even for biography than for
the common things which make the great akin to little men. The age of
heroes and of hero worship concentrated on the distinguishing features
which raised men up above their fellows: democracy dotes on the defects
which bring them down to a common level understanded of the people.
If we cannot share the greatness of men, our self-esteem seeks fellow
feeling in their foibles. Some of the Tudors are immune from this ignomin-
ious popularity: even Shakespeare wrote no play about Henry VII, who
would paralyze any film; for he merely conducted the most successful
foreign policy in English history and established a throne on foundations
invisible to opera glasses. Edward VI died at 15, disqualified by disease
and early death from admission to the school for scandal, while Mary
was too conscientious or too plain. Elizabeth was anything but either,
and Lytton Strachey's book *Elizabeth and Essex* were better named
Elizabeth and her Sex. Martin Hume was more polite in his *Courtships of
Queen Elizabeth* than in his *Wives of Henry VIII,* and it is Henry's wives
who qualify him for posthumous popularity. The grave and right reverend
Bishop Stubbs[1] did, indeed, confess (while he was only a professor) that
the portraits of those wives "were, if not a justification, at least a colour-
able occasion for understanding the readiness with which he put them
away." But the more wives he put away, the more they cling to his
memory.

Marriage was doubtless—though murder was not—one of the matters
the Apostle had in mind when he counseled moderation in all things.
The morality of the problem is obscure. Six mistresses would have been
no news at a royal court; they would have eluded the film altogether,
like the 45 debited to Henry of Navarre or the unspecified number George
II had in mind when he protested in tears to his dying Queen that he
could not bear the thought of marrying again. Mere mistresses might,
perhaps, have cast over Henry VIII the meretricious halo which now
adorns the brow of that prince of profligates, Charles II. Even four wives
might not have mattered: Henry's last queen, Catherine Parr, had four
husbands without leaving a stain on her character; his brother-in-law the
Duke of Suffolk had four wives and his sister Margaret Tudor, Queen of
Scotland, three husbands. Six seems to have been the limit which divided

---

[1] William Stubbs, Anglican bishop of Oxford and distinguished constitutional
and medieval historian.

the silly sheep from the giddy goats. The gravamen of the charge against
Henry is not that he seduced the ladies of his court, but that he married
them. The papal curia itself was lenient to mistresses; it was, indeed, as
Mr. Hilaire Belloc has noted, "a common practice" for his "greater ecclesi-
astics" of that time to take a mistress, and Anne Boleyn only encountered
papal censures when Clement VII discovered that Henry really meant
to marry her.

Henry could have had, if he wanted them, as many mistresses as
Francis I without raising a ripple on the surface of English history. He
had at least one, Bessie Blount, the mother of the Duke of Richmond,
and almost certainly another, Mary, the elder sister of Anne Boleyn—both
before he was 30 years of age. If there were others they have entirely
escaped the records, his correspondence, and the chronicles of the time;
not one has ever been named, and a hundred thousand contemporary documents can be searched in vain for any reference to a child of Henry's other
than the Duke of Richmond, Edward VI, Mary, and Elizabeth. There
was no secrecy about any of these, and total silence with regard to others
is fairly conclusive proof that they never existed.

The King, indeed, was not in search or in need of a mistress, or even
of a wife, so much as of a son to succeed him, carry on the Tudor succession, and avert a recrudescence of the Wars of the Roses. That was
his engrossing problem throughout almost the whole of his reign; and it
was only solved in the end by an act of parliament, to the terms of which
—in spite of religious passions and rival claims—England stood staunch
so long as a Tudor remained to fulfill them. Catherine of Aragon, whom
he had not chosen himself, failed him: one miscarriage or stillborn child
succeeded another, and in 1514, after five years of parental misfortune
Henry—or Wolsey—petitioned Leo X to annul the marriage with his
brother's wife which another pope had sanctioned, doubting the validity
of his own dispensation. Then in 1516 came Mary, who was welcomed,
not for her own sake, but as an earnest of the son to follow. No woman
had yet reigned in England, and Henry VII had secured the throne, not
only by ending a civil war, but by excluding from the throne his mother,
from whom he derived whatever hereditary right he possessed. The expected heir never followed Mary, and by 1527 it was certain that Henry
VIII would have no legitimate son so long as Catherine remained his
wife. He ceased to cohabit, though not to live, with her from that date,
and fell a victim to the one grand passion of his life. It might provide a
better hope for the succession than the *marriage de convenance* with
Catherine. He was the second English king to marry for love and nothing
else, and its ripe and refreshing fruit was Queen Elizabeth. But for five

years he waited; the child must be legitimate, and a divorce from Catherine was confidently expected from Clement VII in 1529. It was refused: if, wrote the Pope's secretary, it is granted, "The Church cannot escape utter ruin, as it is entirely in the power of the Emperor's servants." Charles V's armies had almost turned Italy into a province of Spain; Catherine was his aunt, and Mary his cousin whose succession to the English throne he was bent on securing.

The papacy was immovable: so was Henry on the question of the succession to his throne. So, too, was the Queen: her honor was involved, the legitimacy of her child, that child's prospects of a crown, and the Spanish alliance of which they were the emblems and the agents. The women of England supported her on the grounds of morality and sentiment; their husbands opposed on those of national policy. It was not yet a question of religion or the faith: the Lutherans and Tyndale, the Protestant martyr, denounced the divorce; and, could Clement VII have been constrained or persuaded to grant it, there might have been no immediate breach with Rome and no Act of Supremacy. France, for the sake of the English alliance and her ambitions in Italy, supported Henry, and the diplomatic struggle raged for three years. But, meanwhile, the Reformation Parliament assembled in November, 1529, and gave voice to the anticlerical tide which Wolsey had damned for 15 years. It overflowed, swept away some of the more notorious privileges and abuses, and enabled Henry to extort from the church itself a reluctant admission of his supremacy. Warham died, protesting in vain, and Cranmer became Archbishop of Canterbury, while Cromwell succeeded to Sir Thomas More's and Stephen Gardiner's place in Henry's counsels. The Act of Annates robbed the papacy of its revenues from English benefices, and the Acts of Appeals made England independent of its jurisdiction. Henry married Anne Boleyn about the end of January, 1533, in the confidence born of her pregnancy, and on September 7, she gave birth to the future queen, Elizabeth. Finally, in 1534, the Royal Supremacy was enshrined in a parliamentary statute, where it has remained ever since, save for Mary's Catholic reign and the Puritan regime a century later.

Never was revolution more skillfully draped as reform; it was made respectable, like treason, by success. Its path had, indeed, been prepared by centuries of struggle between church and state, in which the church had grown weaker and the monarchy stronger through the decline of ecclesiastical unity and the rise of secular nationalism; and the church in England had already proved too weak to resist the royal demand that it should become the Church of England. Nevertheless, Henry VIII was the parent of what Lord Acton justly termed "a new polity." Hitherto there had been no "state" in England, but various estates, of which the ecclesiastical were subject to papal, and the secular to royal, sovereignty. The Act of Supremacy brought all under one sovereign and created out of them a single, novel state which also claimed to be an empire, independent alike of Holy Roman Emperor and Holy Roman Pope; and, what was more, the emancipator became dictator, and the father of all the fascists[2] in the world. The Middle Ages passed away in childbirth, and its child was what Michelet calls "le nouveau Messie, le Roi."

[2] In understanding Pollard's selection and use of words, it may be helpful to note that this article was written in 1935 just as Fascist Italy and Germany were threatening the peace of Europe.

2. KING OR MINISTER?

G. R. Elton is to the contemporary study of Tudor history what Pollard was a generation ago. In his major work, The Tudor Revolution in Government, *he argues that the major development of Henry's reign was not the religious crisis but the evolution of a bureaucratic administration separate from the personality and court of the monarch and endowed with a life and independence of its own—in other words, a national, as opposed to a royal, government. His hero is Thomas Cromwell, the very model of a modern majordomo, and his archenemy is A. F. Pollard.*

G. R. ELTON[*]

The question whether Henry VIII or Thomas Cromwell supplied the ideas and the policy which underlay the break with Rome is of more interest than may be imagined. Until it is answered neither the men nor the event can really be understood. The English Reformation gave to England, the English monarchy, and the English church a character quite their own: this makes it important to know just how and why and through whom it happened. . . . Here I shall attempt only to elucidate the true relationship between the two leading personalities of that age, for the prevailing notions seem to me to do scant justice to the genius of the minister and vastly to overrate the genius of the King. One's opinion of Henry VIII must stand by one's view of his part in the Reformation. The

[*] From G. R. Elton, "King or Minister?: The Man Behind the Henrician Reformation," *History*, Vol. XXXIX (October, 1954), pp. 216–18, 220–22, 224–25, 228–32. By permission of the author and editor of *History*.

positive achievements of his long reign were crowded into its middle years; if he deserves the high opinion of his skill and understanding which so many moderns seem to hold it must be because he was "the architect of the Reformation." But whether he was that remains to be seen. . . .

It is time to turn from what has been said about Cromwell and Henry to what can be found in the evidence. Is it, in fact, possible to come to conclusions in this matter which are more than opinions? Can one decide with any degree of certainty whether Thomas Cromwell or Henry VIII evolved the plan which led to the schism and the establishment of the royal supremacy, especially since both men must have worked together and much of the story must lie forever hidden in unrecorded conversations, council meetings, and even private thoughts? I believe that despite these obstacles an answer is possible. In the first place, we can investigate the relations between King and minister to see whether they permit an insight into their position toward each other. Second, a reinterpretation of the course of the Henrician Reformation collated with Cromwell's career will, it is hoped, offer a solution of the problem. . . .

The question here is whether it was Cromwell's mind or Henry's that evolved the plan for breaking the deadlock created by Wolsey's failure to get the King his divorce. What has been shown so far is that there is no justification for the frequent assertion that Cromwell was a mere "instrument"; in government and affairs he followed his own mind. But while this makes it possible to see in him the maker of the Reformation if further proof is forthcoming, it does not do so by itself. The answer can only be found in a reinterpretation of the meaning, and especially of the chronology, of the Henrician Reformation.

The whole interpretation depends on chronology because Cromwell did not immediately succeed Wolsey as the King's chief minister. If he represented a policy of his own one might expect to see it appear with his arrival in power in 1532; and this is what happened. It is necessary to keep in mind what the "Henrician Reformation" really meant: the break with Rome—the withdrawal from the papal obedience—the creation of a schismatic English church—the setting up of the royal supremacy. All these are different, and in part tendentious, descriptions of one thing: the definition of independent national sovereignty achieved by the destruction of the papal jurisdiction in England. There lay the supremely important constitutional achievement of the 1530's. It came about because of the King's desire for a divorce from his first wife; it was greatly facilitated by the dislike of clergy and papacy which prevailed among the English laity; it may even have been assisted by the supposed spread of new and reformist ideas, whether Lutheran or humanist, though here the present writer would advocate the utmost caution. But in none of these things lay the essence of the change. Henry's campaign to have his marriage annulled is one thing; his break with the pope is another. The break was the means by which in the end the marriage was annulled; but Henry tried other means, and the historical importance of the break did not consist even mainly in the accomplishment of the divorce. To understand the years 1527–34 one must indeed start from the divorce, but one must try to follow events without allowing one's knowledge of the outcome to influence interpretation. One must attempt to discover what the king was up to as time went on.

This goes counter to Pollard's view that "the general course of the Reformation was a perfectly natural development from existing circumstances which it is idle to attribute to the influence of any one man." It was his opinion that Henry knew from the beginning where he was heading, though he had hopes that he would not be driven all the way but might compel the pope to surrender before the break came. In Pollard's own metaphor, the outworks were sapped and the fortress taken step by predetermined step. Gairdner,[1] too, thought that Henry from the first "claimed spiritual as well as civil supremacy in his own kingdom" since he never intended "to accept the jurisdiction of the Roman Curia," an extremely doubtful statement indeed. This I believe to be now the accepted view: it credits the King both with farsighted plans and with an immediate ready radicalism of action. But it cannot be reconciled with those six long and tiresome years spent over the business. More than 60 years ago, Brewer[2] rightly asked why Henry did not assert his own supremacy as early as 1529 but continued to prosecute the divorce at Rome even after Wolsey's failure. He answered that Henry "never, in the first instance, seriously contemplated separation from Rome." This view makes better sense. Unable to see how he could legitimately marry Anne without the pope's connivance, and unaware of the possible implications of a royal supremacy in the church, Henry did not at first plan anything as extreme as a break with Rome. The ideas on which the revolution rested only appeared in the course of time.

To make the disagreement plain: Pollard held that a policy which relied on bringing Clement VII to compliance was the natural preliminary to a policy which solved the problem by ignoring the pope altogether. Put like this, it surely looks as though there were two radically different

---

[1] James Gairdner, *Lollardy and the Reformation in England*, 4 vols. (London, 1908–13).

[2] J. S. Brewer, *The Reign of Henry VIII from his Accession to the Death of Wolsey*, 2 vols. (London, 1884).

lines of approach rather than one naturally developing single line. With dubious logic, Pollard argued that the ultimate outcome, being inevitable (which one may doubt), was therefore envisaged from the first. What proof is offered? The Reformation was "so far dictated by circumstances that intelligent observers could predict its general tenor" even before November, 1529. "General tenor" is a question-begging phrase; of course, intelligent observers could foresee some of the issues that were going to be raised, but did they forecast, and did Henry show signs of aiming at, something very like the royal supremacy and break with Rome ultimately established? The alleged evidence—commonly cited from a calendar which at times mistranslates tendentiously—will not bear this out. . . .

It is fair to say that no one can be shown to have prophesied in 1529, or even in 1530, the complete separation of England from the papacy, though many expected attacks on specific forms of papal authority. Among them was the Venetian envoy, also put in evidence by Pollard, who in December, 1530, remarks that the English government were trying so to arrange affairs that they no longer needed the pope in administrative matters. Charles V similarly heard that Henry would "degrade" the pope whom he allegedly called heretic. The King was thought to desire a reduction of English dependence on Rome such as had long been achieved in France, not the overthrow of the pope's entire temporal and spiritual authority. After all, England, having been the most papalist and pope-ridden of countries in the 15th and early 16th centuries, had some way to go to attain the relative independence of France or even of Spain. Henry's continued stand against Lutheran heresy made plain that he was not following the German example, and no one as yet—including Henry—could visualize a Catholic country without the pope.

What matters are not the words of observers but the deeds and intentions of Henry's government. Wolsey's failure to free Henry from Catherine of Aragon by means of the legatine court at Blackfriars was followed by the revocation of the case to Rome (July, 1529), and for the three years after that everything turned on the issue whether Henry could be compelled to attend a trial at Rome or persuade the pope to let the case be decided in England. All the maneuvers on the King's part revolved around this central point. His intention was clear throughout: he wished to impress on Clement VII how much more comfortable it would be if he complied with the King's wishes. As a first step he called parliament. Left to themselves, the commons could be trusted to attack the church; they had shown their temper in 1515 and had been restive in 1523. The anticlericalism of that first session was neither king-imposed nor king-inspired; at most it was permitted by the King. The commons' spontaneous action put pressure on the church and supplied Henry with ammunition for his attack at Rome—at Rome but not on Rome, for it is patent that Henry thought a divorce not sanctioned by the papacy insufficient to secure a legitimate succession. The real purpose of parliament was to overawe the church; it is too readily forgotten that Henry could no more afford opposition among his own clergy if the pope permitted them to try the case in England than if he acted (as ultimately he did act) entirely without the pope. Attacks on the independence of the English church were not synonymous with attacks on Rome: hitherto King and pope had more commonly joined hands against the liberties of the English church....

It would be tedious and pointless to follow the negotiations at Rome which throughout 1531–32 turned on the small technical point whether the curia should hear Edward Carne, sent to Rome as *excusator* to plead that Henry should not be compelled to appear in a foreign court in person or by proxy. For two more years the pope held off both parties, refusing to let the case proceed in England, but also refusing to decide against Henry in Rome as the Spaniards demanded. All this time Henry continued his policy of convincing the pope of the justice of his case, showing so little decision that hostile observers repeatedly concluded that he would give in, put Anne away, and return to Catherine. Reginald Pole[3] heard similar reports: he alleged that Cromwell's advice rescued Henry from a fit of depression induced by his inability to see any way out. The King was bankrupt in ideas. He knew what he wanted; that neither he nor his ministers knew how to obtain it is proved by those years of bootless negotiations. Strong words having failed, he was less violent in language in 1531 than in 1530. In July he again suggested that Canterbury might be allowed to adjudicate; so far from wishing to withdraw from the Roman obedience, he still hoped to get papal approval for a trial in England. New envoys were despatched, only to report the obvious fact that nothing could be hoped for from Rome. By December, 1531, Henry was so far reduced that was ready to have the case tried in France, a safe enough compromise no doubt, but an astonishing surrender of his claims as a sovereign prince and greatly at variance with the high language of 1530. The letter ended in threats so vague as to lack all import: if the King knew what he meant he carefully hid his knowledge. Early in 1532, when the pope seemed at last about to pronounce, Henry was desperate to have the case deferred; throughout 1531 and 1532 there run like a thread the silly machinations designed to bribe some cardinals to Henry's side and

---

[3] Cardinal Reginald Pole, cousin of Henry VIII, descendant of Edward IV, and leader of the Catholic opposition to Henry's break with Rome.

so prevent a decision in consistory. As late as this Henry was so firmly stuck in the mental processes of the past that he hoped to obtain his ends by the bestowal of English sees on Italians. Small wonder that early in 1532 Norfolk and Gardiner allegedly counseled the King to give up: it was about the only piece of advice they had left.

By this time, however, Norfolk and Gardiner[4] were no longer the leading advisers, and diplomatic pressure at Rome was no longer the only policy. Late in 1531 Cromwell was ... admitted to that inner circle of councilors who really advised the King and governed the realm. ... At last parliament was turned against the pope. However harshly the sessions of 1529 and 1531 had dealt with the English clergy, they had not touched the papacy. But in 1532 parliament passed the first Act of Annates by which an important source of papal revenues was cut off and promoted the "Supplication against the Ordinaries" which enabled Henry to follow up his nominal triumph of 1531 with a real triumph over the English clergy by forcing it to accept his control of ecclesiastical legislation. Since—as Maitland has taught us—the English church had no legislative independence in the later Middle Ages, this meant that its dependence was transferred from pope to King; the maneuver based on the Supplication—the "Submission of the Clergy"—was a real though a masked attack on the pope's authority in England.

Thus 1532 saw the inauguration of the policy which was to culminate in the complete destruction of the Roman jurisdiction in England and England's complete withdrawal from the Roman obedience. It also saw the first use for that purpose of the instrument by means of which the revolution was to be accomplished, a point of great significance which can only be hinted at here: there is good reason for supposing that Cromwell, who deliberately made a career in parliament, introduced the King to the potentialities of statute. In the sudden eruption of a new policy, Cromwell's hand is manifest. ...

In the session of February–April, 1533, the Act in Restraint of Appeals to Rome, with its great proclamation of national sovereignty, signaled the triumph of the radical policy—the break with Rome. The prehistory of this act provides the last proof of the two separate policies which have been traced in this paper, and of the fact that Cromwell sponsored the one that proved successful. There survive two drafts for acts of parliament in the hand of Sir Thomas Audley, who had succeeded More as keeper of the great seal in May, 1532, which indicate that even late in 1532 some doubt remained as to the best way of getting the divorce

---

[4] Thomas Howard, 3rd duke of Norfolk, and Stephen Gardiner, bishop of Winchester.

legalized in the realm. One of them would have given parliamentary endorsement to a divorce pronounced by the archbishop of Canterbury; this represented only an ex post facto sanction and not a parliamentary policy. The other intended to give to the archbishops parliamentary authority to act in the divorce in the pope's place; it is the climax of that policy which had persistently endeavored to get Rome to remit the case to England—the culmination of all those complaints, recitals of privileges, and vague threats of hostile action in which Henry had indulged ever since Wolsey's failure in the summer of 1529. It used parliament, but only to permit Canterbury for once to stand in Rome's stead: not based on any profound principle, it was the halfhearted sort of thing that the lawyers' decision had held up in 1530. Its preamble recites the divine law against a man marrying his brother's wife, laments the long delays, and accuses the pope of aspiring to usurp the rights of princes; it is throughout full of apologies, self-justification, and polite references to "the popes holynes."

The statute actually passed on the other hand not only provided for a general prohibition of appeals to Rome—that is, it dealt with a wide issue of general significance instead of confining itself to the particular matter of the divorce—but also included a preamble which described in unequivocal language a theory of England as a sovereign state in which no other potentate might interfere. That it was Cromwell who evolved this measure, and how he overcame some remaining fears and doubts which proclaimed themselves in apologetic and justificatory phrases, has been described elsewhere. Right to the end of the long-drawn conflict the two policies—one pursued since 1529, the other introduced by Cromwell in 1532—vied with each other for the King's approval. So reluctant was Henry to take the decisive step that even toward the end of 1532 he could still toy with a partial measure designed to keep the door open at least an inch or two, even while a simple and thorough policy based on a devastating principle was offered to him. Cromwell's grandiose conceptions triumphed, but it seems to have been a near thing.

The Reformation, then, was not the inevitable development of the textbooks. Whether it would have come anyway it is idle to speculate; but it came in the 1530's simply because Henry's desire for his divorce was balked by an international situation which made cooperation with the papacy impossible, and it came as it did because Thomas Cromwell produced a plan which achieved Henry's ends by destroying the papal power and jurisdiction in England and by creating in England an independent sovereign state. This policy was not present from the start; it had to overcome much caution and conservatism as well as fear of the consequences before its bold simplicity was permitted to develop. The Henrician Reformation reflects the ideas—one may say, the political philosophy—of Thomas Cromwell.

3. SOCIAL DISCONTENT AND LUTHERAN INFLUENCE

Henry Osborn Taylor was one of the outstanding American intellectual historians of the 20th century. His most distinguished work is The Medieval Mind. *The following selection comes from volume two of* Thought and Expression in the Sixteenth Century *in which he develops the link between ideas and action: When an institution, regardless of its honesty or corruption, no longer meets the intellectual, social, and economic needs of society, it must either change or be overthrown.*

HENRY OSBORN TAYLOR[*]

Turning the pages of Gascoigne,[1] one hears the resonant echoes of ancient denunciations—of mankind, of knights and bourgeoisie, and so often of the church. These satires or denunciations might be general, or specifically pointed at the particular abuse or crime. Much also has been recorded, or more lately has been written, upon the state of the church in England, and especially upon the state of its monasteries, at the time when Henry VIII bestrode the throne. Yet just how good or bad the church and its monasteries were, one queries still.

The church had been and still was part of English society, in which the gentry were the favorite sons, and estates were inherited from one generation to the next. The landed classes furnished the church's maintenance, and the nobility and gentry put their younger sons and needy relations into the bishoprics and other goodly benefices. This regular operation of family interest was but one remove from the law of inheritance of secular landed estates. It was much the same in Germany and elsewhere. The condition of the church paralleled that of society at large; it was not abnormally bad, but merely permeated with normal human

---

[*] From Henry Osborn Taylor, *Thought and Expression in the Sixteenth Century* (New York: Macmillan Company, 1920), Vol. II, pp. 50–53. By permission of the President and Fellows of Harvard College.

[1] Doctor Thomas Gascoigne was a 15th-century scholar and a critic of the laxity, worldliness, and corruption of the English clergy.

slackness, selfishness, materialism, and ignorance, with occasional instances of a better energy and enlightenment in its upper or lower orders. The monasteries possessed large revenues or small; the denizens managed their fat lands, or subsisted leanly; generally they lived slackly enough and, like normal human beings, were disinclined to exert themselves beyond the goading of their needs. The monasteries also exercised charity and hospitality, and the richer ones provided funds for the support of scholars at the universities. Probably the poorer monasteries were spiritually the more squalid and inert.

Sadly general statements these, sounding like truisms: the clergy are part of society, and made what they are by education, convention, and environment; they are good or bad, but on the whole tending, by virtue of their education, to be a little better than the corresponding upper or middle classes from which they are drawn. And as one part of society is jealous of another, and not apt to sympathize with its difficulties and temptations, so the laity tended to be captious as to the clergy and to envy them the wealth which they did not seem to earn. It was thus in England, as we might assume, if we were not so informed.

The matter may, however, be regarded in another light. There come times when some order in society fails to function in correspondence with the demands of society at large. Or the ideas conventionally represented by a certain order may no longer meet the best thoughts of contemporaries. This touches the clergy and their functions. The needs of society, and its somewhat clearer or advancing ideas, may pass beyond the current observances and practices of the church. And therefore, from this point of view, the question of church abuses and clerical corruption resolves itself into the question whether the habits of the clergy and the methods and institutions of the established religion fittingly correspond with the ideas, and meet the needs, of the time. An answer in the negative means that church and clergy are no longer suited to the time, and reform is needed. Contemporary verdicts will declare that church and clergy are corrupt. The clergy may be as good, as moral, as the laity, or even better; but methods and institutions, and perhaps principles of belief, need refashioning. What is called for is the application of intelligence and the best available knowledge in matters of religion.

In fact, to make one more general statement before turning to specific illustration of the English situation, it may be said that the German, French, and English reformations represent intellectual advance rather than moral or religious improvement, except as the latter is involved in the former. For example, to give up image worship, relics, pilgrimages, and indeed to renounce the authority of the Roman bishop, was to become more intelligent rather than better.

In the reign of Henry VIII two currents, or perhaps three, of popular criticism assailed the established church. Distinguishable in origin, in their working they tended to unite. The one was the surviving loosely heterodox dissent of the so-called "lay party," which was no longer (if it ever was) a "party," or anything so concrete and articulate. The other current, confused Lutheran or Zwinglian, came from the Continent, where it also may have had its ancient sources. But in England it represented the "new learning."[2] The third current, if one will, was social and economic discontent, the stress of poverty, the sense of disadvantage. This was aggravated by the enclosure of parks and pastures by great proprietors, which dispossessed many tenants, and by the middle of the 16th century may have thrown out of employment 10 percent of the Kingdom's population. Such sense of poverty and oppression had always made part of the indigenous condemnation of the clergy's wealth, and readily combined with the "new learning" when it came from the Continent. Indeed one may say that most reforms which have issued out of Christianity against its own corruptions, as they have been called for by the avarice and lusts of priests and prelates and rich seculars, so have they carried the motive of relieving the distress of the poor. In some way they all seem popular movements, and to represent some assertion of popular rights as against the oppression of the rich. So had it been with Wyclif and the Lollards,[3] so was it with the Lutheran reform, in spite of Luther's violent protests, and so was it to be in England. Thus, although distinguishable, these three factors in English 16th-century disaffection toward the church often joined together, and became as indigenous soil, with native harrowings and foreign informing seed.

It was none too easy for clever contemporaries to distinguish them; and dispute arose as to which cause to ascribe the dissatisfaction (the degree was in dispute) with the church. A notable debate took place between a clever lawyer, Saint-German, and Sir Thomas More, in the years 1532 and 1533, when the King already had proceeded far in his conflict with the pope. Saint-German contended that "the division between spiritualitie and temporalitie," in other words, the laity's dissatisfaction with the wealth

---

[2] The "new learning" is often associated with humanism: the critical, sometimes secular, approach to religious matters.

[3] John Wyclif (1320?–1384) was an English reformer and proto-protestant who preached a heresy not dissimilar to that of Martin Luther. His followers, who during the 15th century may have numbered as many as a third of the English population, were called Lollards.

and laxity of the clergy, was both general and of long standing; while More insisted that it was special or local, and of recent origin: "The division is nothing such as this man makes it, and is grown as great as it is only since Tyndale's books and Frith's and Friar Barnes' began to be spread abroad."[4]

Probably Saint-German was right in contending that the disaffection was old, in its roots at least, and that it was then general; and More was doubtless right in ascribing its current prevalence largely to the recently disseminated literature. That contained social protest as well as religious novelty; yet the proportions varied with the writers. Instances may be given, first, of those in which the social protest outbulks all else, and then of those in which principles of religious reform are clear and trenchant.

---

[4] William Tyndale, John Frith, and Robert Barnes were Protestant polemical writers and martyrs.

4. THE MEDIEVAL BACKGROUND

Professor Powicke was a medieval historian whose work spilled over into the 16th century. His essay, The Reformation in England, *is the classic statement of the thesis that the institutional cart in England preceded the spiritual horse. He sees the break with Rome from a medieval perspective: the disruption of the delicate balance between the secular and spiritual authorities which constituted the very essence of medieval Christendom.*

F. M. POWICKE[*]

The one definite thing which can be said about the Reformation in England is that it was an act of state. The king became the head of the church, the king in parliament gave a sanction to the revised organization, formularies, liturgy, and even in some degree to the doctrine of the church. The king's council and ministers took cognizance of ecclesiastical affairs. The king cooperated with the bishops and convocation in the government of the church, and he appointed commissions to determine appeals in ecclesiastical cases. All this amounted to a revolution. In earlier times there had, of course, been constant cooperation between secular and ecclesiastical authorities in matters ecclesiastical. Movements of thought

---

[*] From F. M. Powicke, *The Reformation in England* (London, 1941), pp. 1–7. By permission of the Oxford University Press.

tending to the isolation of the two authorities from each other had not been successful in the Middle Ages. Although there was much difference of opinion about the origin and rights of secular authority, some saying that it had a divine sanction as part of the nature of things, others contending that after the coming of Christ it was derived from the successors of Christ, that is from the church, and in particular from the pope, very few were prepared to deprecate it, to regard it as a necessary evil. Indeed, in the best thought, human society was one, held together and inspired by belief in and obedience to God in a visible church which comprised all Christian people, but also directed in this life by various kinds of secular authority. As is well known, idealists still believed in the necessity, if not in the actual existence, of a single secular ruler, to whom other rulers could look as subordinate authorities looked to them; but this theory was going out of fashion before the Reformation. In actual fact secular authority was bound up with the traditions of the group or community in which it resided; it could be regarded as democratic in its origin, although its justification depended upon its harmonious reaction to the moral law. But it was not sufficient in or for itself. It could not claim to lead its fraction of the whole Christian society in all the social activities of this life. It was so important that its cooperation was desired, it might be so powerful that the limits which it imposed upon the activities of the ecclesiastical authorities—who were linked together under the pope in the government of the whole society—might have to be treated with acquiescence or even made the matter of formal agreement, but, strictly speaking, such limitations were forms of usurpation. For example, it was not unfitting that a king should have some voice in the election of a bishop; society was so intricate, secular and ecclesiastical functions so bound up together, that the royal license to elect a bishop must be requested and given, and it was more than discourteous to elect a man who was not likely to be useful or was known to be distasteful to the king; or, again, friendly joint pressure on the part of king and pope in favor of a particular candidate or a combined nomination actually overriding the electing body might be advisable. But brutal insistence that such and such a man must be elected was a gross interference with canonical order. It would be hard to say, here and in many other ways, where agreement ended and usurpation began. The tactful exercise of papal authority, by the use of dispensations or of the papal "plentitude of power," was required all the time in the later Middle Ages to oil the wheels. Yet that, ecclesiastically, society was one, greater than any political divisions, was a fundamental doctrine; nay, it was regarded as a natural fact. Hence the action of Henry VIII and his successors amounted to a revolution.

It is hard to resist the conclusion that the ease with which this revolution was effected was due to the prevalent system of compromise and not to any widespread belief in the necessity of change. As we shall see later, the momentous step was so easy that its significance was not faced. Facts, as usually happens, were more potent than theory, and when the time came for elaborate explanation, it was maintained that, as a matter of historic fact, the development of a united Christendom under papal guidance had itself involved a gross usurpation of the rights of bodies politic, and that Christian unity was not bound up with the supremacy of Rome. Indeed, so it was claimed, the usurpation of the pope was such a monstrous perversion of the true nature of the church as to stamp him as Antichrist. At first this rereading of history was confined to a very few. Henry VIII and his parliament were content with the statement, surprising enough to us, but a very significant description of policy, that "by divers sundry old authentic histories and chronicles it is manifestly declared and expressed that this realm of England is an Empire . . . governed by one supreme head and king . . . unto whom a body politic, compact of all sorts and degrees of people, divided in terms and by names of spiritualty and temporalty, be bounden and ought to bear, next to God, a natural and humble obedience." In any "cause of the law divine," it was within the power of the spiritualty "now being usually called the English Church" to declare and determine "without the intermeddling of any exterior person or persons." To maintain the independence of England as against any foreign interference was the first concern. Hence in 1534 a definite "conclusion" was proposed in accordance with royal mandate to the convocations of Canterbury and York and to the Universities of Oxford and Cambridge; it was in the simple form "Whether the Roman Pontiff has any greater jurisdiction bestowed on him by God in the Holy Scriptures in this realm of England than any other foreign bishop?" There were four votes in favor of papal jurisdiction in the convocation of Canterbury, none in that of York. But the problems which are raised by the attempt to observe the "law divine" in an independent state, and still more by the attempt to base national policy on the teaching of Holy Scripture, were not faced at this stage. Yet they are the fundamental issues in the development of the Reformation.

The cause of a united Christendom was not left without witness; yet it is to be observed that, with two great exceptions, only two or three cartloads of monks were willing to die for it. One of these monks, Dr. Richard Reynolds of Sion Monastery, had some reason for asserting that at heart the greater part of the kingdom was of their opinion, but opinion was not deep-rooted and was easily stifled by fear and bewilderment.

Even the friars, the old militia of the church, were divided, and the practical opposition of a few was soon checked. The Carthusians, most remote from the world and also the least numerous in England of monks of the great medieval orders, were the most determined in opposition. The two great exceptions to the acquiescence of the laity and clergy were Bishop Fisher of Rochester and Sir Thomas More. After sentence had been passed upon him, More, for the first time, gave free expression to his views. No temporal lord could be head of the spiritualty; just as a child cannot refuse obedience to his natural father, so the realm of England could not refuse obedience to the see of Rome. His isolation signified nothing: for every bishop opposed to him, he could call upon a hundred saints, against every parliament he could appeal to the general councils of a thousand years:

You have no authority, without the consent of Christendom, to make a law or act of Parliament contrary to the common body of Christendom.

This was the witness of a man who had brooded long over the state of Christendom. He was wise, witty, urbane; observant, critical, caustic, yet full of pity. In his inner life he was austere, and could withdraw himself easily from the society in which he always shone, with a charm that captivated kings and bishops, nobles and all scholars, and brought him near to the common man. He found every place home in which he could be near to God. He believed as easily and intimately in the communion of saints as the ordinary citizen believed in the reality of the passerby who jostled him in the street. Erasmus says of him that he talked with his friends about the future life as one speaking from the heart, with full hope; and it has been observed that what seemed to him "the most terrible thing in the clamour for the plunder of church endowments was that it involved, not only social injustice, but the cessation of prayer for the dead": in his own words, "that any Christian man could, for very pity, have founden in his heart to seek and study the means, whereby a Christian man should think it labour lost, to pray for all Christian souls." The two cardinal tenets in the religion of Utopia[1] are the belief in Divine Providence and in immortality. Such was More in his inner life. But he was also a public man, shrewd and clear-sighted, compact of observation and pity. He had no illusions about the state of Europe. He was not a fanatical churchman, nor a thoroughgoing papalist. Indeed it would appear that at one time he was ready to welcome a general council which might even depose the pope. He was a leader in the new learning and interested in the discovery and exploitation of the empty spaces of the

---

[1] This refers to Sir Thomas More's masterpiece, *Utopia*, written 1516.

earth. What he could not stand was the denial of the unity of Christendom, and that men should take advantage of the troubles of the time to
decry this unity for the sake of power or money. He could see no rhyme
or reason in the incessant wars, no justice in movements which spoiled
the poor, no wisdom in the destruction of great institutions and ancient
loyalties because they were not all that they should be. Hence, while nobody was more conscious than he of the impossibility, if not the folly, of
trying to restrain the individual conscience, he was indignant against all
disturbers of the peace in matters of opinion. There he was last in line
with the new point of view. The state of things was precarious; so
many people were headstrong, vain, ignorant, and irresponsible, fostering schisms which they could not control. In his public capacity he would
naturally be expected to issue, and did issue, certificates which would give
effect to the ecclesiastical law against heretics; although it is untrue that
he actively set the law in motion—which was not his business—and insulted
or persecuted heretics, he would see no inconsistency with his general
outlook on life in the attempt to suppress the spread of Lutheran doctrines,
especially if they were expressed with clamor or ostentation. With the perplexed, on the other hand, he was patient and persuasive; his own son-in-
law was for a time, while a member of his household, attracted by the new
views. Similarly, he took no public part in opposition to the royal policy
and its developments. He refused to take the Oath of Supremacy, and
rather than take it he died, but he would not have raised his voice if he
had not been faced with the necessity of decision. Only if we had been
in his position could we tell if his conduct was too cautious, whether he
delayed unduly in putting his principles of order and loyalty before his
duty to God. In his *Utopia* he had conveyed his deepest convictions in
the fanciful form congenial to a child of the new learning. He was one of
the first men to introduce the spirit of Plato into political discussion, but
it never could have occurred to him, any more than it occurred to the
long line of Platonic divines in the later Anglican Church, that his loyalty
to the church could be questioned. His Utopian people were dressed in
Franciscan garb. They worshiped in the dark, mysterious, sumptuous
churches which he loved. They recognized in European monasticism an
institute with which they could sympathize. They would have nothing to
do with violence and intransigence of thought. It is possible to push the
analogy between the society of Utopia and the society of united Christendom too far, but the two societies are not inconsistent in principle. More
wished to see, as so many idealists in the Middle Ages had wished to see,
a really united and peaceful Christendom, striving energetically to prepare itself for the life with God, despising and rejecting capitalistic divi-

sions in society, confident in the fundamental harmony of reason and beauty and law with the experience of the church. Such faith in the possibilities of the future may well astonish us. For all his wit and shrewdness, Sir Thomas More was a dreamer, not reckoning enough with the untidy, disrespectful adventurousness in the spirit of man. He had no experience of the explosive power of conviction, whether it is right or wrong. But he stands out as the one person who saw quite clearly what Henry VIII's revolution meant; and, in the contrast between him and the people about him, we can see how far religous society had drifted in the current of secularism and compromise from the acceptance of the medieval system, however irksome or imperfect, as beyond question. Other interests and loyalties were now so natural, so much a matter of course, that, if need be, the old could go. The thoughtless could safely feel indifferent to them, not caring much what came to take their place. More's wife, Mistress Alice, could not understand why, for the sake of an oath, Master More should suffer himself to lie in a close filthy prison, shut up among mice and rats.

'Is not this house,' quoth he, 'as nigh heaven as mine own?' To whom she, after her accustomed homely fashion, not liking such talk, answered 'Tilly vally, Tilly vally.'

In the course of the century men gradually entered upon a view of life, or rather upon several views of life, very different from that of Sir Thomas More, though equally important in their eyes, and maintained with conviction and passion. Doubtless a few saw their way clearly, even in the early days of change. There had been little groups of men who at the universities had been inspired by the teaching of Luther. In various parts of England, for example in the Chiltern Hills and the Forest of Dean, were families which held Lollard views as part of their inheritance. The skepticism which frequently went with the new learning had in some minds, especially the minds of courtiers and men of affairs, given a sharper edge to religious indifference. But Sir Thomas More was undoubtedly right in thinking that he was faced by men who, for the most part, did not know and did not seem to care where they were going. The more light is thrown upon the feelings of men at this time, even of the inmates of monasteries, the clearer this incapacity for sustained conviction seems to be. There was widespread indignation against the King's treatment of Queen Catherine; the royal insistence that More and Fisher should declare themselves was probably due to the fear that, if criticism and passive resistance were not quelled in high quarters, the management of the public temper might become too difficult; yet the general acquiescence is one of the most mysterious things in our history, and remains, from the point of view of the historian, the chief explanation of the drastic treatment of the church and the ruthless spoliation of the religious houses.

5. A SPIRITUAL REFORMATION?

There still remain three aspects of the Reformation which require explanation: the intensity of the appeal of Protestant doctrines, the speed with which those ideas spread throughout England and the Continent, and the international nature of the Reformation. The root of the Reformation crisis, according to Professor Smith, was spiritual; late medieval society was in a state of spiritual shock, and it found relief and satisfaction in an approach to God which was in no way unique to Luther and was appearing, in one form or another, throughout Europe.

LACEY BALDWIN SMITH[*]

Professor Strayer[1] once wrote that "No civilization can endure unless its members are occasionally willing to sacrifice immediate personal advantage for ultimate social gain. Obviously, this willingness to cooperate for the good of the group requires general agreement on values and objectives." Social cooperation also requires that the "values," the "objectives" or the ideals of a society, must be considered both worthy of attainment and possible of attainment. It is this aspect of the late medieval world which should be emphasized—the conflict which existed between the officially sanctioned ideals of society and the actual practices of the average man. . . . The underlying dilemma lay in the fact that it was increasingly difficult to realize in one's own life the ideals of medieval society. The church preached that the surest road to salvation was to be found in the seclusion of a monastery where the temptations of the world could be minimized. Should this prove to be impossible, then the average man was expected constantly to remind himself that it was his duty to approach God as closely as possible and that this life was a testing ground studded with pitfalls to ensnare the unwary sinner. Despite the lurking

[*] From L. B. Smith, "The Reformation and the Decay of Medieval Ideals," *Church History*, Vol. XXIV (September, 1955), pp. 4–11. By permission of the author and editors of *Church History*.

[1] J. R. Strayer and D. C. Munro, *The Middle Ages* (New York, 1942), p. 440.

dangers, however, the church always extended the hope that with reasonable caution and care the ordinary man might expect salvation. Unfortunately, as life became more complex and commercial, the pitfalls became more numerous and more difficult to avoid. Though the church fathers might warn that "Riches exist for man, not man for riches," most reflective people were well aware that merchants and bankers were growing fat and prosperous and daily risking their immortal souls with apparent impunity. . . .

Not only were individuals failing to make the necessary sacrifice to maintain their ideals but the church itself was forsaking those ideals. Ideally the church was catholic and universal; in fact, it was racked by schism and degrading internal anarchy throughout most of the century. In theory the church was designed to minister to things of the spirit; in fact popes and cardinals, bishops and abbots were worldly prelates more interested in the fleshpots and the lawyer's brief than in the "cure of innumerable souls." On almost every level of society the gulf between what was and what ought to be, though perhaps no greater than in the past, was at least much more apparent than before. . . .

The effect of this tension within the medieval structure can be seen in two aspects of the 15th and early 16th centuries. It can be perceived first in the gloom, despair, and almost pathological sense of guilt which pervades so much of the literature of these years and in the rather unhealthy and neurotic emphasis placed upon the theme of death. Second, the growing strain became manifest in what I can only describe as the tendency to replace the qualitative approach to life with a quantitative one.

It is not necessary to reiterate Huizinga's thesis[2] or to present examples of the depression which seems to have settled upon the soul of Europe. I would like to point out, however, that just as many, if not more, examples of necrophilia, the Black Mass, witchcraft, and the Villonesque literature of despondency can be found in the early 16th century as in the previous age so ably described by Huizinga. The calamities of the previous century were still vivid in men's minds—the black death, the civil and national wars, the schism, the atrocities, heresies, and brutalities remained a part of the conscience of northern Europe. We should not allow the humanistic optimism of a man such as Erasmus to blind us to the morbid fascination with death which still existed. This undertone of fear and the obsessive preoccupation with death is clearly seen in a sermon of Bishop Longman of Lincoln preached in 1536. This is the warning he thundered from the pulpit.

[2] J. Huizinga, *The Waning of the Middle Ages.*

I was born and came into this world bare and naked, and bare and naked I shall go from it. . . . This fair body of thine which you make so much of, which you deck so preciously, which you set so much by: it shall away. . . . It is but earth, ashes, dust and worm's meat. . . . Serpents, worms and toads shall inherit thy body . . . shall gnaw, eat and devour thy beautiful face, thy fair nose, thy clear eyes, thy white hands, thy goodly body. Remember this thou lord and lady. Remember this thou Christian man and woman. . . .

Finally, we have what I described as the quantitative approach to life —the assumption that if something is good, then it must be three times as good when repeated thrice over. In fact, there seems to be a direct relationship between loss of faith and increase of form and ceremony. In almost every aspect of medieval life one finds this aimless reiteration of the ceremonial as if sheer weight of repetition could make acceptable what one actually doubted. It has sometimes been pointed out that this process of galloping mechanization was striking at the very heart of the medieval creed, the mass itself. If the benefits accruing from the sacrifice of the mass were to be desired, then the logical assumption followed that the more masses you heard or paid for, the more fruits and benefits you would obtain. For example, Henry V of England in his will ordered and paid for the saying of 20,000 masses for his soul, while the Earl of Oxford on a less royal scale financed the saying of 2,000 masses. Moreover, there was growing up around the mass a number of quantitative beliefs such as that a man never grew old while attending mass and if he could attend mass constantly one might expect to live forever. It was Savonarola who put his finger on and condemned most vigorously this tendency of his age to obscure with the weight of elaboration and repetition the thing worshiped, when he warned:

All fervour and inward worship are dead, and ceremonies wax more numerous, but have lost their efficacy. Wherefore we are come to declare to the world that outward worship must give way to inward, and that ceremonies are naught, save as a means of stirring the spirit. . . .

These then are the characteristics of the later Middle Ages which bear most directly upon the Reformation, for it is here that we can detect the explanation for the speed, internationalism, and conviction bred by the Protestant revolution. In relating these movements to the Reformation I want to turn briefly to the life of Martin Luther, who in a very real sense was the embodiment of a late medieval man. One cannot read his life without sensing the despondency which weighs so heavily upon his mind and the sense of guilt which dominates his early career. If there is any one thing predominant in this youthful Luther, it is his conviction that he did not merit salvation. Like his age he was fearful, oppressed, and insecure. He endeavored to relieve this gloom through a preoccupation with form and ritual on the assumption that the observance of detail, of the rules of his monastery, could substitute for conviction. In the midst of his despair he turned to the only way out open to him—to the reiteration of the old, to endless fasting, praying, mortification of the flesh, and rigid self-discipline. And the less they satisfied, the more he was induced to reassert them. "True it is," Luther confessed in later life, "I was a good monk, and I kept the rules of my order so strictly that I may say that if ever a monk got to heaven by monkery, it was I." Luther's actions seem to me to be very similar to those of the Earl of Oxford and his 2,000 masses. Well might Dr. Staupitz's[3] condemnation of Luther's methods stand as an indictment of his entire age when he warned: "Thou art a fool, God is not angry with thee, it is thou who art angry with God." If indeed Luther was plagued by troubles common to his century, then, when he found personal peace of mind, and the sense of forgiveness, his solution was the answer to the despair of his contemporaries.

Luther's solution to his mental and spiritual anguish was, of course, the doctrine of Justification by Faith. It is not necessary to reiterate the details of the new creed. Two aspects of Luther's solution, however, should be noted. First of all, Luther afforded for his age a method by which a man could bridge the gap between the ideal and the real, and in a very immediate sense he overcame the dichotomy between the divine and the profane. In transforming the whole world into a monastery Luther may have been insisting on a more difficult spiritual standard than the medieval world which had been content with its double road to salvation —the path of the saint and the path for those of merely mortal clay. But Luther's ideals when translated into the patterns of normal life meant that salvation and the bliss of paradise could be attained within this world and not by renouncing this world. In a way the ideal life was made more available, and in making it more available, he somehow made it more worthwhile. Moreover, he made it possible for men to live with the knowledge that the path of the saints could not in fact be attained, for, as Professor Bainton[4] has said, "The Christian is bound every day to fail, yet he is never sunk. He is at once a sinner and yet saved." It is very consoling to realize that the impossible is not expected of you and that even as a pedestrian sinner, the gates of the kingdom of heaven are open to you. Whether this ideal is very far removed from the original medieval con-

---

[3] John von Staupitz was a distinguished scholar, Vicar of the Augustinian Order and one of Luther's early mentors and friends.

[4] Roland H. Bainton, *Here I Stand, a Life of Martin Luther* (Boston, 1952), p. 53.

cept is difficult to say, but it was certainly a marked change from the distortion of ideals so characteristic of late medieval society, and it did apparently supply the North of Europe with a solution to its problems.

Second, I would emphasize the sense of hope and optimism which accompanied Luther's discovery. The endless days and nights of anguish and terror vanished. So also did the repetition of ceremonies; likewise the feeling of guilt. There are endless passages bubbling over with this sense of joy and I merely quote from one of the most famous.

Thereupon I felt myself to be reborn and to have gone through open doors into paradise. The whole of Scripture took on a new meaning, and whereas before the "justice of God" had filled me with hate, now it became to me inexpressibly sweet in greater love. This passage of Paul became to me a gate to heaven. . . .

Though the idea that the "just shall live by their faith" was the key to heaven for Luther, it was also the magic formula which seemed to lift the burden, the gloom and depression which had settled upon the soul of much of northern Europe. In order to appreciate the international nature of the problem let us turn to another reformer, who quite independently of Luther seems to have reenacted with only slight variation Luther's early history.

Little Thomas Bilney was a student at Trinity Hall, Cambridge, and like his German contemporary he also was headed for the bar. Also like Luther, Bilney was an obsessively conscientious individual who was tortured by a sense of his own inadequacy and sinful nature. And he too turned to the quantitative way out of his difficulties. Sir Thomas More wrote of Bilney's early addiction to form for form's sake saying that Bilney was "very fearful and scrupulous and began at the first to fall into such a scrupulous holiness that he reckoned himself bounded so straitly to keep and observe the words of Christ after the very letter, that, because our Lord biddeth us when we will pray [to] enter into our chamber and shut the door to us, he thought it therefore a sin to say his service abroad, and always would be sure to have his chamber door shut unto him while he said his matins." Thus did this introverted and conscience-stricken young man attempt to find solace. Again like Luther, Bilney turned to the Scriptures to find relief and though he was working quite independently, his solution bears striking resemblance to that of the Wittenberg monk. In 1516 he was reading Erasmus' translation of the New Testament when, as he relates in his own words, "he chanced upon this sentence of St. Paul's, 'It is a true saying and worthily of all men to be embraced, that Jesus came into the world to save sinners of whom I am the chief and principle.'" Bilney no less than Martin Luther found consolation in his discovery, a sense of the lifting of sin and oppression, and as he confessed he found "marvellous comfort and quietness so much so that his bruised bones leaped with joy."

It would appear to me that both Luther and Bilney are part of their age—the waning of the Middle Ages. These men were the leaders, the articulators, but they had followers by the legions only because they were themselves part of this movement. That Thomas Bilney was burned at the stake for his mild Protestantism while Luther lived to lead a vast revolutionary movement is eloquent evidence of the importance of local variations, of political forces, and of chance, but the initial inspiration which moved these men was the same, as it was the same in all Europe. If the Reformation is viewed as a part of the closing years of the Middle Ages and as a solution to problems caused by the decay of medieval ideals and institutions, then the speed with which the revolt gained momentum becomes understandable; its European and international aspect becomes fully recognizable; and finally the conviction and courage of the martyrs becomes comprehensible since they now have something worth dying for: they had found "marvellous comfort and quietness" in the intimate knowledge of a God both more merciful and more powerful than the visible church.

6. THE ENGLISH ACCIDENT

Hilaire Belloc, a belligerent but capable Catholic polemical writer, wrote in 1928 a slim volume entitled How the Reformation Happened. *Almost by definition he branded the Reformation as a bad thing and Henry VIII as an incompetent king and a despicable man. More important than Belloc's religious bias, however, is his argument that the English Reformation was essentially an accident devoid of economic, intellectual, social, or institutional causation.*

HILAIRE BELLOC*

I call this the most important division of my subject, the English *Accident*. I have chosen the word with care.

If ever there were, in all history, an event not desired by its agents; not

* From Hilaire Belloc, *How the Reformation Happened* (London, 1928), pp. 90–94, 109–11. Reprinted by permission of A. D. Peters and Co., London.

understood by those who suffered it; coming by no design, but as the prodigious effect of comparatively small and quite incongruous causes, it was the gradual, mechanical, and disastrous destruction in the English mind of that Faith which had made England.

Most histories written in the English language represent the English movement as something at once national and inevitable—something that the English nation desired and necessarily, in due course, achieved. At the same time, while giving in different degrees some hint of the European background, they center the Reformation upon the English story.

The first of these characteristics, the treating of what happened here as national and inevitable, is historically nonsense. The second is historically sound. Though England was then but a small nation, yet the blunder of the English government in separating from European unity *was* of capital effect in the success of the Reformation.

There was no national movement against the Catholic Church in England: the little that happened at first was a government movement, and not even a doctrinal movement. It was a mere political and even personal act. What followed it was not a normal process generally desired by the people. It was an artificial process managed by a very few interested men, and these acting not on a religious fad, but for money; what is more, it was a process which, in its first beginnings, gave even these few actors no conception of what was ultimately to come of their greed and folly.

But the concentration upon the English Reformation as being of special importance, is, oddly enough, and in spite of the intention of the official legend in our anti-Catholic academic textbooks, true history.

This concentration upon the English story of the Reformation has indeed hidden from the great run of our educated men the general nature of the Reformation, and especially (what I shall come to later) two main points: that Holland was the example, and that France was the battleground. But it is certain that if England had not left the unity of Christendom, that unity would be fully recovered today—and long before today.

Until England was cut off from that unity of which the papacy is the living principle, the trouble had stirred in a confused but violent fashion throughout the Germanies and little affected the rest of Europe. Even in the Germanies it had not principally affected the strongest, oldest, and most civilized body of Germans. It had less deeply involved those Germans who had been originally disciplined by the Roman culture.

The statement is general only. Exceptions swarm. Thus Strasbourg, a Roman city (if ever there was one!), counted among those that cut themselves off by the "protest" at Spires.

But, whatever might happen in the Germanies, and especially in the less civilized Germanies, in England it was otherwise.

England was an ancient province of the Roman Empire, with Christian traditions twice as old as, and far stronger than, those northern districts of Germany which the Gallic armies of Charlemagne and his successors had compelled by conquest to accept Christian doctrine and practice and to abandon barbarism. Had the English government not moved, the reaction for unity when it came would have been overwhelming. In a word, it was the separation of England from the unity of the church, which was, amid a host of other factors, greater and less, the *chief* factor in the final event of our disruption. It was the artificial removal of the English from the main body of Europe which made the breakup of Christendom permanent.

It therefore is no exaggeration due to patriotic bias, or to local distortion of perspective, which makes any sound historian insist upon the capital importance of the Reformation in England; though no one with historical sense can pretend that the English desired that ruin of their traditions.

Moreover, the English movement was the first great *official* or government movement away from unity. The nominal head of the German States had stood firm for the Faith; many even of the German independent regions had stood firm. Scotland was, so far, well secured; equally well secured (so far) were the great and dominating French monarchy, the already united Spanish monarchy, and the various Italian States. But for the gradual and half-blind destruction of the Faith in England, what we now call the Reformation would today appear in history as no more than one of the many outbreaks against the necessary discipline of our culture: a spiritual dissension gradually confined to but one district of Christendom, and that among the least important, northern Germany with its lordlings. At last the anomaly would have been brought to an end by the pressure of all the rest of Europe. . . .

How, then, did the Reformation in England originate, and how was it confirmed and made enduring? That is the question I must attempt to answer. . . .

First, as to motive. I have called the very first act—Henry VIII's breach with the papacy—an *accident,* because I think that word the closest to the truth. An accident—for instance, the swerving of a motorcar—is not intentional of its effect. It is due to miscalculation upon the part of the driver who, attempting one thing, does another. The miscalculation can often be redressed and its consequences eliminated. It was not desired by him. . . .

[Belloc then tells the story of the divorce and the break with Rome.]

Yet was the breach not irrevocable. It could have been mended. Unity could have been restored, had it not been for a second act which was of permanent effect: the seizure of the Abbey lands.

For the break between the government of England and the Holy See was followed in a couple of years, and on for four years more, by the dissolution of the monasteries and convents, and the seizure of their wealth; immediately by the Treasury, ultimately (and soon) by the landed gentry, by speculators and by a number of adventurers, obscure in origin.

The unwitting character of the English separation from the church is nowhere better seen that in the loot of ecclesiastical endowments which thus followed the quarrel between Henry and the pope.

When I say "unwitting" I do not mean "aimless." The aim was obvious: enrichment of the looters. I mean accomplished without calculating the consequences that would follow. Thomas Cromwell, the author of this policy as he had been of the schism, had personal fortune for his motive in both cases, and, in both cases, the acquirement of that fortune by pampering the King. That it would have, ultimately, the effect of a religious revolution was not conceivable to him and his contemporaries.

The breach with Rome had been a chance act which, I repeat, would almost certainly have failed—if left unsupported—to be permanent: it was but an episode in a violent but essentially personal and restricted struggle. It hinged wholly upon those two points: Catherine's tenacious resistance and Anne Boleyn's equally tenacious ambition—with Henry for puppet. It had no general basis of policy behind it, still less any national feeling. But quite a short time after it had taken place Anne Boleyn herself had been put to death and Catherine of Aragon had died: all obstacles to reconciliation had disappeared. Henry—and England—abhorred essential doctrinal change; what had been done had no outward effect on national life.

The mass went on as usual, the Sacraments, the daily life of a somewhat slack but thoroughly Catholic populace was, on its religious side, exactly what it had been for generations. Everyone had heard or read of past quarrels between King and pope, or papal claims. This was but another. It would blow over. Other sovereigns had threatened to break with the pope. It had all come right in the end.

But the dissolution first of the lesser, then of *all* the monasteries, and the later seizure of much other clerical endowment, made the breach with Rome continue. A strong motive for prolonging it was henceforward present in the wealthier and governing classes. Not that renewed communion with Rome would necessarily mean restoration of the stolen land. In point of fact, when communion was, for a few years, restored, the looted property was left in the hands of its new owners. But that the old full religious life would *tend* to create, sooner or later, a demand for the reparation of sacrilege, to ruin the new millionaires, and to diminish the recently increased incomes of the older gentry who had shared in the adventure.

This second step, the loot of ecclesiastical endowment, was not designed as a profound religious change. There was no deep-seated scheme for making the breach with Rome more permanent. It was not one further step in a long process of gradual edging away from the mass of civilized Europe. It was adventitious, mechanical, a thing which was an end in itself—and that a sordid but wholly terrestrial end: the enrichment of Thomas Cromwell and (temporarily) of the Treasury.

Orest Ranum, Associate Professor of History at Columbia University, was born in Lyle, Minn., in 1933. A graduate of Macalester College, he received his M.A. and Ph.D. degrees from the University of Minnesota. He was a Fulbright fellow at the Sorbonne and a Fulbright teaching fellow at the University of Strasbourg and has taught history at the University of Southern California. At Columbia he is chairman of the College's program in Contemporary Civilization. He is the author of *Richelieu and the Councillors of Louis XIII* (Oxford, 1963) and of a history of Paris in the 17th century published in 1966. He is a member of the American Historical Association and of the Society for French Historical Studies.

CHAPTER FIVE

OREST RANUM

Columbia University

Religion and International Politics
in the Early Seventeenth Century

In 1600 Europe lay in the eye of a giant hurricane of war and violence, in momentary calm after decades of fighting; soon more decades of storm and death would again sweep the continent in the Thirty Years' War. Political assassination, burnings at the stake, treason, rebellion, riots, pillaging, subversion, maurauding bands, and large-scale military campaigns all came together in a complex blending of hatreds and hopes.

The reasons for all this violence were numerous and complex. They could not have been the same in every part of Europe. Political and social conditions in far-off Bohemia differed from those in the Netherlands, southern Switzerland, Spain, or England, but once violence broke out in 1618 it continued to spread until every area and people in Europe were marked by it. From Sweden to Naples, and from Scotland to Poland an intricate combination of political and religious factors would set off violence that would change radically the political climate of Europe and cause the death of several hundreds of thousands of Europeans. Not since the Black Death nor until the 20th century would Europeans suffer such a loss of life and destruction of property.

It was tempting to contemporaries, and it is tempting to historians today, to seek some "common cause" or general explanation for all this violence. What could have been the catalyst which made the European political climate so unstable? Contemporaries, that is the participants in the Thirty Years' War and the civil wars of the 1640's, tended to believe

141

that religious fervor had stirred up every heart and nation to violence over religious beliefs. A sermon, divine inspiration to assassinate some prince, the harsh process of "converting heretics," the struggle for control of church wealth and education, and the intense quarrels over doctrine provided a climate for violence.

This, for modern historians, has led to the fascinating problems of defining and seeing the connections between religion and politics in the early 17th century. They find that treason and heresy, both punishable by death, cannot be clearly distinguished, and that no clear distinction existed between the civil and the religious life. Furthermore, in studying European political thought they found a prevalent conception of the state and the church as sorts of individuals or super persons. Each "body politic" and "body religious" was thought to have its own traditions, ego, needs, aims, strengths, and weaknesses. This conception of the state implied, of course, that states had souls and profound religious convictions. Since the Peace of Augsburg in 1555 each prince had the sanction to determine the religion of his subjects and, in turn, assumed the obligation to answer before God for their spiritual welfare. This religious element provided the modes of thought, the rhetoric, even the ideology for most actions of men and of states. Princes undisputably believed that one aspect of their power was the control of the religious belief of their subjects. Though perhaps not religiously fervent themselves, they nevertheless insisted on conformity of beliefs in a period of shifting and conflicting dogmas and doctrines.

The consequences of this religious orientation for international politics are difficult to pin down. How seriously should the religious ideology be taken? Was it a mere cover for the aims of conquest and the ambition to dominate first subjects, then states? The insistence on religious conformity determined the ethical considerations of foreign policy as much as it did the moral conformity of members of the state. This blending of religion and ethics in a crusade, with what would later be considered secular aims, such as conquest and trade rivalries, makes the problem of discerning motives for policy extremely complex. Did the kings and princes of Europe actually create the conditions which caused the violence, or were they responding to those conditions themselves?

Attacked from within by "subversive" religious minority groups, and faced with hostile coalitions of foreign powers supporting these minorities, Catholic and Protestant princes were caught in an ideological and religious cross-current which forced them to engage their states in a struggle for survival. Historians looking at this combination of subversion and war usually emphasize religion as the prime source of instability, but none would deny the importance of other factors. Geographic, economic, social, and dynastic conditions, all intertwined in a religious setting, contributed to the instability. Religious convictions may have served as the catalyst to bring them together.

Miss C. V. Wedgwood examines the 16th-century settlements after the Reformation and the Counter-Reformation and, finding them fragile, suggests that the Thirty Years' War, the Puritan Revolution, and other outbreaks of violence were an extension of the violence of the 16th century. The Hapsburg-Valois conflict is seen as an early phase of the Thirty Years' War. Then Miss Wedgwood insists on how Calvinist doctrine remained an internal threat to the state. Finally, by examining the issue of toleration she demonstrates the fundamental unity of political and religious attitudes.

Hajo Holborn, in his monumental *History of Modern Germany*, sees the prime source of conflict as a struggle between estates—chiefly the nobility—and the Hapsburg monarchy. Religion served to "rationalize actions motivated by secular interests," while single individuals contributed to European instability. The dreams and actions of Christian of Anhalt and Mansfeld make it abundantly clear how individuals, and not merely general forces, contributed to the violence.

Through analyzing the correspondence of Spanish ambassadors, Charles H. Carter recreates the conceptions of strategy and the aims of one of the greatest states in Europe. Heady and amoral theorizing, rather than lofty idealism and religion, suggests that the secular aims of conquest and trade rivalries remained uppermost in the formulation of Spanish policy.

At one point a Spanish ambassador observes that there was "a very important Reason of State" for a certain policy. The phrase would have delighted Friedrich Meinecke, the author of a classic work, *The Idea of Reason of State*. Tracing the history of secularized, national policymaking from Machiavelli down through the reports of diplomatic observers (Relations), Meinecke suggests that secular or nonreligious principles provided the foundation for Richelieu's foreign policy. France placed the preservation, interests, and power of the state above religious considerations. Does Holborn agree with Meinecke's contention when he stresses the rapid secularization of French politics?

Finally, George L. Mosse suggests that the idea of reason of state was not necessarily as secular as Meinecke thought. By analyzing the works of Christian theologians and statesmen, both Puritan and Catholic, Mosse discovers that they incorporated Machiavelli's conception of the ends justifying the means into Christian ethics and into foreign policy. Did reason of state then strengthen the religious bases of foreign policy?

The final answer to the question of the role of religion in international politics will, of course, never be found. But in their attempts to answer it, and even in their disagreements, historians have greatly enriched our knowledge of the connections between moral, religious, and political factors contributing to violence.

1. THE DIVISIONS HARDEN

C. V. Wedgwood (1910–   ) published her second book at the age of 28. Entitled The Thirty Years' War, *it established her reputation as an outstanding historian, not only of her native country, England, but of all Europe in the 17th century. Concealed beneath vivid prose and forceful narrative style, Miss Wedgwood's powers of analysis go almost unnoticed as she depicts the political and religious stage of Europe. Notice how she brings sources to bear on the crucial concerns of the 17th century.*

C. V. WEDGWOOD[*]

Was the question of the Reformation in England settled by 1603 when Queen Elizabeth died? Was it settled for the other nations of Western Europe? Luther had been dead for more than half a century. There had been three generations of knotted argument, wars, martyrdoms, massacres—justification enough for Francis Bacon's comment:

Surely this is to bring down the Holy Ghost, instead of the likeness of a dove, in the shape of a vulture or raven; and to set out of the bark of a Christian church a flag of a bark of pirates and assassins.

Another Englishman, that great Anglican Richard Hooker, ... writing at the close of the troubled 16th century, breathed a spirit of reconciliation and compromise over England. On the mainland of Europe it appeared that rulers and churchmen of different faiths were content, or at least resigned, to accept coexistence with one another. The princes of the numerous German states were, since the Peace of Augsburg, free to impose their own religion on their subjects, so that Roman Catholic and Lutheran states existed together (and within a few years Calvinist states also) within the loose framework of the Holy Roman Empire and under the suzerainty of a Roman Catholic emperor. In France the Huguenots

[*] C. V. Wedgwood, "The Divisions Harden," from *The Reformation Crisis*, ed. by Joel Hurstfield (London: Edward Arnold, Ltd., 1965), pp. 107–15.

had, by the Edict of Nantes, gained the right to practice their religion, a right further secured by military and territorial concessions. Though the dominions of the king of Spain remained closed to Protestant influences, the hereditary lands of their Hapsburg cousins in Austria, Hungary, and Bohemia were infiltrated with Protestantism, and in 1609 the Protestants of Bohemia secured a guarantee of toleration. Such arrangements made it look as though, after a long period of struggle, diversity of religion and coexistence would be henceforward accepted.

But what in fact happened in the 17th century—that century which we see, in the perspective of time, as the beginning of the modern world: the scientific age, the century of Galileo and Newton? Contrary to what might have been expected, religious passions blazed up afresh. One after another settlements which had seemed to promise peace were violently overthrown. Thus in England the armed forces of Puritanism for a time destroyed the Anglican settlement and sent both the Archbishop of Canterbury and the King to scaffold. In France the Huguenots were attacked and gradually deprived of their special privileges, until in 1685 the Edict of Nantes was withdrawn and thousands were compelled either to change their religion or to go into exile. In Central Europe, in 1618, more than a century after Luther had nailed up his theses at Wittenberg, the Thirty Years' War began. It started as a Protestant rising in Bohemia, and developed into the bloodiest and the most bitter of the wars stemming from the Reformation. It was also the last. When it came to an end, at the exhausted Peace of Westphalia in 1648, Protestantism had suffered heavy losses. It had been suppressed in Bohemia, in all the Austrian domains, and in large areas of south Germany.

But how important was the religious element in the conflicts which mark the second century after the Reformation? It is true, as indeed it had been in the earlier stages of the story, that princes and governments of the same religion were by no means always on the same side. The dynastic rivalry between the ruling families of France and Spain in this century, as in the previous one, prevented united action on the part of the Roman Catholic powers.

Statesmen living at the time would often assert that the religious aspirations of their opponents were nothing but a cover for political ambition or economic greed. Their own religious motives, on the other hand, were wholly sincere. Thus, for instance, Father Joseph, the pious adviser of Cardinal Richelieu in France, was convinced that the King of Spain and the Hapsburg dynasty in general only upheld the Roman Catholic cause so that, under the pretext of religion, they could increase their own power. To take an example from the other side: the revolt of the Presby-

terian Covenanters in Scotland against King Charles I was described
by his authoritarian minister Strafford in these terms:

This is not a war of piety for Christ's sake, but a war of liberty for their own
unbridled inordinate lust and ambition, such as threw Lucifer forth of heaven.

Nothing in history is harder to establish than motive, and religious
fervor had never been the only motive in the disputes arising from the
Reformation. It is none the less apparent that beliefs, sincerely held,
played a part which was never negligible and was sometimes significant.
With some individual protagonists religious zeal was undoubtedly the
dominant force, although it was rarely free from an admixture of other
elements. The renewed violent wave of religious conflict which swept
over Europe in the 17th century arose, in great part, from the material
rivalry of growing nation-states, but national and dynastic antagonism
were heightened and inspired among Catholics by the crusading spirit
of the Counter-Reformation, and among Protestants by the influence of
Calvin and his followers.

The idea of a powerful centralized nation-state, usually, though not
always, a monarchy, had developed fast in the 16th century. It continued
to do so in the 17th, and reached its most formidable expression in the
France of Richelieu and later of Louis XIV. A religion therefore which
challenged the authority of the ruler or was potentially hostile to the
interests of the state was bound to become an object of persecution. Calvinism, the most dynamic of the Protestant creeds, presented an obvious
challenge to the secular state and particularly to monarchy because it
aimed at a theocracy and the rule of God's elect.

The persecution of the Huguenots in France, of the Puritans in England, and of the Presbyterians in Scotland was the logical expression of
the centralizing policy of the Crown. But the religious motive cannot be
discounted. Richelieu thought it a principal duty of a sovereign to recon-
vert his heretical subjects to the true faith, and the genuine piety of
Louis XIV under the austere influence of Madame de Maintenon was
undoubtedly a factor in the ultimate repeal of the Edict of Nantes. The
devotion of Charles I to the Church of England is, of course, unquestionable.

On the other hand, the resistance aroused in the Puritans by persecution in Scotland and England undoubtedly gained much of its force from
the religious fervor which transfigured and accompanied the more
worldly motives of these rebels. The Covenanting movement in Scotland
began as a protest against episcopal government and the Anglican liturgy, but in its earliest form it was by no means a purely religious pro-

test. National pride, resentment against the English, the fear of the nobles that the spoils of the Reformation might be taken from them, and personal ambition for power: all these things played a part. But the history of the movement is remarkable for the emergence of a dominant rigidly religious group; these men, rather than compromise with their consciences, excluded potential allies, purged the military command, and so narrowed the range of their supporters as to bring inevitable disaster to their cause. There was more faith than self-interest here.

In England the motives behind what used to be called the Puritan revolution were more complex. We know it as a constitutional struggle between Parliament and the Crown. The desire of the gentry in Parliament to extend their political power, to maintain and improve their economic position, and to establish their freedom of action against the authority of the Crown—these things have become evident in the light of modern research. But we must not leave out of account the organic links between the English struggle and the religious war which was raging in Europe. Calvinist doctrine captured a high proportion of the English gentry in the earlier part of the 17th century, so that Puritanism became the religion of the opposition to the Crown. The situation was made more acute after the outbreak of the Thirty Years' War by the foreign policy of James I and Charles I, who—apart from a short interlude— aligned themselves with the Spanish-Austrian Hapsburg, that is with the militant Roman Catholic party in Europe: this meant, of course, with the traditional enemy, the Spaniard, whose sea power was still a block to English maritime and colonial expansion. Religious and economic objections to the king's policy thus reinforced each other.

The position was further complicated by the favor shown by the King to the Arminian clergy in the Anglican church. Arminius was a Dutch reformer whose lenient views on predestination, election, and Grace had been declared heretical by the Synod of Dort in 1619. The Synod of Dort was for orthodox Calvinists what the Council of Trent was for Roman Catholics: hence educated Puritans in England were dismayed at the encouragement of Arminian influence in the Anglican church. But what perturbed educated and uneducated alike was not so much the doctrine of Arminius as the ritual which his Anglican followers reintroduced into worship. Candles, vestments, genuflections—they took these for popery.

A king who encouraged these unwelcome elements in the Church and also maintained an alliance with Roman Catholic Spain could hardly fail to provoke opposition, some of it sincerely religious. After all, fellow Protestants in Europe were suffering heavy reverses in the 1620's and

1630's. Bohemia was lost, the Rhineland occupied by Spanish troops; destitute Protestant refugees were familiar figures in England. Such things provoked righteous indignation against the King's policy.

Turning from England to Europe we find an equal confusion of motives. The Bohemian revolt of 1618, which began the Thirty Years' War, was partly religious, partly nationalist, and partly the work of an ambitious faction among the nobility. In putting down the revolt and suppressing all forms of Protestantism in his hereditary dominions the Hapsburg emperor Ferdinand II consolidated his power. He also found it convenient to pay his supporters and the commanders of his army by grants of Bohemian land. An enlightening comparison can be made between the expropriation of the Protestant Bohemians by Ferdinand and of the Catholic Irish by Oliver Cromwell for similar reasons. But, although Ferdinand had strong secular motives for his attack on Protestantism, he was also acting in accordance with a solemn vow which he had made in his youth at the shrine of Our Lady of Loretto, to extirpate heresy in his lands.

Much of the literature and many private letters and diaries of this period bear witness to a deep and far-reaching renewal of religious faith. Among extremists, both Catholic and Protestant, there are even signs of a renascent hope that, through a Holy War, Christendom may be united in one faith once again. A French ambassador in Scotland in 1643 reported the opinions of the Covenanters in these words:

They say openly they will push their fortune as far as France . . . they are convinced that they would beat all the princes in Christendom . . . General Leslie lately in a large meeting of nobles said: Consider what a glorious thing it would be before God and man, if we managed to drive the papists out of England and follow them to France . . . and plant *nolens volens* our religion in Paris and thence go to Rome, drive out anti-Christ and burn the town that disseminates superstition.

Of course, this was ridiculous boasting, but it was not isolated. The same idea occurs, for instance, in Andrew Marvell's *Horatian Ode on Cromwell's Return from Ireland:*

> What may not then our Isle presume
> While Victory his Crest does plume!
> What may not others fear
> If thus he crown each Year!
> A Caesar he ere long to Gaul,
> To Italy an Hannibal,
>   And to all States not free
>   Shall clymacterick be!

On the Roman Catholic side it certainly looked at one time as though the reconquest of Europe for the Church might be achieved. In 1629 the imperial armies of Ferdinand II reached the Baltic and the extinction of Protestantism in northern Europe seemed almost a possibility.

What prevented the work of the Counter-Reformation from going farther was, once again, the rivalry between the two leading Roman Catholic powers, France and Spain.... The Hapsburg-Valois conflict favored the spread of the Reformation up to 1555. Nearly a century later the basic pattern is unchanged. The Hapsburg still ruled over the Spanish-Austrian combine, and the dynastic jealousy of the Valois in France had been inherited by their successors, the Bourbon. When Austrian Hapsburg armies, sweeping up from South Germany and Bohemia, reached the Baltic, when Spanish Hapsburg armies were on the Rhine, it was high time for France to act. And so Cardinal Richelieu subsidized Gustavus Adolphus, the Protestant King of Sweden, to invade Germany and turn the tide of war. After his death at the Battle of Lutzen in 1632 the Protestant cause came to rely more and more on French money and French troops. Just as the Valois-Hapsburg rivalry had favored the spread of the Reformation, now Bourbon-Hapsburg rivalry checked the further advance of the Counter-Reformation.

In the face of the renewed Roman Catholic attack there had been some movements toward unity among Protestants. But these came mostly from preachers and thinkers and were not reflected in the views of Lutheran or Calvinistic rulers. For more than 40 years, from 1630 onward, the sad figure of John Dury flits through Protestant courts and assemblies. Himself a Calvinist, he longed for a union of the Protestant churches and worked for it vainly all his life. Time and again, in private letters and public statements, he urged on rulers and theologians the need for mutual trust:

Let our aim be . . . to purge our heart from a design to serve the interests of one side, mainly to cross another. For he that looks upon his brother with the eye of a party, has put out the eye of a Christian . . . He that doth not confide in his neighbours, doth hinder them to confide in him, and he that doth fear others, doth beget in them causes of fear against himself . . . For if I cannot bring my spirit to trust my neighbour, how can I expect that his spirit should be brought to trust me?

Dury aimed at *union:* he did not aim at toleration, and he did not believe in it. In a closely wrought argument, published in 1644, he rejected the plea of the English Independents to a separate existence and form of organization:

The liberty whereunto we are called in Christ, doth not give occasion to singularity, or permission to break the bonds of spiritual unity; which by the allowance of a public toleration of different Church Government may be occasioned.

Toleration was still in the middle years of the 17th century regarded with dismay even by moderate men. The ideal of union, by which different but not dissimilar beliefs could find room in a single church—this had been Hooker's ideal. It was also John Dury's. Union and conciliation were good, but toleration was bad because it led to licentious excesses. There had been the frenzied outburst of the Anabaptists at Münster in the previous century which had frightened Protestants as much as, or even more than, Catholics. It was generally felt that if religion was not in some way controlled there would be no end to ignorant self-appointed prophets teaching blasphemous and immoral doctrines. Amsterdam, where a large measure of freedom was permitted, was notorious for the number of sects which had sprung up, and jocose references were often made to their "Amsterdamnable opinions."

During the Civil War in England, when government censorship was relaxed, preachers of all kinds multiplied, and some valuable ideas took root, and have survived to this day. The Baptists were the most widespread of the numerous Independent groups. Scores of prophets and preachers appeared during this period of religious anarchy; George Fox, the founder of the Quakers, was to prove in the end the most remarkable and the most influential. Many were, however, merely ignorant and hysterical ranters, condemned, not without justification, by the more sober Anglicans and Puritans alike:

> These kind of vermin swarm like caterpillars,
> And hold conventicles in barns and cellars,
> Some preach or prate in woods, in fields, in stables,
> In hollow trees, in tubs, on tops of tables,
> To the expense of many a tallow taper
> They toss the holy scripture into vapour . . .
> I write of separatists and schismatics
> Of shallow-pated, hair-brained heretics . . .
> Whom neither law nor sense can curb or bridle,
> Who ne'er are well employed, nor never idle.

Toleration it was widely believed would only encourage such people. The desire for it came therefore in the first place only from the "separatists and schismatics" themselves. Roger Williams, for instance, left England for greater liberty in New England, but withdrew from the more rigid Calvinism of Massachusetts to found his own colony in Rhode Island. In his famous attack on what he called the "Bloody Tenet of Persecution" published in 1644 he asserted that it was consonant with the spirit of Christianity to tolerate pagans, Jews, and Turks as well as all kinds of Christians. His ideas combined a wide vision with practical sense:

An enforced uniformity of religion throughout a nation or civil state confounds the civil and religious, and denies the principles of Christianity and civility. . . . The permission of other consciences and worships than a state professeth, only can, according to God, procure a firm and lasting peace; good assurance being taken, according to the wisdom of the civil state, for uniformity of civil obedience from all sorts.

Roger Williams put his finger on a critical point. If civil obedience could be assured, there ought to be no difficulty in tolerating purely religious opinions. The unsolved problem was that so many religious opinions still at this date involved political action that could endanger the state. As long as religion was a pretext for war between nations, so long differences of religion within the state might cut across national loyalties.

2. THE THIRTY YEARS' WAR

Born and educated in Germany, Hajo Holborn (1902–   ) was one of the first outstanding young scholars to emigrate to the United States as a result of Hitler's impact on the intellectual and civil life of Germany. In his career of over 30 years at Yale University he has studied and taught the intellectual, political, and social history of modern Europe and Germany from the Reformation to World War II. Interested in historiography himself, Holborn's influence on it in his own time has been great because his scholarship represents the German tradition of writing history at its best. In this sense Holborn is an heir of Ranke, Hintze, and Troeltsch.

HAJO HOLBORN*

It was not a conflict among European powers, not even an acute controversy between the emperor and the princes of the Empire or among these princes themselves that led to the outbreak of the long war that

* Hajo Holborn, *A History of Modern Germany, The Reformation* (New York: Alfred A. Knopf, 1959), pp. 305–9. © Copyright 1959 by Hajo Holborn. Reprinted by permission of Alfred A. Knopf, Inc.

lived on in the memory of the German people as the "Great War" and in the books of the historians as the Thirty Years' War. Rather, it was a struggle between the estates and the monarchy in the territories of the Hapsburg dynasty which set fire to all of Germany and to the European continent. Without the grave crisis in the constitutional life of the Empire, the weakness of the German states, and the ambitions of the great powers of Europe, the events that occurred in Bohemia could not have developed into a disaster from which Germany was to emerge crippled and mutilated.

It is difficult to determine to what extent differences in the interpretation of Christian faith were a direct cause of the catastrophe. There is no doubt but that religious motivation was strong in the lives of individuals and societies, and even in the relations among states and nations, in this age. But the confessional war started at a time when enthusiasm for the religious revivals, both Protestant and Catholic, had lost much of its original force and religious ideas had again become conventionalized. Frank skepticism was rare in Germany, but ever larger groups of people had ceased to find in religious ideals the full satisfaction of their human aspirations. Nevertheless, the reality of heaven and hell was nowhere questioned, nor was the necessity of basing the political and social order on principles that would keep Satan from undoing the work of God. Religious zeal found expression not only in the ghasty fury of witch trials, which reached its climax during these years, but also in the care with which all governments attended to the direction of church life in their dominions. Yet while on the one hand religion deteriorated into superstition, on the other it tended to become formalized and to lose genuineness. Every political action was publicly cloaked in religious terms, but religion seemed to be used more and more to rationalize actions motivated by secular interests. Under the general cover of Christian orthodoxy there came to be a separation of religion and politics. It is usually assumed that the failure of the religious reunification of Germany during the Thirty Years' War led to toleration and to the secularization of politics. But the process was more complex. In countries such as France, where the religious division was overcome at an early date, the secularization of politics went forward at a much faster pace than in Germany. It began in Germany before the Thirty Years' War, and although in the end it limited the influence of religion on politics very considerably, the survival of denominational churches contributed in some measure to the strong position of religion in the intellectual life of Germany well into the 18th century.

Already under Emperor Matthias the Austrian government had made strenuous efforts to strengthen the position of the Catholic Church in Bohemia and to counteract the Protestant movement, which had won great liberties with Emperor Rudolf's Letter of Majesty of 1609 granting all Bohemians protection against a forceful imposition of religion. Much power still rested with the crown and the old Church. Particularly in the royal and ecclesiastical lands, much activity on behalf of the old faith was possible, and both crown and Church had the support of a strong group of the Bohemian nobility as well as of such cities as Pilsen and Budweis. After the accession of Ferdinand II to the throne, action favorable to Catholic institutions was intensified and carried on openly. The Protestant opposition among the nobility was incensed by a number of incidents, and it pressed for strict adherence to the Letter of Majesty. On May 23, 1618, a large group of noblemen appeared at the castle of Prague to protest to the royal governors, Martinitz and Slavata. The meeting was a stormy one. A minority in the group managed to turn a verbal exchange into a physical scuffle. The governors and one of their secretaries were thrown out of the window in deliberate imitation of the defenestration that had started the Hussite revolution two centuries before. Only one of the governors suffered bodily harm, but the incident had a symbolic quality that made any compromise in the future practically impossible.

A radical group of Bohemian magnates and squires was in the saddle. With the approval of the majority of the estates, they succeeded in setting up a directorate of 30 men, which was to organize the defense of the rights of the country. Wenzel von Ruppa was made president of the government formed by the estates; Count Matthias Thurn, commander of the army that was to be mobilized. The revolt was declared directed, not against King Ferdinand, but against his governors and the bad priests, the Jesuits. It was almost inevitable, however, that such distinctions would be dropped once the movement gathered sufficient strength. From the outset, hopes were entertained of forming a union with the Protestant estates of the other Hapsburg lands, particularly with those of the Wenceslas crown—Bohemia, Silesia, Lusatia, and Moravia—but also those of Lower and Upper Austria. The revolt of the Protestant Netherlands against Spain could not fail to throw a shadow over the Danube. But with the exception of Silesia, the estates of the other Hapsburg territories were slow in joining Bohemia.

It was apparent that the attitude of the German and European states was of paramount importance for the ultimate outcome of the Bohemian revolution. The Union of the Protestant German princes had become a rather small and pronouncedly defensive association, slow to reach decisions. In the fall of 1618, however, it did announce that it considered the violations of the Letter of Majesty as endangering the evangelical faith and German liberty, and that its members were expected not to tolerate the recruitment of soldiers for war against the Bohemian estates or the passage of troops through their territories. But some members of the Union such as the margrave of Ansbach were already convinced that the Bohemian events were the last warning to Protestants that they must fight if they did not wish eventually to be submerged by the Catholic reaction. This was also the opinion of Prince Christian of Anhalt, who was still virtually in control of the policy of the Palatinate.

Christian of Anhalt was a man of large conceptions and an untiring inventor and promoter of political projects, though of projects that were not always founded upon a realistic appraisal of persons and conditions. His greatest diplomatic success had been the marriage between the young Elector Palatine, Frederick V, and Princess Elizabeth, the cultured, beautiful, and vivacious daughter of King James I of England. Planned as an ordinary political marriage with a view to strengthening the ties between England and the Union, it did not in the end achieve this aim. At the time of the Bohemian crisis, King James was pursuing the dream of a conciliation between England and Spain, an occupation that made him neglect his role as the self-styled leader of European Protestantism.

The marriage of the young couple—both were only 16 at the time of their wedding in 1613—was an unusually happy one. They shared an interest in the arts and fine aesthetic judgment. The last addition to the Heidelberg castle, as well as its magnificent terrace and garden, is a lasting monument to their happy days in the Palatinate. But Frederick had little political acumen and even less energy. On the whole, he depended on his councillors. His wife was often suspected of having persuaded him to accept the Bohemian crown. This accusation is unjust. But the Stuart princess, who showed much greater fortitude and pride than her husband during the long years of exile in the Hague, which followed the Bohemian adventure, had no knowledge of the intricacies of German politics.

Only one European prince was willing immediately to assist the Bohemian estates. Charles Emanuel, the ambitious duke of Savoy, saw in the Bohemian revolt an opportunity to wreck the position of the house of Hapsburg. Together with Venice, he hoped to break the Spanish domination of Italy. At the same time he wished to thwart the election of Ferdinand in Germany and win both the Bohemian and German crown for Savoy. He offered the leaders of the Union an army of 2,000 men to be employed at their discretion. They accepted the offer and placed the troops, which were under the command of Ernst von Mansfeld, at the disposal of the directorate in Prague.

Mansfeld was the first of a number of adventurous military captains to enter the stage. For the next decades these captains were to play roles out of all proportion to their station and character, even for so martial an age. Nothing showed so clearly the breakdown of the traditional political order and the complete failure of the German princes to set a model of leadership as the rise of these "soldiers of fortune," as they called themselves. Religion and fatherland meant nothing to them. They talked boisterously about their honor, but it actually consisted only of physical courage; their actions revealed the most unscrupulous pursuit of personal advantage and the most flagrant disregard of all commitments and common decency. Ernst von Mansfeld was an illegitimate scion of the Belgian, Catholic line of the Counts Mansfeld. He had served in the Spanish army in the wars against the Netherlands. In the Jülich war he had commanded troops of Archduke Leopold. But the unwillingness of the Spanish government to recognize him as a count drove him to embrace Calvinism and serve the Union. Simultaneously, he took service under the duke of Savoy. While in Bohemia, he negotiated with every faction, always eagerly looking for the turn of fortune that would serve his own interests best. His gift for tactics was only moderate, but he had a talent that every military entrepreneur of the age needed, a knack for recruiting soldiers and keeping them even without regular pay. Lack of funds made the quartering of troops among the civilian population inevitable. Foraging developed quickly into plundering, regardless of whether the soldiers were in the country of friends or foes. The conduct of campaigns was greatly affected by these conditions. Valuable strategic positions often had to be given up because an army had eaten everything that could be wrung from a region. Like a swarm of locusts it would then descend upon greener fields and continue its destructive work. Economic conditions go far to explain the rise of the cold-blooded managers and profiteers of war. But the appearance of these self-serving men was a reply to the political and moral failings of the German princes as well.

3. THE ULTIMATE QUESTION:
WAR OR PEACE?

Charles H. Carter (1927–   ) studied under Garrett Mattingly at Columbia University before joining the faculty of Tulane University. His extensive researches in the Spanish archives and his insight into the thinking and language of diplomats enables him to re-create the thought behind the decisions made by the highest officials of government. Carter's achievement is enhanced by his gift for letting evidence speak for itself.

CHARLES HOWARD CARTER[*]

In spite of the great number and variety of questions that came before policymakers for consideration, there was underlying each one the same fundamental problem, the same basic decision which, directly or indirectly, had to be made over and over as each important issue came up for discussion. Whatever the specific subject might be, the ultimate question was the same: the simple, impossible choice between war and peace.

The constant presence of this factor, of this ultimate question lying behind all questions of substance, has been alluded to previously, and some of its more conspicuous manifestations have been discussed—the peace treaties, the Cleves-Jülich crisis, disputes such as those over commerce and piracy which threatened to lead sooner or later to war. Yet one aspect remains unmentioned: the immense complexity, not only of the tangle of surface issues and current developments, but of reaching a decision on the ultimate question itself.

For Spanish policymakers this complexity existed even in the years just prior to the Treaty of London, when the Spanish Netherlands especially felt a desperate need for at least temporary respite from war and when in the circumstances one might have expected the decision, bitter though it was, to be a fairly simple one to make. Yet the determination for peace with England was reached only after a great many facts, factors,

* Charles Howard Carter, *The Secret Diplomacy of the Habsburgs, 1598–1625* (New York: Columbia University Press, 1964), pp. 53–59.

and arguments had been considered; even then there remained councillors who were not convinced that peace was the proper course.

The need for peace in Albert's domains was not just a matter of the government's financial straits, nor even of the chaotic state of the country itself (in purely economic terms); it also involved the more fundamental political problem of making at least possible the difficult task of governing the restive population.

Albert was advised on this point that the treaty under discussion would:

give satisfaction and contentment to the people, who, seeing that Your Highness has already brought about peace with two such great and powerful enemies, will enter into firm expectation that the third peace settlement, which is that with Holland and the most important, must now follow, and in this expectation they will [no longer] stir up trouble; on the contrary they will bear all things more patiently, [will show] more love, more respect, more obedience to the prince and will yield more and more to his will and commandments. In the same way, they will be rid of the suspicion that some have conceived (although in error) that one tries only to perpetuate war here in order to maintain the domination of the foreigner, and meanwhile the prince will have some months in which to put his affairs in order, which will be enough time.

It will cast great credit on Your Highness and bring stabilization to Your Highness's affairs, which is no small thing at this conjuncture, and will serve as honey to sweeten the gall of so many mutinies and so much bad news, which embitter and cast down the hearts of the people completely.

Still, the wisdom of this was not so certain as it was made to sound. If the people were led to such expectations of benefit from the peace and were then disillusioned, they might very well, it was pointed out, become even harder to govern than they were now.

In any event, however, domestic considerations were far from the only ones which had to be taken into account. Until 1603, for example, there was the fact that heretic England was ruled, as one unfriendly critic put it, by "a decrepit princess on the edge of the grave." The fact that Elizabeth, childless, was nearly 70 was to the Hapsburgs a vital statistic indeed, and one whose implications were frequently discussed. Opinion on what course of action the bare fact dictated for Spain was, as usual, at opposite poles.

"By means of this peace," it was argued by one side, "one will be able to go freely all over the kingdom and gain supporters there for the eventuality of the death of the Queen (which according to the course of nature can hardly delay much longer) in order to advance our affairs in the best way it can be done." Making peace at this conjuncture would be "the true road to the installation there of a prince of the House of Austria, or at least some Catholic prince with the heiress of that kingdom, which would not be a small foundation for maintaining there the good friendship and correspondence between [us] which can never be firm and durable between princes of contrary religion."

Against this it was urged that there was "a great likelihood of a war for the crown," and that "if the Queen should die during this peace . . . the King of Spain could not then interpose himself in it with as much claim and foundation as he could being in open war with that kingdom."

It is worth noting that, while both sides in the above exchange were concerned with putting a Catholic on the English throne, neither mentions anything about the advancement of the faith there (though both may simply have felt it too obvious to mention). The one in favor of making peace is concerned with maintaining long-term peaceful relations—with making the English government friendly, not with making the English people Catholic.

The other debater, a sanguine type who thought England's power far overrated and was sure the island could be taken by Spanish invasion simply by avoiding the now obvious mistakes made in '88, advocated a new "Enterprise of England" simply because, from a strategic point of view, that was the most advantageous country the Spanish crown could possess, carrying with it domination of the Narrow Seas and of all Spain's enemies in northern Europe.

The latter's argument that there would be no great difficulty in invading England was based on a whole series of doubtful assumptions but his motives were sound enough, for he viewed the invasion as a single solution to Spain's three greatest problems: the Indies, the Dutch rebellion, and the danger from France. How peace with England would affect these three problems informs much of the debate on the subject.

The importance of the overseas empire (for which the all-inclusive term "Indies" was commonly used) was so basic that the above adviser's opponent not only ranked the beneficial effects he foresaw for it first among the reasons for making peace with England but so thoroughly identified the two that he began his discussion of the Indies by saying, "First of all to speak of Spain. . . ."

He was certain that once peace was made "the fleet from the Indies will be able to come and go more surely without being troubled and belabored." Leaning heavily on the sort of imagery common at the time, he described the flow of treasure from the Indies and commerce with them as "the lifeblood of the kingdom and of all the others that depend upon it," and the routes to the Indies as "the very veins which give life to this great and vast body." As for the English raiders, "with this peace they will immediately and completely withdraw all their armadas, without farther molesting either the states or the shipping of Spain."

But this was the optimistic view, and it had ample (and more prescient) opposition. Now that she was delivered from the Irish war that had been causing her so much travail, it was pointed out, Elizabeth was free once again to infest the seas with her ships, treaty or no treaty, just as she had done before when "her Drake" had robbed the king of Spain of so much treasure, excusing his acts under various pretexts, even before the opening of the war. As for promises Elizabeth might make, Spain had had plenty of such assurances in Drake's time, but that had stopped him not at all. And if the treaty did stop openly English raids, it would in fact stop nothing, for the Hollander would not leave off "playing his game," the English would simply "mix themselves in pell-mell" with the Dutch, and they would all go divide up their booty in Holland.

This seeming certainty was just one more reminder to Spanish policymakers of how circumscribed they were by simple, unpleasant facts, and this one, the continuing war with the Dutch, was the bitterest of all. Much consideration had to be given to the effect peace with England would have on that war.

It was frequently argued that the rebel provinces would "be left alone, feeble, fearful, without support other than that of two or three princes on the German frontier." But would peace with England really end aid to the Dutch from that quarter? Not likely. Even with fine promises aid would continue covertly, just as French aid continued regardless of the Treaty of Vervins.

For one thing, the cause which had led Elizabeth to take up the defense of the rebels in the first place would be motive enough for continuing it. For another, she knew her own interest and could be counted on to continue sustaining the weaker side, thus nourishing a perpetual war between "these lands" in order to extend her own—an unkind but not wholly inaccurate description of English balance-of-power tactics. Her motives hardly mattered, however, for "the effects will always be the same."

The critic quoted here often vented his spleen in rather rabid vilification of Elizabeth, but he had considerable respect for her judgment, just as others had. She was a heretic, but she was certainly no fool, and she was credited, if not with having a proper sense of honor, at least with having sensible care for her reputation. Appreciation of these elements in the queen could, when applied to specifics, lead to a sound estimate of probabilities. The question of what could be expected to happen to the strong places she held in the Low Countries provides a case in point.

The same critic said:

If there were at least some appearance of enfeebling Holland, or of putting them in a worse case by this peace, which would be done if she liquidated with us in terms of close alliance or returned into our hands the places she holds . . . that would be an advantageous peace in all ways. But it cannot at all be presumed that she would ever do such a thing, as much so as not to wound her honor and reputation as not to increase our forces by this means, in spite of the fact that she well knows that others hold these places only by usurpation. And thus, in place of begrudging them to them, she will strengthen them by turning these places over to them, and thus they will come to the capping of their little act and render themselves stronger and more powerful than before, having their hands freer and the control over their state more absolute.

The same critic also expressed an opposite view of the value of the United Provinces' German allies, asserting that they formed a more important *appui* than England—and implying as well that they were less troublesome as allies than Elizabeth was. To draw England out of Holland's set of alliances would be, he said, like plucking a feather from an eagle: "it is nothing done."

Ridicule by metaphor is a standard weapon in debate, and this sally may have brought the derisive laughter desired, but the man who made it did not really believe that depriving the Dutch of English support (even if it could be contrived) would have no effect. On the contrary, his real convictions he showed in a maxim counseling against any such attempt: "Il ne faut jamais remuer les choses non nécessaires."

This advice to let sleeping dogs lie (and eagles as well) was based on a commendably frank estimate of the Dutch attitude toward reunion with the southern provinces. If deprived of English support, the Dutch, seeing that in the end they could not survive by themselves, would give themselves up "body and soul" to the king of France—or to the Turk, if they could. They would do this, even this, this realist said, "to avoid falling into our hands."

This was, he said, "a very important Reason of State" for not taking their English ally away. Obviously not the strongest of arguments against a treaty with England, it was really a warning not to make the rebels too desperate for outside help. The reason for his warning and his worry is not far to seek, for, in a world a great part of which was ruled by the Spanish Hapsburgs and much of the rest of which lived in mortal terror of their power, they and their counselors pondered the problems of empire, of war and peace, sitting nervously in the growing shadow of France—a source for them of much worry and no little irony.

Of the three most important considerations involved in making peace with England, that of the Indies was a special case, one of guarding a necessary source of revenue; that of Holland was largely a short-term matter of effects on a war which the archdukes hoped to end soon anyway; but that of France was of a special seriousness, for it was a long-term problem which made unusual demands on policymakers' powers of insight and foresight. There was considerable of both in Spanish counsels, and the possible effects on the growing French danger were thoughtfully weighed—as always—in considering peace with England.

It was hoped that once peace was made there would be "a renewal of the old alliances that have always been between these provinces and England," alliances which had seldom been infringed because of their mutual profitability, and which had often served to guarantee the Burgundian lands from French invasion.

What was needed in the present circumstances was

a salutary counterweight to the grandeur and might of France, which nation, because of the repose and order which [that] king has at present, will soon be in a position to terrorize all the princes of Christendom, who are for the most part at war while he takes the high road and forges his grandeur from the ruin of these provinces. I say this principally because of the manufacturing industries [migrating] to France, to the great and irreparable damage of these provinces. For, if France should break with Spain, and if England should not be in amity with Spain, obviously Spain will suffer, which is surely one of the most pregnant considerations which ought to make these three states [England, Spain, and the Spanish Netherlands] come together, and the strongest bond of this peace (*ommunio necessita facit communes amicos*), and the same reason which brought about the confederation of France and England in these latest wars, that is, the grandeur of the King of Spain, should now bring together Spain, England and this country.

4. SECULARISM AND REASON

OF STATE

Friedrich Meinecke (1862–1954) spent his long and extremely influential career as a historian entirely in Germany. Preoccupied as much by the philosophical and political upheavals in his own lifetime as by the study of the past, Meinecke lacks the detachment found in the work of his hero, Leopold von Ranke. Bold and controversial, Meinecke's work on Machiavellism served, at least for some, as an apology for Bismarck's Realpolitik.

FRIEDRICH MEINECKE[*]

One can readily understand that it was not in Italy, the classic native land of modern statecraft, but, on the contrary, in France that the new feeling arose. Italy provided the political thinker with the choicest material for observation in the form of small states and petty despots, who were accustomed to keeping their heads above water only by exercising a masterly technical skill in the matter of spying out and making use of human passions and weaknesses. Hense arose the tendency to produce general recipe books of *arcana imperii*, a kind of psychology for practical use in politics.

In spite of all the interest shown in the policy and governmental methods of the existing great powers, there was a complete absence of the impulse (which can only be aroused by a participation in the misfortune and destiny of a great state) to rise above the mere application of human knowledge, and to comprehend, not only the subjective aspect of statecraft, but also the objective interconnections of state activity. But in France people had been forced out of this petty preoccupation with self-interest by the bitter experiences of the Huguenot Wars. It was, in fact, just this profound religious and political division of the nation that brought political thought to fruition and impelled it to seek out a new intellectual and spiritual cohesive force for a state threatened with dissolution. As we have already seen, a cohesive force of this kind on a grand scale was provided by Bodin's doctrine of the sovereignty and centralization of state authority. And another such cohesive force, too, would be the recognition of the true collective interest of the whole of France, which was at present obscured by the fanaticism of the opposing parties. The problem of the division of creed led directly on to the supreme political problem of French power and independence in Europe; for the ruthless struggle over the old Church could not fail to drive the state into the arms of Spain and to lead to the abandonment of all those power aims which could only be achieved by struggling against Spain. After 1562 there arose the party of the *Politiques* who recognized this fact, and who at once concentrated all their energies on establishing once more a real

---

[*] Friedrich Meinecke, *Machiavellism, The Doctrine of Raison d'Etat and Its Place in Modern History*, trans. Douglas Scott (New Haven: Yale University Press, 1957), pp. 151–56.

peace by granting toleration to the Huguenots; and then they also went on (and in this they quickly found themselves at one with the Huguenots) to take up a political front against Spain. The fact that the modern idea of toleration is founded on realistic policy appears very clearly here. The true interest of France made it imperative to exercise toleration, in order to keep the state free from foreign influence and to enable its strength to be deployed abroad.

These ideas of the *Politiques* (which have been described, somewhat erroneously, as "the first signs of Chauvinism") continued to shine right through the following decades like a guiding star above the thunderclouds of the Civil War. They came to be realized in the monarchy and in the system of Henry IV. His death once more threw France off the path of a rational policy of interest. But the tradition of the *Politiques* remained alive, and reawoke at the very moment when France was preparing once more to take up the work which had been begun by Henry IV but interrupted by his death, and to enter the lists against Spain. At the beginning of the 1620's, thinking politicians in France were painfully conscious of the loss in European power which their country had suffered owing to the internal chaos of the regency and on account of the weak attitude of the Queen-Regent Maria and the first advisers of Louis XIII toward Spain. Spain was about to strike at the land routes, which led from Milan by way of the Valtelline, over the Passes of the Grisons, and across the Austrian countryside on the Upper Rhine. Together with the emperor, Spain dominated western Germany, and also dominated (it was generally assumed) imperial policy; with the result that sooner or later Spain might become permanently established on the territory of the Upper Rhine, and the Republic of the Netherlands might be completely overthrown. Simultaneously, since the summer of 1623, negotiations had been going on for a marriage between Charles, the heir to the English throne, and a Spanish infanta, which might very possibly lead to England becoming tied to the Spanish system for some considerable time to come. It certainly seemed high time that France tore herself free from these clutches; and just as Henry IV had succeeded formerly, by means of an internal pacification of the parties, in deploying abroad once again the strength of his country, so also it now appeared that with the Peace of Montpellier, which the government concluded in 1622 with the Huguenot rebels, the internal split had been resolved once more, and the possibility was created for a new deployment of power abroad.

It was in this situation that there appeared the book entitled *Discours des Princes et Estats de la Chréstienté plus considerables à la France, selon leurs diverses qualitez et conditions.*

It exists in two editions, the first of which appeared toward the turn of the years 1623–24, and the second (an edition which expanded the book in some places and shortened it in others) can be dated pretty exactly as having appeared at the end of March or beginning of April, 1624—that is to say, shortly before Richelieu began to take part in the counsels of the king, which occurred on April 24, 1624. The authorship has been ascribed to no less important a person than Father Joseph, Richelieu's intimate friend and assistant; though up to the present it has not been proved that there is anything more than a possibility that he might have been the author. It is certain, however, that the author of the book was a man of first-rate political training and wide information; and it is also certain that his work was more or less closely connected with the ascending fortunes of Richelieu. It belongs to a whole group of pamphlets, which appeared during those years, and in which the French nationalist ideas of the former *Politiques,* the "good Frenchmen" (as they now called themselves), came to life once more in the form of a reaction against the Spanish-Catholic line taken by Luynes. During those same weeks in which the work must have originated, Father Joseph was actually living with Richelieu; and Richelieu himself was struggling hard to win the King over to a policy of glory and grandeur, and combat the weak policy of the existing minister, in order thereby to pave his own way to the ministry. Other possibilities, however, must be considered, besides that of Richelieu's circle. The author might also have been in close touch with the Connétable Lesdiguières; for this former Protestant (who had negotiated the Peace of Montpellier) was also strongly in favor of taking up again the policy of Henry IV, and particularly advocated (just as the author of our book did) a struggle for the Valtelline and a closer union with the Italian rulers.

This is not the place, however, to deal with the contemporary significance of the book for French policy at the time, and we must pass on. We shall only use it to show how the vital impulses in the sphere of the European states were reflected in contemporary minds, and what it was capable of offering toward a deeper historical and political understanding.

What it had to offer was considerable, and is in no way impaired by the shortcomings in the form of the work. The ponderous diction may be excused on account of the existing state of French prose; and in any case, in the matter of flexibility, it still surpasses the style of German political writings of the time. Though copiously sprinkled with historical facts and allusions, it never becomes bogged down among crude matters of fact and antiquarian detail; on the contrary, it gathers all the historical threads tightly together in the service of the immediate political aim. Historical knowledge is, for the author, a prerequisite of all political thought and action. "The best advice one can give in matters of State," thus it begins, "is based on special knowledge of the State itself." One must know what the state is in itself and what relation it bears to other states, how it is governed, what the relationship is between ruler and subjects, and how it behaves with reference to foreign countries. For there exists—and here speaks the bitter experience of half a century of French history—a necessary and inevitable correlation between internal and external affairs, good as well as bad, and the slightest disorder within the state has its effect on the conduct of foreign powers toward it; whereas every internal gain in strength leads on at once to the task of repairing the damage which has taken place in the outward situation of the state during its convulsions and sicknesses. For, since all rulers in the world are only guided by their own interests, and their impulse to action comes from the fortune or misfortune of their neighbors, who can doubt that a sovereign, who is weak and not respected by his subjects, will be considered by his neighbors and allies to be of less importance than a ruler who enjoys obedience and fear in his own country? In the last troubled times of King Henry III, France found herself being treated quite badly by old allies and friends; whereas immediately after Henry IV's internal victory almost all the European powers, with the exception of the House of Austria, drew closer to France, in order that by uniting themselves with her they could reestablish the balance of power against Austria. The French body politic was, by the mercy of God, quite sound; and so now once more, after a happy settlement of the internal confusion, the time had come to take up one's position again in the face of the foreign powers. And it was worth studying these foreign powers now, in order to know what there was to be hoped or feared from each of them.

The states of Europe were to be viewed and depicted, then, solely from the point of view of the special interests of France; and Europe alone was to constitute the range of vision. For this reason, therefore, the author specifically refused to consider the Spanish sphere of power beyond the seas. This also shows, what can still be observed in all attempts of this kind, namely that the practical political aim was always bound to narrow down the field of view. In return for this, the political aim sharpened one's perception for the business of distinguishing all the peculiar phenomena inside the field of vision. One or two examples will be enough to show this.

First and foremost, a very significant and clear picture is given of the Spanish power in Europe: its various main and subordinate spheres, its resources, and its principles and methods of government. Then, with a general survey of its geographical disposition throughout southern and western Europe, we are shown how it is linked together in the form of a chain and joins hands with the German and East European possessions of the House of Hapsburg, so that it threatens to encircle all the states lying in between. Its immediate appearance is that of a still unfinished system of waterways, whose aim it must be to clear out of the way all those obstacles to union which lie in between; then, particularly, it becomes obvious why the Valtelline is important, *comme une galerie et un chemin aisé entre les montagnes pour passer de l'une à l'autre.* From this composite picture one gets a distinct idea of the main territory of Spain, entrenched behind its Pyrenean rampart which seems to have been created by nature as if for an exalted type of fortification, dominating everything around (*comme un cavalier eslevé pour lui commander*); a picture of a land complete and at unity with itself ever since the grandees had lost their political power a hundred years before, of a country which is underpopulated and yet capable of exerting immense strength in order to keep neighboring countries under its yoke.

5. RELIGION AND REASON

OF STATE

Born and educated in Germany, George L. Mosse (1918–   ) is professor of European history at the University of Wisconsin. His intensive researches into the connections between intellectual, religious, and political history have culminated in several important publications on the Reformation, 17th-century English history, and German history in the 20th century.

GEORGE L. MOSSE[*]

Friedrich Meinecke has told us how, in the early modern period, powerful religious ideas faced the equally powerful idea of reason of state: "hard and brittle as these ideas were in confrontation, were the people themselves." Yet Meinecke's statement is misleading. The two complexes

---

[*] George L. Mosse, *The Holy Pretence, A Study in Christianity and Reason of State from William Perkins to John Winthrop* (Oxford, Eng.: Basil Blackwell, 1957), pp. 11–14.

of ideas were not so rigid or unyielding that a union between them could not be forged. It was, as a matter of fact, of the greatest importance to the future of both reason of state and the Christian ethic that such a task should have been attempted by both Protestants and Catholics alike.

To demonstrate the close connection between religion and reason of state in the minds of men in the 16th century, so different from the modern approach, we may take a speech made on the floor of the Elizabethan House of Commons: "We may not trust only to the sword, lest the common saying of Cicero should turn to our shame: *parva sunt foris arma, nisi consilium domini.* Neither our preaching nor our praying to God are sufficient, but withal we must do our endeavour, and help each other; since for the driving away of a dog there is (as the countryman says) some virtue in a stone, if it be conjoined with St. John's Gospel." How then is the stone to be conjoined to the Gospel?

One answer to this problem was given by the distinguished Puritan, Sir Francis Hastings, speaking also on the floor of the Elizabethan House: "Religion and policy may well stand together; but as that policy is most detestable which hath not religion to warrant it, so is that religion most happy which has policy to back and maintain it." Another and similar answer to this question was given by a Jacobean pamphleteer who advised his king that if his people be unreasonable he must bring them to do his bidding, little by little, through "some craft or by some holy pretence." The "holy pretence" in this quotation has furnished the title for our study: it has come to symbolize that relationship between Christianity and reason of state which the Divines managed to establish. Thomas Edwards did have reason, during the Civil War, to accuse all sides of "pious frauds, holy deceits." However, he failed to see that such frauds and deceits imply much more than mere hypocrisy, but were, perhaps, sincere attempts to meet the challenge of "policy" and reason of state. Nor can we agree with Friedrich Meinecke when he sums up the 16-century answer to this conjoining of the stone and St. John's Gospel in the phrase: "follow the Church and all will be well." If the process of conjoining did not imply a deeper meaning than the mere citing of this phrase conveys, it would be difficult to see more in our problem than a thinly disguised acceptance of reason of state. This is the impression Meinecke conveys to his readers. Croce has rightly remarked that Meinecke himself rejected the moral theory of politics as well as the political theory of morals. It is for this reason, perhaps, that the great German historian showed little comprehension for the significance of the phrase he cites.

For all this Friedrich Meinecke has shown us how the idea of reason of state and the Christian ethic confronted each other on the continent of Europe. They confronted each other in England as well: by the Elizabethan age there were many who had a grasp of the concept of reason of state, and during the reign of James I it was becoming widely accepted as an axiom in politics. At first reason of state tended to be a royal doctrine based upon the king's "absolute power" which Justice Fleming described as a power for the "general benefit of people." By 1610, the House of Commons saw clearly the dangers implied in this royal use of the concept. Carleton then attempted to defend the idea before his fellow members: "you must know that this reason of state is not such a monster as this gentleman here made it. Reason of state is preservation of the state and not the ruin of the state." Carleton here shows a realization of the nature of this concept as defined by continental theorists: that of preserving, not expanding, the state.

Furthermore, to quiet the tempers of the House, Carleton contrasts reason of state with the law of the land. It was not the intention of the government to apply reason of state to the matter of impositions, but instead to aid in clarifying the common law of England. Here, too, Carleton seems to be cognizant of the emergency nature of the concept, of its essential opposition to the laws of the land, which would be transcended by the necessity of state.

By 1621 the House of Commons itself was no longer attacking reason of state, but taking the concept over into its own vocabulary. "To reason of state and the preservation of state is most fit in this place." Thus, in the struggle for sovereignty between the king and the Parliament, the concept of reason of state became a part of the arsenal of arguments on both sides. Beyond this, it lent itself to use by the war party in their urgings to have England enter on the side of the hard-pressed German Protestants in the Thirty Years' War. For example, Denzill Holles, of that party, added to his religious arguments for war the following: the Bohemian situation ". . . relates to us not only as we are fellow members with them of the Church . . . but does more particularly concern us in point of policy and reason of state, by supporting our allies to advance this Kingdom to the highest pitch of greatness and reputation."

These random examples should serve to show that the idea of reason of state had found a home in England. However, the concept did not stand alone: it had an all-important consequence. If reason of state were the goal, then all actions must be attuned to the realities of political life, inasmuch as these lead to this greatest good. In this way the concept of "policy" becomes a part of reason of state, or rather the necessary implementation of it. In its most basic definition, policy connotes an expedient but wicked action for reason of state. Here is the crux of the matter. Men might speak about reason of state, but were they ready to face the consequences, to resort to policy?

The overt 16th-century reaction to this question would have been in the negative: policy was rejected as a desideratum of political action. This condemnation took the form of a rejection of "Machiavellism," for the Florentine seemed to stand for just this combination of reason of state and policy. In order, therefore, to see how these new Renaissance concepts penetrated into England, we must first consider what kind of reception this Machiavellism had there. We shall then realize to what extent the idea of reason of state with policy as its consequence confronted the Christian ethic in England. Then, too, we can better understand the linkage between the two concepts which the Casuists of this study attempted to make.

David E. Underdown, Associate Professor of History at
the University of Virginia, was born at Wells, Somerset,
England, in 1925. He received the degrees of B.A., M.A.,
and B. Litt. from the University of Oxford and an M.A. from
Yale. He formerly taught history at the University of the
South. He is the author of the book *Royalist Conspiracy in
England, 1649–1660* (New Haven, Conn., 1960) and of articles in various historical journals. He recently discovered
two hitherto unpublished speeches of Oliver Cromwell. He
received recently a Guggenheim Fellowship to prepare a
book on Pride's Purge. He is a member of the American
Historical Association and of the Conference on British
Studies.

CHAPTER SIX

DAVID UNDERDOWN

University of Virginia

Oliver Cromwell: Puritan Idealist

or Conservative Statesman?

THE CAREER of Oliver Cromwell is inextricably entangled with one of the great revolutions of European history—the English Puritan Revolution which in part shaped, and was shaped by, him. Both the revolution and the man have never failed, and never will fail, to arouse controversy among historians. In both can be found an endlessly varied mixture of causes and motives, about whose relative importance historians can disagree even after the most scrupulous analysis of the evidence.

About the facts of Oliver Cromwell's career, however, there need be no dispute. A modern entry in *Who's Who* might read something like this:

Cromwell, Oliver. Born Huntingdon, England, 1599, son of Robert and Elizabeth (Steward) Cromwell. Education: Huntingdon Free Grammar School and Sidney Sussex College, Cambridge. Married (1620) Elizabeth Bourchier; four sons, four daughters. Member of Parliament for Huntingdon, 1628–29; for Cambridge, 1640–53. Cavalry officer for Parliament in Civil War; Captain 1642, Colonel 1643, Lieutenant-General 1644, second-in-command of New Model Army 1645. Supported Army in quarrel with Parliament 1647, negotiated with Charles I 1647–48, but prominent in securing his execution 1649. Member of Commonwealth Council of State 1649–53. Commander in Ireland 1649, in Scotland 1650–51. Lord General (Commander-in-chief) 1650. Expelled Long Parliament April 1653. Lord Protector December 1653 until death, 3 September 1658.

Bare facts, however, tell us little about the man's opinions and motives. To understand these a brief review of some of the major events of the

171

early 17th century is required. Cromwell's formative years coincided with the intensification of the religious conflict between Calvinism and the Counter-Reformation, which exploded as the last and greatest of the wars of religion in 1618. To Cromwell and thousands of other passionately Protestant (that is, Puritan) young Englishmen, the Thirty Years' War appeared as the great climactic confrontation between the forces of light and darkness, truth and error, and they felt bitter humiliation at the refusal of the Stuart kings, James I and Charles I, to intervene effectively on the Protestant side. In these same years Cromwell also witnessed the growing, and related, struggle between the Stuarts and their parliaments. He was himself an inconspicuous member of the parliament which in 1628 attempted the first major limitation of the king's prerogatives, by the Petition of Right. Inconspicuous Cromwell may have been in the House of Commons, but the fact that he was elected to it at all is an indication of his local prominence. Cromwell was no social upstart. He came of a substantial (though not extravagantly wealthy) landowning family, one of the governing oligarchy of country gentry of an England in which the right to political power was automatically assumed to depend on the ownership of property.

Between Cromwell's two spells in parliament, separated by the years 1629–40, occurred the 11 years in which Charles I tried to govern as an almost absolute king. This in itself would have been enough to alienate Cromwell and his fellow gentry, but Charles also pursued an ecclesiastical policy based on a strong episcopacy and the repression of the rigorously Calvinist Puritans. What was this, to men like Cromwell, but an attempt to lead the country back to Rome? When at last the Long Parliament met in 1640 the institutions of absolute monarchy were unanimously dismantled, but civil war followed when the more radical ("root and branch") Puritans tried to deprive the king of his militia powers and to achieve the total destruction of episcopacy. As in most revolutions, the revolutionaries soon split into their moderate and extremist wings. The moderates wanted a compromise peace with the king, wished to keep the parliament's forces under the charge of safe aristocratic generals like the ineffective Earls of Essex and Manchester, and aimed at a religious settlement that, while abolishing bishops, would retain a disciplined and intolerant national church: they were, therefore, often called Presbyterians, though not all of them were in the strictly religious sense. The extremists, who included Cromwell, wanted total victory over the king even at the risk of opening the door to social disorder, recruited and officered their regiments (for example, Cromwell's famous Ironsides) from Puritan enthusiasts rather than from men of rank, and wanted a religious settlement that would permit wide toleration for Puritans of all varieties and in which authority would rest with local, independent congregations. They were, therefore, usually called Independents, though again the term has its limitations.

An Independent army, a parliament with a Presbyterian majority; in 1647 the split came into the open. In December, 1648, the Independents purged parliament of the now backsliding Presbyterians, executed the king, abolished the House of Lords, and governed England as a republic under the title of a commonwealth. Cromwell's role in the Commonwealth should not be exaggerated (for much of it he was engaged in conquering Ireland and Scotland), but it was he who in April, 1653, decided that it had outlived its usefulness and expelled the "Rump" of the Long Parliament by force. He and his fellow officers now had to devise a substitute. At first they tried a nominated assembly of Puritan enthusiasts, the so-called Barebones Parliament, or Parliament of Saints. Then, when that went too far in its reforming zeal, they installed Cromwell himself as Lord Protector, governing with the aid of a council, and with a parliament meeting for short periods under a reformed, but still restricted franchise. This constitution, the Instrument of Government, was revised in 1657 after a "Humble Petition and Advice" which gave Cromwell almost monarchical powers even though he declined the title of king that was offered him.

Efforts to resolve the paradoxes of Cromwell's career have been many and varied, ranging from the satanic figure depicted by royalist writers after the restoration of Charles II in 1660 to the almost godlike hero discovered by Thomas Carlyle in the 1840's. Each generation of historians has tended to revise its verdict according to its own assumptions and preoccupations; there was, for example, a significant spate of books in the 1930's in which Cromwell appeared as a sort of 17th-century fascist dictator, surrounded by the trappings of jackbooted militarism. In the four selections that follow, the student might ask himself to what extent the authors were affected in their evaluations by the climate of their own times. Was Macaulay, for instance, influenced by the Whig achievements of his own day, by the apparent triumph of representative parliamentary government following the passage of the 1832 Reform Bill? Was Harrison inspired in part by enthusiasm for Britain's imperial greatness when he wrote in the heyday of empire building, the "braggart years" at the end of the 19th century?

Cromwell was obviously a Puritan idealist, inspired by Protestant enthusiasm both at home and abroad. He was also, equally obviously, a conservative country gentleman who revered what he believed to be the traditional English constitution, the mixed monarchy based on a division of powers between king and parliament, and the common law. These two sides of Cromwell's character are conveniently illustrated by his behavior in 1653. Having got rid of the Rump because of its members' insistence on retaining power for its own sake, without pressing on with the construction of the Puritan "New Jerusalem," Cromwell welcomed the Barebones Parliament in a speech on July 4 which is perhaps the most inspirationally religious of his many biblical utterances. In it he looked forward to the establishment of a godly commonwealth by men whose sole qualification to rule was their sense of religious calling. Here is the climax of the Puritan Revolution—the rule of the saints on earth. Yet within six months Cromwell had decided that the Barebones Parliament was dominated by nothing more than a desire to "overturn, overturn," and that by trying to abolish tithes and reform the legal system it was destroying the very foundations of the rights of property. And so he turned to the Instrument of Government, to an attempt at "settlement" and conciliation on the basis of a conservative constitution which outwardly resembled the traditional one, though in practice it rested ultimately on the sword. His subsequent difficulties with his parliaments, discussed in one of the following selections, may have been in part the inevitable result of his conservative constitutionalism.

The student must find in the four selections his own answers to the questions that arise from this inner tension in Cromwell's makeup. Which of the two sides of Cromwell, the Puritan idealist or the conservative constitutionalist, was the more important? Were there times at which one or other was uppermost, and if so, why? Do any of the four authors suggest a change in Cromwell's thinking as the years passed as a possible means of resolving his apparent contradictions? Did the Protectorate, conservative as it was in form, with its return to single-person government and even a House of Lords, mark a complete repudiation of Cromwell's Puritan ideals? It is a mere cliché to say that Cromwell's government was like Napoleon's in being both a product of the earlier revolution and a reaction against it; the important question is in precisely what ways was it either a product or a reaction? Finally, the student should bear in mind that his answers about Cromwell will be to some extent answers to questions about the nature and meaning of the Puritan Revolution itself. Was that movement, as Trevor-Roper has said, merely a struggle of "outs" against "ins," a blind revolt of the country gentry against the court, the work of "mutinous, impoverished, backward-looking provincial squires"? Or can we say, as Macaulay claimed for the Long Parliament, that it was a great force for liberty, "justly entitled to the reverence and gratitude of all who, in any part of the world, enjoy the blessings of constitutional government"? Finally, are even these last questions mutually exclusive?

1. CROMWELL THE WHIG

Thomas Babington Macaulay (1800–59), created Lord Macaulay in 1857, was the greatest of the English Whig historians. Brought up in the reformist Evangelical atmosphere of the "Clapham Sect," he was an active politician as well as a man of letters. Member of parliament from 1830, holder of administrative office in several Whig governments, member of the Supreme Council of India, he was also the most popular historian of his age, perhaps of any age. His brilliant contributions to the famous Edinburgh Review, *his separately published* Essays, *and above all the best-selling* History *from which the following selection is taken, all display the same polished style and sometimes overconfident certainty of judgment. The first two volumes of the* History *originally appeared in the "year of revolutions," 1848, and consciously point up the moderate Whig reformer's preference for the pragmatic, cautious Revolution of 1688 (the central event of the* History), *compared with the violent, ideologically inspired events taking place across the Channel in Macaulay's own time.*

THOMAS BABINGTON MACAULAY*

There had been from the first, in the parliamentary party, some men whose minds were set on objects from which the majority of that party would have shrunk with horror. These men were, in religion, Independents. They conceived that every Christian congregation had, under Christ, supreme jurisdiction in things spiritual; that appeals to provincial and national synods were scarcely less unscriptural than appeals to the Court of Arches or to the Vatican; and that popery, prelacy, and Presbyterianism were merely three forms of one great apostasy. In politics the Independents were, to use the phrase of their time, root-and-branch men, or, to use the kindred phrase of our own time, radicals. Not content with limiting the power of the monarch, they were desirous to erect a common-

* Thomas Babington Macaulay, *The History of England from the Accession of James the Second* (New York: Harper & Brothers, 1879), Vol. I, pp. 115–19, 122–25, 127, 129–30, 132–36.

wealth on the ruins of the old English polity. At first they had been inconsiderable, both in numbers and in weight; but before the war had lasted two years they became, not indeed the largest, but the most powerful faction in the country. . . .

The soul of that party was Oliver Cromwell. Bred to peaceful occupations, he had, at more than 40 years of age, accepted a commission in the parliamentary army. No sooner had he become a soldier than he discerned, with the keen glance of genius, what Essex and men like Essex, with all their experience, were unable to perceive. He saw precisely where the strength of the royalists lay, and by what means alone that strength could be overpowered. He saw that it was necessary to reconstruct the army of the parliament. He saw also that there were abundant and excellent materials for the purpose, materials less showy, indeed, but more solid, than those of which the gallant squadrons of the king were composed. It was necessary to look for recruits who were not mere mercenaries, for recruits of decent station and grave character, fearing God and zealous for public liberty. With such men he filled his own regiment, and, while he subjected them to a discipline more rigid than had ever before been known in England, he administered to their intellectual and moral nature stimulants of fearful potency. . . .

Cromwell made haste to organize the whole army on the same principles on which he had organized his own regiment. As soon as this process was complete, the event of the war was decided. The Cavaliers had now to encounter natural courage equal to their own, enthusiasm stronger than their own, and discipline such as was utterly wanting to them. It soon became a proverb that the soldiers of Fairfax and Cromwell were men of a different breed from the soldiers of Essex. At Naseby took place the first great encounter between the royalists and the remodeled army of the Houses. The victory of the Roundheads was complete and decisive. It was followed by other triumphs in rapid succession. In a few months the authority of the parliament was fully established over the whole kingdom. . . .

But, while the Houses were employing their authority thus, it suddenly passed out of their hands. It had been obtained by calling into existence a power which could not be controlled. In the summer of 1647, about 12 months after the last fortress of the Cavaliers had submitted to the parliament, the parliament was compelled to submit to its own soldiers.

Thirteen years followed, during which England was, under various names and forms, really governed by the sword. Never before that time, or since that time, was the civil power in our country subjected to military dictation. . . .

And now a design, to which, at the commencement of the civil war, no man would have dared to allude, and which was not less inconsistent with the Solemn League and Covenant than with the old law of England, began to take a distinct form. The austere warriors who ruled the nation had, during some months, meditated a fearful vengeance on the captive king. When and how the scheme originated; whether it spread from the general to the ranks, or from the ranks to the general; whether it is to be ascribed to policy using fanaticism as a tool, or to fanaticism bearing down policy with headlong impulse, are questions which, even at this day, cannot be answered with perfect confidence. It seems, however, on the whole, probable that he who seemed to lead was really forced to follow, and that, on this occasion, as on another great occasion a few years later, he sacrificed his own judgment and his own inclinations to the wishes of the army. For the power which he had called into existence was a power which even he could not always control; and, that he might ordinarily command, it was necessary that he should sometimes obey. He publicly protested that he was no mover in the matter, that the first steps had been taken without his privity, that he could not advise the parliament to strike the blow, but that he submitted his own feelings to the force of circumstances which seemed to him to indicate the purposes of Providence. It has been the fashion to consider these professions as instances of the hypocrisy which is vulgarly imputed to him. But even those who pronounce him a hypocrite will scarcely venture to call him a fool. They are, therefore, bound to show that he had some purpose to serve by secretly stimulating the army to take that course which he did not venture openly to recommend. It would be absurd to suppose that he, who was never by his respectable enemies represented as wantonly cruel or implacably vindictive, would have taken the most important step of his life under the influence of mere malevolence. He was far too wise a man not to know, when he consented to shed that august blood, that he was doing a deed which was inexpiable, and which would move the grief and horror, not only of the royalists, but of nine tenths of those who had stood by the parliament. Whatever visions may have deluded others, he was assuredly dreaming neither of a republic on the antique pattern nor of the millennial reign of the saints. . . . Cromwell had, at one time, meant to mediate between the throne and the parliament, and to reorganize the distracted state by the power of the sword, under the sanction of the royal name. In this design he persisted till he was compelled to abandon it by the refractory temper of the soldiers, and by the incurable duplicity of the king. . . .

Cromwell had to determine whether he would put to hazard the attachment of his party, the attachment of his army, his own greatness, nay, his own life, in an attempt, which would probably have been vain, to save a prince whom no engagement could bind. With many struggles and misgivings, and probably not without many prayers, the decision was made. Charles was left to his fate. . . .

England was declared a commonwealth. The House of Commons, reduced to a small number of members, was nominally the supreme power in the state. In fact, the army and its great chief governed everything. Oliver had made his choice. He had kept the hearts of his soldiers, and had broken with almost every other class of his fellow citizens. Beyond the limits of his camps and fortresses he could scarcely be said to have a party. Those elements of force which, when the civil war broke out, had appeared arrayed against each other were combined against him; all the Cavaliers, the great majority of the Roundheads, the Anglican Church, the Presbyterian Church, the Roman Catholic Church, England, Scotland, Ireland. Yet such was his genius and resolution that he was able to overpower and crush everything that crossed his path. . . .

But the alliance which had been cemented by danger was dissolved by victory. The parliament forgot that it was but the creature of the army. The army was less disposed than ever to submit to the dictation of the parliament. Indeed, the few members who made up what was contemptuously called the Rump of the House of Commons had no more claim than the military chiefs to be esteemed the representatives of the nation. The dispute was soon brought to a decisive issue. Cromwell filled the House with armed men. The speaker was pulled out of his chair, the mace taken from the table, the room cleared, and the door locked. . . .

King, lords, and commons had now in turn been vanquished and destroyed; and Cromwell seemed to be left the sole heir of the powers of all three. Yet were certain limitations still imposed on him by the very army to which he owed his immense authority. That singular body of men was, for the most part, composed of zealous republicans. . . . The object of the warlike saints who surrounded Cromwell was the settlement of a free and pious commonwealth. For that end they were ready to employ, without scruple, any means, however violent and lawless. . . .

The sentiments of Cromwell were widely different. He was not what he had been; nor would it be just to consider the change which his views had undergone as the effect merely of selfish ambition. He had, when he came up to the Long Parliament, brought with him from his rural retreat little knowledge of books, no experience of great affairs, and a temper galled by the long tyranny of the government and of the hierarchy. He had, during the 13 years which followed, gone through a political education of no common kind. He had been a chief actor in a succession of revolutions. He had been long the soul, and at last the head, of a party. He had commanded armies, won battles, negotiated treaties, subdued, pacified, and regulated kingdoms. It would have been strange indeed if his notions had been still the same as in the days when his mind was principally occupied by his fields and his religion, and when the greatest events which diversified the course of his life were a cattle fair or a prayer meeting at Huntingdon. He saw that some schemes of innovation for which he had once been zealous, whether good or bad in themselves, were opposed to the general feeling of the country, and that, if he persevered in those schemes, he had nothing before him but constant troubles, which must be suppressed by the constant use of the sword. He therefore wished to restore, in all essentials, that ancient constitution which the majority of the people had always loved, and for which they now pined. The course afterward taken by Monk[1] was not open to Cromwell. The memory of one terrible day separated the great regicide forever from the House of Stuart. What remained was that he should mount the ancient English throne, and reign according to the ancient English polity. . . .

His plan bore, from the first, a considerable resemblance to the old English constitution: but, in a few years, he thought it safe to proceed further, and to restore almost every part of the ancient system under new names and forms. The title of king was not revived: but the kingly prerogatives were entrusted to a lord high protector. The sovereign was called not His Majesty but His Highness. He was not crowned and anointed in Westminster Abbey, but was solemnly enthroned, girt with a sword of state, clad in a robe of purple, and presented with a rich Bible, in Westminster Hall. His office was not declared hereditary: but he was permitted to name his successor; and none could doubt that he would name his son.

A House of Commons was a necessary part of the new polity. In constituting this body, the Protector showed a wisdom and a public spirit which were not duly appreciated by his contemporaries. The vices of the old representative system, though by no means so serious as they afterward became, had already been remarked by farsighted men. Cromwell reformed that system on the same principles on which Mr. Pitt, 130 years later, attempted to reform it, and on which it was at length reformed in our own times. Small boroughs were disfranchised even more unsparingly than in 1832; and the number of county members was greatly increased. Very few unrepresented towns had yet grown into importance. Of those towns the most considerable were Manchester, Leeds, and Halifax. Repre-

---

[1] George Monck, the general who in 1660 restored Charles II.

sentatives were given to all three. An addition was made to the number
of the members for the capital. The elective franchise was placed on such
a footing that every man of substance, whether possessed of freehold
estates in land or not, had a vote for the county in which he resided. A
few Scotchmen and a few of the English colonists settled in Ireland were
summoned to the assembly which was to legislate, at Westminster, for
every part of the British Isles. . . .

How Oliver's parliaments were constituted, however, was practically
of little moment; for he possessed the means of conducting the administration without their support, and in defiance of their opposition. His wish
seems to have been to govern constitutionally, and to substitute the empire of the laws for that of the sword. But he soon found that, hated as
he was both by royalists and Presbyterians, he could be safe only by
being absolute. The first House of Commons which the people elected by
his command questioned his authority, and was dissolved without having
passed a single act. His second House of Commons, though it recognized
him as Protector, and would gladly have made him king, obstinately refused to acknowledge his new lords. He had no course left but to dissolve
the parliament. "God," he exclaimed, at parting, "be judge between you
and me!"

Yet was the energy of the Protector's administration in nowise relaxed
by these dissensions. Those soldiers who would not suffer him to assume
the kingly title stood by him when he ventured on acts of power as high
as any English king has ever attempted. The government, therefore,
though in form a republic, was in truth a despotism, moderated only by
the wisdom, the sobriety, and the magnanimity of the despot. The country
was divided into military districts. Those districts were placed under
the command of major generals. Every insurrectionary movement was
promptly put down and punished. The fear inspired by the power of the
sword, in so strong, steady, and expert a hand, quelled the spirit both of
Cavaliers and Levellers. . . .[2]

Had he been a cruel, licentious, and rapacious prince, the nation
might have found courage in despair, and might have made a convulsive
effort to free itself from military domination. But the grievances which
the country suffered, though such as excited serious discontent, were by
no means such as impel great masses of men to stake their lives, their
fortunes, and the welfare of their families against fearful odds. The taxation, though heavier than it had been under the Stuarts, was not heavy
when compared with that of the neighboring states and with the re-

---

[2] A party among the army rank and file, headed at first by John Lilburne, which
demanded a more democratic franchise.

sources of England. Property was secure. Even the Cavalier, who re-
frained from giving disturbance to the new settlement, enjoyed in peace
whatever the civil troubles had left him. The laws were violated only in
cases where the safety of the Protector's person and government was
concerned. Justice was administered between man and man with an
exactness and purity not before known. Under no English government
since the Reformation had there been so little religious persecution. The
unfortunate Roman Catholics, indeed, were held to be scarcely within the
pale of Christian charity. But the clergy of the fallen Anglican Church
were suffered to celebrate their worship on condition that they would
abstain from preaching about politics. Even the Jews, whose public
worship, had, ever since the 13th century, been interdicted, were, in spite
of the strong opposition of jealous traders and fanatical theologians, permitted to build a synagogue in London. . . .

While he lived his power stood firm, an object of mingled aversion,
admiration, and dread to his subjects. Few indeed loved his government;
but those who hated it most hated it less than they feared it. Had it been
a worse government, it might perhaps have been overthrown in spite of
all its strength. Had it been a weaker government, it would certainly
have been overthrown in spite of all its merits. But it had moderation
enough to abstain from those oppressions which drive men mad; and it
had a force and energy which none but men driven mad by oppression
would venture to encounter.

It has often been affirmed, but with little reason, that Oliver died at a
time fortunate for his renown, and that, if his life had been prolonged,
it would probably have closed amid disgraces and disasters. It is certain
that he was, to the last, honored by his soldiers, obeyed by the whole
population of the British islands, and dreaded by all foreign powers, that
he was laid among the ancient sovereigns of England with funeral pomp
such as London had never before seen, and that he was succeeded by his
son Richard as quietly as any king had ever been succeeded by any
Prince of Wales.

2. CROMWELL THE LIBERAL IMPERIALIST

*Frederic Harrison (1831–1923) was a far less distinguished historian
than Macaulay, but his study of Cromwell, first published in 1888 in the
popular* Twelve English Statesmen *series, is an interesting product of his*

time. Rejecting organized Christianity, Harrison became a disciple of Auguste Comte and a prominent English exponent of positivism. Whereas Macaulay's old-fashioned Whiggism looked back to the two previous centuries, regarding 1832 as merely a desirable broadening of a constitution still based on property, Harrison was a more progressive Liberal, looking ahead to a more democratic era and welcoming further reforms. Strongly nationalistic, he saw in the emergence of Germany a menace to Britain, and in his old age wrote violent propaganda during World War I.

FREDERIC HARRISON*

The internal policy of the Protector can only be understood if we regard him as a temporary dictator set up to close an epoch of revolution and war. His rule was avowedly provisional and summary; based on expediency, necessity, and public peace. Constitutional right it could have none: it rested on the sword, as in times of revolution and civil war all government must rest. Cromwell's nature and genius were those of the practical man, dealing with the exigencies of the hour. He made no attempt to recast the political organism, or to found a brand-new set of institutions. As he said in parliament, healing and settling were the crying needs of the time. He was the typical opportunist, doing what seemed best for the hour with the actual materials at hand. He did things quite as arbitrary as any Tudor or any Stuart. He did violent things—even odious things. He governed at times by sheer military force. But the true tests by which he must be judged are these. Was not his task essentially different from that of any Tudor, Stuart, or legitimate king? Was not his task an indispensable duty? Did he erect military government into a system, or carry arbitrary action beyond the immediate necessity? Was his government as a whole, given its revolutionary origin and its military basis, that of the self-seeking military tyrant? These questions each of us must answer according to his general view of this momentous epoch.

The first duty of the Protector was to keep order. He was the constable set to keep the peace in the parish. In a country torn by rebellion and war for 14 years and on the verge of social dissolution, external order was the first pressing need. No English government had ever kept it better— not even that of Henry VIII or Elizabeth at their best. . . .

Penruddock's insurrection[1] led to the very severe policy against the royalists, by which they were amerced in the tenth of their fortunes. It

---

* Frederic Harrison, *Oliver Cromwell* (2d ed.; London: Macmillan & Co., 1890), pp. 208–9, 212–16, 218–22.

[1] A minor royalist rebellion in 1655.

was a crushing measure, but it can hardly be called vindictive or wanton. The system of major generals by which it was carried out was an antici- pation of the modern method of government by prefects and military governors of provinces. Oliver called it his "little poor invention," and it was undoubtedly an engine of terrible power. It was in the highest degree arbitrary and without a shadow of legal right. It was, in fact, the military occupation of a country after insurrection, declared, as we now say, to be in a state of siege—a condition with which in modern Europe we are but too familiar, and one which no government can absolutely renounce. It was a war measure, to be justified only, if at all, by the exigencies of war. It lasted in vigor somewhat more than a year, and was a terror to the royalists, but not to the public. Having served its turn, it was dropped, partly in consequence of the odium it caused, partly because it served as an expedient to undermine the Protector's authority.

Most of the 82 ordinances passed by the Protector and his council were subsequently confirmed by parliament. They consisted of measures to con- tinue taxes and excise, for reorganizing the church, reforming the law, for union of Scotland with England, for consolidating the Treasury, for the reform of colleges, schools, and charitable foundations, and for the suppression of cockfighting, dueling, etc., etc. On the whole, this body of dictatorial legislation, abnormal in form as it is, in substance was a real, wise, and moderate set of reforms.

Taxation was throughout the great difficulty of the Protectorate, owing entirely to this: that parliament so long occupied itself with checkmating or upsetting the Protectorate itself. This drove Oliver to measures which in point of constitutional law are quite as illegal as any device of James or Charles. And when he proceeded to procure the conviction of Cony,[2] and actually sent to the Tower three eminent lawyers who claimed in his defense the ancient law of the land, it is open to anyone to argue that this was as arbitrary as anything in the case of ship money or the Impositions. The question for us is this: Was his arbitrary government in spirit and effect the same as that of Charles or James? As a matter of constitutional law the Protectorate as a whole is out of court altogether. Its sole plea is necessity. And though necessity is for the most part, as we know, the tyrant's plea, it is also at times the plea of the wise and just man in a great crisis.

If this arbitrary government had settled into a system, if it did not prepare for a return to a legal government by consent, Oliver stands con- demned as a tyrant and not a Protector. It is possible that the situation

---

[2] A merchant who refused to pay customs duties on the grounds that the Pro- tector had no right to tax without consent of parliament.

was itself inherently impracticable, and the difficulties it presented may have been insuperable. But such as they were, each year of Oliver's short rule showed them as diminishing, and his power to control them as growing. The ancient organization of England, political, judicial, administrative, ecclesiastical, and social—law, police, taxation, education, and government—had rested since the Conquest upon a king, a territorial church, and a privileged territorial aristocracy. First the church, and then the aristocracy, had broken away from the revolutionary movement and rallied round the king. Oliver found both fanatically hostile to Commonwealth and to himself. And he had to found order—parliamentary, judicial, administrative, and ecclesiastical—in a society where the old ministers of such order were bent on producing disorder. A permanent settlement was beyond the reach of human genius. Such temporary settlement as was possible Oliver made.

Apart from its dictatorial character, the Protector's government was efficient, just, moderate, and wise. Opposed as he was by lawyers, he made some of the best judges England ever had. Justice and law opened a new era. The services were raised to their highest efficiency. Trade and commerce revived under his fostering care. Education was reorganized; the universities reformed; Durham founded. It is an opponent who says: "All England over, these were Halcyon days." Men of learning of all opinions were encouraged and befriended. "If there was a man in England," says Neal, "who excelled in any faculty or science, the Protector would find him out, and reward him according to his merit." It was the Protector's brother-in-law, Warden of Wadham College, who there gathered together the group which ultimately founded the Royal Society.

Noble were the efforts of the Protector to impress his own spirit of toleration on the intolerance of his age; and stoutly he contended with parliaments and council for Quakers, Jews, Anabaptists, Socinians, and even crazy blasphemers. He effectively protected the Quakers; he admitted the Jews after an expulsion of three centuries; and he satisfied Mazarin that he had given to Catholics all the protection that he dared. . . .

Apart from opposition from his parliaments, the Protectorate was one unbroken success. Order, trade, commerce, justice, learning, culture, rest, and public confidence returned and grew ever stronger. Prosperity, wealth, harmony were restored to the nation; and with these a self-respect, a spirit of hope and expansion such as it had not felt since the defeat of the Armada. Never in the history of England has a reorganization of its administrative machinery been known at once so thorough and so sound. No royal government had ever annihilated insurrection and cabal with such uniform success, and with moderation so great. No government, not even that of Henry VII or of Elizabeth, had ever been more frugal; though none with its resources had effected so much. No government had ever been so tolerant in things of the mind; none so just in its dealings with classes and interests; none so eager to suppress abuses, official tyranny, waste and peculation. No government had been so distinctly modern in its spirit; so penetrated with desire for reform, honesty, capacity. For the first time in England the republican sense of social duty to the state began to replace the old spirit of personal loyalty to a sovereign. For the first and only time in modern Europe morality and religion became the sole qualifications insisted on by a court. In the whole modern history of Europe, Oliver is the one ruler into whose presence no vicious man could ever come; whose service no vicious man might enter.

But it was in foreign policy that the immediate splendor of Oliver's rule dazzled his contemporaries. "His greatness at home," wrote Clarendon, "was but a shadow of the glory he had abroad." Englishmen and English historians have hardly even yet taken the full measure of the stunning impression produced on Europe by the power of the Protector. It was the epoch when supremacy at sea finally passed from the Dutch to the English. It was the beginning of the maritime empire of England. And it was the first vision of a new force which was destined to exercise so great an influence, the increased power of fleets and marine artillery to destroy seaports and dominate a seaboard. Hitherto fleets had fought with fleets. But Blake taught modern Europe that henceforward fleets can control kingdoms. It was the sense of this new power, so rapid, so mobile, with so long an arm and practically ubiquitous, that caused Mazarin and Louis, Spain and Portugal, pope and princes of Italy to bow to the summons of Oliver. England became a European power of the first rank, as she never had been since the Plantagenets, not even in the proudest hours of Wolsey or Elizabeth. From the Baltic to the Mediterranean, from Algiers to Tenerife, from Newfoundland to Jamaica, were heard the English cannon. And the sense of this new factor in the politics of the world produced on the minds of the age such an impression as the rise of the German Empire with the consolidation of the German military system has produced upon our own. . . .

Cromwell's foreign policy had one consistent aim: to form a great Protestant alliance, and to place England at its head. It was a policy not of war but of defense; though peace was to be secured by the assertion of armed might on land and on sea. As a means to this end, it involved the destruction of the mercantile monopoly, first of the Dutch in Europe, and then of Spain in the west. In result, it placed England by one bound at the head of the powers of Europe; it laid the foundations of the naval supremacy of England, and also of her transmarine empire; could it have been maintained unbroken down to the age of William III, it would have changed the whole history of Europe, and the latter half of the reign of Louis XIV would have told a very different tale. Coming after the wars of religion, and before the dynastic wars and the commercial wars of the next hundred years, Cromwell's foreign policy was founded in part on religion, in part on trade. It was in no sense a policy of dynasty or of conquest. Had it been continued, it might have done much to prevent wars of dynasty and conquest. When the Commonwealth opened on the death of Charles I, England had sunk, both in credit and in power, to one of the lowest points known to her history. At the death of the Protector, she held a rank in the eyes of Europe such as she had never reached since the days of the Plantagenets, such as she has never reached since but in the time of Marlborough, Nelson, and Wellington.

The war which finally wrenched from the Dutch the supremacy at sea was the work of the Commonwealth. In this Cromwell shared, but his part was not so great as that of Vane or Blake. But it was his privilege to tell his first parliament, as Protector, that he had already made four honorable treaties of peace. Within four months he made peace with Holland, with Sweden, with Denmark, with Portugal; and was negotiating peace with France. "Peace is desirable with all men," he said, "so far as it may be had with conscience and honour!" "There is not a nation in Europe but is very willing to ask a good understanding with you." It was a proud saying—and it was true.

Though he long made some politic hesitations, it is plain that, from the first, he honestly designed an alliance with France and not with Spain. And in this he was right, not only from the point of view of his time, but on a just estimate of the state of Europe. The safety of the Protestant cause was by no means yet secured; Spain, and not France, was then the head of the Catholic and retrograde forces; and the free commerce of the ocean was impossible while the exclusive pretensions of Spain existed. When Blake's guns destroyed fleet after fleet of Spain, when Penn and Venables conquered Jamaica, when Lockhart's redcoats swept away Don John's veterans, Cromwell was true to his idea of a great Protestant alliance, with England at its head.

All through his rule he labored to unite the non-Catholic states— Sweden, Denmark, Holland, Brandenburg, and the other North German duchies, Switzerland, even Russia—"All the interests of the Protestants," he said, "are the same as yours"—regarding himself as the heir to the policy of Henry IV, of Elizabeth, of Gustavus Adolphus; preparing that of our own William of Orange. This policy reached its highest point in the magnificent burst of pity and indignation with which he championed the Vaudois against extermination: one of the noblest memories of England. It is seldom that in the history of a country national pride and moral elevation surround the same deed. It is seldom that the foremost states-man of an age joins to himself the foremost poet of his time in expressing in one voice the religion, the sympathy, the power, the generosity of a great nation. "Avenge, O Lord, Thy slaughtered Saints," wrote Oliver's secretary in verse....

The ... war policy of Oliver in Europe ... was an unbroken and daz-zling triumph. The history of England offers no such picture to national pride as when the kings and rulers of Europe courted, belauded, fawned on the farmer of Huntingdon. The record of English arms has no more brilliant page than that of Blake at Tenerife, of Lockhart at Dunkirk and Morgan at Ypres, when the Ironsides stormed unbreached forts and an-nihilated Spanish battalions, to the amazement of Turenne, Condé, and Don John.... "It was hard to discover," wrote Clarendon, "which feared him most, France, Spain, or the Low Countries"; "There is nothing he could have demanded that either of them would have denied him." But, as in his own age, so perhaps still, the memory of Cromwell has impressed itself on the imagination of foreigners more deeply than on that of his countrymen.... It is a philosopher of another country who has said: "Cromwell, with his lofty character, is the most enlightened statesman who ever adorned the Protestant world."

3. CROMWELL THE PURITAN IDEALIST

Dr. Robert S. Paul, Waldo Professor of Church History at the Hartford Seminary Foundation, Connecticut, has written perhaps the most favor-able study of Cromwell to appear since World War II, a period in which Cromwell has generally had a "good press." It will be evident from the following extract from his concluding chapter that Dr. Paul's principal interest is in Cromwell as a religious leader. But he is also concerned to assess the interaction between religion and politics, in a period when it is impossible to understand one without the other. His book was first published in England in 1955.

DR. ROBERT S. PAUL*

All through his life there is the consistent evidence of sincere personal religion and the influence of his theological and ecclesiastical concepts is too evident to be disregarded or explained away as merely the thought forms of his day. They were the thought forms of his day, but there was all heaven and hell behind them.

In 1656 the Venetian ambassador wrote of the Protector, "It cannot be denied that by his ability and industry he has contributed to his own greatness," but he added, "with all his abounding courage, good sense and natural prudence, all these qualities would have served him for nothing if circumstances had not opened the way to greatness." The Italian envoy perhaps would not have appreciated the religious significance of his own words, but it was in the amazing circumstances of his own career that Cromwell discerned and tested the validity of the divine call that he believed was his. That strict doctrine of Providence which held with John Calvin that "the righteous are the special objects of His favour, the wicked and profane the special objects of His severity" was not only the stimulus of Cromwell's single-minded purpose throughout the civil wars, and the foundation of his claim to a vocation of statesmanship, but during the vicissitudes of the Protectorate it was also the one sure anchor of hope that God would be with him to the end. It is possible to criticize this interpretation of Providence, or the exclusive view of "Election" and "Grace" in Calvinism, or the literal biblicism and extravagant apocalyptic hopes of Puritanism, but however much these ideas may be criticized, they were factors, and often governing factors, in conditioning the life and thought of 17th-century England, and we disregard them only at the expense of misinterpreting the period.

In the same way it is possible to ridicule the idea of a troop of cavalry or council of army officers organized as a "gathered Church," but it was recognized by Richard Baxter[1] after Naseby, and that keen critic admitted the honesty of Cromwell's intention when he said, "I conjecture, that at his first choosing such men into his Troop, it was the very Esteem and Love of Religious men that principally moved him." Sir Ernest Barker has commented that "The habit of the Independents was always a habit of congregationalism. Even the Independent army debated, because it

---

* Robert S. Paul, *The Lord Protector: Religion and Politics in the Life of Oliver Cromwell* (Grand Rapids, Mich.: William B. Eerdmans Publishing Co., 1964), pp. 384–87, 390–93. Reprinted with permission of William B. Eerdmans Co.

[1] One of the leading Presbyterian clergy, and therefore not a wholehearted admirer of Cromwell.

was a congregation as well as an army." In Baxter's testimony, in the nature of the army council and its discussions, and in the continuous influence of the army's opinion on Cromwell's own decisions, we see that these words were true not only in a general sense, but also in the particular and personal sense of a man's relationship with his "Church."

It is within this kind of setting that Oliver Cromwell saw his own divinely appointed task on behalf of the people of England—or perhaps more accurately, on behalf of the "godly" people of England. He was only accidentally—or "providentially"—a soldier and a statesman, and he owned few political theories that could be regarded as inviolable. It was "lawfull to passe through any formes of Government for the accomplishing his ends," and he reminded the army officers in 1647 that the Hebrews had experimented with several different kinds of government. "If you should change the government to the best of it," he commented, "it is but, as Paul says, 'dross and dung in comparison of Christ'": forms of government, no less than individuals, were to be brought under the judgment of the biblical revelation, and the proof of divine approval was to be sought in that "chain of Providence" by which nations and individuals are led.

It might be thought at first that because Cromwell's sense of vocation was based upon personal experience it therefore must have been entirely subjective—an arbitrary declaration of his own purpose that brooked no argument or interference: "Come, come, I will put an end to your prating... call them in, call them in!"[2] A closer study, however, will show that his sense of vocation is not to be dismissed so summarily, for it was endorsed not only by the actual success of his undertakings, but it was also tested by the Word of Scripture. The importance of these factors can be seen when Cromwell's career is compared with more modern dictators, for whereas his conception of duty might lead him to act dictatorially, it could never lead him to act amorally, much less contrary to biblical morality insofar as he understood it: Cromwell might misinterpret the biblical standards, he might be guilty of faulty exegesis, but he could never deliberately mishandle Scripture, for he had placed himself under the judgment of its revelation. Similarly with regard to the doctrine of Providence, he could not believe that God was with him, unless he could assure himself of a clean conscience; for, according to his own beliefs, his success was entirely due to the singleness of purpose with which he and his troops had tried to obey God's will. There may be occasions when we are able to discern beneath Oliver's passionate assertions of high calling

---

[2] Cromwell's words when he called in his soldiers to dissolve the Rump in April, 1653.

the shape of less worthy motives, but he never gives any indication in private letter or public utterance that these motives were consciously recognized by him: Cromwell acted like a prophet, and the true prophet "is one who can say with Paul, 'I was not disobedient to the heavenly vision.'"

Throughout his public life we see the future Lord Protector struggling to reconcile these fundamental convictions first with the military and political needs of the nation, second with his own responsibility within the nation, and finally with the position of the English Protectorate within the context of world affairs. . . .

Of all the Protector's experiments, the one which would most repay careful study is his settlement of religion. Since 1660 it has never received the attention it deserved, no doubt partly because it had had such a short time in which to justify itself—a matter of five or six years—and partly because it had been brought into being by a discredited government.

By the *Instrument of Government* and the *Humble Petition and Advice,* "the Christian religion as contained in the Scriptures" was established as the officially recognized religion of the three nations of Britain. A Profession of Faith was compiled, and all ministers who agreed with this statement, although differing in matters of worship and discipline, were to be "fit and capable . . . of any trust, promotion or employment whatsoever in these nations." By this means the Protector established not a particular church with its individual orders and theory of church government but the Christian Protestant religion; for the first time in history the state had established an ecclesiastical system in which more than one form of churchmanship was recognized and was able to take its full part. . . .

Cromwell became a "dictator," but it was not from choice. Events had their own way of pushing him to the fore and ultimately to the head of affairs, and the very circumstances of his rise prevented that popular recognition which would have set the seal to his mission. Nevertheless, although only a person "mistaken and greatly mistaken" would imagine that he consciously schemed for the position which he came to occupy, when the chance of taking the government presented itself he took it firmly. It is within that paradox that what he did sometimes seems to belie what he said.

Yet to suggest a fundamental hypocrisy—whether on the grounds advanced by 17th-century royalists, or on those put forward by 20th-century realists—is to offer a solution too simple to be acceptable. It is too simple because it ignores what is perhaps the most singular fact of Cromwell's career—that throughout the vast accumulation of his uttered thought that has come down to us, never once does he admit a lesser motive in private conversation, public speech, or in his most intimate correspondence. No man could have forwarded his own self-interest to achieve a public career of such magnitude without giving some hints of his ambition in word or letter, if personal ambition were the only or even the predominant motive of the career; and yet few men in history appear to have acted more consistently and with a clearer conscience than Oliver Cromwell. The explanation of this can only be that within Cromwell's own mind his ambition was itself the instrument of a greater cause which he served with absolute sincerity.

When we have given due weight to the motives of self-interest and preservation, and when we have faced the fact that the Independents had either to rule or pay the penalty for their rebellion, there remains a paradox within Cromwell's career which has a religious cause; for although religion was not the original occasion for the outbreak of civil war, "God brought it to that issue at last," Oliver said, "and gave it unto us by way of redundancy, and at last it proved to be that which was most dear to us." To Oliver himself the issue of religion had become central, and it was simply the issue of winning liberty for "all species of Protestants, to worship God according to their own light and consciences," but the paradox is in the fact that this liberty could be guaranteed in no other way but by his own personal rule: Episcopalian king, Presbyterian parliament, Sectarian convention—they all gave ample evidence of the "strange itch" of persecution that Cromwell feared and detested. He had to rule, or else be prepared to see the religious freedom that he prized above all other earthly benefits disappear either into the prison of uniformity or into a madhouse of anarchy. It was the major tragedy of his rule that in defending one liberty he seemed to threaten all the rest, that in standing as the champion of freedom he often appeared as the epitome of tyranny.

Nevertheless we must ask ourselves whether at that time religious liberty could have been won in any other way. Amid the political dangers of our own day, if this essential freedom should again be put in jeopardy, who could say now how it could best be defended, or what forms of government would be justifiable in its defense? Perhaps a good dictatorship must always be bad government but Oliver Cromwell believed that both spiritual coercion and political anarchy were infinitely worse. It was for this reason that his deepest convictions and his own advancement became identified, and the Lord's "unprofitable servant" accepted the call to become his country's Lord Protector.

4. CROMWELL THE CONSERVATIVE
BACKBENCHER

Hugh Trevor-Roper, Regius Professor of Modern History at Oxford, is one of the most pungent and iconoclastic of living British historians. Besides a brilliant book on Adolf Hitler, and many provocative essays and reviews on modern subjects, he has published a study of Charles I's great adviser, Archbishop Laud (1940), and several important contributions to the recent acrimonious debate over the social causes of the Puritan Revolution. In the most elaborate of these, The Gentry, 1540–1640 *(1953), he attacked R. H. Tawney's hypothesis that the Revolution was the work of a "rising gentry" class. Trevor-Roper advanced instead the argument, reflected in the following essay, that the parliamentarians, especially the Independents, represented a "declining gentry" unable to survive during a period of inflation on the revenues of their lands alone, and thus desperately seeking to capture the vast patronage resources of the court, but with few constructive aims of their own.*

HUGH TREVOR-ROPER*

Oliver Cromwell and his parliaments—the theme is almost a tragicomedy. Cromwell was himself a member of parliament; he was the appointed general of the armies of parliament; and the Victorians, in the greatest days of parliamentary government, set up his statue outside the rebuilt Houses of Parliament. But what were Cromwell's relations with parliament? The Long Parliament, which appointed him, he first purged by force and then violently expelled from authority. His own parliament, the Parliament of Saints, which to a large extent was nominated by his government, was carried away by hysteria, rent by intrigue, and dissolved, after six months, by an undignified act of suicide. Of the parliaments of the Protectorate, elected on a new franchise and within new limits determined by the government, the first was purged by force within a week

* H. R. Trevor-Roper, "Oliver Cromwell and his Parliaments," in Richard Pares and A. J. P. Taylor (eds.), *Essays Presented to Sir Lewis Namier* (London: Macmillan & Co., Ltd., 1956), pp. 1–3, 5–11, 45–48. This essay will also appear in a forthcoming collection of essays by Trevor-Roper, *Religion, the Reformation, and Social Change,* to be published by Macmillan. Reprinted with permission of Macmillan & Co., Ltd.

and dissolved, by a trick hardly distinguishable from fraud, before its legal term; the second was purged by fraud at the beginning and, when that fraud was reversed, became at once unmanageable and was dissolved within a fortnight. On a superficial view, Cromwell was as great an enemy of parliament as ever Charles I or Archbishop Laud had been, the only difference being that, as an enemy, he was more successful: he scattered all his parliaments and died in his bed, while theirs deprived them of their power and brought them both ultimately to the block.

Nevertheless, between Cromwell and the Stuarts, in this matter, there was a more fundamental difference than this; for even if he could never control his parliaments in fact, Cromwell at least never rejected them in theory. This is not because he was deliberately consistent with his own parliamentary past. Cromwell was deliberately consistent in nothing. No political career is so full of undefended inconsistencies as his. But he was fundamentally and instinctively conservative, and he saw in parliament part of the natural order of things. He did not regard it, as Archbishop Laud had regarded it, as "that hydra" or "that noise": he regarded it as the necessary legislature of England; and it was merely, in his eyes, an unfortunate and incomprehensible accident that his own particular parliaments consistently fell below the traditional standard of usefulness. Therefore again and again he summoned and faced them; again and again he wrestled with the hydra, sought to shout down the noise; and again and again, in the end, like the good man in a tragedy, caught in the trap of his own weakness, he resorted to force and fraud, to purges, expulsions, and recriminations. He descended like Moses from Sinai upon the naughty children of Israel, smashing in turn the divine constitutions he had obtained for them; and the surprised and indignant members, scattered before their time, went out from his presence overwhelmed with turbid oratory, protestations of his own virtue and their waywardness, romantic reminiscences, proprietary appeals to the Lord, and great broken gobbets from the Pentateuch and the Psalms.

Why was Oliver Cromwell so uniformly unsuccessful with his parliaments? To answer this question we must first look a little more closely at the aims and character both of Oliver Cromwell and of that opposition to the court of Charles I of which he was first an obscure and ultimately the most powerful representative . . . the backwoods gentry who, in 1640, sat on the back benches of parliament, but who, as war and revolution progressed, gradually broke through the crumbling leadership which had at first contained them: the "Independents."

Now these "Independent" gentry, it is important to emphasize, were not, as a class, revolutionary: that is, they did not hold revolutionary ideas.

There were revolutionaries among the Independents, of course. There were revolutionaries in parliament, men like "Harry Marten and his gang" . . . ; just as there were also revolutionaries outside parliament: the Levellers and the Fifth Monarchy Men.[1] But if these men were the successive sparks which kindled the various stages of revolution, they were not the essential tinder of it. The majority of the members of parliament, who at first accidentally launched the revolutionary movement and were afterward borne along or consumed by it, were not clearheaded men like these. They were not thinkers or even dreamers, but plain, conservative, untraveled country gentlemen. . . . These were the men who formed the solid stuff of parliamentary opposition to Charles I: men whose social views were conservative enough, but whose political passions were radical, and became more radical as they discovered depth below depth of royal duplicity. These were the men who became, in time, the Independents; and Cromwell, though he transcended them in personality and military genius, was their typical, if also their greatest, representative. . . .

And what were the positive ideals of these outraged but largely unpolitical conservative gentry? Naturally, in the circumstances, they were not very constructive. These men looked back, not forward: back from the House of Stuart which had so insulted them to the House of Tudor of which their fathers had spoken, and in the reign of Elizabeth they discovered, or invented, a golden age: an age when the court had been, as it seemed, in harmony with the country and the Crown with its parliaments; an age when a Protestant queen, governing parsimoniously at home and laying only tolerable burdens on "her faithful Commons," had nevertheless made England glorious abroad—head of "the Protestant interest" throughout the world, victor over Spain in the Indies, protector of the Netherlands in Europe. Since 1603 that glorious position had been lost. King James had alienated the gentry, abandoned Protestantism for Arminian policy at home and popish alliances abroad, made peace with Spain, and surrendered, with the "cautionary towns," the protectorate over the Netherlands. When the religious struggle had broken out anew in Europe, it was not the king of England who had inherited the mantle of Queen Elizabeth as defender of the Protestant faith: it was a new champion from the North, the king of Sweden. . . .

Such were the basic political views, or prejudices, of the English backbenchers who poured into parliament in 1640. But they had social views also, and these too led them back to the same golden age of the

---

[1] The most extreme Puritan enthusiasts, who anticipated the imminent establishment of the "Fifth Monarchy," the reign of King Jesus, in which the saints would rule.

Protestant queen. First there was the desire for decentralization—the revolt of the provinces and of the provincial gentry not only against the growing, parasitic Stuart court but also against the growing, "dropsical" city of London, against the centralized church, whether Anglican or Presbyterian, and against the expensive monopoly of higher education by the two great universities. All this was implied in the Independent program. And also, what we must never forget, for it was a great element in the Protestant tradition, there was the demand for an organic society responsible for the welfare of its members. . . .

Such was the common denominator of positive philosophy shared by many of the backbench members of parliament in 1640, as it emerges, by way of protest, from their pamphlets, their diaries, their letters to their patrons, their parliamentary ejaculations both before and after that crucial date. It is astonishing how faithfully it is reflected in the letters and speeches, as afterward in the groping policy, of Oliver Cromwell. "Reformation of law and clergy," social justice for the "poor people of God" secured not by radical revolution but by patriarchal benevolence, a revival of the glories of "Queen Elizabeth of famous memory"—a protectorate over the Netherlands, a privateering war in the West Indies, and the leadership of "the Protestant interest" in Europe—all these recur in his later policy. Even the uncritical worship of Gustavus Adolphus is there. . . .

In 1640 Oliver Cromwell was still, like the other country gentry who had followed their patrons to Westminster, a mere backbencher, a lesser ally of his relatives the Barringtons, John Hampden, and Oliver St. John, a client of the earl of Warwick. . . . None of them dreamed, in 1640, of revolution, either in church or in state. They were neither separatists nor republicans. What they wanted was a king who, unlike Charles I, but like the Queen Elizabeth of their imagination, would work the existing institutions in the good old sense; bishops who, unlike the Laudian bishops, but like Bishop Hall or Archbishop Ussher, would supervise their flocks in the good old sense of "the sweet and noble" Anglican, Richard Hooker. At first they hoped that King Charles would adjust himself, would jettison a few Stuart innovations, give a few guarantees, and become such a king of the state, such a supreme governor of the church. It was only when King Charles had shown himself quite unadjustable that revolution, though unwanted, took place, generating its own momentum and driving basically conservative men to radical acts such as they would never have imagined before and would shudder to recollect afterward, and facing them with fundamental problems of which they had never previously thought. It was only by an extraordinary and quite unpredictable turn of events that one of these backbenchers, Oliver Cromwell, having ruined all existing institutions, found himself, in 1649, faced with the responsibility of achieving, or restoring, the lost balance of society. . . .

Cromwell was not a radical or an intellectual or a young man. He did not want to continue the revolution, which had already, in his eyes and in the eyes of his fellow gentry, got out of control. He wanted to stop it, to bring it under control, to bring "settlement" after an unfortunate but, as it had turned out, unavoidable period of "blood and confusion." Nor did he believe in new constitutions, or indeed in any constitutions at all. He did not believe, as some of his more wooden colleagues believed, in the divine right of republics any more than in the divine right of kings. Forms of government were to him "but a mortal thing," "dross and dung compared with Christ," and therefore in themselves quite indifferent. He was not, he once said, "wedded or glued to forms of government": had not the ancient Hebrews, God's own people, fared equally well, according to circumstances, under patriarchs, judges, and kings? Acceptability, or as he called it, "acceptance," was to him the only test of right government. In his indignation against Charles I he might denounce monarchy, but in cooler moments he would admit that a government "with something monarchical in it" was probably the most acceptable, and therefore the best. In his indignation against the earl of Manchester he might express his hope of living "to see never a nobleman in England"; but in cooler moments he could insist that "a nobleman, a gentleman, a yeoman" were "the ranks and orders of men whereby England hath been known for hundreds of years," and that "nobility and gentry" must be kept up. Fundamentally, in his eyes, it was the fault of persons, not of institutions, which had been fatal to the *ancien régime:* "the King's head was not taken off because he was King, nor the Lords laid aside because Lords, neither was the Parliament dissolved because they were a Parliament, but because they did not perform their trust." In politics Oliver Cromwell was not a theorist or a doctrinaire, but an opportunist.

Opportunists who do not believe in the necessity of particular constitutions take what lies nearest to hand, and what lay nearest to Cromwell's hand when he found himself called upon to restore his ideal Elizabethan society was naturally the surviving debris of the Elizabethan constitution. Parliament had been savaged—and by none more than himself—but its rump was there; the king had been destroyed, but he himself stood, if somewhat incongruously, in his place. Naturally he saw himself as a new Queen Elizabeth—or rather, being a humble man, as a regent for a new Queen Elizabeth; and he prepared, like her, to summon a series of deferential parliaments. Surely, since he was one of them, and since they all earnestly pursued the same honest ideal, the members would agree with him, just as they had agreed with "that Lady, that great Queen"? Surely he had only to address them in the Painted Chamber, to commend them in a few eloquent phrases, to leave them to their harmonious deliberations, and then, having received from them a few "good laws," to dismiss them, in due time, amid applause, complimentingly, with a "Golden Speech"?

Alas, as we know, it did not happen thus. It was not with golden speeches that Cromwell found himself dismissing his parliaments, but with appeals to heaven, torrents of abuse—and force. This was not merely because the basis of legitimacy and consent were lacking: Queen Elizabeth, like Cromwell, was disputed in her title, and Cromwell, like Queen Elizabeth, was personally indispensable even to those extremists who chafed at his conservatism. The fatal flaw was elsewhere. . . .

Oliver Cromwell's successive efforts to govern with and through parliament failed, and failed abjectly. They failed through lack of that parliamentary management by the executive which, in the correct dosage, is the essential nourishment of any sound parliamentary life. As always with Cromwell, there is an element of tragic irony in his failure: his very virtues caused him to blunder into courses from which he could escape only by the most unvirtuous, inconsistent, and indefensible expedients. And the ultimate reason of this tragic, ironical failure lies, I think, in the very character of Cromwell and of the Independency which he so perfectly represented. Cromwell himself, like his followers, was a natural backbencher. He never understood the subtleties of politics, never rose above the simple political prejudices of those other backwoods squires whom he had joined in their blind revolt against the Stuart court. His first speech in parliament had been the protest of a provincial squire against popish antics in his own parish church; and at the end, as ruler of three kingdoms, he still compared himself only with a bewildered parish constable seeking laboriously and earnestly to keep the peace in a somewhat disorderly and incomprehensible parish. His conception of government was the rough justice of a benevolent, serious-minded, rural magistrate: well-intentioned, unsophisticated, summary, patriarchal, conservative. Such was also the political philosophy of many other English squires who, in the 17th century, turned up in parliament and, sitting patiently on the back benches, either never understood or, at most, deeply suspected the secret mechanism whereby the back benches were controlled from the front. In ordinary times the natural fate of such men was to stay at the back, and to make a virtue of their "honesty," their "independency." . . . But the 1640's and 1650's were not ordinary times. Then a revolutionary situation thrust these men forward, and in their indignation they hacked down, from behind, the sharp politicians and courtiers, the royalists and Presbyterians, who had first mobilized them. Having no clear political ideas, they did not—except in the brief period when they surrendered to the republican usurpers—destroy institutions, but only persons. They destroyed parliamentarians and the king, but not parliament or the throne. These institutions, in their fury, they simply cleaned out and left momentarily vacant. But before long the vacancy was refilled. By careful tests and a new franchise, parliament was reopened—to Independents (that is, backbenchers) only; under careful reservations and a new title, the throne was reoccupied—by an Independent (that is, a backbench) ruler. At last, it seemed, Crown and Commons were in natural harmony.

Alas, in political matters natural harmony is not enough. To complete the system, and to make it work, something else was necessary too: an Independent political caucus that would constitute an Independent front bench as a bridge between Crown and parliament, like those Tudor privy councillors who gave consistency and direction to the parliaments of Henry VIII and Elizabeth. Unfortunately this was the one thing which Cromwell always refused to provide. . . . His ideal was an Elizabethan parliament, but his methods were such as would lead to a Polish Diet. Consequently, each of his parliaments, deprived of leadership from him, fell in turn under other leadership and were then treated by him in a manner which made them feel far from free. . . .

Ironically, the one English sovereign who had actually been a member of parliament proved himself, as a parliamentarian, the most incompetent of them all. . . . He failed even more dismally than the Stuarts. The tragedy is that whereas they did not believe in the system, he did.

Leonard M. Marsak, Professor of History at the University of California, Santa Barbara, was born in New York City in 1924. He received B.S., M.A., and Ph.D. degrees from Cornell University and formerly taught history and the humanities at Reed College, Wellesley, Massachusetts Institute of Technology, and Rice University. He is the author of *Bernard de Fontenelle: The Idea of Science in the French Enlightenment* (Philadelphia, 1959); and of numerous articles in the field of intellectual history and the social history of science. He also is the editor of *French Philosophers from Descartes to Sartre* (Cleveland, 1961); *The Rise of Science in Relation to Society* (New York, 1964); and *The Achievement of Bernard le Bovier de Fontenelle* (New York, 1967). He is a member of the American Historical Association.

CHAPTER SEVEN

LEONARD M. MARSAK

University of California at Santa Barbara

The Contribution of
Sir Isaac Newton

THE ACHIEVEMENT OF Sir Isaac Newton is normally accounted the zenith of the scientific revolution of the 17th century, and with good reason. Newton accomplished the great synthesis of terrestrial and celestial mechanics, and did so in a ratio that is notable for its simplicity: every particle of matter attracts every other with a force varying directly as the product of their masses, and inversely as the square of the distance between them. This law is taught to students everywhere. Once the law is learned by the prospective scientist he can turn with comfort to more contemporary problems in science. There is no Newton problem for him unless he should try to fathom the mathematics that Newton employed in his proofs. Then why should historians and scholars concern themselves with Newton, and in ways that seem purely antiquarian to the scientist? The answer lies partly in the difference between science and history, partly in the fact that knowledge of the law does not provide us automatically with knowledge about it, that while we know the meaning of Newton's work, we are not sure about its significance. Insofar as Newton exemplifies the Scientific Revolution of the 17th century, when science was called "The New Philosophy," we are asking questions about the significance of science itself. What then are the questions that historians and philosophers ask about Newton?

Newton's impact on the 18th century has often been described in terms of the watchmaker God who set the world in motion and then left

201

it to run by itself, with only a little tinkering needed from time to time to keep it in repair. But is this the God Newton himself worshipped? Is it the only God compatible with the new view of the universe? Newton set the keystone to the work of Kepler and Galileo, thus completing the arch of classical physics through which formal philosophy progressed to the conclusions of David Hume and Immanuel Kant. Galileo, Descartes, and Newton had stripped the world bare of sensible reality to define it anew as matter in motion. Such a redefinition of subject matter, Hume and Kant insisted, can be given only in terms of the scientists' methodology, or the way scientists themselves construct truths. Is scientific reality, then, a creation of the human mind to be compared with other creations, like poetry, that satisfy man's longing for truth? If so, what becomes of science's much-vaunted objectivity? Why do many of us find its explanations more satisfying than those of poetry or religion? In asking these questions we seek to know three things: what Newton really said about the universe and our capacity for knowing it; what his assumptions were, and their implications for an understanding of the origins of modern science; and finally, how we may assess the Newtonian achievement in its impact on our lives.

Historians of science like A. Rupert Hall have pointed out the importance of mathematics to the scientific revolution of the 17th century; for mathematics became at that time the language of science, the shorthand or language of metaphor, a necessary complement to experiment's language of analysis. Hence Sir Francis Bacon's inattention to mathematics gave rise to the charge that he criticized science like a lord chancellor. No such charge could be leveled against Newton. He was perhaps the greatest mathematical genius in a century that counted many; but he was a scientist as well, who successfully linked mathematics to experiment to become a model methodologist for his successors. However, mathematics was more than a useful tool of exposition to Newton. At its deepest level it expressed to him God's law of nature. We know that Newton became a secret Unitarian; some scholars have argued for the Jewishness of his God. Whether Newton's God was lawgiver in the scientific or in the biblical sense, he was at any rate, as Professor Hall says, "a God of law and certainty, not a God of hope and fear, of punishment and reward," and not the Christian God of his contemporaries. This was understood in the 18th century by philosophers who were intent on secularizing their world and who, as a consequence, believed in the warfare of science with theology. Newton himself believed otherwise. Nevertheless, from Newton's time man has had to reckon with the universe knowing that it is no longer comfortably closed but infinite, and has had to find his satisfaction in the universe in accordance with that knowledge.

J. M. Keynes would have us view Newton not as the first of the modern scientists but as the last of the magicians who sought to read the riddle of God's universe. It was less an exercise in conscious methodology, Keynes argued, than superb intuition that provided Newton with the answer to the riddle. Perhaps Newton's science was magical in substance too, for what else is magic but the effort to dominate nature by penetrating her secrets? If such is the case then science in general may be simply a variety of magic more successful than earlier efforts to win power over nature. So successful has science been in this endeavor that, dazzled by it, we are on the point of losing interest in other human goals equally traditional though less power seeking. And what becomes of our quest for control over nature should the sorcerer's apprentices in our midst act as we can expect them to do, with less than full responsibility? To judge by the reaction of his contemporaries to his discoveries, Newton's mathematics had provided them with a magical formula that in its various scientific and social applications would make all things possible, including happiness for the human race.

Newton supplied us with the law of universal gravitation, but as Professor E. W. Strong points out the law "explains" nothing. It simply describes or gives an operational definition of the phenomena. Newton never pretended to know what gravitation is (unless it is synonymous with God), but only how it works. Strong sees Newton, therefore, as the model of the modern scientist, which is to say, as a master methodologist who made his imagination conform to the exigencies of verifiable fact. Even so, Newton made certain assumptions of a metaphysical kind that are unproved and perhaps unprovable. Foremost was his assumption that nature is uniform, which was essential to his work. Indeed, without it no science would ever be done, for if we changed our view of nature with every exception to its behavior we would never come to those generalized explanations which are the mark of science. Denoting each and every specific form of behavior is the way of the primitive mind. Yet the assumption of uniformity cannot be proved until all the evidence is in, and this can never be the case till man has reached the end of his career, or at least the end of his scientific endeavors. Scientific knowledge, therefore, is probable knowledge only. David Hume understood this perfectly when he devised a skeptical philosophy based entirely on the Newtonian achievement. He even went so far as to announce that the principle of cause and effect is another metaphysical assumption that may rest on nothing more firm than our faith in its occurrence. Science is forced to its own act of faith which can never yield absolute certainty.

What then are we to make of Newton's statement that he feigned no hypotheses when we note that they lie at the heart of his work? As S. I.

Vavilov demonstrates, Newton sought additional hypotheses in the works of antiquity, and his borrowings turned out to be especially fruitful for the subsequent development of science. Historians of science would insist that by hypotheses Newton meant the "philosophical romances" he sought to avoid, and these he would bar from the scientific enterprise. But how are we to know before the fact which are romances and which are not? Is Newton's reliance on God to explain action at a distance, and his obvious reverence for Him, to be dismissed as a philosophical romance? We can do altogether without God in the Newtonian system if we can be satisfied with less than certainty, but the evidence suggests that Newton himself sought absolute certainty in scientific fact. The Newtonian world view looks very much like any other, a conceptual system that turns gradually to complete the circle, but such a one as to be without peer in the modern world.

Here we offer a dissenting view by R. G. Collingwood, who argues that the metaphysical assumptions Newton made and accepted from antiquity were not handled well at all, and that without a suitable metaphysics the Newtonian achievement is not very much. Doubtless Newton remains a superb mathematician, but this does not speak for the profundity of his mind, which is revealed, in fact, to be shallow in his philosophical and historical speculations. Newton stood on the shoulders of giants, and his contribution was simply one more brick, although a large one, to the scientific edifice. If that is the case, then what can we say about science itself, which is epitomized by Newton's achievement? In its facticity science is the work of gifted minds that may never be given to self-conscious thought. Even the most gifted scientist may be no more than a highly trained technician. Insofar as the scientist is a self-conscious thinker he must be judged as a philosopher, and it is here that Collingwood's bias is revealed; for in *The Idea of History* he concludes that history and philosophy are more subtle and profound studies than science, which cannot in itself give meaning to our lives. It may be the task of science in our time to clear the underbrush for more fruitful mental activity that will allow us to feel at home in our world.

We are the heirs to the mathematical dispensation of the 17th century. For those of us who enjoy the power of mathematics Newton is the Moses of the modern age. But for those who seek other satisfactions Newton has often seemed an arid personality, and his achievement a mixed blessing. The student of history who approaches Newton has more to think about than Newton's contribution to science, for inevitably the question is raised which only the student himself can answer: What is the meaning of the Scientific Revolution of modern times and what is its present significance? His view of Newton and of modern science will be governed by the answer he gives to that question.

1. NEWTON, THE MATHEMATICIAN

Professor A. Rupert Hall is a historian of science who has published extensively on the 17th century. In the accompanying selection he tells how the Principia *came to be written, and suggests that it was as a mathematician that Newton made his distinctive contribution to science.*

A. RUPERT HALL*

How the *Principia* came to be written is a well-known story. By 1684, besides Newton and Hooke, Halley and Wren were intuitively convinced of the inverse-square law of gravitation. None of the three last could derive orbits from that law mathematically. Halley, a young and energetic man, made a special journey to Cambridge to put the problem to the mathematical professor: "What would be the curve described by the planets on the supposition that gravity diminished as the square of the distance?"

Newton immediately answered, *an Ellipse.* Struck with joy and amazement, Halley asked him how he knew it? Why, he replied, I have calculated it; and being asked for the calculation, he could not find it, but promised to send it to him (Halley).[1]

Newton had carelessly mislaid what other brilliant men with their best efforts could not find out! Reworking his calculation, Newton realized it could hardly stand by itself; it required, to be convincing and clear, axioms, definitions, subsidiary propositions—in short, a demonstration of the use of mathematical reasoning in handling problems of mechanics. Within a few days or weeks he had decided to devote his lectures of the approaching Michaelmas Term, 1684, to *The Motions of Bodies.* Two or three months later, in October, he began to read a text that is substantially that of Book I of the *Principia.* Next month some of its propositions were despatched to Halley, in fulfillment of his promise, who hastened off to

---

* Pp. 292–98, 301–4 *From Galileo to Newton 1630–1720* by A. Rupert Hall. Copyright © 1963 by A. Rupert Hall. Reprinted by permission of Harper & Row, Publishers.

[1] The quotations are from the account of Newton's nephew-in-law John Conduitt (Ball, 26 etc.), which is confirmed by Halley's letters.

Cambridge a second time to persuade Newton to lay his work before the Royal Society. His wish prevailed, and Newton set to work to revise and expand his lectures, but the *Philosophiae Naturalis Principia Mathematica* ("Mathematical Principles of Natural Philosophy") assumed its ultimate form only gradually during the next two years.

In 1686, when Book I was duly presented to the Royal Society, Hooke and Newton quarreled for the fourth and final time. It was a quarrel that led to Hooke's virtual retirement from the Society during the last years of his life; that strengthened Newton's desire to abandon the university and science; and that prevented the publication of *Opticks* until after Hooke's death. No doubt Hooke's charge of plagiarism against Newton was no more unjust than Newton's neglect of Hooke's just claims to recognition. Yet Newton could rightly assert that he had far surpassed Hooke— no comparison between their achievements is possible; his countercharge that he had learned nothing from Hooke, who had proved nothing, was fair; but his jealous temperament swayed him into injustice when he proceeded to deny that Hooke had accomplished anything at all. In the course of his outpourings against Hooke, in letters to Halley (who had undertaken to pay for the printing of the *Principia* and see it through the press), Newton made some remarks of more than partisan importance underlining the obstacles that he had surmounted before the *Principia* could be written. The first, naturally, was the proof that the inverse-square law yielded an elliptical orbit. (Or, more generally, a conic which may be closed [ellipse and circle] or open [parabola].) To the discovery of the law itself he attached little importance, since it was obvious after Huygens' book of 1673. The difficulty was to prove it for the astronomical ellipses as a mathematically exact law, not to infer it for circles.

There is so strong an objection against the accurateness of this (inverse-square) proportion (Newton added) that without my demonstrations, to which Mr Hooke is yet a stranger, it cannot be believed by a judicious philosopher to be anywhere accurate.[2]

By this Newton meant that on the evidence any competent physicist would recognize the impossibility of the law's exactness; only a mathematician could turn the tables and demonstrate that—paradoxically—it was perfectly exact and physically sufficient. Kepler, said Newton (rather unreasonably), had guessed that the planetary ovals were geometric ellipses; his own demonstrations proved at one and the same time the mathematical precision of both the inverse-square law and the ellipses.

Secondly, Newton recollected,

---

[2] *Correspondence*, Vol. II, p. 437, Newton to Halley, June 20, 1686.

I never extended the duplicate proportion lower than to the superficies of the Earth, and before a certain demonstration I found the last year (1685), have suspected it did not reach accurately enough so low.[3]

It was a ready inference for Newton that the gravitational force must reside in the ultimate particles of matter, if it is a property of gross bodies. Now, even such astronomically adjacent bodies as the earth and moon are so distant that the lines drawn between any two particles in these bodies could be considered parallel and of the same length, hence it was easy to see that the total force was the sum of the forces of the particles. In the case of a body only a few feet above the earth's surface, like an apple on a tree, the situation was quite different. How could the summation of particulate forces be effected in this case, and where would the center of force in the earth be located? In the *Principia* Newton confessed his doubt that the common-sense way of thinking would work:

After I had found that the force of gravity towards a whole planet did arise from and was compounded of the forces of gravity towards all its parts, and towards every one part was in the inverse proportion of the squares of the distances from the part, I was yet in doubt whether that proportion as the square of the distance did accurately hold, or but nearly so, in the total force compounded of so many partial ones; for it might be that the proportion that was accurate enough at greater distances would be wide of the truth near the surface of the planet, where the distances of the particles are unequal, and their situations dissimilar.[4]

Doubt was removed by a group of theorems in which Newton integrated mathematically the individual forces arising from the infinitely numerous particles of two solid spheres. (*Principia*, Book I, Propositions LXX to LXXVII.) They proved that the centripetal (or gravitational) forces between two spheres "increases or decreases in proportion to the distance between their centers according to the same law as applies to the particles themselves. And this is a noteworthy fact."[5] Once more mathematics demonstrated a physical improbability as truth: the sphere acted on any body outside it, however close, from its own center; and this was true of any law of attraction. But if the inverse-square law applied outside the sphere, then inside it the attraction to the center was directly as the distance.

Here were at least two instances where the physical or imaginative implausibility of the inverse-square law could only be corrected by mathematical reasoning. Newton was claiming, in effect—and he was

---

[3] *Ibid.*, p. 435.

[4] *Principia*, Motte-Cajori, pp. 415–16.

[5] *Ibid.* (1687), p. 203. I have tried to improve upon Motte-Cajori, pp. 202–3.

right—that his great achievement lay not in imagining a physical hypothesis (to which there were grave objections that qualitative physical thinking could not surmount) but in proving mathematically that what seemed to be objections were on the contrary, when properly analyzed, decisive testimonies to the accuracy of the theory. In other words, the theory of universal gravitation was only worth anything when it was a mathematical theory; and only as a mathematical theory could it be verified by observation in such a way as to sway conviction. Hooke, from the opposite pole, made a remark that provoked one of Newton's most furious outbursts:

(Hooke) has done nothing, and yet written in such a way, as if he knew and had sufficiently hinted all but what remained to be determined by the drudgery of calculations and observations, excusing himself from that labour by reason of his other business, whereas he should rather have excused himself by reason of his inability. For 'tis plain, by his words, that he knew not how to go about it. Now is not this very fine? Mathematicians, that find out, settle, and do all the business, must content themselves with being nothing but dry calculators and drudges; and another, that does nothing but pretend and grasp at all things, must carry away all the invention, as well as those that were to follow him, as of those that went before.[6]

Imagination, the ability to feign hypotheses, could give only the beginning of a theory in physics. To find out, to do everything, was to make a mathematical theory and confirm it by experiments or observations.

That is why Newton entitled his great work *The Mathematical Principles of Natural Philosophy* rather than, as he once thought, simply *On the Motion of Bodies.* To Newton, the laws of nature were not certainties of introspection, but those derived by mathematical reasoning. The method of explaining phenomena by reference to these laws was not by ingenious hypotheses, but again by mathematical reasoning. Galileo's proclamation of faith, tinged still with numerical or geometrical mysticism of Pythagorean or Platonic origin, became for Newton a plain, stern rule of procedure:

The whole burden of philosophy seems to consist of this: from the phenomena of motion to investigate the forces of nature, and then from these forces to demonstrate the other phenomena.[7]

To follow any other course than the mathematical in this was quite simply to fail to comprehend the nature of physics. Yet even Newton was not quite free of the ancient delusion that mathematics is something more than logic, that it has in itself the roots of harmony and order, since

---

[6] *Correspondence,* Vol. II, p. 438.

[7] *Principia,* Preface.

he could find repeated in the colors of the spectrum the ancient divisions of the musical chord.[8]

The *Principia* was, and is, a difficult book. Few of Newton's contemporaries were capable of working systematically through it, so that his celestial mechanics became widely known either through popularizations like Henry Pemberton's *View of Sir Isaac Newton's Philosophy* (1728) or through the "translation" of its theorems into the language of calculus. As Newton wrote at the opening of Book III, *The System of the World,*

. . . not that I would advise anyone to the previous study of every Proposition of (the First and Second) Books; for they abound with such as might cost too much time, even to readers of good mathematical learning. It is enough if one carefully reads the Definitions, the Laws of Motion, and the first three Sections of the First Book. He may then pass on to this Book. . . .[9]

John Locke, it is said, sought an assurance from Huygens that Newton's mathematics could be relied upon; he then read the *Principia* for its scientific ideas (which he adopted). No doubt many others approached it in the same way. Within only a few more years another difficulty came between Newton and the reader. Newton had the ill-luck to write at the moment when the new mathematics was born, at the very moment of Leibniz's first paper on the calculus. Within a generation continental mathematicians had adopted Leibnizian methods of handling such problems as Newton had treated in the *Principia*, while the British were turning rather less rapidly to Newton's own fluxional analysis. But Newton's mechanics was fossilized in the geometrical proofs of an older generation of mathematicians—Huygens, Wallis, Barrow, Gregory; in a sense, it was the last great piece of mathematical physics composed in the Greek tradition. Its form was soon to seem both old-fashioned and laborious.

Nor were the difficulties merely mathematical. To mathematicians comparable in stature to Newton, such as Huygens and Leibniz, it was his philosophy that proved unacceptable. Did the theory of gravitation assume that bodies are capable of acting upon each other at a distance without mechanical connection? Were space and time to be conceived of as Newton required? Was he perverting the apparently triumphant metaphysic of mechanism? Did he make God, as Leibniz alleged, an imperfect workman who needed to tinker continually with His creation? These were questions that transcended mathematical reasoning and experimental decision, yet until they were settled the status of Newton's work remained, in a measure, in suspense. . . .

---

[8] *Opticks* (1931), pp. 126–28, 154, 212.
[9] *Principia,* Motte-Cajori, p. 397.

No other work in the whole history of science equals the *Principia* either in originality and power of thought, or in the majesty of its achievement. No other so transformed the structure of science, for the *Principia* had no precursor in its revelation of the depth of exact comprehension that was accessible through mathematical physics. No other approached its authority in vindicating the mechanistic view of nature, which has been so far extended and emulated in all other parts of science. There could be only one moment at which experiment and observation, the mechanical philosophy, and advanced mathematical methods could be brought together to yield a system of thought at once tightly consistent in itself and verifiable by every available empirical test. Order could be brought to celestial physics only once, and it was Newton who brought order. His is the world of law. Since everything that happens in this world is the effect of motion, the primary, never-failing laws are the laws of motion defined at the beginning of Book I. Motion—except in the rare event of pure inertial motion—is the product of force; therefore in physics the next set of laws should define the forces that operate in nature. Of these Newton succeeded in defining only one, the law of gravity: the *Principia* is for the most part his treatise on this one force and the phenomena that arise from it. In it, such older descriptive laws as Kepler's and Boyle's are deduced as consequences of the basic law of force (though in the latter case the force is not that of gravity). Newton's deduction of Boyle's Law from a repulsive force between the particles of a gas varying inversely as the distance (Book II, Proposition XXIII) must be considered a noble failure, however. Third, there are the laws of mathematics, belonging to the sphere of reason and logic indeed rather than to the sphere of physical reality, yet laws which physical reality obeys, and which scientific reasoning must not ignore. Nothing happens by chance, nothing is arbitrary, nothing is *sui generis* or a law unto itself. The philosophy of both *Principia* and *Opticks* insists that however varied, disconnected, and specific the almost infinite range of events in nature may seem to be, they are so in appearance only: for in reality all the phenomena of things and all their properties must be traceable to a small set of fundamental laws of nature, and by mathematical reasoning each of them is deducible again from these laws, once they are known.

Yet Newton shrank from the belief that these laws are innate in nature; that in his view would lead to necessitarianism and the deification of matter. Matter and material properties could not be eternal and uncreated; rather matter is, and the laws of nature are, because God has willed them. The perfection of the laws implied for him a lawgiver, as the perfection of the architecture of the universe implied a cosmic design:

Though (the planets and comets) may indeed continue in their orbits by the mere force of gravity yet they could by no means have at first derived the regular positions of their orbits from those laws ... it is not to be conceived that mere mechanical causes could give birth to so many regular motions, since the comets range over all parts of the heavens in very eccentric orbits ... and in their aphelions, where they move the slowest and are detained the longest, they recede to the greatest distances from each other, and hence suffer the least disturbance from their mutual attractions. This most beautiful system of the sun, planets, and comets could only proceed from the counsel and dominion of an intelligent and powerful Being. And if the fixed stars are centres of other like systems these, being formed by the like wise counsel, must be all subject to the dominion of One; especially since the light of the fixed stars is of the same nature as the light of the sun, and from every system light passes into all the other systems; and lest the systems of the fixed stars should, by their gravity, fall on each other he hath placed those systems at immense distances from each other.[10]

The ideas that Newton expressed in the General Scholium with which he concluded the second edition of the *Principia* (1713) had persisted throughout his life, for they occur in a document he wrote as a young man, before 1669. Like Descartes and Boyle, Newton saw the mechanistic universe as an argument against atheism, not in favor of it. But Newton's God—it will now be clear—was no Christian deity, nor the God of any sect. The attributes Newton conferred upon Him are unexceptionable: He is living, intelligent, omnipotent, eternal, omniscient, and most perfect, but He is a God of science, not theology. His kingdom is in the brain rather than the heart, for He is a God of law and certainty, not a God of hope and fear, of punishment and reward.

2. NEWTON, THE MAGICIAN

The late Lord Keynes was fascinated by Newton's personality. Keynes likens Newton's power of penetration to mystical intuition and sees in it the key to Newton's excellence and a motive for his achievement.

J. M. KEYNES[*]

Newton was not the first of the age of reason. He was the last of the magicians, the last of the Babylonians and Sumerians, the last great mind

---

[10] *Ibid.*, pp. 543–44.

[*] J. M. Keynes, "Newton, The Man," from *The Royal Society Newton Tercentenary Celebrations*, Cambridge University Press, pp. 27–29.

which looked out on the visible and intellectual world with the same eyes as those who began to build our intellectual inheritance rather less than 10,000 years ago. Isaac Newton, a posthumous child born with no father on Christmas Day, 1642, was the last wonder child to whom the Magi could do sincere and appropriate homage. . . .

In vulgar modern terms Newton was profoundly neurotic of a not unfamiliar type, but—I should say from the records—a most extreme example. His deepest instincts were occult, esoteric, semantic—with profound shrinking from the world, a paralyzing fear of exposing his thoughts, his beliefs, his discoveries in all nakedness to the inspection and criticism of the world. "Of the most fearful, cautious and suspicious temper that I ever knew," said Whiston, his successor in the Lucasian chair. The too well-known conflicts and ignoble quarrels with Hooke, Flamsteed, Leibniz are only too clear an evidence of this. Like all his type he was wholly aloof from women. He parted with and published nothing except under the extreme pressure of friends. Until the second phase of his life, he was a rapt, consecrated solitary, pursuing his studies by intense introspection with a mental endurance perhaps never equaled.

I believe that the clue to his mind is to be found in his unusual powers of continuous concentrated introspection. A case can be made out, as it also can with Descartes, for regarding him as an accomplished experimentalist. Nothing can be more charming than the tales of his mechanical contrivances when he was a boy. There are his telescopes and his optical experiments. These were essential accomplishments, part of his unequaled all-around technique, but not, I am sure, his *peculiar* gift, especially among his contemporaries. His peculiar gift was the power of holding continuously in his mind a purely mental problem until he had seen straight through it. I fancy his preeminence is due to his muscles of intuition being the strongest and most enduring with which a man has ever been gifted. Anyone who has ever attempted pure scientific or philosophical thought knows how one can hold a problem momentarily in one's mind and apply all one's power of concentration to piercing through it, and how it will dissolve and escape and you find that what you are surveying is a blank. I believe that Newton could hold a problem in his mind for hours and days and weeks until it surrendered to him its secret. Then being a supreme mathematical technician he could dress it up, how you will, for purposes of exposition, but it was his intuition which was preeminently extraordinary—"so happy in his conjectures," said de Morgan, "as to seem to know more than he could possibly have any means of proving." The proofs, for what they are worth, were, as I have said, dressed up afterward—they were not the instrument of discovery.

There is the story of how he informed Halley of one of his most fundamental discoveries of planetary motion. "Yes," replied Halley, "but how do you know that? Have you proved it?" Newton was taken aback— "Why, I've known it for years," he replied. "If you'll give me a few days, I'll certainly find you a proof of it"—as in due course he did.

Again, there is some evidence that Newton in preparing the *Principia* was held up almost to the last moment by lack of proof that you could treat a solid sphere as though all its mass was concentrated at the center, and only hit on the proof a year before publication. But this was a truth which he had known for certain and had always assumed for many years.

Certainly there can be no doubt that the peculiar geometrical form in which the exposition of the *Principia* is dressed up bears no resemblance at all to the mental processes by which Newton actually arrived at his conclusions.

His experiments were always, I suspect, a means, not of discovery, but always of verifying what he knew already.

Why do I call him a magician? Because he looked on the whole universe and all that is in it *as a riddle,* as a secret which could be read by applying pure thought to certain evidence, certain mystic clues which God had laid about the world to allow a sort of philosopher's treasure hunt to the esoteric brotherhood. He believed that these clues were to be found partly in the evidence of the heavens and in the constitution of elements (and that is what gives the false suggestion of his being an experimental natural philosopher), but also partly in certain papers and traditions handed down by the brethren in an unbroken chain back to the original cryptic revelation in Babylonia. He regarded the universe as a cryptogram set by the Almighty—just as he himself wrapped the discovery of the calculus in a cryptogram when he communicated with Leibniz. By pure thought, by concentration of mind, the riddle, he believed, would be revealed to the initiate.

He *did* read the riddle of the heavens. And he believed that by the same powers of his introspective imagination he would read the riddle of the Godhead, the riddle of past and future events divinely foreordained, the riddle of the elements and their constitution from an original undifferentiated first matter, the riddle of health and of immortality. All would be revealed to him if only he could persevere to the end, uninterrupted, by himself, no one coming into the room, reading, copying, testing—all by himself, no interruption for God's sake, no disclosure, no discordant breakings in or criticism, with fear and shrinking as he assailed these half-ordained, half-forbidden things, creeping back into the bosom of the Godhead as into his mother's womb. "Voyaging through strange seas of thought *alone*," not as Charles Lamb, "a fellow who believed nothing unless it was as clear as the three sides of a triangle."

And so he continued for some 25 years. In 1687, when he was 45 years old, the *Principia* was published.

3. NEWTON, THE METHODOLOGIST

Professor E. W. Strong is a philosopher of science. In the following selection he considers Newton's famous declaration that he feigned no hypotheses, and distinguishes between legitimate and illegitimate hypotheses in science. Strong describes Newton as an early positivist, hence essentially modern in his methodology.

E. W. STRONG[*]

In view of Newton's position with regard to principles to be admitted into mathematical-physical science, what is one to make of his definitions of absolute, true, and mathematical time and space and motion? Newton writes that parts of an absolute space, like parts of an absolute time, are not

distinguished from one another by our senses, therefore in their stead we use sensible measures of them. For from the positions and distances of things from any body considered as immovable, we define all places; and then with respect to such places, we estimate all motions, considering bodies as transferred from some of those places into others. And so, instead of absolute places and motions, we use relative ones; and that without any inconvenience in common affairs; but in philosophical disquisitions, we ought to abstract from our senses, and consider things themselves, distinct from what are only sensible measures of them. For it may be that there is no body really at rest, to which the places and motions of others may be referred.

Similarly, Newton states, "It may be, that there is no such thing as an equable motion whereby time may be accurately measured. All motions may be accelerated and retarded, but the flowing of absolute time is not liable to any change."

The abstracting "from the senses" here recommended, in view of Newton's own admission that there may be no equable motion and no

[*] E. W. Strong, "Newton's Mathematical Way," *Journal of the History of Ideas*, Vol. XII, 1951, pp. 100–102.

body absolutely at rest, strongly suggests that absolute space, time, and motion are being proposed as postulates and hence as a possible or pre-supposed system. Undoubtedly Newton believed that the "absolutes" he postulated were not conventional constructs but were a real order of nature, yet lack of empirical confirmation restrained him from asserting this as a matter of knowledge. ". . . there may be some body absolutely at rest," Newton writes, "but impossible to know, from the position of bodies to one another in our regions, whether any of these do keep the same position to that remote body." It follows "that absolute rest cannot be determined from the position of bodies in our regions." Newton thought that the matter was not "altogether desperate" empirically with regard to absolute motion if one considered the evidence in determining angular velocity from the rotation of vessels filled with water. The experiment, however, does not provide empirical warrant for absolute rectilinear motion implied in the first Law: "every body continues in its state of rest, or of uniform motion in a right line, unless it is compelled to change that state by forces impressed upon it."

There is no conflict or confusion in Newton's reasoning regarding an absolute, true, and mathematical system provided he does not employ the asserted "absolutes" as more than postulates. Newton does assume absolute coordinates from which to compute sensible measures of bodies and motions, but in so doing the expressions are unexceptionable if asserted not as *physical* but only as *mathematical*. A careful reading of Newton supports the following conclusions concerning abstracting from the senses. In effect, Newton distinguishes three levels. In a first level of abstracting, propositions are said to be inferred or deduced from phenomena. In a second level, the propositions are "rendered general by induction," for example, the two theorems in optics previously discussed. As derived from mathematical experimentation, these principles are *mechanical* principles, or mathematical-physical formulas. When Newton postulates absolute, true, and mathematical space, time, and motion, he introduces principles which are not evinced by experiments. Such principles, so far as Newton believes they express a real order of nature, are thereby metaphysical in the sense of being unverified assumptions. They are constructs introduced on the second level of abstracting, but not themselves inductively derived and thereby empirically grounded. So far as Newton's scientific purpose is concerned in his mechanics, nothing more need be asserted or assumed. Yet a third level appears in Newton's views expressed in the General Scholium at the end of the *Principia* and in the conclusion of the *Opticks* where Newton attributes the order of nature to God as the first Cause.

Where interpreters of Newton have gone astray is in supposing that

Newton held that Space and Time constitute the "sensorium of God" in order to preserve empiricism in principle for the atomic ingredients and absolute structure of his system. Yet Newton *added* the General Scholium in the second edition of the *Principia* in 1713, 26 years after the first edition; and the theological views expressed in the *Opticks*, Queries 28 and 31, did not appear in the first edition of 1704. Had Newton supposed these discussions to be fundamental to his science, he would hardly have omitted them originally. Newton, of course, believed that his system of the world was not incompatible with a traditional conception of God which he never questioned. He wrote the General Scholium at the urging of Cotes, who became alarmed by the criticism of Leibniz to the prejudice of a work in which God had not been employed. Newton, however, did not suppose that his scientific theorems either proved the theological doctrine or needed to assume it. His famous statement, "Hypotheses non fingo (I feign no hypotheses)," is his judgment upon the pertinence of the theological discussion which immediately precedes it. The philosophers who take this third level to be a subscription on Newton's part to theological foundations of his physical science have not followed Newton in his own disavowal. Science proper is limited, by Newton, to the first two levels of abstracting.

4. NEWTON, THE METAPHYSICIAN

S. I. Vavilov, Soviet Academician, tells of Newton's metaphysical borrowings and the important role they played in his work.

S. I. VAVILOV*

Lagrange considered Newton not only the greatest but the most fortunate of men of genius: "On ne trouve qu'une fois un systeme du monde à établir (It is given to only one man to discover the system of the world)."[1]

Newton's good fortune, in Lagrange's opinion, consisted in the fact that his system was the only correct one, and comprised an eternal, infallible truth.

---

* S. I. Vavilov, "Newton and the Atomic Theory," from *The Royal Society Newton Tercentenary Celebrations,* Cambridge University Press.

[1] Delambre, 1812, "Notice sur la vie et le travail de M. Lagrange," *Mem, Classe Sci. Math. Phys. Inst. France,* pp. 13, 46.

During the two and a half centuries which have elapsed since Newton's *Principia* and his investigations in the field of optics were first published, physics has been developing by leaps and bounds. But the fundamental principles of Newton's physics—his theory of gravitation, his general conception of central forces acting at a distance, his doctrine of monochromatic colors and their periodicity—have stood the hard test of time marvelously well and have fully retained their vast significance to this day. Time has only generalized and supplemented them to some extent, and has given them a new interpretation.

The secret of the "immortality" of the main points of Newton's physics is known to lie primarily in Newton's rigid, faultless method. Taking Bacon's elementary induction as his basis, Newton built up his own ingenious and difficult method, which may be termed the "method of principles" and is a blend of rationally generalized quantitative experiment and quantitative logic, that is, mathematics.

Newton's "principles" in physics are quite analogous in function to axioms in geometry, but they are extremely difficult to reveal. As a matter of the utmost importance he considered that

To derive two or three general Principles of Motion from Phenomena and afterwards to tell us how the Properties and Actions of all corporeal Things follow from those manifest Principles, would be a very great step in Philosophy, though the Causes of those Principles were not yet discover'd.[2]

Indeed, this "very great step in philosophy" was achieved in the field of mechanics by Newton himself, in his *Principia*, in a clear, distinct, and conscious form, and was undertaken by him, but not quite completed, in the field of optics. On the basis of this method the generations of scientists that followed created thermodynamics, electrodynamics, the theory of relativity, and quantum mechanics. Modern science has supplemented Newton's method of divining "principles" with a mighty method of mathematical generalization, of which examples are to be found in the equations of Maxwell, Schrödinger, Dirac, and others. It is Newton's supreme ability in discerning effective "principles," his art in apt quantitative experiment and his great skill in mathematics, that account for the immortality of his scientific works.

At first sight Newton's hypotheses seem to be quite opposite to "eternal truths." Newton's distrustful, skeptical, even sarcastic attitude toward other scientists' hypotheses, and toward his own, is, quite naturally, associated primarily with his personal qualities, his extraordinary severity in judging himself and his own statements. . . .

---

[2] Newton, *Opticks* (2d ed.; 1717), Query 31, p. 377. Also *Opticks*, reprint of 4th ed., London, 1931, p. 401.

Still, nothwithstanding Newton's rigid attitude toward hypotheses, it is a well-known fact that he was the author of a large number of correct as well as incorrect hypotheses, which were always, however, clearly and sharply distinguished from the indubitable truths upon which he insisted. It is precisely on account of Newton's skepticism that his hypotheses were of comparatively small importance in the subsequent development of science. But these hypotheses are of great interest in understanding Newton's world outlook.

In our time, when atoms have graduated from the category of hypotheses into the class of the most potent realities, it is especially interesting to review the atomistic conceptions of the author of "Hypotheses non fingo."

Newton never expounded his atomic conjectures in consecutive order. But they can be traced by fragments in all his works throughout his life, beginning with his *Lectiones Opticae* and right up to the last edition of his *Opticks*.

There is no difficulty in determining the sources of Newton's first conceptions of the atomic theory. The first of these was the tradition originated by the ancient atomists, Democritus, Epicurus, and Lucretius. There is no doubt that Newton had read and knew well the work of the last named: there was a copy of the works of Lucretius in his private library.[3]

Further, Newton derived his atomistic conceptions from some of his contemporaries and predecessors, such as Galileo, Gassendi, Descartes, and, probably most extensively, from his teacher and friend Isaac Barrow. Barrow's theological works and his *Lectiones Mathematicae* are full of references to Democritus, Epicurus, and Lucretius. . . .

But the power of tradition and of current ideas could hardly have made a decisive impression on Newton's independent and critical mind. There must have been some other arguments which convinced Newton of the truth of his atomism. . . .

The arguments of the ancients, reproduced by Lucretius, are irrefutable to this day and remain an indisputable and at the same time a very comprehensible proof of atomism. Only toward the end of his life, as we shall see, in the last editions of his *Opticks*, does Newton mention the argument of the ancients as his own fundamental one. This argument was essentially strong enough to turn the hypothesis into a principle, but to the end of his days Newton could not make up his mind to do so.

Newton retained his formal neutrality with respect to atomism, ex-

---

[3] R. de Villamil, *Newton, the Man*, London, 1931.

pressed in his *Lectiones Opticae,* through all his subsequent memoirs and letters concerning discoveries in optics, and particularly in his large "hypothetical" memoir of 1675, entitled *An Hypothesis explaining the Properties of Light, discoursed of in my Several Papers,* which was read before the Royal Society, but was not published during Newton's lifetime.[4]

In this memoir, which deals mainly with ether and vibrations caused in it by light, Newton refers to the atomistic conception as a thing to be taken for granted. In many places he mentions "parts, particles, corpuscles" of matter without further explanation. . . .

He concludes with words that show how concrete were his conceptions of this hypothesis.[5]

. . . it is not impossible, but that microscopes may at length be improved to the discovery of corpuscles of bodies, on which their colours depend. For if those instruments could be so far improved, as with sufficient distinctness to represent objects five or six hundred times bigger than at a foot distance they appear to our naked eyes, I should hope, that we might be able to discover some of the greatest of those corpuscles. And by one that would magnify three or four thousand times, perhaps they might all be discovered but those, which produce blackness.

These words bring out clearly the consistency of the physicist-experimenter. For the first time, apparently, in the history of science, Newton derived from the atomistic conception a conclusion which was in principle subject to experimental verification, and showed that it would be an *experimentum crucis* in the future. We know now that Newton was mistaken in his quantitative estimation by about two orders, but in principle he was right, and the electron microscope had already brought into our field of vision at least the larger molecules. In the memoir just mentioned Newton expounds a large number of hypotheses, after having acquitted himself at the beginning of responsibility for them:

And though I shall not assume either this or any other hypothesis, not thinking it necessary to concern myself . . . yet while I am describing this, I shall sometimes, to avoid circumlocution, and to represent it more conveniently, speak of it, as if I assumed it, and propounded it to be believed.[6]

While displaying great skill in the application of the atomistic hypothesis, Newton, notwithstanding, nowhere professes to be an adherent of this hypothesis.

At the time when he was writing his memoir, Newton's position on physics was as yet quite vague. His memoir is imbued to a considerable

---

[4] T. Birch, *The History of the Royal Society of London,* 1757, Vol. 3, p. 248.

[5] T. Birch, *loc. cit.,* p. 303.

[6] *Ibid.,* p. 249.

extent with the spirit of Descartes. In it, for instance, one reads about "aethers in the vortices of the sun and planets,"[7] nor is this written by way of criticism. During this period Newton apparently still hesitates to make his choice between the matter-filled space of Descartes and the void of Epicurus and Lucretius.

However, investigations in the fields of mechanics and astronomy, and the discovery of the law of gravitation, which was made known to the world through his *Principia*, evidently brought a radical change in Newton's outlook. He replaces Descartes's purely mechanical conception of direct contacts and shocks between bodies as the only cause of the acceleration, by his own formal, dynamical scheme. According to the latter, bodies are regarded as the centers of forces which act on one another at a distance. Newton eliminates mechanical ether—the medium between bodies—as an impediment to the regular motion of the heavenly bodies. His conception of the universe, from a formal standpoint at least, is that of a void with bodies traveling through it and acting on one another at a distance. The atoms of Epicurus and Lucretius become the incarnation of Newton's universe. The difference from the conceptions of the ancients is that the particles are now provided with forces acting between them.

In the *Principia* itself the author intentionally evades the problem of atoms. In speaking, for instance, about forces of attraction and repulsion acting between the particles in a fluid, Newton prefers to remain on the standpoint of mathematical formalism:[8]

But whether elastic fluids do really consist of particles so repelling each other, is a physical question. We have here demonstrated mathematically the property of fluids consisting of particles of this kind, that hence philosophers may take occasion to discuss that question.

Newton even goes so far as to give a figure illustrating the arrangement of the particles in a fluid,[9] still retaining, nonetheless, his formal standpoint.

At the same time, behind the rigorous mathematical screen of his *Principia*, Newton's "hypothetical" mind was unquestionably hard at work. There can be no doubt that he pondered incessantly over problems concerning the structure of bodies and atomism, especially in connection with the experiments constantly conducted in his chemical laboratory, which for many years took up the greater part of his time. Unfortunately, to this day we know very little about these chemical studies of Newton's.

---

[7] *Ibid.*, p. 253.

[8] F. Cajori, Sir Isaac Newton's *Mathematical Principles of Natural Philosophy* (Berkeley, California, 1934), p. 302.

[9] *Ibid.*, p. 367.

It can, however, be definitely stated that during these years Newton, as a result of the conclusions reached on the basis of his mechanics and astronomy and the vast amount of physical and chemical data at his disposal, built up a picture of the microstructure of matter, remarkable for its profundity, foresight, and correctness....

The author of the *Principia,* who from his early years, as we have already mentioned above, put forth the slogan "Hypotheses non fingo," was nevertheless, as we have convinced ourselves, one of the greatest masters of physical hypothesis. Only in our time, when the atom has become an indisputable reality, when man has begun to master the atom and its depths, can Newton's gift of hypothetical intuition be appraised in full. A large part of this field of his work remained incomprehensible and inaccessible to his contemporaries and successors, and did not have the influence it should have had on the development of science. But there is no doubt that Newton's atomistic conceptions raise him to an even higher level in our eyes, and make him an even more attractive and unique figure. It may be said that Newton saw through "classical physics," right down into its profoundest depths, and right out into its ultimate scope.

5. THE NEGATIVE VIEW

The late R. G. Collingwood, philosopher and historian, devoted much of his work to a criticism of method. In this final selection he notes his objections to Newton's metaphysics and concludes that Newton's "careless and secondhand thinking on fundamental questions of cosmology ... proved his undoing in the end."

R. G. COLLINGWOOD*

If Spinoza's theory of the relation between body and mind is at bottom unintelligible, it is obviously the work of an exceedingly intelligent mind which has understood the weak point of Descartes's theory and has worked heroically to amend it. This is more than can be said of Newton (1642–1727). Newton's work has placed him securely among the great thinkers; but when Wordsworth described his statue in Trinity as

> The marble index of a mind for ever
> Voyaging through strange seas of thought alone

* R. G. Collingwood, *The Idea of Nature,* by permission of the Clarendon Press, Oxford, 1960, Galaxy edition, pp. 106–10.

he overestimated not so much Newton's greatness as his loneliness and the strangeness of the ideas which he explored. In mathematics, it is true, he was an innovator and a notable one in discovering the differential calculus; but in this he was so far from being alone that the simultaneous and independent discovery of the same method by Leibniz gave rise to a squabble between the two great men which reflects ill on the moral character of both; and in any case the seeds of the discovery were obtained by each of them from a far more important invention, the analytical geometry of Descartes. The genius of Newton lay in the patient thoroughness with which he worked out the details of what he called, on the title page of his immortal work, the "Mathematical Principles of Natural Philosophy" (1687; ed. 2, 1713; ed. 3, 1726). But the main idea of that work is nothing more nor less than Descartes's idea of a "universal science" mathematical in its form; the rules of method which he lays down at the beginning of his third book are drawn from Bacon; and the cosmology which he develops is nothing but Galileo's cosmology, according to which the natural world is a world of bodies possessing extension, figure, number, motion, and rest, modified by Kepler's idea of force and Gilbert's hypothesis of universal attraction between body and body: this natural world being regarded in the fashion of Galileo as a machine made by God and known by human beings who, in their capacity as sentient creatures, invest it with "secondary qualities" of color, sound, and so forth, which in its own right it does not possess.

Newton also owed something to the neo-Epicureans. Following them, he believed that all bodies consisted of minute particles surrounded by empty space. Their rest or motion in this empty space was determined, he thought, by forces of two kinds: *vis insita, or* inertia (an idea derived from Galileo), because of which they either rested or moved uniformly in a straight line; and *vis impressa,* which caused accelerated motions, and of which he recognized that there was more than one kind; he mentions two: (1) gravity or weight, which he defined mathematically as a force of mutual attraction varying directly as the product of the masses of the bodies concerned (where mass is defined as quantity of matter) and inversely as the square of the distance between their centers (where center is circularly defined as center of gravity); and (2) electricity, of which he characteristically refuses to say anything on the ground that our experimental knowledge is at present inadequate.

Of the theoretical difficulties lurking among the foundations of his natural philosophy Newton seems quite unaware, although many of them had been familiar for a very long time. In the *Scholium* appended to his definitions he distinguishes absolute time, which "in itself and without relation to anything external flows at a uniform rate," from relative time, which "is measured by movement," without asking whether the two are really distinct, how anything can be said to "flow" except relatively to something that stands still, or how it can be said to flow "at a uniform rate" unless its flow is measured by movement. He distinguishes absolute space which "is defined by our senses by its position relatively to bodies," again without asking any questions. He distinguishes absolute motion from relative motion, again in a quite uncritical way. And these uncritical distinctions form the groundwork of his entire treatise. To a critical eye they vanish as soon as they are looked at, leaving the conclusion, which Newton's successors have at last consciously embraced, that for what he called "experimental philosophy" the only kind of time is relative time, the only kind of space relative space, and the only kind of motion relative motion.

Similarly, in the *Scholium Generale* at the end of the work he demolishes by unexceptionable arguments the Cartesian theory of vortices (that is, Descartes's view that the space vulgarly called empty is full of a continuous and very subtle matter in constant motion, which revolves in eddies round every body of gross matter, and that the rotary movement of a planet, for example, is caused by its floating in this subtle matter and being carried round in the solar vortex) and thinks that in this way he has demolished the doctrine that all space is full of matter and established the reality of empty space. He argues that since we cannot on his own principles explain why all the planets revolve in the same direction round the sun, or why their orbits are so disposed that they never bump into one another, this "supremely elegant structure of the solar system cannot have arisen except by the device and power of an intelligent being," thus exalting the limitations of his own method into a proof of the existence of God. Finally, in the last paragraph of the whole work, as if to apologize for not having carried out the Cartesian program of a universal mathematical science, he calls attention to some of the things he has left out. I will translate the whole paragraph.

I should have liked to say something of the highly subtle spirit which pervades crass bodies and lurks in them, by whose force the particles of bodies attract each other to within minute distances and cohere in this contiguity; electrical bodies act at greater distances, repelling others as well as attracting them; light is emitted, is reflected, is refracted, is inflected, and warms bodies; and sensation is excited, and the limbs of animals are moved at will, by vibrations of this spirit propagated through the solid nerve-filaments from the external sense-organs to the brain and from the brain to the muscles. But these matters cannot be expounded in a few words; nor is there a sufficiency of the experiments by which the laws of this spirit's action would have to be accurately determined and demonstrated.

There speaks a man great enough to be aware of his own work's shortcoming. He knows that his program has been carried out only in part. But he is not great enough to be aware that the questions he has left unanswered bear upon those which he has answered. For example: Are the phenomena of light consistent with his doctrine of empty space? Is the admission that a body coheres in virtue of a mutual attraction between its parts which is not gravitation consistent with his doctrine that mass is simply quantity of matter? Is the admission that nature contains repulsive forces, as well as attractive ones, consistent with his doctrine that only an omnipotent God can prevent the planets from colliding with one another? And what reason has he for asserting that all the phenomena cataloged in this paragraph are due to one and the same *spiritus subtilissimus?*

Newton had become professor at the age of 27. He published the *Principia* at 43; from 54 to 85 he was controlling the Mint and living in the retirement of old age. One of the unsolved problems, mentioned in the paragraph I have quoted, we know that he tried to solve: that of light. He published the results in his *Optics* in 1704, at the age of 62; but he himself, as well as the friend to whom he submitted them for criticism, found them unsatisfactory. He had tried conclusions with that *spiritus subtilissimus,* and had suffered defeat. It is perhaps legitimate to infer that the careless and secondhand thinking on fundamental questions of cosmology, to which I have called attention, proved his undoing in the end.

Charles Morley, Professor of History at The Ohio State University, was born in Cleveland, Ohio, in 1913. A graduate of Ohio State, he received his M.A. and Ph.D. degrees from the University of Wisconsin. He was a Kosciuszko Foundation scholar at the University of Warsaw and has taught history at the University of North Dakota. He is the author of *Guide to Research in Russian History* (Syracuse, 1951) and *Portrait of America: Letters of Henry Sienkiewicz* (New York, 1959). He is a member of the American Historical Association and of the American Association for the Advancement of Slavic Studies.

CHAPTER EIGHT

CHARLES MORLEY

The Ohio State University

Peter the Great

THE IMPORTANCE of the reign of Peter the Great (1682–1725) can best be illustrated by a brief quotation from V. O. Kliuchevsky's *A Course in Russian History*. In his concluding chapter dealing with this period, the famous 19th-century Russian historian wrote as follows: "For almost two hundred years Russians have written a great deal, and talked even more, about Peter's activities. . . . At times, in fact, the whole philosophy of our history became confined to an evaluation of Peter's reforms; by means, so to speak, of a certain scholarly foreshortening, the entire perspective of Russian history was telescoped into a single question concerning the relationship of Peter's transformed new Russia to the old Russia."[1]

Although it has become customary to speak of "old" Russia and "new" Russia, with the line of demarcation being the reign of Peter the Great, historians have been far from agreement on this concept. While it is true that many have accepted the ancient distich

> Russia was covered in darkness for many years;
> God said: let there be Peter—and there was light in Russia!

others have rejected outright the interpretation of Peter's role in Russian history implied by this verse.

To understand completely the importance of Peter the Great and the differences of scholarly opinion about him would really require a thorough knowledge of Russian history both before and after his reign. Here we can hope only to introduce the problem of Peter's role in Russian history

---

[1] Vasilii O. Kliuchevskii, *Kurs russkoi istorii* (5 vols.; Moscow, 1937), Vol. IV, p. 211.

228 INTERPRETING EUROPEAN HISTORY

by presenting some of the necessary background and a few examples of conflicting interpretations of this problem.

By the time Peter ascended the throne, the Russian lands had been consolidated into a unified state and the Romanov dynasty had been firmly established on the throne. It is true that members of the Romanov family quarreled from time to time, especially in the 18th century, over the right to wear the crown. Peter had to contest this right with his stepsister Sophia, but once the contest was resolved, Peter's authority within the country remained generally unchallenged.

But the Russian state faced serious threats from without. Although Turkish power had passed its zenith, the Turks and their Crimean Tartar vassals continued to menace the borderlands of the South and blocked Russia's access to warm water ports. In the North, Sweden, which had played such a decisive part in the Thirty Years' War, was ruled by a young monarch of military genius, Charles XII. Sweden sat squarely astride the Baltic provinces, prevented Russia from reaching the sea, and even threatened to extend still further her influence, if not her possessions, on the Continent.

In meeting the dual danger from Turkey and Sweden, Peter sought assistance from Western Europe. He thought not only in terms of military alliance but even more in terms of learning from the West, especially its technology and military science. Thus he made two separate trips to Western Europe, invited many Western technicians to Russia, and sent numerous Russians abroad to study. At home, Peter began to introduce changes in the economy, in the governmental organization, in the military system, and even in society. While carrying out these internal reforms, Peter was engaged throughout his reign in almost continuous warfare. Although his military efforts against the Turks ultimately failed, he proved to be successful against the Swedes: he conquered the Baltic coastline and built the new capital, St. Petersburg, to serve as a window on the West.

Few will deny Peter credit and praise for his achievement vis-à-vis Sweden: Russia replaced Sweden as the strongest military power in northern and eastern Europe and henceforth played an active and important part in European international affairs. But Peter's total effect on the internal development of Russia raises numerous questions, some of which are basic. For example, is it really correct to speak of pre-Petrine Russia as "old," "backward," "prehistoric"? Does "modern" Russian history begin only with the reign of Peter the Great? Is Russia European or Asiatic? Or neither? Or a little of both? Does Russia differ from Europe only *in degree* or *in kind*? Should Russia's ancient institutions have been preserved in their pristine purity? Did Peter merely continue a process of westernization which had already begun under his predecessors in the 17th century? Or was he a genuine revolutionary? Would the reforms have come in due course even without Peter the Great? How rapid and how durable was Russia's progress under Peter? Did she, thanks to Peter, make more progress in 50 years than any other nation by itself in 500 years, as Voltaire suggests? Is it true that if Peter had not hurried in transforming Russia, she would have become a Swedish province? What about Peter's harsh and autocratic methods? Was Peter's use of "barbarous means of struggle against barbarism," to quote Lenin, a justifiable or, indeed, the only way to effect change in a lagging society? Were the reforms really necessary? Finally, did he exert a beneficial or detrimental influence on the development of Russia?

The answers that have been given to these questions have varied with virtually each new generation. Nor have they always been based on fact; personal motives and prejudices or an unrealistic nostalgia for a little-known past have often influenced the attitude of writers toward Peter the Great. Two of the Tsar's collaborators set the pattern for the views of Peter the Great that were generally expressed during the 18th century. Feofan Prokopovich, rector of the College of Theology in Kiev, delivered a sermon following the victory of Poltava which was in reality a panegyric upon the Tsar. By the time of Peter's death, Prokopovich had risen to the position of vice president, and therefore virtual head, of the Holy Synod. Preaching the funeral oration, he heaped endless praise upon his bene-factor who "raised Russia from a state of death" and whom he compared with such heroes of Biblical fame as Sampson, Japhet, Moses, Solomon, and David.[2]

After 14 years of service as a hydraulic engineer under Peter the Great (for which, incidentally, he was very poorly compensated), John Perry returned to his native England where he wrote his *Present State of Russia....* (London, 1716). Although the book served to a large extent as a record of Perry's financial grievances against the Russian government, its author expressed great enthusiasm for both the person and policies of the Tsar. Later English and French writers echoed Perry's views and some even plagiarized his book. Voltaire used Perry's work extensively when he wrote his own *Histoire de Russie sous Pierre-le-Grand* (2 vols.; Paris, 1759–63). Since this book was based on Perry and since Voltaire was commissioned by Peter's daughter, the Empress Elizabeth, to write

[2] For the text in English of Prokopovich's funeral oration see T. Consett, *The Present State and Regulations of the Church of Russia....* (London, 1729), pp. 279–87.

it, the famous French philosophe's "portrait of the superman could hardly be expected to reproduce every wart on his swarthy countenance" (G. P. Gooch). Quite the contrary, excessive glorification of the Tsar and his reforms characterized the *Histoire de Russie.*

A final example of the general attitude toward Peter the Great during the 18th century deserves to be cited. The Empress Catherine II (1762– 96), who greatly admired Peter and who considered herself the continuator of his work, invited the well-known French sculptor Falconet to the Russian capital to carve the impressive equestrian statue of the Tsar which still stands in the city that once bore his name.

It was during the first half of the 19th century that the discussion concerning the significance of Peter the Great and his reforms became most animated. There appeared in Russia at that time two conflicting schools of philosophy of history. In essence, their differences centered around Russia's relationship to the West. While the Slavophiles might be regarded as exclusively Russian in their orientation, the Westerners championed a European orientation. The Slavophiles extolled the inherent virtues of Russia's ancient institutions and identified Russia with the Greek Orthodox faith. Russian civilization differed *in kind* from that of the West and was superior to it, they claimed. The civilization of old Russia must, therefore, be preserved from contamination by the West. Having faith in Russia's own institutions and customs, the Slavophiles were antiforeign, anti-European.

The Westerners, on the other hand, believing in the universality of human culture, argued that Russian civilization differed from that of the West only *in degree,* not *in kind.* Due to certain historical circumstances Russia had fallen behind in the development of her institutions and culture and the Westerners urged that Russia must proceed ever more rapidly along the road of westernization in order to overtake the more advanced European nations.

One can readily see how the Slavophiles and the Westerners, differing fundamentally in their attitude toward the West, would also differ in their views on Peter the Great. To quote one Russian historian, "the Slavophiles knew of no man who embodied the true Russian principles as effectively as Peter the Great embodied their antithesis."[3] They held Peter responsible for destroying Russian national traditions, indiscriminately copying everything from the West, and imposing by force a foreign civilization on Russia. To the Westerners, on the contrary, Peter the Great was a "divine Hercules" who had set Russia on the road to progress and enlightenment.

---

[3] Nicholas V. Riasanovsky, *Russia and the West in the Teaching of the Slavophiles* (Cambridge, 1952), p. 183.

Nikolai M. Karamzin (1766–1826) and Peter IA. Chaadaev (1794–1856) were really precursors of the Slavophiles and the Westerners. Even though they actually belonged to neither movement, excerpts have been chosen from their writings as being among the best expressions of the ideas of these two schools of thought.

By the second half of the 19th century Russian historians were delving more deeply and more scientifically into their country's past and were basing their studies on a thorough examination of the source materials available to them. In their analysis of Peter's reign, they eschewed the extremes of Slavophilism and Westernism. Although they did not question Peter's reputation as a great monarch, they regarded his reign as an integral part of Russia's historical evolution. They looked upon many of his reforms as a natural continuation of innovations already begun in the 17th century; others they regarded as a direct consequence of the exigencies of the military situation created by the wars with Turkey and Sweden. Illustrative of this line of approach to Peter the Great are V. O. Kliuchevsky (1841–1911) and Paul N. Miliukov (1859–1943); likewise included in this category is the noted English historian of Peter the Great, B. H. Sumner (1893–1951).

Following the collapse of Imperial Russia, the Communists replaced the scientific, objective study of history with the revolutionary, Marxist interpretation of their past. But the new interpretation did not mean a single, uniform point of view toward any historical period or person. Rather, since history had become the handmaid of politics under the Soviet regime, there have been frequent changes in historical interpretation, depending on the needs of the Communists Party line at any particular moment. On the eve of World War II and during the war years, for example, the party was eager to arouse the patriotic sentiments of the Russian people. Thus Peter was portrayed by the novelist Alexei Tolstoi as a great national hero who repulsed foreign invaders. Marxist historians, however, de-emphasizing the role of the individual in history, have paid more attention to economic forces at the beginning of the 18th century than to the personal leadership of the Tsar. To illustrate the Marxian approach, excerpts are cited from the writings of Mikhail N. Pokrovsky (1868–1932) and from the official history of this period published by the Academy of Sciences of the U.S.S.R.

Reading and thinking about the selections below, each student will no doubt reach his own conclusion about the meaning of Peter the Great in Russian history. He may, however, find it interesting to speculate about the relevance of the reign for the world today. Here is a prototype of the problems that arise when a less advanced country endeavors to adopt the technology and techniques of more advanced nations. Peter's controversial reign provides a graphic example of the stresses and challenges inherent in the ordeal of change, whether in the 18th or in the 20th century.

1. EARLY 19TH-CENTURY VIEWS

A.

Nikolai M. Karamzin (1766–1826) has sometimes been called "the first Russian historian." This title stems from his appointment as court historiographer under Alexander I and from his 12-volume History of the Russian State.

Alexander's contemplated reorganization of the government aroused deep opposition on the part of Karamzin and other conservatives. From Karamzin's pen came a bitter and elaborately stated criticism of Western innovations entitled Memoir on Ancient and Modern Russia *written in 1811 for private perusal by the Tsar. Those parts of the* Memoir *which touch upon the reign of Peter the Great follow below.*

NIKOLAI M. KARAMZIN*

At this point Peter appeared. In his childhood, the license of the lords, the impudence of the *Streltsy,* and the ambition of Sophia had reminded Russia of the unhappy times of boyar troubles. But deep inside of him the youth already had the makings of a great man, and he seized hold of the helm of state with a mighty hand. He strove toward his destination through storms and billows. He reached it—and everything changed!

His goal was not only to bring new greatness to Russia but also to accomplish the *complete* assimilation of European customs.... Posterity has praised passionately this immortal sovereign for his personal merits as well as for his glorious achievements. He was magnanimous and perspicacious, he had an unshakable will, vigor, and a virtually inexhaustible supply of energy. He reorganized and increased the army, he achieved a brilliant victory over a skillful and courageous enemy, he conquered Livonia, he founded the fleet, built ports, promulgated many wise laws,

* Reprinted by permission of the publishers from Richard Pipes: *Karamzin's Memoir of Ancient and Modern Russia,* Cambridge, Massachusetts: Harvard University Press, Copyright 1959, by the President and Fellows of Harvard College, pp. 120–27.

improved commerce and mining, established factories, schools, the academy, and, finally, he won for Russia a position of eminence in the political system of Europe. And speaking of his magnificent gifts, shall we forget the gift which is perhaps the most important of all in an autocrat: that of knowing how to use people according to their ability? Generals, ministers, or legislators are not accidentally born into such and such a reign—they are chosen.... To choose good men one must have insight; only great men have insight into men. Peter's servants rendered him remarkable assistance on the field of battle, in the Senate, and in the Cabinet. But shall we Russians, keeping in mind our history, agree with ignorant foreigners who claim that Peter was the founder of our political greatness? ... Shall we forget the princes of Moscow, Ivan I, Ivan III, who may be said to have built a powerful state out of nothing, and—what is of equal importance—to have established in it firm monarchical authority? Peter found the means to achieve greatness—the foundation for it had been laid by the Moscow princes. And, while extolling the glory of this monarch, shall we overlook the pernicious side of his brilliant reign?

Let us not go into his personal vices. But his passion for foreign customs surely exceeded the bounds of reason. Peter was unable to realize that the national spirit constitutes the moral strength of states, which is as indispensable to their stability as is physical might. This national spirit, together with the faith, had saved Russia in the days of the Pretenders. It is nothing else than respect for our national dignity. By uprooting ancient customs, by exposing them to ridicule, by causing them to appear stupid, by praising and introducing foreign elements, the sovereign of the Russians humbled Russian hearts. Does humiliation predispose a man and a citizen to great deeds? The love of the fatherland is bolstered by those national peculiarities which the cosmopolite considers harmless, and thoughtful statesmen beneficial.... The Russian dress, food, and beards did not interfere with the founding of schools. Two states may stand on the same level of civil enlightenment although their customs differ. One state may borrow from another useful knowledge without borrowing its manners. These manners may change naturally, but to prescribe statutes for them is an act of violence, which is illegal also for an autocratic monarch. The people, in their original covenant with the king, had told him: "Guard our safety abroad and at home, punish criminals, sacrifice a part to save the whole." They had not said: "Fight the innocent inclinations and tastes of our domestic life." In this realm, the sovereign may equitably act only by example, not by decree.

Human life is short, and the rooting of new customs takes time. Peter confined his reform to the gentry. Until his reign all Russians, from the plow to the throne, had been alike insofar as they shared certain features of external appearance and of customs. After Peter, the higher classes separated themselves from the lower ones, and the Russian peasant, burgher, and merchant began to treat the Russian gentry as Germans, thus weakening the spirit of brotherly national unity binding the estates of the realm.

Over the centuries the people had become accustomed to treat the boyars with the respect due to eminent personages. They bowed with genuine humbleness when, accompanied by their noble retinues, with Asiatic splendor, to the sound of tambourines, the boyars appeared in the streets on their way to church or to the sovereign's council. Peter did away with the title of boyar. He had to have ministers, chancellors, presidents! The ancient, glorious Duma gave way to the Senate, the *prikazy* were replaced by colleges, the *diaki* by secretaries, and so it went. Reforms which made just as little sense for Russians were introduced into the military hierarchy: generals, captains, lieutenants took the place of *voevody, sotniki, piatidesiatniki,* and so forth. Imitation became for Russians a matter of honor and pride.

Family customs were not spared by the impact of the tsar's activity. The lords opened up their homes; their wives and daughters emerged from the impenetrable *teremy;* men and women began to mingle in noise-filled rooms at balls and suppers; Russian women ceased to blush at the indiscreet glances of men, and European freedom supplanted Asiatic constraint. . . . As we progressed in the acquisition of social virtues and graces, our families moved into the background; for when we have many acquaintances we feel less need of friends, and sacrifice family ties to social obligations.

I neither say nor think that the ancient Russians who had lived under the grand princes or the tsars were in all respect superior to us. We excel them not only in knowledge but also in some ways morally; that is to say, we are sometimes overcome with shame by things which left them indifferent, and which indeed are depraved. However, it must be admitted that what we gained in social virtues we lost in civic virtues. Does the name of a Russian carry for us today the same inscrutable force which it had in the past? No wonder. In the reigns of Michael and of his son, our ancestors, while assimilating many advantages which were to be found in foreign customs, never lost the conviction that an Orthodox Russian was the most perfect citizen and *Holy Rus'* the foremost state in the world. Let this be called a delusion. Yet how much it did to strengthen patriotism and the moral fiber of the country! Would we have today the audacity, after having spent over a century in the school of foreigners, to boast of our civic pride? Once upon a time we used to call all other Europeans *infidels;* now we call them brothers. For whom was it easier to conquer Russia—for *infidels* or for *brothers?* That is, whom was she likely to resist better? Was it conceivable in the reigns of Michael and Fedor for a Russian lord, who owed everything to his fatherland, gaily to abandon his tsar forever, in order to sit in Paris, London, or Vienna, and calmly read in newspapers of the perils confronting our country? We became citizens of the world but ceased in certain respects to be the citizens of Russia. The fault is Peter's.

He was undeniably great. But he could have exalted himself still higher, had he found the means to enlighten Russians without corrupting their civic virtues. . . .

National inclinations, habits, and ideas were still sufficiently strong to compel Peter, in spite of his theoretical liking for intellectual liberty, to resort to all the horrors of tyranny in order to restrain his subjects, whose loyalty, in fact, was unquestionable. The Secret Chancery of the Preobrazhenskoe operated day and night. Tortures and executions were the means used to accomplish our country's celebrated reform. Many perished for no other crime than the defense of the honor of Russian caftans and beards, which they refused to give up, and for the sake of which they dared to reproach the monarch. These unfortunates felt that by depriving them of their ancient habits Peter was depriving them of the fatherland itself.

The extraordinary efforts of Peter reflect all the strength of his character and of autocratic authority. Nothing frightened him. The Russian church had had since time immemorial its head, first in the person of the Metropolitan, and lastly in that of the Patriarch. Peter proclaimed himself the head of the church, abolishing the patriarchate as dangerous to unlimited autocracy. But, let us here note, our clergy had never contended against secular authority, either princely or tsarist. Its function had been to serve the latter as a useful tool in affairs of state, and as a conscience at times when it occasionally left the path of virtue. Our primate had one right: not to act, not to rebel, but to preach the truth to the sovereigns—a right which carries blessings not only for the people but also for the monarch whose happiness consists in justice. From Peter's time on the Russian clergy had deteriorated. Our primates turned into mere sycophants of the tsars, whom they eulogized in biblical language from the pulpits. . . .

Shall we close our eyes to yet another glaring mistake of Peter the Great? I mean his founding a new capital on the northern frontier of the state, amid muddy billows, in places condemned by nature to barrenness and want. Since at that time he controlled neither Riga nor Reval, he might have founded on the shores of the Neva a commercial city for the import and export of merchandise; but the idea of establishing there the residence of our sovereigns was, is, and will remain a *pernicious* one. How many people perished, how much money and labor was expended to carry out this intent? Truly, Petersburg is founded *on tears and corpses.* A foreign traveler, upon entering a country, usually looks for its capital in localities which are most fertile and most propitious for life and health. In Russia, he sees beautiful plains, enriched with all the beauties of nature, shaded by groves of linden trees and oaks, traversed by navigable rivers whose banks please the eye and where, in a moderate climate, the salutary air favors long life. He sees all this, and regretfully turning his back on these beautiful regions, enters sands, marshes, sandy pine forests, where poverty, gloom, and disease hold sway. This is the residence of the Russian sovereigns, who must strive to the utmost to keep the courtiers and guards from starving to death, as well as to make good the annual loss of inhabitants with newcomers, future victims of premature death! Man shall not overcome nature!

But a great man demonstrates his greatness with his very errors. They are difficult if not impossible to undo, for he creates the good and the bad alike forever. Russia was launched on her new course with a mighty hand; we shall never return to bygone times! It would have taken another Peter the Great at least 20 or 30 years to establish the new order much more firmly than all the successors of Peter I up to the time of Catherine II had done. Notwithstanding his marvelous diligence, Peter left much to be finished by his successors. Menshikov, however, was concerned only with his personal ambition, and so were the Dolgorukis. Menshikov intrigued to pave the road to the throne for his son, while the Dolgorukis and Golitsyns wanted to see the pale shadow of a monarch on the throne, and to rule themselves in the name of the supreme council. Impudent and dastardly plots! Pygmies contending for the legacy of a giant. The aristocracy, the oligarchy was ruining the fatherland.... And could Russia at this time have dispensed with monarchy, after she had changed her time-sanctioned customs, and undergone internal disorders as a result of new, important reforms which, by dissociating the customs of the gentry from those of the people, had weakened spiritual authority? Autocracy became more essential than ever for the preservation of order.

B.

Peter IA. Chaadaev (1794–1856), a political thinker and essayist, had traveled widely in Europe and become as much a European as a Russian. His views first attracted attention in 1836 when his "First Philosophical Letter" appeared in print. The letter expressed the dismal conclusion that

Russia as a nation had stood apart from world civilization, had contributed nothing to it, and had learned nothing from it. In the ensuing patriotic furor the publisher was exiled, the censor who passed the letter was dismissed, and Chaadaev was officially declared insane by Czar Nicholas I.

In his "Apology of a Madman" written soon afterward but only published posthumously, Chaadaev expressed a more complimentary interpretation of Russia's past and especially of Peter the Great's role in that past. The excerpt which follows is from the "Apology."

PETER IA. CHAADAEV*

For 300 years Russia has aspired to consort with Occidental Europe; for 300 years she has taken her most serious ideas, her most fruitful teachings, and her most vivid delights from there. For over a century Russia has done better than that. One hundred and fifty years ago the greatest of our kings—the one who supposedly began a new era, and to whom, it is said, we owe our greatness, our glory, and all the goods which we own today—disavowed the old Russia in the face of the whole world. He swept away all our institutions with his powerful breath; he dug an abyss between our past and our present, and into it he threw pell-mell all our traditions. He himself went to the occidental countries and made himself the smallest of men, and he came back to us so much the greater; he prostrated himself before the Occident, and he arose as our master and our ruler. He introduced occidental idioms into our language; he called his new capital by an occidental name; he rejected his hereditary title and took an occidental title; finally, he almost gave up his own name, and more than once he signed his sovereign decrees with an occidental name.

Since that time our eyes have been constantly turned towards the countries of the Occident; we did nothing more, so to speak, than to breathe in the emanations which reached us from there, and to nourish ourselves on them. We must admit that our princes almost always took us by the hand, almost always took the country in tow, and the country never had a hand in it; they themselves prescribed to us the customs, the language, and the clothing of the Occident. We learned to spell the names of the things in occidental books. Our own history was taught to us by one of the occidental countries. We translated the whole literature of the Occident, we learned it by heart, and we adorned ourselves with its tattered garment. And finally, we were happy to resemble the Occident, and proud when it consented to count us as one of its own.

We have to agree, it was beautiful, this creation of Peter the Great, this

* Hans Kohn (ed.), *The Mind of Modern Russia* (New Brunswick, N.J.: Rutgers University Press, 1955), pp. 50–54, 56–57.

powerful thought that set us on the road we were to travel with so much fanfare. It was a profound wisdom which told us: That civilization over there is the fruit of so much labor; the sciences and the arts have cost so much sweat to so many generations! All that can be yours if you cast away your superstitions, if you repudiate your prejudices, if you are not jealous of your barbaric past, if you do not boast of your centuries of ignorance, if you direct your ambition to appropriating the works of all the peoples and the riches acquired by the human spirit in all latitudes of the globe. . . .

Never was a people less infatuated with itself than the Russian people, such as it has been shaped by Peter the Great, and never has a people been more successful and more glorious in its progress. The high intelligence of this extraordinary man guessed exactly the point of our departure on the highway of civilization and the intellectual movement of the world. He saw that lacking a fundamental historical idea, we should be unable to build our future on that impotent foundation. He understood very well that all we could do was to train ourselves, like the peoples of the Occident, to cut across the chaos of national prejudices, across the narrow paths of local ideas, and out of the rusty rut of native customs; that we had to raise ourselves, by one spontaneous outburst of our internal powers, by an energetic effort of the national conscience, to the destiny which has been reserved for us. Thus he freed us from previous history which encumbers ancient societies and impedes their progress; he opened our mind to all the great and beautiful ideas which are prevalent among men; he handed us the whole Occident, such as the centuries have fashioned it, and gave us all its history for our history, and all its future for our future.

Do you not believe that if he had found in his country a rich and fertile history, living traditions, and deep-rooted institutions, he would have hesitated to pour them into a new mold? Do you not believe that faced with a strongly outlined and pronounced nationality, his founding spirit would have demanded that that nationality itself become the necessary instrument for the regeneration of his country? On the other hand, would the country have suffered being robbed of its past and a new one, a European one, being put in its place? But that was not the case. Peter the Great found only a blank page when he came to power, and with a strong hand he wrote on it the words *Europe and Occident:* from that time on we were part of Europe and of the Occident.

Don't be mistaken about it: no matter how enormous the genius of this man and the energy of his will, his work was possible only in the heart of a nation whose past history did not imperiously lay down the road it had to follow, whose traditions did not have the power to create its future, whose memories could be erased with impunity by an audacious legislator. We were so obedient to the voice of a prince who led us to a new life because our previous existence apparently did not give us any legitimate grounds for resistance. The most marked trait of our historical physiognomy is the absence of spontaneity in our social development. Look carefully, and you will see that each important fact in our history is a fact that was forced on us; almost every new idea is an imported idea. But there is nothing in this point of view which should give offense to the national sentiment; it is a truth and has to be accepted. Just as there are great men in history, so there are great nations which cannot be explained by the normal laws of reason, for they are mysteriously decreed by the supreme logic of Providence. That is our case; but once more, the national honor has nothing to do with all this.

The history of a people is more than a succession of facts, it is a series of connected ideas. That precisely is the history we do not have. We have to learn to get along without it, and not to vilify the persons who first noticed our lack. . . .

We are situated to the east of Europe; that is a positive fact, but it does not mean that we have ever been a part of the East. The history of the Orient has nothing in common with the history of our country. As we have just seen, the history of the Orient contains a fertile idea which, in its time, brought about an immense development of the mind, which accomplished its mission with a stupendous force, but which is no longer fated to produce anything new on the face of the earth. . . .

Believe me, I cherish my country more than any of you. I strive for its glory. I know how to appreciate the eminent qualities of my nation. But it is also true that the patriotic feeling which animates me is not exactly the same as the one whose shouts have upset my quiet existence, shouts which have again launched my boat—which had run aground at the foot of the Cross—on the ocean of human miseries. I have not learned to love my country with my eyes closed, my head bowed, and my mouth shut. I think that one can be useful to one's country only if one sees it clearly; I believe that the age of blind loves has passed, and that nowadays one owes one's country the truth. I love my country in the way that Peter the Great taught me to love it. I confess that I do not feel that smug patriotism, that lazy patriotism, which manages to make everything beautiful, which falls asleep on its illusions, and with which unfortunately many of our good souls are afflicted today. I believe that if we have come after the others, it is so that we can do better than the others; it is so that we may not fall into their faults, their errors, and their superstitions. . . . I believe that we are in a fortunate position, provided that we know how to appreciate it. It is a wonderful privilege to be able to contemplate and judge the world from the height of independent thought, free from unrestrained passions and petty interests which elsewhere disturb man's view and pervert his judgment. More is to come: I am firmly convinced that we are called on to resolve most of the social problems, to perfect most of the ideas which have come up in the old societies, and to decide most of the weighty questions concerning the human race. I have often said it, and I like to repeat it: in a way we are appointed, by the very nature of things, to serve as a real jury for the many suits which are being argued before the great tribunals of the human spirit and of human society.

2. VIEWS OF SCIENTIFIC HISTORIANS

A.

Vasili O. Kliuchevsky (1841–1911) was Russia's outstanding historian of the 19th century. At the early age of 28 he succeeded his teacher, Soloviev, in the chair of Russian history at the University of Moscow. His brilliant lectures attracted crowds of students and his numerous writings revealed exceptional literary talent.

Only toward the end of his life was Kliuchevsky persuaded to prepare his university lectures for publication. The result was A Course in Russian History (Kurs russkoi istorii) *(5 vols.; Moscow, 1904–21); the last volume was published from the notes of one of his students only after Kliuchevsky's death. Remarkable for its scholarship, for its synthesis of Russian history, for its vivid characterization of Russian leaders, and for its literary style, the work has been one of the most widely read histories of Russia.*

The following selection is taken from a recent translation of the lectures in Volume IV which deal with the reign of Peter the Great.

VASILI O. KLIUCHEVSKY*

First of all, how did Peter become a reformer? The name of Peter makes us think of his reforms, and indeed "Peter the Great and his reforms" has become a cliché. "Reformer" has become his sobriquet, and the name by which he is known to history. We tend to believe that Peter I was born with the intention of reforming his country, and that he believed that

---

* Vasili O. Kliuchevsky, *Peter the Great*, trans. Liliana Archibald (New York: St. Martin's Press, Inc., Macmillan & Co., Ltd., 1958), pp. 254–57, 262–65, 270–72.

this was his predestined historical mission. Nevertheless it was a long time before Peter took this view of himself.... Peter acted on the spur of the moment, and was not concerned with making plans for the future; he regarded everything he did as an immediate necessity rather than a reform, and did not notice how his actions changed both people and established systems. Even from his first foreign tour he brought back, not plans for reform, but impressions of a civilization which he imagined he would like to introduce into Russia; and he brought back, too, a taste for the sea, that is to say, a desire to wage war against the country which had won access to the sea away from his grandfather. Indeed it was only during the last decade of his life, when the effect of his reforms was already fairly obvious, that he realized that he had done something new and spectacular. His better understanding of what he had done, however, did not help him to understand how he might act in the future. Peter thus became a reformer by accident, as it were, and even unwillingly. The war led him on and, to the end of his life, pushed him into reforming.

In the history of a country, war generally impedes reform, since foreign war and domestic reform are mutually exclusive and reform prospers best in times of peace. But in the history of Russia the correlation is different. Since a successful war has always served to secure the status quo, and an unsuccessful war, by provoking internal discontent, has always forced the government to review its domestic policy and introduce reforms, the government has always tried to avoid war, often to the detriment of its international position. Reforms at home were commonly achieved at the price of disaster abroad. In Peter's time the relationship between war and domestic change was different. Reforms were stimulated by the requirements of war, which indeed dictated the nature of the reforms that were undertaken. In other times the effect of war has been to force change on an unwilling government, but Peter, as he said himself, was able to learn from war what changes were needed. Unfortunately the attempt to carry on both war and reform simultaneously was unsuccessful: war slowed up reform, and reform prolonged the war because there was opposition and frequent revolt, and the forces of the nation could not be united to finish the war.

There were also interminable controversies about whether the reforms had been sufficiently elaborated, and whether they were introduced to meet the needs of the people, or had been forced on them as an unexpected act of Peter's autocratic will. In these discussions the preparations for reform were examined. It was asked whether they were deliberately calculated to bring about improvement, or were simply forced upon Peter by urgent difficulties, and were therefore only by accident measures which led to new possibilities and a new way of life. Soloviev's view was that the reforms had been prepared by Russia's past history, and even that "they had been demanded by the people." Some changes had been borrowed from the West and introduced in Russia as far back as Peter's grandfather, and after him by Peter's father, elder brother, and sister. Long before Peter's reign, indeed, a fairly extensive plan for reforms had been drawn up, which in many ways anticipated his own. . . .

Peter's first reforms were adapted from the Dutch and then from the Swedish systems. Moscow was replaced by St. Petersburg, a city built on the swamps, and Peter forced the nobility and merchants to build their houses in his new capital; to achieve his purpose he transported thousands of laborers from Central Russia. The reform as carried out by Peter was his personal enterprise, and though it was an enterprise of unexampled ruthlessness, it was not arbitrary and was, indeed, necessary, otherwise Russia could not have developed fast enough to deal successfully with the dangers that threatened her. . . .

What was Peter's attitude to Western Europe? He had inherited the precept "Do everything after the example of foreign countries," that is to say Western European countries. This precept combines large doses of despondency, a lack of confidence in Russia's strength, and self-denial. How did Peter interpret this precept? What did he think of Russian relations with Western Europe? Did he see in Western Europe a model to imitate or a master who could be dismissed at the end of the lesson? Peter thought that the biggest loss suffered by Muscovy in the 17th century had been the Baltic littoral, by which Russia was deprived of contact with the civilized nations of the West. Yet why did he want this contact? Peter has often been accused of being a blind and inveterate Westerner who admired everything foreign, not because it was better than the Russian, but because it was unlike anything Russian; and it was believed that he wanted rather to assimilate Russia to Western Europe than to make Russia resemble Western Europe. It is difficult to believe that as sensible a man as Peter was troubled by such fantasies.

We have already seen how, in 1697, he had traveled incognito with the Great Embassy, with the intention of acquiring general technical knowledge and recruiting West European naval technicians. Indeed it was for technical reasons that the West was necessary to Peter. He was not a blind admirer of the West; on the contrary, he mistrusted it, and was not deluded into thinking that he could establish cordial relations with the West, for he knew that the West mistrusted his country, and was hostile to it. On the anniversary in 1724 of the Peace of Nystadt, Peter wrote that all countries had tried hard to exclude the Russians from knowledge in many subjects, and particularly military affairs, but somehow the countries had let information on military affairs escape them, as if their sight had been obscured. . . . We would gladly believe the legend which has come down to us, that Peter once said, as Osterman records it: "We need Europe for a few decades; later on we must turn our back on it." Thus for Peter association with Europe was only a means to an end, and not an end in itself.

What did Peter hope to gain from a rapprochement? Before answering this question, we must remember why Peter sent scores of young Russians to study abroad, and ask what type of foreigner he attracted to Russia. The young Russian was sent to study mathematics, the natural sciences, naval architecture, and navigation; the foreigners who came to Russia were officers, naval architects, sailors, artisans, mining engineers, and later on jurists and specialists in administration and finance. With their help Peter introduced into Russia useful technical knowledge and skills lacked by the Russians. Russia had no regular army: he created one. It had no fleet: he built one. It had no convenient maritime commercial outlet: with his army and navy he took the eastern littoral of the Baltic. Mining was barely developed, and manufacturing hardly existed, yet by Peter's death there were more than 200 factories and workshops in the country. The establishment of industry depended on technical knowledge, so Peter founded a naval academy, and many schools of navigation, medicine, artillery and engineering, including some where Latin and mathematics were taught, as well as nearly 50 elementary schools in provincial and subprovincial main towns. He even provided nearly 50 garrison schools for soldiers' children. There was insufficient revenue, so Peter more than trebled it. There was no rationally organized administration capable of managing this new and complicated business, so foreign experts were called on to help to create a new central administration.

The above is, of course, an incomplete account of Peter's achievements, but it does show what he hoped to do with the help of Western Europe. Peter called on Western Europe to work and train Russians in financial and administrative affairs, and in the technical sciences. He did not want to borrow the results of Western technique, but wanted to appropriate the skill and knowledge, and build industries on the Western European model. The intelligent Russian of the 17th century realized that it was essential to increase Russia's productive capacity, by exploiting the country's natural and virgin riches, in order that the increased requirements of the state might be more easily met. Peter shared this point of view, and gave effect to it as did nobody before or after him, and he is therefore unique in the history of Russia. In foreign policy he concentrated on solving the Baltic problem.

It would be difficult to assess the value of the many industries he introduced. The evidence of the increased wealth was not a higher standard of living, but increased revenue. All increased earnings were, in fact, used to pay for the war. Peter's intention had been general economic reform, but the only evidence of success was the improved financial position. . . . Were we to draw up a balance sheet of Peter's activities, excluding those affecting Russia's security and international position, but including those affecting the people's welfare, we would find that his great economic ambitions (which were the basis for his reforms) failed in their purpose, and, in fact, their only success was financial.

Thus Peter took from the old Russia the absolute power, the law, and the class structure; from the West he borrowed the technical knowledge required to organize the army, the navy, the economy, and the government. Where then was the revolution which renewed or transformed the Russian way of life, which introduced not only new institutions but new principles (whether they were good or bad is, for the moment, immaterial)? Peter's contemporaries, however, thought that the reforms were revolutionary, and they communicated their opinion to their descendants. But the reforms did not stop the Russians from doing things in their own way, and it was not the innovations that agitated them so much as the methods Peter used. Some of the results of the reforms were only felt in the future, and their significance was certainly not understood by everyone, and contemporaries anyhow only knew the effect the reforms had on them. Some reactions, however, were immediate, and these Peter had to account for. . . .

Let us end by giving our opinion of Peter's reforms. The contradiction in his work, his errors, his hesitations, his obstinacy, his lack of judgment in civil affairs, his uncontrollable cruelty, and, on the other hand, his wholehearted love of his country, his stubborn devotion to his work, the broad, enlightened outlook he brought to bear on it, his daring plans conceived with creative genius and concluded with incomparable energy, and finally the success he achieved by the incredible sacrifices of his people and himself, all these different characteristics make it difficult to paint one painting. Moreover they explain the diverse impression he made on people; he sometimes provoked unqualified admiration, sometimes unqualified hostility. Generally the criticism prevailed because even his good actions were accompanied by disgusting methods.

Peter's reforms were the occasion for a struggle between the despot and the people's inertia. The Tsar hoped to arouse the energies and initiative of a society subdued by serfdom with the menace of his power, and strove, with the help of the noblemen, the oppressors of serfs, to introduce into

Russia the European sciences and education which were essential to social progress. He also wanted the serf, while remaining a serf, to act responsibly and freely. The conjunction of despotism and liberty, of civilization and serfdom, was a paradox which was not resolved in the two centuries after Peter. . . .

Autocracy as a political principle is in itself odious. Yet we can reconcile ourselves to the individual who exercises this unnatural power when he adds self-sacrifice to it, and, although an autocrat, devotes himself unsparingly to the public good, risking destruction even on difficulties caused by his own work. We reconcile ourselves in the same way to the impetuous showers of spring, which strip branches from the trees, but nonetheless refresh the air, and by their downpour bring on the growth of the new seed.

B.

Paul N. Miliukov (1859–1943) achieved distinction not only as a historian but also as a political leader. In the last years of the imperial regime he was the recognized head of the Russian liberals (Constitutional Democrats) and in the Provisional Government of 1917 he served briefly as foreign minister.

A student of both Soloviev and Kliuchevsky, Miliukov also taught at the University of Moscow. He first attracted attention as a historian with his master's thesis entitled State Economy in Russia during the First Quarter of the Eighteenth Century and the Reforms of Peter the Great *(St. Petersburg, 1892). Based on extensive use of hitherto unexploited archival material, the book inspired other scholars to do further research on the Petrine period. Miliukov's most important work, which best reflected the breadth of his erudition, was* Outlines of Russian Culture *(3 vols.; St. Petersburg, 1896–1903).*

A refugee from the Communist revolution, Miliukov spent his last years in France. It was here that he wrote, in collaboration with other scholars, his Histoire de Russie *from which the following selection is taken.*

PAUL N. MILIUKOV[*]

The reign of Peter the Great marks the beginning of a new era in the history of Russia. The tradition of modern Russia, of civilized Russia, originates in this period. What is most characteristic of this new period,

[*] Pavel N. Miliukov, *et al., Histoire de Russie* (3 vols.; Paris: Librairie Ernest Leroux, 1932–33), Vol. 1, pp. 267–68.

whose gestation may be observed in pre-Petrine times, is that Russia definitely assumes the stature of a European power and becomes an important factor in international politics, while internally a new social class is formed which immediately assumes the character of a privileged nobility. With the reign of Peter begins the gradual formation of new generations which, having been subjected rather closely to foreign influences for a long time, now begin to emancipate themselves little by little and in the end create Russian civilization by assimilating the national spirit.

There has long been dispute over the personal role of Peter in this new evolution of the Russian national character. For his supporters, his role has been very important; his detractors, on the other hand, refuse to accord him any credit and are of the opinion that he only caused Russia to embark upon a wrong track. Using different arguments, both sides arrive at the same conclusion: that the principal element in Peter's reform activity was his personal will or whim.

Recent historical studies have shown that there are closer ties than was previously thought between the epoch of Peter the Great and the one which preceded it. These studies amount to denying the existence of the break which some have wished to see at this juncture of Russian history and have viewed the reigns of Peter and his predecessors as successive stages of a single organic historical evolution. If, as the result of this evolution, the Russian nation has assumed a more European character, this proves that all the facts of her historical development place her rather in Europe than in Asia, even though the Russian nation does serve as a kind of intermediary between these two parts of the world. But, while affirming the organic nature of Russia's historical evolution, these studies seek, contrary to earlier ones, to diminish the personal role of the czar-reformer. . . .

Generally speaking, one may state that Peter's epoch marks the transition of Russia from an unconscious or spontaneous evolution, attributable to the national spirit, to a more conscious, planned evolution that was more directed toward a goal. Nevertheless, Peter's first reforms, when contrasted with the general character of his work, appear rather to be the outcome of whim and appear to interrupt the organic evolution. It is in this sense that one may call Peter the Great "the first Russian revolutionary." In fact, his first efforts at reform were rather destructive; it is only later that he undertakes the task of reconstruction. This change from the unconscious and impulsive to the conscious and systematic is the distinctive attribute of the great reform undertaken by Peter which stamps this period as one of transition.

C.

A leading English historian of Russia, B. H. Sumner (1893–1951) spent most of his life at Oxford University where he was both student and teacher. Because of the restrictive travel policies of the Communist regime, he lacked the kind of knowledge of Russia that comes with direct experience. Yet this very remoteness gave his writings a certain detachment and objectivity that add to their value.

Sumner's deep interest in Russia's relationship to Europe inevitably led him to a study of Peter the Great. On this subject he wrote several books, including a small popular volume entitled Peter the Great and the Emergence of Modern Russia *(London, 1950). The following selection is a summary of his views on Peter from a paper he read at a scholarly meeting in 1945.*

B. H. SUMNER[*]

Peter was an iconoclast: he broke with many externals, and with the ritualistic, traditional orthodox manner of life that hitherto had been part and parcel of the nationalism and religion of the court and the magnates and landed families, and in some degree of the bulk of the Russian people. He was lay and secular in his interests, aims, and habit of mind and of life; rationalism and utility were uppermost. He had dynamic energy, violent unbreakable determination, and unfailing courage: therewith he triumphed in the long run over all his adversities, defeats, and setbacks—except one, and that one curiously enough his defeat at the hands of the Turks, in 1711, on the Pruth. He was a patriot, devoted to Russia, not sparing his subjects, but least of all himself, in unremitting service to her. He worked upon her "like nitric acid on iron." He was untiring in his plans for the development of Russia's economic resources, particularly her industries, and among those especially metallurgy. In this he had much success, and the great iron and copper industries in the Urals owe their origin to Peter. He was the initiator of what may be called modern education in Russia, not confined to one class, though mainly confined to the immediately useful and the technical. He devoted great attention to Asiatic lands and to Siberia, marched in person into Transcaucasia in war against Persia, sought out Central Asian routes to India, and initiated the final

[*] B. H. Sumner, "Peter the Great," *History*, Vol. XXXII (March, 1947), pp. 42–44, 47.

successful search for a northeast passage, discovered shortly after his death by Behring. He made the Russian navy out of nothing. He remade the Russian army, on the model of the up-to-date European armies of that day, armed for the greater part with flintlocks and bayonets, well-equipped with a varied artillery, munitioned in the end for the most part from Russian resources. With this army and navy he defeated Sweden, ultimately, after 21 consecutive years of war; and Sweden ranked among the foremost military powers of the day, and had in her King Charles XII a military leader who was the compeer of Marlborough and Prince Eugene, however lacking he was as a statesman. . . . With this army and navy Peter gained for Russia the Baltic provinces and the mouth of the Neva, where he founded his new capital St. Petersburg, achievements which obviously enough during the last seven years have been brought home again and again to the Russian people.

Such are some of the salient aspects of Peter's character and deeds which link up easily enough with much that is of absorbing interest to the Soviet Union. But I would like at this point to utter a caveat against facile comparisons which are often made between Peter and Stalin or Lenin, or between what was accomplished under Peter and what has happened in the last 30 years in Russia. There is, in my opinion, nothing truly corresponding to the October Revolution in Peter's transformation of Muscovy into Russia—or indeed in any period of Russian history. Peter stood for a new outlook on life, but not for a radically new type of society or of state. He has often been compared to a thunderstorm, with blinding, searing lightning, with drenching but fruitful and irrigating rain, a thunderstorm in spring *from a clear sky*. That is an untrue comparison. The thunderstorm had been slowly working up, growling and flickering on the horizon, long before it burst with Peter. His methods were extreme and violent and shocking to many, perhaps most, of his subjects—so had been Ivan the Terrible's methods a century and more before him—and in that sense he may be called revolutionary; as Herzen styled him: "*un jacobin anticipé et un terroriste révolutionnaire*," who wrought "grimly and terribly against the will of the people, relying on autocratic authority and personal strength." But he did not seek either to build upon entirely new foundations or to sweep away the essentials of the Muscovite social structure. Especially, he not only did not change the basic fact of serfdom: in various ways he extended serfdom and clamped it down more heavily. His achievements were very great, even though many of them were undone or warped after his death, but they constituted a great era of reforms, rushed through at breakneck speed, rather than a revolution in comparison with so all-embracing and far-spreading and profound a revolution as that begun in 1917. . . .

If you take eight essential fields in which Peter wrought profound changes, you will find that in all of these there were beginnings in the generation before him, and sometimes much farther back than that. That applies to the greater part of his foreign policy, to his army reorganization, to his reorganization of the central government, to his reorganization of taxation and serfdom, to his employment of foreigners in Russia and education reforms, to his insistence on compulsory service, to his economic and industrial developments, and lastly to his break with the prevailing traditional and ritualistic ordering of life typified in so much of 17th-century orthodoxy. I can think of only four changes wrought by Peter (though they were great and lasting) which had either nothing leading toward them in the immediate past or so very little that it scarcely counts. These were the education of Russians abroad, the abolition of the patriarchate, the creation of the navy, and the making of a new capital, St. Petersburg. Further, however much in many ways Peter was enamored of the West and borrowed from it, he did not do so indiscriminately or wholesale, and he remained thoroughly Russian.

3. VIEWS OF SOVIET HISTORIANS

A.

After completing his studies at the University of Moscow, Mikhail N. Pokrovsky (1868–1932) taught history in the secondary schools of Moscow. In 1905 he joined the Bolshevik wing of the Social Democratic party and became a very active member. In 1908 Pokrovsky emigrated to France where he wrote some of his most important historical works, including his Russian History from the Earliest Times (5 vols.; Moscow, 1910–14).

Pokrovsky returned to Russia on the eve of the Bolshevik Revolution and soon became the most influential historian under the new regime. He was responsible for organizing Communist historical studies and editing the principal historical journals. His writings met with Lenin's approval and remained the official Marxian interpretation of Russian history for about 15 years. The Party began to find fault with Pokrovsky's interpretations, however, as its needs changed with the growing international ten-

sions of the early 1930's, and it repudiated his views completely within two years of his death.

The following selection is taken from Pokrovsky's Russian History *from the Earliest Times.*

MIKHAIL N. POKROVSKY[*]

Thus in the Russia of the end of the 17th century there were present all the conditions requisite for the development of large-scale production: there was capital (though in part foreign); there was a domestic market; there were working hands. These factors are more than sufficient to prevent comparison of Peter's factories with artificially forced hothouse plants. And nevertheless the collapse of Petrine large-scale industry is a fact just as indubitable as the other facts we have just stated. The manufactures founded under Peter failed one after another; hardly a tenth part of them dragged out their existence to the second half of the 18th century.

A closer examination of this, the first industrial crisis in Russian history, shows that nothing could have been more natural, and that it is to be explained by the very fact formerly assigned as the cause of the rise of large-scale industry in the reign of Peter. It is an absolutely mistaken opinion that political conditions forced the growth of Russian capitalism in the 17th and 18th centuries; but it is quite true that the political framework of a state that was controlled by the nobles prevented this capitalism from developing. Here, as in other fields, Peter's autocracy could not create anything, but it did destroy much; in this respect the history of the Petrine manufactures supplies a perfect parallel to the picture of administrative havoc so well depicted by Mr. Milyukov in his book.

"The merchantry of Your Majesty are very few, and it may be said that already there are none," as an unknown Russian "who was in Holland" wrote to Peter in 1715. His explanation was the competition of "exalted personages." But, over and above competition, Peter's very method of influencing industry was such as to frighten capital away rather than to attract it. Even in the Muscovite period industry had been hampered enough by monopolies and privileges; but both of these restricted the application of capital negatively, so to speak, by showing it what it could not do. Peter tried to teach capital what it must do and where it ought to go, and he executed his task with the energy and force ever native to him, but with a naïveté that might vie even with the methods of Pososhkov,

---

[*] Mikhail N. Pokrovskii, *History of Russia from the Earliest Times to the Rise of Commercial Capitalism,* trans. and ed. by J. D. Clarkson and M. R. M. Griffiths (New York: International Publishers, 1931), pp. 283–87.

who made the amount of trading profit depend on the trader's firmness of character. Commands in the spirit of Pososhkov (and in the spirit of medieval mercantilism in general)—for example, that serfs should wear Russian cloth only and should not dare to wear imported cloth, and in case cloth failed should sew clothes of kersey, or that no one should dare to wear clothes with galloon, "for the English are richer than we, and they do not wear galloon"—were the mildest and most indirect methods employed by Peter to influence the development of industry.

He was capable of acting far more directly and simply. An edict to the senate (January, 1712) prescribed: "so to multiply plants, and not in one place, so as in five years not to purchase an imported uniform, and to give an establishment to the trading men, having collected a company, whether they are willing or not, and not to assess this plant heavily so that they should have encouragement to earn in that business." We have heard a good deal about serf labor under Peter; but of serf entrepreneurs we have heard far less often, and this type is incomparably more interesting. In 1715 it came to Peter's ears that Russian leather was not thought much of abroad since dampness soon spoiled it, thanks to the Russian method of tanning it. Immediately it was prescribed that the leather be made in a new way, for which purpose craftsmen were despatched through the whole empire; "for this instruction a term of two years is to be given, after which if any one makes leather in the old way, he shall be sent to penal servitude and deprived of all his property."

The results of such paternal care are shown by the well-known fate of the North Russian linen weavers. As we know, Russian linen and linen cloth went abroad in large quantities. Foreign merchants chanced to reproach the czar because the Russians sent them very narrow linen cloth, which was disadvantageous in use and therefore was priced far more cheaply than if it had been broad. Immediately Peter most strictly forbade the weaving of narrow linen cloth and linens; but in the huts of the Russian domestic workers there was no room to set up broad looms, and the domestic weaving of linen languished, ruining many merchants engaged in the marketing of this merchandise. Similar were the results of prohibiting the men of Pskov from trading in flax and flax products with Riga, a measure designed to stimulate the trade of the port of St. Petersburg. That this whole campaign against domestic weaving was intended to support the large-scale manufactories of linen cloth which were then being established (one of them belonged to the empress) can hardly be doubted.

But Peter lacked the patience to wait until capital began of itself to flow into the business, and he tried to drive capital into the manufacture of linen cloth with a club. As a result, in place of the tens of thousands of weavers now ruined, he got only the linen cloth manufacture conducted by a certain Tamesz; it is true, this establishment made goods, as foreigners declared, no worse than foreign goods, but it could make ends meet only thanks to the fact that it was bolstered up by having ascribed to it a large village (Kokhma) of 641 peasant homesteads. A factory that had to be maintained by the labor of serfs was no capitalistic enterprise. It was flaunted before foreign travelers as a nursery of Russian craftsmen, but it does not appear that they later found application for their skill.

Peter firmly believed in the club as a tool of economic development. "Is not everything done by compulsion?" he asked his imaginary opponent in an edict of 1723. . . .

The most European measure in this catalog of compulsions was the protective tariff; "whatever factories and manufactures are established among us, it is incumbent to impose on such imported articles a duty on everything except cloths." In fulfillment of this desire of the edict of 1723 the tariff, published in the following year, imposed on a large part of the manufactures imported from abroad a duty of 50–75 percent ad valorem. . . .

In a different, but just as unhealthy, way Peter's mercantilism manifested itself in the iron industry; almost prohibitive duties were imposed on iron, and at the same time the treasury plants at Tula were wholly absorbed (from 1715) in the manufacture of the arms needed in such quantities for the army as reformed by Peter. Supply of the popular demand was wholly in the hands of privileged monopolist entrepreneurs like the celebrated Demidov or the czar's kinsman, A. L. Naryshkin. It was more advantageous to the Treasury, both politically and financially, to have its own small arms and its own cannon than to be dependent on Holland for them. But probably more favorable for the development of the iron industry in Russia on a large scale had been the times when Marselis made poor cannon and good frying pans.

The intensive and compulsory development of Russian manufactures under Peter had, of course, another consequence, one long since noted by historians; Peter's reign marks the beginning of the bondage factory. The advantages of free labor in manufacture were as well recognized then as in the preceding period; Tamesz was bound by contract, like Vinius and Marselis in their time, "to hire as apprentices and workmen free men and not serfs, with payment for their labour of a worthy wage." But when it was a matter of putting a hundred enterprises into operation all at once, including some very large ones . . . the small number of free workers available could not be sufficient. On the other hand, the monopolist entrepreneur was not much interested in the quality of his products. The quality did not matter, for there was no one else to buy from. Hence arose a natural tendency to replace free labor with substitutes, and the government was willing to meet this effort halfway. "By the edict of February 10, 1719, it was prescribed to send off to the linen-cloth factories of Andrew Turchaninov and his colleagues, 'for the spinning of flax, the women and girls, who, whether by the central offices at Moscow or by other provinces, are punished for their faults.' By an edict of 1721 this measure was made general; women guilty of various offences were sent, at the discretion of the Collegium of Manufactures and Mines, for work in company factories for a certain term or even for life." The edict of January 18, 1721, permitting merchants to purchase inhabited hamlets for factories and workshops, definitely legalized this state of affairs. But if the factory owner could now carry on his business with the labor of serfs, who prevented the serfholder from establishing a factory? Peter's measure brought little advantage to Russian industrial capitalism, but it was one of the forerunners, remote enough as yet, of bondage, or landlord, capitalism. Given a uniform character, and consequently uniform quality of labor, the landlord's factory had every chance of defeating the merchant's; and so it turned out in the course of the 18th century. By drawing the string too taut, Petrine mercantilism broke it altogether.

B.

Little need be said by way of introduction to the last selection in this chapter. Since 1953 more than a half dozen volumes of an official history of Russia have appeared in a series entitled Studies in the History of the U.S.S.R. *(Ocherki istorii SSSR). The series is published by the Institute of History of the Academy of Sciences and one of the volumes of more than 800 pages is devoted exclusively to the first quarter of the 18th century. It is from the conclusion of this volume that the following passage has been translated and abridged. While the names of Marx, Lenin, and Stalin are cited, the summary contains no mention of Peter the Great.*

INSTITUTE OF HISTORY OF THE ACADEMY OF SCIENCES[*]

In the first quarter of the 18th century the productive forces were developing at an accelerated pace and the political and economic independence of our country was gaining ground. A struggle was being waged against the economic as well as the military, administrative, and

---

[*] Akademiia Nauk SSSR. Institut Istorii. *Ocherki istorii SSSR. Period Feodalizma. Rossiia pervoi chetverti XVIII v. Preobrazovaniia Petra I* (Moscow, 1954), pp. 766–74.

cultural backwardness of Russia. It should be kept in mind, however, that these achievements failed to benefit all classes: they increased the domination of the landed gentry and the oppression of the serfs. A heavy price was being paid for any successes.

Most notable in the economic development of the time was the rise of large industrial undertakings. Within a quarter of a century 180–200 big industrial enterprises arose in the Ural area, in Karelia, Moscow, Petersburg, and other localities. In the field of agriculture the changes were less impressive. The growing social division of labor brought about a greater specialization of the various agricultural regions. On the hereditary estates (*votchiny*) outside the black earth area the system of rent paid by the peasants (*obrok*) made headway, while in the black earth South the economy based on compulsory labor (*barshchina*) became prevalent. The area of the cultivation of flax and hemp expanded, and attempts were made to improve livestock breeding. The growth of industry and the partial advance in agriculture were accompanied by expanding commerce, both domestic and foreign.

In the social-economic development of Russia during the first quarter of the 18th century elements of primitive accumulation were more in evidence than in the preceding century. Under primitive accumulation Marx understood the accumulation of capital that is not the result of the capitalistic system of production but its starting point. The essence of primitive accumulation consists in the separation of the immediate producers from all property in the means of production, and in the concentration of wealth converted into capital. Expropriation of the land, bloody legislation against the workers, heavy taxation, trade, protectionism, the colonial system—these are the methods of primitive accumulation. Marx emphasized, however, that the history of primitive accumulation "in different countries, assumes different aspects, and runs through its various phases in different orders of succession, and at different periods."

It was the peculiarity of primitive accumulation in Russia that it proceeded within the framework of the social system of serfdom. Serfdom hampered the expropriation of small producers; it also impeded the transformation of impoverished peasants into free sellers of labor. Moreover, the system of serfdom allowed the landowner to control the accumulation of capital by the upper stratum of the peasantry and to appropriate a part of this accumulated wealth under the guise of increased rent (*obrok*). It was another distinctive feature of the primitive accumulation in Russia that it owed much less to colonial depredations than the same process in England and the Netherlands. . . .

One of the sources of primitive accumulation during the period under study was the budget of the state. Tax revenues tripled between 1680 and 1728.... The threefold increase of the state budget imposed a heavy burden on the working population, both peasants and townsfolk. Peasants had to look for work in various trades outside agriculture. Frequently an impoverished peasant abandoned husbandry altogether and, while still his landlord's serf, hired himself out to work in town, in water or land transportation, or in a factory. A significant number of serfs escaped to the borderlands of the state—the Don, the Ural, Siberia.

The increased budget allowed the government to spend large sums on building up vast industrial undertakings, to be later transferred into private ownership. In many cases the initial capital would pass directly from the Treasury to the manufacturer in the form of a subsidy for the establishment of a factory. Large sums went also to contractors who supplied the state with equipment, clothing, provisions. The merchant and the contractors, in their capacity of middlemen between production and markets, exploited the immediate producers.

The state tended to meet the demands of the manufacturers halfway, and along with granting them privileges for the construction of manufactories it restricted or prohibited the importation of the respective goods from abroad.... Protectionism and monopolies enriched the rising bourgeoisie at the expense of the masses of the people.

A part of the capital accumulated by the merchants was being invested in industry. For the first time manufacturers were now coming from different backgrounds—big merchants (Shchegolin, Miklaev), prosperous artisans (Demidov, Batashov), well-to-do peasants (the Miliakovs). Still, the accumulation of capital and its transfer from the sphere of circulation into that of production was a comparatively slow process.

According to the testimony of contemporaries, the workers in some manufactories were paid no more than it cost to keep a prison inmate. The dispossessed producers were taught the discipline of a large enterprise by means of harsh punishment and fines.

The influx of impoverished peasants did not ensure a sufficient labor force to the factories. The government therefore used various methods to provide manpower to the manufacturers—forcibly assigning peasants to industrial plants; permitting manufacturers to buy serfs; allocating recruits, convicts, prisoners of war, beggars, vagabonds, and so forth to factories.

Thus, in the first quarter of the 18th century various developments were taking place in Russia that are characteristic of a period of primitive accumulation: the impoverishment of a part of the immediate producers, and the accumulation of wealth in the hands of merchants and

industrialists. The state played an active part in this process inasmuch
as it "manufactured manufacturers" by feudal methods—by providing
additional labor power to the factories, and also directly by organizing
commercial and industrial companies in a compulsory manner....

In noting the advances of metallurgy in the Ural area in the course
of the 18th and 19th centuries, V. I. Lenin discerned two stages of its
development: the first, when the system of serfdom still contributed to
the growth of the Ural industry, which reached a high mark in the 18th
century, and the second, when that system became a handicap and
caused the decline of the Ural in the 19th century....

The growth of feudal exploitation and the process of the accumulation of capital by merchants, manufacturers, and the upper stratum of
the peasantry brought about the intensification of the class struggle. In
1705 a riot broke out at Astrakhan; in 1707–08 antifeudal rioting occurred on the Don; the years 1705–11 saw uprisings in Bashkiria. Peasant uprisings occurred even in the central and southern provinces of
the realm. All the rebellions, whether of peasants or townspeople, were
put down with the utmost cruelty. New forms of the class struggle originated in the factories, with workers rising up against the owners.

The Russian empire of the first quarter of the 18th century represented
an absolutist state dominated by landowners and the rising mercantile
class and administered by bureaucratic institutions....

The efforts to overcome the economic and military backwardness of
Russia went together with measures to develop culture and learning. The
growing industry, the reorganized army, and the reformed bureaucratic
machinery required well-trained officers, competent officials, skilled workmen. During that period the foundations were laid for specialized school-
ing.... The spread of education did much to consolidate the position of
the landed gentry and the upper merchantry, since education was available mainly to these classes.

By the end of the first quarter of the 18th century the gap between
backward Russia and the advanced states of Western Europe had been
reduced; the productive forces of the country were developing faster
than in the preceding period. The role of Russia in international affairs
had grown immeasurably.

Nevertheless, the reforms failed to put an end to Russia's backwardness, inasmuch as they were carried out within the narrow frame of a
feudal system based on serfdom and were ultimately aimed at strengthening that system. Neither the feudal aristocracy nor the rising bourgeoisie
were equal to the task of overcoming backwardness.

In the long process of the formation of the Russian nation, the period under study represents an important stage. The process had begun in the 17th century with the emergence of an all-Russian market and bourgeois relationships.

Territorial unity, one of the attributes of nationhood, had been achieved in the preceding period.... Economic unity, another attribute of a nation, was steadily growing during the period under study in connection with the increasing social division of labor.... A national market was gaining ground.

Superstructural factors also influenced the formation of the nation. The greater centralization of the state authority with the establishment of absolute monarchy, the organization of a regular army and navy, the mobilization of manpower for construction, the transfer of artisans from one region to another—all this contributed to the emergence of a linguistic and psychological community....

During the period under consideration some changes occurred in another sphere characteristic of nationhood: the common language. The first quarter of the 18th century represents an important stage in the evolvement of a language of literature and its gradual liberation from the influence of the church-Slavonic language....

Psychological unity, in other words the "national character," is a historical category. J. V. Stalin points out that "the national character is not an entity given once for all but is subject to change in accordance with changing conditions; yet insofar as it exists at any given moment, it puts its stamp on the face of the nation."

Victorious wars, tenacious labor in agriculture and industry, as well as the fierce struggle against the exploiters, provided vast opportunities for the display of the remarkable qualities of the Russian national character: a lucid mind, fortitude and endurance. The victories at Azov and Poltava ... the leadership of Russia in the Northern Alliance intensified Russian national consciousness, raised Russian patriotism to a higher level, strengthened common psychological attitudes which found expression in a common culture....

To sum up: The main historical significance of the processes that took place at the end of the 17th and in the first quarter of the 18th century lies in the growth of the productive forces of the country—the rise of manufacturers, the construction of waterways, the expansion of commerce, and so on. The organization of a regular army, the creation of a navy, the administrative reforms contributed to progress; and the achievements in the field of foreign policy brought about a definite solution, favorable to Russia, of the perennial Baltic problem.

In the cultural field the reforms resulted in the establishment of a series of general and special schools, the increase in technical knowledge, the creation of the Academy of Sciences. A theater came into being, as well as secular painting; architecture, literature, and political writing achieved a flourishing state.

The people, however, had to pay a high price for the progress achieved: the aggravated oppression of the peasantry. The cultural and all the other advances profited mainly the ruling class of the landowners and, in some measure, the merchantry.

While the system of feudalism and serfdom proved still able to ensure a certain growth of the productive forces, the bondage of the peasantry restricted its scope. Neither the landowning class nor the bourgeoisie were capable of overcoming the backwardness of the country. Only the proletariat, two centuries later, in carrying through the great socialist October revolution and seizing the power, opened the way to the unprecedented cultural and material advance of the masses.

John B. Wolf, Professor of History at the University of Illinois, Chicago Circle, was born in Ouray, Col., in 1907. A graduate of the University of Colorado, he received his M.A. from that institution and his Ph.D. from the University of Minnesota. He was a Guggenheim fellow, Paris, and a Fulbright research professor at the Sorbonne, and formerly taught history at the University of Missouri and the University of Minnesota. He is the author of *Diplomatic History of the Bagdad Railroad* (1936); *France 1815 to the Present* (1940; paperback, 1962); *The Emergence of the Great Powers, 1685–1715* (1961; paperback, 1962); and, soon to appear, a biography of Louis XIV and, with Hutton Webster, a two-volume *History of Civilization*. He has written many articles and has contributed chapters to co-operatively written books. A member of the American Historical Association and past chairman of its European section, he belongs to other French and American historical societies.

CHAPTER NINE

JOHN B. WOLF

University of Illinois, Chicago Circle

Louis XIV

AT THE DEATH of his father in 1643, Louis XIV became King of France; his personal rule began in 1661 when Cardinal Mazarin, his minister and mentor, passed from the scene; the reign lasted until 1715, and when Louis finally died, there was no one alive who could remember any other king. A career so long and so eventful quite naturally has attracted the attention of many historians, so many, indeed, that in a short chapter it would be impossible to present more than a small sample of their works. The selections that have been made were chosen to illustrate both the historian's attitude toward the reign of Louis XIV and his conception of the nature of history, for this latter usually conditions his approach to his problems as well as the material that he chooses to illustrate his story. There is good reason to argue that the historian's conception of the nature of history can be more important in forming his interpretations than his class, his nationality, or his political philosophy. While we find that rightist-oriented historians generally treat Louis XIV kindly and more or less approve of his actions, and that leftist-oriented historians tend to be critical, their basic assumptions about the historical process are often more important than their political views in conditioning the form of the presentation of their history.

The many aspects of the reign of Louis XIV that could be used to illustrate the varieties of historical interpretation make it difficult to choose among them. However, since the historian's opening gambit will often reflect his attitudes, it seems suitable to present the different ways in which historians have introduced their readers to the opening years of Louis's personal reign.

The first selection was written by one of the most famous men of letters of the 18th century. Voltaire was historian, playwright, poet, novelist, critic, a man of caustic wit and of passionate devotion to his profession. His was not the first history of the reign of Louis XIV, but it was unquestionably the most widely read of all such histories written in the 18th century. In some of his works Voltaire shows insight into history as a process, but in the selection presented here he writes like most other historians of his time, that is to say, he rarely rises above a chronological account. He presents one event after another with little or no discussion of their interrelationships or of the forces in society that were probably responsible for them. The sequence is orderly, but without explanation. Voltaire's history is like his account of the career of Candide; it is a series of events held together by time, but in the end the series becomes the basis for a moral judgment. Thus history is not an organic story or even a philosophical analysis; it is the raw stuff for moral preachments. Voltaire opens his account of Louis' personal government with a relatively colorless presentation of the problems of foreign affairs. There seems to be little organic connection between events, but they will become the framework upon which the author can erect an ethical statement. As a man of letters, Voltaire approved of Louis' search for *la gloire* by supporting and patronizing the arts and the sciences, but he disapproved of the Sun King's wars, of any king's wars, and used chronology of events to show the folly and wickedness of such wars. Voltaire does not try to understand the King's foreign policy; he wants to use it to teach his philosophy about the world.

The next selection is from Guizot's *History of France*. Guizot, professor of history at the Sorbonne, became prime minister (1841–48) under Louis Philippe. His history only slightly reflects the understandings that he might have gained from active participation in the affairs of state, but it does well illustrate his basic assumption that the emergence of the bourgeoisie as a class capable of exercising power was the most important event of modern history. Guizot's history is largely based upon *mémoires*, and as a result of this sort of material, his account often becomes little more than a series of anecdotes. It is not surprising that the Fouquet incident introduces Guizot's story of the reign, for in it we find a bourgeois figure to be the victim of prejudice and tyranny. Guizot's sympathies, like those of most of the memoirists upon whose accounts he relies, are with Fouquet. It is interesting that he calls attention to the fact that Louis' arbitrary action against Fouquet was probably motivated, among other things, by his fear that the fallen minister might dominate him. Most historians have pointed to Fouquet's wealth, his display, suspicions of his dishonesty and Colbert's hostility, and have overlooked this psychological insight into Louis' acts. Nonetheless, Guizot's history is the old-fashioned variety; with its anecdotal frame of reference and its reliance upon *mémoires* for its material, his account is in the mold of the humanist historians rather than that of his contemporaries in the German seminars where von Ranke's teachings were being taken seriously.[1]

The next selection is one of the finest fruits of 19th-century French historical scholarship. In the decade before the opening of the war of 1914–18 French academic historians undertook to write a multivolume history of France under the general editorship of Professor Ernest Lavisse.[2] Lavisse himself projected and wrote most of the three books in this series dealing with Louis XIV's reign. This work is "scientific history" at its best: objective, concise, and complete within the framework of its author's conceptions. Like much of French thought in the 19th century, it is Cartesian in its form, that is to say, rigorously logical within a mechanistic frame of reference. As Lavisse introduces us to the reign of the young King, he presents the mechanism of government, the machine of state. It is an analysis that assumes a sort of static reality; the state becomes a social mechanism that can be understood in terms of its structure. Lavisse relies upon the academic research of his generation for his material; the "facts" are dredged up from the archives and libraries and allowed to "speak for themselves." In this passage Lavisse remains objective and dispassionate, but he was a "republican" historian of the generation that fought the battles of the Dreyfus case, and his final assessment of monarchy is critical of the institution as well as of the King.

The next selection is by Louis Bertrand, a man of letters turned historian, who regarded history as both literature and polemic. In nice contrast to Lavisse who tried to allow "the facts to speak for themselves," Bertrand uses the facts to prove his point. He wanted to show that France achieved *gloire* and *grandeur* under the monarchy that, by implication, would be impossible under a republic, and to prove that the frontiers of France vis-à-vis Germany were justified by history. Bertrand's *Louis XIV* is more interesting reading than Lavisse's, but it is literature or propaganda

---

[1] "Scientific history," taught in Germany, proposed that history be written as "it actually happened" by rigorous analyses of sources, broad research in archives, and a neutral presentation that would allow the facts of history to speak for themselves. The new schools of historians may never have achieved their goal, but they did introduce a vigorous and important element into historical thought.

[2] E. Lavisse, *Histoire de France*. The first series of nine volumes (eighteen books) is subtitled *Depuis les origines jusqu'à la Revolution*. The second series, largely written immediately after 1918, takes the story from 1815 to the end of the war of 1914–18.

rather than history. In the selection presented below, Bertrand prepares his readers for the great events of the reign by showing how Louis was aware of his mission; a closer reading of the letters of the King would have forced him to modify his simplified interpretation.

The next selection was written by Professor André Latreille of the University of Lyon. It is part of a two volume cooperative history of France, published in 1950 and written, so say its authors, "for all the French." Since France has so long had history written for the "left" or for the "right," this becomes a formidable task to accomplish. Since the authors intended their book for use in the French *lycées* and for the general readers, they actually did attempt to remain neutral or noncommittal on many of the controversial topics of French history. Professor Latreille has given us a colorful, interesting account of the opening years of Louis's reign; he has emphasized its importance for the great traditions of the French nation. The reader will note that this presentation, in contrast to those of other 20th-century historians, places great emphasis upon the impact of the person and the personality of Louis XIV on the historical process. The King, rather than abstract forces, or deeply flowing movements, or processes that grind on with almost mechanical precision, is at the center of this story; even the King's mistresses find their place in the complex problems of the reign. This approach to history has long been out of style among academic historians except when they engage to write a biography, and even then, the personality of their "hero" is often subjected to the great forces that dominate the era. It may be that even a character as important as Louis XIV was determined by the world into which he was born, yet it is fascinating to speculate upon the possible course of events had another occupied his place. This problem may be at the center of the old controversy between those who believed that "men make their times" and those who insist that "the times determine the character of the men."

The last selection is taken from one of the most distinguished general histories produced by mid-20th-century French academic scholarship. Professor Mousnier has completely abandoned the formal presentation found in Lavisse; his studies have convinced him that the history of Europe following the latter Middle Ages has been given its form by a series of crises that have affected all aspects of European life. The efforts to solve these crises only deepened their impact or imposed upon them as new orientation: thus new crises, according to this theory, appeared with ever increasing severity. According to Mousnier the 16th- and 17th-century political crises created disorders that cried aloud for strong government, for the suppression of the unruly pluralistic forces in the society; he finds that Louis XIV and his advisers were struggling to solve their problems by creating new institutions only to find that the crises continued to expand. Professor Mousnier is also a competent scholar, alert to the necessity of correcting errors that have crept into the corpus of historical learning. Thus we find that in this selection he shows us that the traditional interpretation of Louis' ministers as "bourgeoisie" is not tenable. Louis' ministers were professional royal officials, who, like the professional soldiers who emerged toward the end of the regime, were a new class that cannot be described as bourgeois, "vile or otherwise." Professor Mousnier's approach to history does not end the necessity for deepening our understanding of the past, nor is it probable that it will be universally accepted, but it does give history a meaning that is significant and it evokes many new questions and new avenues for future research.

A character as complex as Louis XIV and a period as important for the history of modern Europe resists simple explanations, but in the discussions of the first steps of the regime we can see the emergence of its characteristic forms. The remolding of the government of the monarchy by bureaucratic organization, and the development of the French army as an instrument of high policy, both contributed to the rise of the modern military-police state and to the emergence of a new order in the international organization of the European world.

1. AN ASSERTIVE POSTURE

Voltaire was an important figure in the history of historical writing, quite aside from his role as a critic and literary giant. Here he describes the young King assuming command at home and asserting the position of France abroad.

VOLTAIRE*

Never were there so many intrigues and expectations in any court as while Cardinal Mazarin lay dying. Women with any pretense of beauty flattered themselves that they would rule a prince of 22, whom love had

---

* Condensed from Voltaire's, *The Age of Louis XIV*, trans. Martyn P. Pollack (New York & London: Dutton & Co., Everyman's Library). Reprinted by permission of E. P. Dutton & Co., Inc.

already so far beguiled as to make him offer his crown to his mistress. Youthful courtiers saw visions of a new reign of favorites. Each minister hoped for the premier place. Not one of them thought that a king brought up in seclusion from affairs of state would dare to take the burden of government upon his own shoulders. Mazarin had prolonged the monarch's childhood so long as he could. . . .

It was so little expected that their sovereign would take up the government himself, that of all those who had hitherto worked with the first minister there was not one who asked the King when he would require his services. They all inquired, "To whom shall we address ourselves?" and Louis XIV replied, "*To me.*" They were still more suprised to see him persevere in his resolution. He had already tested his forces and secretly examined his talent for ruling: his resolution once taken, he kept it to the last moment of his life. He fixed the limits of the power of each minister, requiring them to render a full account to him at stated times, giving them the confidence necessary to the credit of their office, and keeping a watch on them to prevent their abusing it.

Mme. de Motteville informs us that the renown of Charles II, King of England, who was said to govern by himself, aroused the envy of Louis XIV. If such was the case he greatly surpassed his rival. . . . He began by putting his revenues in order, disorganized as they were by prolonged peculation. Discipline was restored among the troops as was order in finance. Magnificence and propriety distinguished his court. Pleasure itself put on splendor and grandeur. All the arts were encouraged, and all dedicated to the glory of the King and of France. . . .

The fantastic point of honor was as keen . . . among crowned heads as was the rage for dueling among private gentlemen.

(1661) It happened that on the arrival of a Swedish ambassador in London, a dispute arose between Count d'Estrades, the French ambassador, and the Baron de Watteville, the Spanish ambassador, as to who should take precedence. The Spaniard with more money and a larger suite had won over the English populace; he began by killing the horses drawing the French carriages, and soon the company of the Count d'Estrades, wounded and scattered, was forced to let the Spaniards pass on with drawn swords as in triumph.

When Louis XIV learned of this outrage he recalled his ambassador from Madrid, dismissed the Spanish ambassador, broke off the conferences which were still being held in Flanders with regard to boundaries, and sent word to his father-in-law, Philip IV, that if he did not acknowledge the supremacy of the French crown and make amends for this outrage by a solemn satisfaction, war would be begun afresh. Philip IV had no desire to plunge his country into a new war on account of an ambassador's precedence; and he sent Count de Fuentes to declare to the King at Fontainebleau in the presence of all the foreign ministers at that time in France (March 24, 1662) that "in future Spanish ministers would not enter the lists against the French." This was not a definite acknowledgment of the preeminence of the French king, but it was a plain enough avowal of the weakness of Spain. . . .

Hardly had he come out of this little affair with such a display of greatness than he showed still more in a matter where his glory seemed less interested. . . . Italy regarded all the nations by whom she was invaded as barbarians, and the French as barbarians who differed only from the rest in being gayer and also more dangerous, since while they introduced pleasures into their houses they also introduced contempt, and added insult to licentiousness. They were feared everywhere, above all at Rome.

The Duke de Créqui, ambassador to the pope, had disgusted the Romans by his arrogance; his servants carrying as usual their master's faults to an extreme. . . .

Some of the lackeys of the Duke de Créqui bethought themselves to charge, sword in hand, a squad of Corsicans (the bodyguard of the pope who see to the execution of justice). The whole company of Corsicans was bitterly offended, and secretly stirred up by Don Mario Chigi, brother of Pope Alexander VII, who hated the Duke de Créqui, they armed themselves and proceeded to attack the ambassador's residence (August 20, 1662). They fired on the coach of his wife, who was returning to the palace; and succeeded in killing one of her pages and wounding several servants. The Duke de Créqui left Rome, accusing the Pope's relations and the Pope himself of having countenanced the murders. The Pope delayed making reparations as long as he could, believing that one has only to temporize with the French and all is forgotten. Finally, at the end of four months, he had a Corsican and a guard hanged, and the governor expelled from Rome who was suspected of having authorized the outrage; but he was astounded to learn that Louis threatened to lay siege to Rome, that he was already marching troops into Italy, and that the Marshal du Plessis-Praslin had been appointed to command them. The affair had become a quarrel between one nation and another, and the King was determined that his country should be respected. Before making the reparation demanded, the Pope implored the mediation of all Catholic princes; he did his best to stir them up against Louis XIV, but circumstances were unfavorable to him. The empire was being attacked by the Turks, and Spain was hampered by an unsuccessful war with Portugal.

The Roman court only succeeded in irritating Louis without being able to do him real damage. The Parliament of Provence subpoenaed the pope and seized the county of Avignon. In former times such outrages would have been followed by excommunications from Rome, but they were now useless weapons and had become ridiculous; the Pope had perforce to give way; he was obliged to banish his own brother from Rome, to send his nephew, Cardinal Chigi, as legate *a latere* to give satisfaction to the King, to break up the Corsican guard and to erect a pyramid in Rome, bearing an inscription relating both the insult and the reparation. Cardinal Chigi was the first legate of the Roman court ever sent to ask for pardon. . . . he forced the Court of Rome to promise the surrender of Castro and Ronciglione to the Duke of Parma, and to compensate the Duke of Modena for his claims on Comacchio; he thus reaped from the insult the substantial honor of becoming the protector of the Italian princes.

While upholding his dignity he did not forget to increase his power (October 27, 1662). The state of his finances wisely administered by Colbert enabled him to buy Dunkirk and Mardick from the King of England for 5 million livres, at 26 livres 10 sous to the mark. . . .

(1663) Louis set 30,000 men to work on the fortifying of Dunkirk, both by land and sea. Between the town and fortress he constructed a harbor large enough to contain 30 ships of war, so that the English had scarcely sold this town than it became a source of dread to them.

(August 30, 1663) Some time afterward Louis forced the Duke of Lorraine to surrender the stronghold of Marsal to him. . . .

Louis extended his territories even in time of peace and held himself always in readiness for war, fortifying his frontiers, keeping his troops well disciplined, adding to their number, and holding frequent reviews. . . .

While openly throwing his weight on the side of the Emperor and adding luster to the French arms, the King directed his policy toward supporting Portugal secretly against Spain. By the treaty of the Pyrenees Mazarin had formally deserted the Portuguese; but Spain had broken several of the smaller provisions of the peace. France now broke out boldly and decisively; Marshal de Schomberg, a foreigner and a Huguenot, marched into Portugal with 4,000 French soldiers, whom he paid with money from Louis XIV, but pretended to do so in the name of the King of Portugal. These 4,000 French soldiers joined with the Portuguese troops and obtained a complete victory at Villa-Viciosa (June 17, 1665) which established the House of Braganza on the throne. Louis XIV was thus already regarded as a warlike and diplomatic prince, and Europe feared him even before he had yet made war.

It was by his diplomacy that he evaded his promise to unite the few vessels he then possessed to the Dutch fleet. He had allied himself with Holland in 1662. About that time, that republic renewed the war with England on the absurd and idle pretext of respecting the national flag, the real issue being the question of trade in the Indies. Louis was delighted to see these two maritime powers launch year by year fleets of more than a hundred vessels, which mutually destroyed one another in some of the most stubborn fights that have ever taken place, the net result of which was weakening of both powers. . . . During the ministry of Richelieu, France thought herself to be powerful at sea, because out of about 60 men-of-war lying in her ports, nearly 30 were seaworthy and one carried 70 cannon. Under Mazarin, the few vessels she possessed were bought from Holland. Sailors, officers, and materials for their construction and equipment were alike lacking. With incredible activity Louis set about reestablishing the navy and providing France with everything she lacked; but in 1664 and 1665, while the English and the Dutch were overrunning the seas with nearly 300 large ships of war, he had as yet but 15 or 16 vessels of the poorest class, which the Duke of Beaufort was employing against the Barbary pirates; and when the Netherland States urged Louis XIV to join his fleet to theirs, only a single fireship could be found in the port of Brest, which he was ashamed to send, but it was necessary to do this at their repeated requests. With all speed Louis XIV hastened to remove this ignominy.

(1665) He rendered more material and creditable aid to the Netherlands with his land forces, sending 6,000 French to defend them against Christopher Bernard Van Galen, Bishop of Münster, a warrior prelate and their implacable enemy, who had been bribed by England to lay waste Holland; but he made them pay dearly for this help and treated them like a powerful man who sells his protection to wealthy merchants. Colbert charged them not only with the soldiers' pay but even with the expenses of sending an ambassador to England to conclude peace with Charles II. Never was help given with so bad a grace or received with so little gratitude. Having thus accustomed his troops to war and made fresh officers on the fields of Hungary, Holland, and Portugal, the King, respected and revenged in Rome, found himself with not a single ruler to fear. With England ravaged by the plague, and London reduced to ashes by a conflagration unjustly attributed to the Catholics, with the perpetual extravagance and poverty of Charles II, as perilous to the state as plague and fire, France had no cause of fear so far as England was concerned. The Emperor was hardly yet recovered from the exhaustion of a war against the Turks. The King of Spain, Philip IV, whose kingdom was as feeble as himself, lay dying and Louis XIV remained the sole powerful and formidable monarch. He was young, rich, well served, blindly obeyed, and eager to distinguish himself by foreign conquest.

2. LOUIS XIV AND FOUQUET

Guizot was an accomplished historian—perhaps the best of an age that had not yet succumbed to the rigorous standards of "scientific" history. As the chief minister of a regime that steadily lost confidence and was widely regarded as corrupt, his account of a monarch's ability to strike down a powerful minister is particularly interesting.

M. GUIZOT*

Cardinal Mazarin on his deathbed had given the young king this advice: "Manage your affairs yourself, Sir, and raise no more premier ministers to where your bounties have placed me; I have discovered, by what I might have done against your service, how dangerous it is for a king to put his servants in such a position. . . ."

The King's councillors were men of experience; and they all recognized the master's tone. From timidity or respect, Louis XIV had tolerated the yoke of Mazarin, not, however, without impatience and in expectation of his own turn [Portraits de la Cour, *Archives curieuses*, t. viii. p. 371]: "The cardinal," said he one day, "does just as he pleases, and I put up with it because of the good service he has rendered me, but I shall be master in my turn. . . ."

A taste for order and regularity was natural to Louis XIV, and he soon made it apparent in his councils.

Under Cardinal Mazarin, there was literally nothing but disorder and confusion; he had the council held while he was being shaved and dressed, without ever giving anybody a seat, not even the chancellor or Marshal Villeroy, and he was often chattering with his linnet and his monkey all the time he was being talked to about business. After Mazarin's death the king's council assumed a more

─────────
* M. Guizot, *France*, trans. Robert Black (New York: P. F. Collier & Son, 1898), Vol. IV, pp. 210–18. This material reprinted with the kind permission of Crowell Collier and Macmillan, Inc.

decent form. The king alone was seated, all the others remained standing, the chancellor leaned against the bedrail, and M. de Lionne upon the edge of the chimney-piece. He who was making a report placed himself opposite the king and, if he had to write, sat down on a stool which was at the end of the table where there was a writing desk and paper [*Histoire de France*, by Le P. Daniel, t. XVI. p. 89].

"I will settle this matter with your Majesty's ministers," said the Portuguese ambassador one day to the young king. "I have no ministers, Mr. Ambassador," replied Louis XIV: "you mean to say my men of business." . . .

At 22 years of age, no more than during the rest of his life, was Louis XIV disposed to sacrifice business to pleasure, but he did not sacrifice pleasure to business. It was on a taste so natural to a young prince, for the first time free to do as he pleased, that Superintendent Fouquet counted to increase his influence and probably his power with the King. "The attorney general [Fouquet was attorney general in the parliament of Paris], though a great thief, will remain master of the others," the queen mother had said to Madame de Motteville at the time of Mazarin's death. Fouquet's hopes led him to think of nothing less than to take the minister's place.

Fouquet, who was born in 1615, and had been superintendent of finance in conjunction with Servien since 1655, had been in sole possession of that office since the death of his colleague in 1659. He had faithfully served Cardinal Mazarin through the troubles of the Fronde. The latter had kept him in power in spite of numerous accusations of malversation and extravagance. Fouquet, however, was not certain of the cardinal's good faith: he bought Belle-Ile to secure for himself a retreat, and prepared, for his personal defense, a mad project which was destined subsequently to be his ruin. From the commencement of his reign, the counsels of Mazarin on his deathbed, the suggestions of Colbert, the first observations made by the King himself irrevocably ruined Fouquet in the mind of the young monarch. While the superintendent was dreaming of the ministry and his friends calling him *the Future*, when he was preparing, in his castle of Vaux-le Vicomte, an entertainment in the King's honor at a cost of 40,000 crowns, Louis XIV, in concert with Colbert, had resolved upon his ruin. The form of trial was decided upon. The King did not want to have any trouble with the parliament, and Colbert suggested to Fouquet the idea of ridding himself of his office of attorney general. Achille de Harlay bought it for fourteen hundred thousand livres; a million in ready money was remitted to the King for his Majesty's urgent necessities; the superintendent was buying up everybody, even the King.

On the 17th of August, 1661, the whole court thronged the gardens of

Vaux, designed by Le Nôtre; the King, while admiring the pictures of Le Brun, the *Fâcheux* of Molière represented that day for the first time, and the gold and silver plate which encumbered the tables, felt his inward wrath redoubled; "Ah! Madame," he said to the Queen his mother, "shall not we make all these fellows disgorge?" He would have had the superintendent arrested in the very midst of those festivities, the very splendor of which was an accusation against him. Anne of Austria, inclined in her heart to be indulgent toward Fouquet, restrained him: "Such a deed would scarcely be to your honor, my son," she said, "everybody can see that this poor man is ruining himself to give you good cheer, and you would have him arrested in his own house!"

"I put off the execution of my design," says Louis XIV in his *Mémoires*, "which caused me incredible pain, for I saw that during that time he was practising new devices to rob me. You can imagine that at the age I then was it required my reason to make a great effort against my feelings in order to act with so much self-control. All France commended especially the secrecy with which I had for three or four months kept a resolution of that sort, particularly as it concerned a man who had such special access to me, who had dealings with all that approached me, who received information from within and from without the kingdom, and who, of himself, must have been led by the voice of his own conscience to apprehend everything." Fouquet apprehended and became reassured by turns; the King, he said, had forgiven him all the disorder which the troubles of the times and the absolute will of Mazarin had possibly caused in the finances. However, he was anxious when he followed Louis XIV to Nantes, the King being about to hold an assembly of the states of Brittany....

On the 5th of September, in the evening, the King himself wrote to the queen mother:

My dear mother, I wrote you word this morning about the execution of the orders I had given to have the superintendent arrested; you know that I have had this matter for a long while on my mind, but it was impossible to act sooner, because I wanted him first of all to have thirty thousand crowns paid in for the marine, and because, moreover, it was necessary to see to various matters which could not be done in a day; and you cannot imagine the difficulty I had in merely finding means of speaking in private to D'Artagnan. I felt the greatest impatience in the world to get it over, there being nothing else to detain me in this district. At last, this morning, the superintendent having come to work with me as usual, I talked to him first of one matter and then of another, and made a show of searching for papers, until, out of the window of my closet, I saw D'Artagnan in the castle-yard; and then I dismissed the superintendent, who, after chatting a little while at the bottom of the staircase with La Feuillade, disappeared during the time he was paying his respects to M. Le Tellier, so that poor D'Artagnan thought he had missed him, and sent me word by Maupertuis that he suspected that somebody had given him warning to look to his safety; but he caught him again in the place where the great church stands and arrested him for me about mid-day. . . .

Three years were to roll by before the end of Fouquet's trial. . . . Fouquet's papers were seized, and very compromising they were for him as well as for a great number of court personages, of both sexes. Colbert prosecuted the matter with a rigorous justice that looked very like hate; the King's self-esteem was personally involved in procuring the condemnation of a minister guilty of great extravagances and much irregularity rather than of intentional want of integrity. Public feeling was at first so greatly against the superintendent that the peasants shouted to the musketeers told off to escort him from Angers to the Bastille: "No fear of his escaping; we would hang him with our own hands." But the length and the harshness of the proceedings, the efforts of Fouquet's family and friends, the wrath of the parliament out of whose hands the case had been taken in favor of carefully chosen commissioners, brought about a great change; of the two prosecuting counsel (*conseillers rapporteurs*) one, M. de Sainte-Hélène, was inclined toward severity; the other, Oliver d'Ormesson, a man of integrity and courage, thought of nothing but justice, and treated with contempt the hints that reached him from the court. Colbert took the trouble one day to go and call upon old M. d'Ormesson, the counsel's father, to complain of the delays that the son, as he said, was causing in the trial. . . .

Fouquet, who claimed the jurisdiction of the parliament, had at first refused to answer the interrogatory; it was determined to conduct his case "as if he were dumb," but his friends had him advised not to persist in his silence. The courage and presence of mind of the accused more than once embarrassed his judges. . . . Nobody had forgotten his conduct during the Fronde. M. d'Ormesson summed up for banishment and confiscation of all the property of the accused; it was all that the friends of Fouquet could hope for. M. de Sainte-Hélène summed up for beheadal. . . .

"If he is sentenced, I shall leave him to die," proclaimed Louis XIV. Fouquet was not sentenced, the court declared for the view of Oliver d'Ormesson. "Praise God, sir, and thank Him," wrote Madame de Sévigné, on the 20th of December, 1664, "our poor friend is saved; it was thirteen for M. d'Ormesson's summing-up and nine for Saint Hélène's. It will be a long while before I recover from my joy; it is really too overwhelming, I can hardly restrain it. The King changes exile into imprisonment and refuses him permission to see his wife, which is against all usage; but take care not to abate one jot of your joy, mine is increased thereby and makes me see more clearly the greatness of our victory." Fouquet was taken to Pignerol, and all his family were removed from Paris. He died piously in his prison, in 1680. . . . Fouquet was guilty; the bitterness of his enemies and the severities of the King have failed to procure his acquittal from history any more than from his judges.

Even those who, like Louis XIV and Colbert, saw the canker in the state deceived themselves as to the resources at their disposal for the cure of it; the punishment of the superintendent and the ruin of the farmers of taxes (*traitants*) might put a stop for a while to extravagances; the powerful hand of Colbert might reestablish order in the finances, found new manufactures, restore the marine and protect commerce, but the order was but momentary and the prosperity superficial, as long as the sovereign's will was the sole law of the state. . . .

3. THE KING AND HIS GOVERNMENT

Ernest Lavisse was one of the finest and most respected products of Third Republican scholarship prior to World War I. This selection is a fine example of the cumulative impact made when statements of fact are allowed to pour out in profusion—"speaking for themselves."

ERNEST LAVISSE[*]

I. The Central Government

To understand Louis XIV's long reign . . . it is necessary to describe, at least briefly, the political structure of France and the [means and] instruments of government employed by the King and his ministers. The political system, "the mechanism," as Saint-Simon called it, was a badly coordinated mélange of old and new parts. Neither Louis XIV nor any of his ministers, Colbert excepted, intended to institute a new system. They preserved the old one while simplifying it and providing it with a more regular procedure.

The king was assisted in the government by the chancellor, the ministers of state, and the councils. The chancellor was the last survivor of the

---

[*] Ernest Lavisse, *Histoire de France illustré depuis les origines jusqu'à la Revolution,* trans. Joseph Klaits; Vol. 7:1 (Paris: Librairie Hachette, 1911), pp. 149–59.

great officers of the feudal kingdom. Chairman of all the councils and head of all the courts and tribunals, he was responsible for the royal seal. Every royal document passed through his hands. "Inspector and controller of all the affairs of France," his was the duty and the right to withhold the seal from documents of which he disapproved. He could not be removed from office unless convicted of a capital crime. . . .

The ministers of state, of modern origin, were simply the king's councillors in his most secret affairs; they were, so to speak, ministers without portfolio and without departments. Before 1661 they had been named by letters patent, but Louis XIV omitted this formality, and whomever he invited to the High Council became a minister. The title was retained for life, but the ministerial function ceased on the day the messenger no longer called a man to council. . . .

The secretaries of state were the administrators of the kingdom. They bought their office, but with the agreement of the king, who could force them to sell it. In 1661, the secretaries of state were Brienne, La Vrillière, Guénégaud, and Le Tellier. Brienne was in charge of Champagne, Provence, Brittany, Metz, Toul, and Verdun; La Vrillière oversaw Languedoc, Bayonne, Guyenne, Brouage, Aunis and La Rochelle, Touraine, Anjou, Maine, Bourbonnais, Nivernais, Auvergne, Picardy, Normandy, and Burgundy; Guénégaud had Paris and the Ile-de-France, Orléanais, Blaisois, Berry, and Béarn; finally, Le Tellier was responsible for Poitou, Saintonge, Augoumois, Marche, Limousin, Lyonnais, Dauphiné, and Catalonia. Thus, each of the secretaries of state was one fourth of a minister of the interior. In addition, the special functions of government were distributed among them: to Brienne, foreign affairs, the Atlantic marine, pensions; to La Vrillière, the affairs of the Huguenots, "the so-called reformed religion"; to Guénégaud, the *maison du roi* and the clergy; to Le Tellier, war, the artillery, and the Levantine marine. Each minister was responsible for the fortifications of places situated in his departments.

Finances were administered separately. After the disgrace of Fouquet the superintendancy of finance was abolished. The King reserved this task for himself with the assistance of a council composed of the chancellor, Marshal Duke de Villeroy, and three others, among whom was an intendant of finance named Colbert. With this rank alone until 1665, and with that of controller general afterward, Colbert was a superintendent without the title, which was suppressed because it had been too ostentatious. Colbert had invented this arrangement, and the King approved of it. The Duke de Villeroy sat in this council only as a figurehead; Colbert was its true master.

There were many councils, for the *ancien régime* believed in polysynody. The High Council, where only the ministers sat, was officially called the Council of State. In it are discussed, wrote Spanheim;

all the great questions of war and peace. In it are read the dispatches of the king's ministers in foreign courts, the responses made there and the instructions given them. Treaties are deliberated as well as the alliances and interests of the crown with foreign powers. In short, in this council are proposed and re- solved all that concerns the government and that might be of some importance to the king, the court and the state both within the kingdom and outside it.

The council was held in the King's apartment before dinner, which was at one, seven times in two weeks: on Sunday, Wednesday, and Thursday of one week and, in the following week, on those three days and on Mon- day. The King sat in his armchair and ministers on their taborets. . . .

The Council of Dispatches, presided over by the king, included the chancellor, the ministers, and the secretaries of state. In it were read "all dispatches from within the kingdom": it was something like a collective ministry of the interior. . . .

The Council of Finance, also called the Royal Council, dealt with the collection of the taille and distributed his tax among the *generalités*. They drew up accounts of the farms and oversaw the conduct of the farmers, managed the royal domain, deliberated on "extraordinary affairs," and examined and controlled the entire state budget. . . .

The High Council, the Council of Dispatches, and the Council of Fi- nances were, so to speak, domestic, that is they met in the royal apartment. The fourth council sat outside the apartment but within the palace. It was a high court which exercised supreme jurisdiction over the whole realm both in civil matters. . . . It was called simply the Council, or the Council of Parties, because of its judicial functions, or the Privy Council, either because it judged private affairs or because it was the king's court and resided near him, whereas the Parliament and the Great Council, at first lodged in the household, had left and had become "Sovereign Courts."

The councillors of state were chosen from among the presidents of the courts, procurators or advocates general, intendants, *maîtres des re- quêtes,* and provosts of the Parisian merchants. They too had many func- tions. . . .

Seven bureaus dealt with civil cases and administrative cases of cas- sation, which were very common. Further, there were three bureaus of finance, the bureau of estates, the bureau of the gabelle, farms, and the taille, and the bureau of financial management. The councillors and *maîtres des requêtes* were distributed among these bureaus and commis- sions, upon which the full weight of the administration of the kingdom converged.

The King appeared at the Council of Parties only rarely. Ordinarily, his throne of red velvet bordered with gold and silver remained empty at the head of the table, which was covered with a cloth of violet velvet edged with gold *fleurs-de-lis*. To the left of the throne sat the chancellor, the chairman of plenary sessions. The councillors, arranged in order of seniority, wore black silk robes with square collars and loose sleeves. Their chairs of black morocco leather were movable as a symbol of their ambulatory habits, for the council followed the King on his journeys unless specially exempted. . . .

These governmental institutions of Louis XIV's reign were imperfectly organized. The ministers—chancellor, ministers of state, secretaries of state, controller general—were not on an even footing. The division of royal administration among four secretaries of state was a vestige of a time when these officials merely dispatched letters and orders; in the 17th century the system was singularly outmoded. There seemed to be no rationale for the way provinces and functions were divided among the secretaries of state. Furthermore, only one of the secretaries of state in 1661, Le Tellier, was also a minister. Brienne, secretary of state for foreign affairs, was not summoned to the High Council, where such matters were handled by Lionne. Brienne received the dispatches, de Lionne reported them; de Lionne prepared the responses, Brienne sent them out. . . .

In addition, work was parceled out among the councils, as among the ministers and secretaries of state, more by amount than by functional division. Spheres of authority were not delineated, undoubtedly because the "certain knowledge" and "full power" of the sovereign king were found wherever he had his throne, and his throne was everywhere. . . .

In 1669 the care of fortifications was still divided among the four secretaries. Later, when Seignelay, Louvois, Colbert de Croissy, and Chateauneuf were secretaries of state, fortifications were entirely under Seignelay in newly conquered territories and under Louvois everywhere else. The provincial division was also better managed: of his father Le Tellier's share, Louvois retained only the frontier provinces. But inexplicable combinations still remained: Colbert's office, for example, included the *maison du roi* and the clergy along with the entire marine. The fractionalization of the secretaries of state and the impotence of the Council of Dispatches also persisted. Saint-Simon says that Louis disliked this council, but perhaps the real story is that the King preferred to deal with each secretary of state individually.

In the same way, each of the councils retained its combination of political, administrative, and judicial powers. Beside them, or rather below them in unacknowledged inferiority, the parliaments, the *chambres des comptes,* the *cours des aides,* and the Great Council preserved their own political, administrative, and judicial functions. This double and triple overlapping, a source of impediment and conflict, persisted for the duration of the monarchy.

There was one novelty, a hallmark of the reign, that compensated for the defects and inadequacy of the mechanism. The administrative personnel—ministers, secretaries of state, and councillors—were all men whose only job was to serve the King because it was his pleasure to be served by them. . . .

In the whole reign, only two dukes received positions in the high administration, both in the Council of Finance, over which they presided: Marshal Duke de Villeroy and the Duke de Beauvilliers. Both were intimates of the King, and the first was of only medium nobility. Louis left to high nobles the title of "Councillor of the King in all his Councils," but this was a title without function. . . . Louis took counsel only from those he selected and paid. Finally, all the King's servants were animated by the same spirit, produced by this fusion of administration and justice, a spirit shrewd, imperious, and single-mindedly ambitious. The ideal of devotion to the state circulated throughout all the councils, while the *maîtres des requêtes* and the intendants carried it to the provinces. They made perpetual war on all dissidence and resistance.

Otherwise, even the defects of the regime were not without their advantages. The fusion of powers . . . broadened the experience of the ministers and gave them a total view of the government. Each day all France passed before the eyes of Colbert, minister of state, superintendent of buildings, controller general, secretary of state, member of all the councils. This system provided the King's councillors with a complete political education.

II. The Role of the King

Louis XIV was equal to the task of presiding over the government. Had he been indolent or vacillating, the internecine conflict of royal institutions would have reduced the kingdom to anarchy, as was the case in the next century. Had he been high-spirited and energetic, the slow, complicated machine of government would have exhausted his patience and worn him down. In fact, he was calm and steady; while not creative himself, he knew how to use the ideas of others. . . . The assiduousness of the King set a brisk pace for the entire government. Ministers, secretaries and councillors of state, *maîtres des requêtes* knew that one day they would be summoned to the King's presence. One had to be ready with counsel;

young men hoped that if they presented a good report their careers would be made. All the personnel of government lived together, observing one another and looking to the King. . . .

It was a proof of his all-powerful authority that he could raise up great lords from nothing, just as God had molded man from a bit of clay. But he observed his creatures suspiciously, lest they persuade themselves that their greatness was of their own making.

The King preferred to have only a small number of ministers, to change them as infrequently as possible, and to replace fathers with their sons. He created two ministerial dynasties, the Le Tellier and the Colbert, and the members of these families succeeded to offices that they considered hereditary. It seemed that the same council endured throughout the period, presided over by one king. . . .

Quite naturally, the two families were not fond of each other, and this was not objectionable to the King; he told his son to "divide your confidence among several, for the jealousy of one serves as a brake on the ambition of others." . . .

There can be no doubt that Louis XIV governed France during his reign. The ordinariness of his mind was overshadowed by the genius of his servants, but they would not have labored so effectively had not the King constantly encouraged them and reviewed their work. Furthermore, Louis XIV perceived correctly that after his servants had done their work something still remained that only a king could provide: "A king, no matter how enlightened and skillful his minister, does not so much as lay hands on a piece of work without making it a reflection of himself."

4. THE KING'S SECRET

In this selection the student will meet a quite different appreciation of Louis XIV. This is a much more humanistic account than one finds in Lavisse. How does it compare with our selections by other authors?

LOUIS BERTRAND*

He is 22 years old, and has long since been crowned. His prime minister has just died. The example of the Cardinal, even more than his formal

---

* Louis Bertrand, *Louis XIV* (London, New York: Longmans, Green and Co., 1928).

instructions, has shown him how to handle men, and how to carry through a sustained political program. His tragic love for Marie Mancini has tested his mettle. The stage is set for him to do something. What will it be?

For some time he has been asking himself the same question. Later, in his *Mémoires*, he wondered whether he made a mistake in not assuming the administration of the state at once. "If it was a mistake," he told his son, "I have done my best to atone for it; and I can assure you, without qualification, that it was due neither to carelessness nor to laxity. From childhood, the mere mention in my presence of the 'Do-nothing Kings' and the Mayors of the Palace was painful to me." He adds that *in his heart he preferred fame to everything else, even to life itself.*

But you should know [he says] that my first steps, those which were either to lay the foundations for that fame or make it foreever impossible, were aided and hindered in almost equal degree by this self-same desire for glory. *However, I first tested myself in secret* without taking anyone into my confidence. I thought out for myself the problems brought up by various events; I was full of hope and joy when I found that *sometimes* my first reactions or my conclusions coincided with those of skilled and experienced men. At heart I was sure that I had not been placed and kept upon the throne, that I could not have such a deep desire to do good, unless I possessed the means necessary to do so. . . . Finally after several years had passed by in this manner, the general peace, my marriage and the death of Mazarin forced me to assume the task which I had so long both longed for and feared.

Note once again his modesty. The King was far from believing that he was born to govern without first learning how, or that conducting the government was an easy matter. It was with fear and misgiving that he assumed control. Yet he did not hesitate to take the step. The nation had besought him to rule alone. He desired, therefore, to have no prime minister. Resolutely he proclaimed his decision to his attendants. At first no one believed him. Even the Queen Mother (proving thereby how little she knew her son) claimed that this laudable enthusiasm would prove to be only a flash in the pan. Already the best informed courtiers spread the rumor that the Cardinal de Retz, then in exile, would be Mazarin's successor. But before that happened, they claimed, the King would appoint him ambassador to the Vatican. To put an end to these rumors, Louis XIV at once demanded the Cardinal's resignation as Archbishop of Paris and immediately appointed his successor. Moreover, he forbade him to come into the vicinity of Paris. Henceforth no one denied that the era of ecclesiastical prime ministers had come to an end.

For a young man of 22 to make such a decision showed a courage that is not sufficiently appreciated. . . .

Here we have him, then, settling down voluntarily to his task. "I began,"

he says, "by glancing rapidly over the various governmental departments
—not casually, *but with the eye of a responsible master.* I was impressed
by the discovery that there was not one of them that was not in imperative need of my personal attention." Before doing anything else, he examined his own conscience, he looked into himself—for on himself, he knew,
everything depended. Exactly what was he?

He was king—that is to say, an extraordinary being—an intermediary
between men and God, and he was entrusted with divine authority. The
Parliamentarians, the Protestants themselves (out of opposition to the
pope) maintained that his authority derived directly from God and that
no power could release his subjects from the allegiance they owed him.
They called him "a living Christ," an "adorable master." All that is forgotten when Louis XIV is accused of arrogance. His detractors forget that
a belief in all that was demanded of him by the nation that he might be a
bulwark against the Pope, who claimed the same prerogatives. Like the
Pope and like the bishops, he too was a priest and had his sacred vocation.

It is to be remembered that after receiving the royal unction at the
time of his coronation he was clothed in tunic, dalmatic, and mantle,
representing "the vestments of a deacon and sub-deacon and the chasuble
of a priest." Like Christ, he performed miracles, cured the scrofulous, and
healed the sick. He was weighed down by appalling responsibilities.
Twenty-five million subjects relied upon him not merely for their livelihood but for happiness and life itself. He was even more the father than
the master. The coronation liturgy specified both his titles and his obligations. Louis recalled vividly one of the most impressive rites of the
ceremony. The presiding bishop, the Duke de Laon, placed a ring on his
finger "to wed him to France." This nuptial rite, according to a contemporary, was "symbolic of the binding union of our Kings with the State;
as a husband loves only his wife, so our monarchs declare that they will
cherish their subjects and grant them protection."

No French king ever took the symbol of this ceremony more seriously.
Louis XIV like his predecessors, had been wedded to France before the
altar at Rheims. Among the items of expense for the coronation, specific
mention is made of "the diamond for the marriage to France." So low
were the funds in the treasury at this time that it was necessary to borrow
a ring from Anne of Austria—it was returned to her immediately after the
ceremony. The lover of La Vallière, the husband of the Infanta, "daughter of the greatest King in the world," never forgot this mystic marriage
performed to the sound of triumphal trumpets in the marvelous basilica,
filled with flying doves released under the high arches, giving the impression that the sculptural seraphim had suddenly spread their wings

and taken flight. Henceforth he was pledged to France by this beautiful and brilliant diamond. What mattered his mistresses and his earthly spouse! It was to France, his spouse of glory, that he had given his heart. What would the young bridegroom, in the full vigor of his youth, do for his beloved Bride, so exacting and so formidable?

With "the assurance of a master" and the tenderness of a lover, he examined conditions in France and in the rest of the world. Despite a long succession of victories and the recent favorable treaty of the Pyrenees, the condition of France, indeed, that of all Europe, seemed precarious. People in general felt that the peace was merely a truce and that it might be shattered at any moment. . . .

Louis XIV shared the impatient desire of his subjects to put an end to the arrogance of his neighbors. He was all the more conscious of it because of the mortification and humiliation he had suffered from the Spanish at his marriage. Lastly, from childhood he had been constantly annoyed by his mother's ceaseless boasting about her country and her family. He came to detest his uncle, His Catholic Majesty, and all the subjects of this conceited monarch. . . .

Glory. What poet refers to it with more emotion, more fervor, than he. The famous passage in his *Mémoires* is known to all. "The love of glory entails the same nicety of handling and it might be said, the same timidity as the more tender passions. . . . The more eager I was to distinguish myself, the more fearful I was lest I fail; since I regarded the slightest mistake as a great disaster, in all that I did I was anxious to take every precaution." Here we have what really lies at the bottom of the King's mind at this time—"to take every precaution." Eager as he was to start things moving, to obey the desires of the nation, to quench his thirst for glory, and to vent his personal grievances, he did not wish to launch France upon any ill-considered enterprise. Moreover after almost half a century of war the country needed a rest, however much it may have desired to put an end to the Spanish threat. For this reason the King held his peace for some time. . . .

The first thought of this man, so often described as a pitiless tyrant, was, therefore, to lighten the burden of his subjects. The paramount duty of a sovereign is, however, to look to their security and, as far as possible, their prosperity; and to do that another war was inevitable. He could not prepare for it too far ahead. Hence he started at once to store up money and to prepare his troops for war; but he did it quietly and without alarming the enemy. If the enterprise was to succeed, it must be shrouded in secrecy until the last moment. Consequently the king attempted to disguise his belligerent projects under an air of frivolity. Those not privy to his secret thought that he was devoting his whole energy to flirtations, to his mistresses, his horses and dogs, military reviews, balls and ballets, open air fetes and fireworks. In reality at this time a thousand plans were taking shape in his head.

For the time being he lived for pleasure, for riches, for splendor, while he awaited the moment when he might live for glory.

5. THE METIER OF LOUIS XIV

Compare this selection especially with those by Lavisse and Mousnier. Though an important consideration of the War of Devolution has been deleted, we have here an excellent piece of historical writing. Is the king one sees here much different than the monarch presented by our other authors?

ANDRÉ LATREILLE[*]

Louis XIV—The Splendor (1661–85)

Foreign historians themselves give the name of *Siècle de Louis XIV* to the second half of the 17th century. From the treaties of Westphalia and the Pyrenees up to those of Utrecht, the French preponderance in Europe and in the world appeared still more evident than had previously been the hegemony of Spain and than must have subsequently been the influence of England. By aims and diplomacy the very Christian king made his will prevail upon the other sovereigns, and then he held his own against their coalition.... Finally, the brilliancy of letters and the arts, the perfection of an ordered and fulfilled civilization gave France a prestige which was to endure beyond her military or economic victories. The Grand Century ... offered the spectacle of the harmonious assembling of all the forces of a nation, then the best endowed and the most vigorous in Europe, under the rule of a king who altogether embodied and directed it.

Louis XIV

Louis XIV is very well known. We possess an enormous number of medals, statues, portraits, prints, engravings of him as well as writings

---

* Edouard Perroy, Roger Doucet, and André Latreille, *Histoire de la France pour tous les Français*, Book I, trans. Donald Bailey (Paris: Librairie Hachette, 1950), chap. XVIII, pp. 375–82.

about him, for French and foreign memorialists accord an unceasing attention to the King. He is especially well reflected in the *Mémoires* which he dictated or inspired in the course of the first years of his reign and in the letters which up to the end he wrote and the style of which, the royal (memorandum) enchanted Voltaire and Sainte-Beuve. That his genius and his role should be the object of very diverse judgments is the ordinary fate of great men, but often those contradictions would be clarified if one took the care to distinguish among the phases of his life and to see in their true colors the Louis XIV of the accession, whom Le Bernin modeled with verve in 1665; the one of the maturity whom Mignard painted in 1674 crowned by Victory; and finally the one of the decline, such as Saint-Simon unpityingly described and as the famous wax of Antoine Benoist preserved in 1706.

He possessed majesty and grace, Saint-Simon admitted, "an incomparable and unique exterior giving an infinite value to the smallest things ... a perfect visage with the greatest appearance and the most distinguished bearing that one has ever seen." At 22 years of age, he added his bodily strength to his handsomeness, "an equal healthiness, firm and almost never interrupted," an astonishing ardor of life. Why would one, like Lavisse, want the son of Anne of Austria to have been from Spain rather than from France? Because of his taste for etiquette and his solemn gravity? But this gravity, which one must not exaggerate—for it never excluded natural, just, moderation,—was possessed by every true man of that time; with even more reason did a prince apply himself to his "métier de roi." ...

Political Doctrine

His political ideas were decided as early as his accession; they had only to be asserted. The experience of his minority, the lessons of Mazarin inspired in him a deliberate and serene doctrine of absolutism. The kings were "absolute masters" and "whoever is born a subject should obey without question"; thus they wanted providential order: "The One who gave kings to men wanted them to respect them as His lieutenants"; the interest of the state, for it believed the Prince alone to penetrate the bottom of affairs; the very interests of the peoples, for "the tranquillity of the subjects was found only in obedience." This authority imposed great duties on the master: the obligation of an assiduous work, and moreover "delightful" for a nature like his, attentive to the well-being of the subjects which is confounded with that of the sovereign, and a constant rule not to sacrifice the state to his passions. But these duties often differed from those of common morals. The reason of state which Richelieu favored,

with Louis XIV in foreign politics took the form of a neo-Machiavel-
lism. . . .

At that time unanimous opinion gave its assent to this doctrine, which
prevailed in all of civilized Europe, in the England of Hobbes and of
Charles II as in the Spain of Philip IV, but which found in France its
clearest and most logical expression. Courtiers, magistrates of the supreme
courts, writers and artists, ministers of the two religions, the Catholic
and the so-called Reformed, revered the king as a visible divinity and professed unconditional loyalty. The intention of the doctrine of divine right
would have been certainly wrongly attributed to Bossuet, whose *Politique
tirée de l'Écriture* did not appear until 1709; it was universally admitted. . . .

The Acceptance of Power

On the day after the death of Mazarin, Louis XIV announced his
resolution to govern himself. In the future he would no longer have a first
minister. To this decision he must have been faithful for more than half a
century, until the last day of the reign.

With a remarkable sense of the necessities of the hour, he attacked
the task of reorganization. The nobility learned that the King waited for
the right occasion to bestow favors personally, that he wanted those who
aspired to his benefices, to be near him, and that he infinitely held to the
minute observance of ceremonial and etiquette; they rushed to the do-
mestication. There was no more room for them in the government except
in some extraordinary councils, when it pleased Louis XIV to call such a
personality judged competent in an affair under consideration. In the
High Council, the ministers were of the common people or men of the
smaller nobility. Three among them were recommended by their aptitudes
and their former services: Michel Le Tellier, secretary of state for war,
Hughes de Lionne at foreign affairs, Nicolas Fouquet, superintendent of
finances. Abruptly in September, 1661, this last one was arrested, tried,
condemned (the will of the King imposing the decision on the judges) to
perpetual seclusion. Louis XIV thus struck a barefaced and ambitious
peculator in whom the spirit of the Fronde perhaps survived; this blow
taught everyone that he would reign truly alone, would tolerate no illegitimate advancement.

A former intendant of Mazarin's, Colbert, received the title of controller
of finances. To wipe out the past he proceeded harshly. A chamber of
justice inquired into the malversations committed since 1635 and constrained certain financiers to restitute about a hundred million. . . .

In justice order had not suffered any less; commissioners departed in rides across the provinces. In 1664–65 Auvergne had its Grand Jours. In this particularly isolated region, rude manners and still feudal customs, and pillaging country gentlemen fostered disorder. An itinerant tribunal, with powers of discretion, examined 2,000 complaints in a few months and struck often very highly placed guilty ones without appeal. It had been a long time ago that the people had had such a direct sensation of the king's justice.

Finally, Louis XIV intended to banish entirely the remainder of the Jansenist sect, for reasons which "considered his honor and the welfare of his State." Pope Innocent X had condemned the theses of the *Augustinus;* he undertook to impose respect for the papal decisions everywhere. . . .

Everything was calm in every place. . . . After one year of marriage, after the happy birth of the Grand Dauphin, the king neglected the insignificant and sullen princess whom reason of state had imposed on him. In the train of his sister-in-law, Henriette of England, he discovered the sweet Louise de la Vallière whom he made his mistress; from this liaison which lasted six years four children were going to be born between 1662 and 1668. The court was quite agitated by the question of whether the young king would abandon himself to a course of carefree voluptuousness which seemed to sweep him away, or if, faithful to his first resolutions, he would hear the exhortations of the *dévots* supplicating him to have regard for the spiritual and temporal health of his people. Finally he worked out an accommodation with his conscience; what he would give to his amours would divert him neither from the accomplishment of the exterior obligations of religion nor from his application to affairs.

Toward Preeminence in Europe

Out of the 54 years of his reign Louis XIV spent 30 making war, offensive at least up to 1688. The first item of royal expenses was at death's door with war and foreign affairs. As early as 1680, the "extraordinary affairs" put the balancing of the budget in peril and the fiscal measures occasioned a very great misery for people.

Thus the external preoccupations dominated the whole reign. Even in the first 25 years, they greatly overshadowed it in importance, and, if they seemed to leave more room for the internal administration than befell it later, it was because the conflicts lasted a shorter time, absorbed fewer forces, and, up to Nimwegen, found a more advantageous conclusion. It may appear to us that the day after the peace of the Pyrenees they ought to have switched over to the second plan, to give way to the tasks of peace and of reform. To read certain historians one might believe that Colbert had offered that option to Louis XIV, but had finally been overthrown by Louvois who dangerously flattered the penchants of the master. The truth of the matter is rather different.

For Louis XIV the *métier de roi* consisted first of directing diplomatic activity and military operations. An already long tradition and the situation in which Mazarin left the kingdom wanted it thus. Since the Capetians, the kings had pursued the territorial building of a France which, toward the continent, was not achieved and which often felt itself exposed to more grave menaces. Against the house of Austria, for a half century, France's military tool had been admirably forged. . . . The feeling of the superiority of France naturally carried a young and proud sovereign to manifestations of prestige, expansion, and war. . . .

Diplomacy

Louis XIV exercised a direct influence over the diplomatic machine, which in his reign attained a high degree of perfection. In 54 years, he had only four ministers of foreign affairs. The first, Hughes de Lionne, knew Europe admirably and handled affairs with "a marvellous facility" and a grandeur of views which did not exclude prudence. At his death (1671), the King chose Pomponne, industrious and useful, but who displeased because "everything which passed by him lost the grandeur and force which one must have in executing the orders of a king of France who is not unfortunate." This disgrace was the only one of the reign. Later, Colbert de Croissy (1679–96) and Torcy (1696–1715) zealously carried the increasing weight of affairs. They kept up an immense correspondence with numerous and often changed ambassadors. The diplomatic service was not settled; for a determined mission the King chose the man whom his dignity and previous services appeared to designate, independently of every consideration of origins or even of religion. They sent him, provided with very full instructions, to his post, where, having "the honor of representing the person of the greatest monarch of the world," he had to assure himself of the first rank over the other legations and to display an ostentatious retinue. Almost always insufficiently paid, the ministers of France scattered money, because at that time all the powers believed in the efficacy of a policy of subsidies. In reality, except at the little German courts and for momentary successes, this manner of persuading was less decisive than the weight of French arms.

In the first years, that weight appeared to be without equal. Louis XIV liked to make it felt not only at London or Ratisbon but even at Rome, imposing on the pope, after the tiny affair of the Corsican guards (1664), a crushing humiliation. . . . If it is incontestable that in this reign diplomacy had "tested its forces in all directions" (Laroche), it would be absurd to attribute to Louis XIV dreams of megalomania. In fact, his policy aspired to well-chosen annexations, sufficiently justified by geographic and human conditions totally to enter the national heritage. It was rarely misled into chimeras. Unfortunately, by exorbitant declarations, by its brutalities, and by his willingness to have recourse to the *ultima ratio* of war, it had too often rendered the French name odious to foreigners.

6. ABSOLUTE MONARCHY:

THE FRENCH MODEL

In this final selection the student should note particularly how the discussion of the government and king in France is presented in a wider perspective. Much detail of the Lavisse variety has had to be deleted but the whole body of data is presented within a larger context.

ROLAND MOUSNIER*

Absolutism was the hope of those who saw their salvation in concentrating power in the single hand of the incarnation of the kingdom, the living symbol of order and unity. Everyone sought to find in the king the image of God: "You are God on earth." Many added the old humanist dream to this conception: the king should be a hero, a lover of glory in the style of antiquity, protector of the arts like Augustus, defender of the church like Constantine, a legislator like Justinian, but with a "predilection for arms," for "the dignity of a conqueror was esteemed the most noble and the most elevated of titles" by all contemporaries.

As the lieutenant of God, the king was sovereign. . . . The public weal is above private right. Thus the church is subordinated to the sovereign and owes him service for its possessions, which were given it "for the general good of the whole kingdom." It follows that:

Just as the sovereign power of the prince is a reflection of the omnipotence of God, so the power of officers is a reflection of the absolute power of the king. . . .

---

* Roland Mousnier, *Les XVIe et XVIIe Siècles, Histoire générale des Civilisations,* trans. Joseph Klaits, Vol. 4 (Paris: Presses Universitaires de France, 1956), pp. 229–36.

As the image of God, the king was obligated to represent Providence on earth. He had to administer justice, "a precious trust that God has delivered into the hands of kings as an element of his wisdom and his power." He ought to promote each of the professions which compose society, for "each of them has its functions, without which all the others undoubtedly would suffer. This is why, far from scorning any of these occupations, or favoring one at the expense of the others, we ought to take care to bring all of them, as far as possible, to the degree of development proper to each." Here is a social ideal which organizes the tasks and occupations of society hierarchically in accordance with human needs. Finally, the king should be the protector of the weak; he ought to "give to people who are subject to us the same proofs of paternal kindness that we daily receive from God," to have "nothing more at heart than to protect the weak from the oppression of the powerful and to provide for the needy some alleviation of their misery." Louis XIV personified these ideas. . . .

Now Louis XIV constructed the same kind of system that Henry IV had planned. He resolved to be his own first minister, so that he alone would be aware of all affairs and become the indispensable man. Thus, the King was led into a more and more bureaucratic life, ordered and organized for efficient output. . . . He was led to isolate himself at Versailles, in a palace and a city constructed for the king's work no less than for his propaganda and his pleasure. It has been said that this bureaucratic routine was an imitation of Spanish procedure. In fact, it was a characteristic of absolutism everywhere, for it derived from necessity.

During the ministerial epoch, institutions were regularized. But institutional development gave rights to dangerous men, *grands* and a first minister. Louis XIV initiated a regression whereby the royal will was left unrestricted. During the ministerial epoch the government was still based on family, birth, titles, and offices. In the High Council sat the members of the royal family, the princes of the blood, the dukes and peers, the chancellors, the superintendent of finance. Ministers were installed by letters patent, and they held their offices as private possessions. Louis XIV wrought a revolution. He removed from the High Council all who could claim political power by birth, title, or office. First his mother, his brother, the princes of the blood: the government ceased to be familial and became truly personal. Then, the chancellor of France, the prelates, the great landowners. Finally, the high officers. . . . The King discussed his affairs at certain times with people whom he was pleased to choose for the purpose. No one, besides the king, had the right to be in the government. All was concentrated in the hands of the monarch. . . .

Louis XIV . . . mistrusted the councils. Unable to do without them, he sought to reduce them to rubber stamps. He worked alone with each of his secretaries of state successively and with his controller general of finance. All important matters were decided by him and passed before the councils only as a formality, if at all. . . .

The King also distrusted his ministers and his secretaries of state. He recast the division of labor by distributing each specialized function of government among several men, so that no expert could be in a position to thwart his will. He set his servants off against one another, provoked them, divided them and fanned their mutual jealousies, for he saw in the opposition of the Colberts and the Le Telliers a guarantee of his power. . . .

More and more, the King made use of commissioners named by him and removable at his will. Further, the councillors of state of the administrative councils were commissioners. Under ministerial rule these councils had been granted by the kings the dignity of the first company of the kingdom with authority over the courts called sovereign, even in the king's absence. After 1632 the councils could nullify and cancel all decrees, including those of the parliaments, that ran against royal authority, against public utility, and against the rights of the crown. The councils intervened in judicial cases, decided them, and took over the functions of sovereign courts. Under Louis XIV the authority of these councils was maintained, but only as a useful fiction, since *arrêts du Conseil* often emanated from the king and his immediate auxiliaries, the secretaries of state and the controller of finance.

In both epochs, the authority of the king "in council" over the sovereign courts was affirmed. In 1641 the king solemnly reserved for himself the management of affairs of state . . . in 1673 he ordered the sovereign courts to register edicts of any kind immediately; remonstrance could only be made afterward, and just once. At most, the courts preferred merely to give an opinion. Thus, the sovereign courts were excluded from general policy decisions and from constitutional questions. . . . The King had codes drawn up (the Civil Ordinance of 1667, the Criminal Ordinance of 1670, the Commercial Ordinance of 1673), which were legal by the king's authority alone, without registration, without consultation, without participation by the constitued bodies. They exhibited a distinct tendency toward unity and equality, the work of a revolution. . . .

The King employed intendants of the army and intendants of justice, police, and finance. These intendants were primarily inspectors, charged with surveying the king's officers and subjects and reporting to the council. The council could then either resolve the question itself by an *arrêt* or delegate to the intendant the necessary power to judge, sentence, or regulate by ordinance. The intendant thus presided over the courts of justice, amended the law in accord with royal ordinances, investigated to see whether officers were carrying out their duties and suspended them if they were not, heard the complaints of the King's subjects and saw to it that justice was rendered them in local courts. The intendants presided over municipal assemblies, supervised elections, verified the debts of communities and watched over the observation of orders and regulations. They inspected the collection of taxes and presided over the bureaus of finance. This is nothing less than an outline of the government's responsibilities. . . .

The intendant was an extremely flexible instrument. In time of war or internal crisis the council could extend his powers indefinitely until the intendant took over all the duties of officers and left them nothing but the title. At these times the intendants and their subordinates formed an administration of commissioners rivaling the administration of officers. The royal government, however, considered these occasions exceptional, an unfortunate necessity. In times of peace the King strove to keep the intendant, always wont to try to extend his power, limited to the role of inspector. . . .

The King strengthened police regulations. These were carried out by intendants, spies, and agents interspersed everywhere. . . . On weak evidence the intendants or the council were prompted to accusations of lese majesty, and judgment was rendered on the basis of simple appearances, for Richelieu, Louis XIII, and Louis XIV held that in matters of conspiracy it was nearly impossible to have mathematical proof and that it was not necessary to wait for the event that would prove and lose everything. The king resorted to preventive prison sentences of indefinite length. . . .

Among all the important officers . . . Louis XIV only wanted those "dévoués" who joined domestic services to their public functions and, like Colbert, transmitted the King's notes to his favorites or received from his mistresses their natural children. He used the sentiment of vassalage, but he wanted to be the sole object of such feelings of dependency. His goal was the establishment of absolutism by the direct connection of all Frenchmen to the king by means of a personal bond, just as vassals had been held to their suzerains. He aspired to be the universal and unique suzerain, or, at all events, the universal patron. . . . All bonds of sentiment and interest converged upon the King who embodied the prayers and hopes of all his subjects and thereby, no less than by the personal exercise of power, concentrated the state in himself and consummated in his person the unity of the state. Thus the King prepared his subjects, by the medium of ancient sentiments, to advance to the conception of the abstract state. Through vestigial instruments of medieval times Louis XIV cleared the way for the modern state.

One of the royal instruments in this accomplishment was the policy of opposing class to class and raising the bourgeois in the social scale. Increasingly in the course of the century the King chose his ministers, his councillors, and his intendants from among the bourgeois in the legal professions. These were men "emerging from complete, simple commonalty" but "exalted above all grandeur." The King ennobled the Le Telliers and the Colberts and made them marquises. They became great seigneurs known by the names of their estates: Louvois, Barbezieux, Croissy, Torcy. He created dynasties of ministers, families and lines whose force he used in opposing noble families and lines. The rolls of the capitation of 1695 put the ministers of state in the first class, the chancellor and the controller general of finance at parity with the princes of the blood. In the administrative sections of the Council of State the proportion of men of the robe increased. The *règlement* of 1673 fixed the number of titled councillors at 24 councillors of the robe, 3 of the church, and 3 of the sword. Further, for the latter, there was no longer the condition of several degrees of nobility: a son of a gentleman of the robe could accede to the nobility of the sword. Among the members of the Privy Council by right, the dukes and peers slowly disappeared. The *règlement* of 1673 omitted them. The councillors of state received nobility transmissible to the first degree. They were presented to the court with their wives and were admitted as courtiers of the king. They held fiefs. Their sons often carried the sword and served in the king's regiments, at least for a time, before beginning to serve in their offices. Thus the King systematically raised up those men of the robe in his service to a nobility of the robe. More and more, it was service to the sovereign, the incarnation of the state, that organized the classes of society.

The nobility grumbled about this. They scorned these bourgeois. "This was a reign of vile bourgeoisie," growled Saint-Simon. They had to endure the leveling accomplished by a state that mowed down all resistance. The jails were full of distinguished prisoners: Comte de Cramaing, Maréchal de Bassompierre, and Baradas, a favorite of Louis XIII. Therefore the kings sought to procure honors and financial perquisites for the nobility. They reserved governorships for them, as well as most of the military ranks; the majority of the ecclesiastical dignities went to their cadets. The kings employed the nobility in their service, inculcated the spirit of subordination, and little by little bureaucratized them. Louis XIV perfected the organization of the royal court. He grouped around him at

Saint-Germain, at Fontainebleau, at Versailles, all who counted in the nobility. He ruined them by the alternation of the onerous life of the camps with the sumptuous environment at court. He was not reluctant to have them find in their military occupations opportunity for glory and reputation. He subdued them with pensions, dowries, and church property. "It can happen that in going to court one will find his true self beneath that self which he has cast away," said Mme. de Sévigné. Moreover, the King found a psychological alibi for this nobility. In a fantastical fete, Louis appeared in the costume of God on Olympus, the courtiers as secondary divinities or heroes. Thus, they could transpose their frustrated dreams of power and grandeur into a copy of the life of the immortals, raised above the common run of mankind and, since they must obey, obeying "Seigneur Jupiter," the God-King. Etiquette accustomed them to see in the king a superhuman being. Men uncovered before the bed of the king, women genuflected, as they did in church before the altar. The princes of the blood quarreled over the honor of holding the king's shirt for him at his *lever*. Reverential ceremony was the rule at the *lever*, when he went to bed, at meals, indeed throughout the daily routine. A courtier said it all at Louis' death when he wrote, "after the death of the King, anything is possible."

Thus, the court and its etiquette were not imitations of Spain at all; they were imposed by the social conditions, by the nature of things.

In sum, the kings divided offices between two classes, but reserved the most important ones to the lesser class, the bourgeoisie, which they fostered systematically and counterposed against the nobility. In this way, they restored the class struggle to a point of equilibrium which assured their personal power and secured unity, order, and hierarchy in the government of the state. But also, perhaps constrained by crisis and without having wanted to change the social structure of the kingdom, the kings increasingly leveled and equalized in regard to service owed to the state and the unlimited obedience required of all men, so that in the person of Louis XIV the royal power became autocratic and revolutionary.

Robert R. Rea, Research Professor of History and Alumni Professor at Auburn University, was born in Wichita, Kans., in 1922. A graduate of Friends University, he received his M.A. and Ph.D. degrees from Indiana University. He has written many articles and reviews, and his publications include *The English Press in Politics, 1760–1774* (Lincoln, Nebr., 1963); *The Spanish Armada* (New York, 1964); *To Prove a Villain* (New York, 1964) with T. D. Littleton; and *The Memoire Justificatif of the Chevalier Montault de Monberaut* (University, Ala., 1965) with M. B. Howard. He has been a fellow of the Folger Shakespeare Library and is a member of the American Historical Association and of the Southern Historical Association.

CHAPTER TEN

ROBERT R. REA

Auburn University

Sir Robert Walpole

No FIGURE looms so large upon the horizon of 18th-century British political history as that of the Squire of Houghton, Robert Walpole. As Newton was to science, so Walpole to politics: before Walpole all was chaos; after Walpole there was order. The decisive character of his impact on British politics has long been acknowledged by historians, but they have by no means agreed upon the nature of his contribution or, for that matter, upon its intrinsic merits. The following selections evaluate Walpole's accomplishments, his methods of operation, the significance of his career and its dramatic end, and the quality of the man who governed England, in Carlyle's words, "in a sturdy, deep-bellied, long-headed, John Bull fashion, not unworthy of recognition."

In outline Walpole's career is plain enough. He was born in 1676 of good county stock, entered the House of Commons by way of a pocket borough in 1701, and being a promising young Whig orator, he was appointed Secretary at War, then Treasurer of the Navy during the War of the Spanish Succession. Ousted with the Whig ministry in 1710, he was made the victim of Tory persecution, a martyrdom for which he gained revenge when the Tories were turned out in 1714 at the accession of George I. A year later Walpole held the offices of First Lord of the Treasury and Chancellor of the Exchequer, offices which he would subsequently transform into something very like that of prime minister.

The Whigs had triumphed over the Tories, but Whig factions soon fell to quarreling over the spoils of office, and their divisions gave the king a decisive voice. Walpole and his brother-in-law, Townshend, lost the king's favor and were maneuvered out of the ministry in 1717 by Stanhope and

Sunderland. For three years Walpole played the opposition game shrewdly, proved his nuisance value, and in 1720, Stanhope invited him back to office. The moment proved fortuitous. Stanhope's unexpected death and the financial crisis caused by the bursting of the South Sea Bubble enabled Walpole to exercise his talents at calming troubled waters. He returned to the Treasury, and from 1721 until 1742, he dominated English political life. During these years he perfected the art of parliamentary management, ingratiated himself with two kings, overrode—or sidestepped —all opposition, and was called prime minister by men who despaired of becoming ministers themselves. It was not intended as a compliment, but it was a most descriptive term: Walpole was the leading minister, the king's "first" minister, and all others paled beside him—or were extinguished.

Thus it was that when the troubles of the Anglo-Spanish War of 1739 —Jenkins' Ear—came upon Walpole, his friends were few and his enemies legion. By 1742, he was old, tired, and ill. Harassed by a brilliant opposition, betrayed by nervous followers, he fought like an aging lion until George II accepted his plea that he might retire from the fray. He fell— but upward, into the House of Lords as Earl of Orford, and those who had cried, "Impeach him!" were not above seeking his advice. He was able to laugh at them before he died in 1745.

Long tenure of office and power led even Sir Robert's contemporaries to confuse the office with the man, and it is not surprising that today he is commonly identified by undergraduates as "England's first prime minister." Eighteenth-century England knew no such office; it knew much, however, about Sir Robert Walpole, who for a generation fulfilled most of the duties later associated with that office. Similarly, it is said that with Walpole "the cabinet" came into being. The early Hanoverian cabinet was little more than the king's spacious "closet" wherein his Majesty and his trusted servants came to agreement on matters of passing importance. The only sort of "cabinet solidarity" was that imposed by Walpole's refusal to tolerate a rival. Lead the House of Commons he did—so well that his baffled opponents, Bolingbroke, Pulteney, Carteret, Chesterfield, and a young cornet of horse named William Pitt, were reduced to crying "Corruption!" for want of any better explanation of their impotence. Not one of them but utilized the same techniques when in office; not one of them did it half so well.

Walpole was a master of politics—the art of the possible—and he wooed power as he wooed his mistress, with infinite patience and care for detail, tantalizing, satisfying, inevitably winning. As the king's minister for the House of Commons, he brought order to that body, harmony to its relations with the Crown, and stable government of a sort that England had never known. Parliament supported the king; the king satisfied the parliamentary majority, and both thereby served the interests of their country without particularly striving to do so. The system could be improved upon, and has been, but it was essentially Sir Robert's system.

The preeminence of Sir Robert Walpole is indisputable, but when it comes to particulars, the colossus appears to have feet of clay. He stirs no high emotions, he stimulates no deep thought, he rouses no enthusiasm. He came to power as the savior of bankrupt investors in the South Sea Bubble, but his salvation was extended rather to the profiteers than their victims. He was praised for financial policies that reduced the national debt, but one of these—the excise scheme—was so unpopular that he was forced to drop it. He maintained peace for England when Europe was in flames, and lost the international influence which Marlborough's arms and Stanhope's diplomacy had won for the British crown. His political as well as his personal morals were no better than they had to be. For all of which his contemporaries showered him with vituperation and blackened his name.

The first significant biography of Walpole was compiled by William Coxe, *Memoirs of the Life and Administration of Sir Robert Walpole* (1798). Coxe's research in private collections of correspondence gave him an appreciation of Walpole's political dexterity, and he became an ardent defender of the statesman through whom "the Protestant succession was established, the Jacobite faction suppressed; the government acquired energy on a constitutional basis; and by the prevention of foreign war, domestic tranquillity was secured. Under the calm stability of such a government, public credit flourished, commerce increased, manufactures were improved, and agriculture ameliorated." Walpole's "uniform principle," wrote Coxe, was "the love of peace." By virtue of his publication of much of the primary material on which he based his work, Coxe became the source of practically every discussion of Sir Robert Walpole for the next 150 years. Subsequent biographers tempered Coxe's eulogy by analyzing the criticism of contemporary pamphleteers, but they could add little to Coxe's portrait. John Morley's *Walpole* (1889) was a Liberal interpretation of the growth of responsible government; F. S. Oliver's *Endless Adventure* (1910–31) was a lengthy discourse on the art of politics; G. R. S. Taylor's *Robert Walpole and His Age* (1931) provided a useful summary of all that had gone before. Not until J. H. Plumb embarked upon his current study, as yet incomplete, did Sir Robert receive the careful attention he deserved. Interestingly enough, the modern scholar's latest appraisal of Walpole at the height of his career attributes to him precisely those achievements hailed by his earliest biographers: political stability, internal prosperity, external peace, and personal power. These were his avowed goals; by their accomplishment the triumphant politician established his right to the accolade of statesman.

1. A TORY DIATRIBE

Sir Charles Petrie is Britain's most eminent royalist historian of the 20th century. The author of numerous biographies of conservative statesmen, his two volumes on The Jacobite Movement *form a passionate appeal for a lost cause. The Four Georges reflects Petrie's inherent distaste for all things Hanoverian—including Sir Robert Walpole.*

SIR CHARLES PETRIE*

Over the whole period was cast the shadow of Sir Robert Walpole. Until 1742 he dominated the scene in person, and for the next 18 years the evil that he did lived after him. More than one of Anne's ministers had broken the laws of conventional morality, but it was left for this Norfolk squire to debase the whole public life of the country, and it was not until the accession to power of the younger Pitt that any real improvement took place. Walpole worked on the assumption that every politician had his price, and long before he resigned it was true:

Had he not been a politician it cannot be doubted that he would have been a great merchant or a great financier. . . . His chief pre-occupation was the keeping out of the rival house of Stuart, which would not have employed the firm of Walpole and the Whigs to keep their accounts. . . . His merciless crushing of any rivals was simply the big firm crushing competition, a familiar feature of commerce.

Externally, Walpole was a bluff, hearty man, whose habit it was always to talk bawdy at table, so that everybody could join in the conversation. Actually, he was jealous and vindictive; the very type of *un faux bonhomme.*

As a political strategist Walpole has had few equals, and hardly a superior. He knew that in the interests of that Whig oligarchy, whose servant he was, the country must be taught to think in terms of material

---

* Sir Charles Petrie, *The Four Georges: A Revaluation of the Period from 1714–1830* (London: Eyre & Spottiswoode, 1935), pp. 77–80.

prosperity alone, and that enthusiasm of any kind must be repressed at all costs. His claim to distinction lies in the thoroughness with which he worked for this end. Walpole was not content merely to avoid measures calculated to excite public opinion, for his passivity was of an active type, if such an expression is permissible. There was no aspect of the national life which he left untouched, one might almost say uncontaminated, and every institution, religious and secular, was carefully lulled to sleep. Whether his policy was right or wrong it was all of a piece. High statesmanship of the type of Bolingbroke and the Pitts was utterly foreign to Walpole, and what he lacked in himself he disliked and mistrusted in others. His task was to let the generation that had been divided by the Revolution die out, and another which only knew the fleshpots of Whig rule grow up in its place. Unhappily for England, the result of this was a stagnation and an apathy which proved a forcing ground for abuses which the statesmen of a later age had the greatest difficulty in eradicating. The Englishman is by nature lazy, and glad of an excuse for doing nothing: Walpole made apathy a political virtue.

It would have been difficult for any man holding these views to have attracted disinterested support, and Walpole signally failed.

He seemed to aim always at getting people to behave like rational human beings, at showing them the folly of running after will-o'-the-wisps or flying into a passion. On the other hand, his words rarely touched their imaginations, still more rarely their consciences. He had little to say about such themes as patriotism, prestige or national glory, and was never heard discoursing on the duty of self-sacrifice or the love of humanity. Walpole had probably a clearer understanding of Everyman in his Everyday humour than any statesman who has ever governed England; but he appears to have had little or no perception of those inward passionate feelings, those tremendous hidden forces, which the elder Pitt, and the younger, and Charles James Fox, each in his different way, knew so well how to evoke and inspire.

For this reason Walpole found, toward the end of his career, all the rising young men banded against him. To some extent, too, this was due to his jealousy of ability, for his cabinets were mediocre in the extreme. In short, Walpole must bear the responsibility for the cynical indifference with which the political system was worked until the younger Pitt took office.

2. A WHIGGISH EULOGY

Thomas B. Macaulay, the great Whig historian, approached the great Whig politician with mixed emotions. The parliamentary reformer was bound to condemn the amoral cynicism and corruption of an earlier age, yet the brilliant young orator could only admire the mature statesman who held the House of Commons in the palm of his hand. Macaulay's essay was originally published in the Edinburgh Review *in 1833.*

THOMAS B. MACAULAY*

He had, undoubtedly, great talents and great virtues. He was not, indeed, like the leaders of the party which opposed his government, a brilliant orator. He was not a profound scholar, like Carteret, or a wit and a fine gentleman, like Chesterfield. In all these respects his deficiencies were remarkable. . . . When he ceased to talk of politics, he could talk of nothing but women; and he dilated on his favorite theme with a freedom which shocked even that plainspoken generation. . . .

That he practiced corruption on a large scale is, we think, indisputable. But whether he deserves all the invectives which have been uttered against him on that account may be questioned. No man ought to be severely censured for not being beyond his age in virtue. . . . Walpole governed by corruption because, in his time, it was impossible to govern otherwise. . . . During the century which followed the Restoration, the House of Commons was in that situation in which assemblies must be managed by corruption or cannot be managed at all. It was not held in awe, as in the 16th century, by the throne. It was not held in awe, as in the 19th century, by the opinion of the people. Its constitution was oligarchical. Its deliberations were secret. Its power in the state was immense. The government had every conceivable motive to offer bribes. . . .

The government could not go on unless the parliament could be kept in order. And how was the parliament to be kept in order? Three hundred years ago it would have been enough for a statesman to have the support of the Crown. . . . A hundred years ago it would not have been enough to

---

* Thomas B. Macaulay, "Letters of Horace Walpole, Earl of Orford, to Sir Horace Mann, British Envoy at the Court of Tuscany," in *Critical and Historical Essays* (12th ed.; London: Longman, 1865).

have both Crown and people on his side. The parliament had shaken off the control of the royal prerogative. It had not yet fallen under the control of public opinion. A large proportion of the members had absolutely no motive to support any administration except their own interest, in the lowest sense of the word. Under these circumstances, the country could be governed only by corruption. Bolingbroke, who was the ablest and the most vehement of those who raised the clamor against corruption, had no better remedy to propose than that the royal prerogative should be strengthened. The remedy would no doubt have been efficient. The only question is whether it would not have been worse than the disease. The fault was in the constitution of the legislature; and to blame those ministers who managed the legislature in the only way in which it could be managed is gross injustice. . . . [Walpole's] crime was merely this, that he employed his money more dexterously, and got more support in return for it, than any of those who preceded or followed him.

He was himself incorruptible by money. His dominant passion was the love of power: and the heaviest charge which can be brought against him is that to this passion he never scrupled to sacrifice the interests of his country.

One of the maxims which, as his son tells us, he was most in the habit of repeating was, *quieta non movere*. It was indeed the maxim by which he generally regulated his public conduct. It is the maxim of a man more solicitous to hold power long than to use it well. It is remarkable that, though he was at the head of affairs during more than 20 years, not one great measure, not one important change for the better or for the worse in any part of our institutions, marks the period of his supremacy. Nor was this because he did not clearly see that many changes were very desirable. . . . Archdeacon Coxe imagined that he had discovered one grand principle of action to which the whole public conduct of his hero ought to be referred. "Did the administration of Walpole," says the biographer, "present any uniform principle which may be traced in every part, and which gave combination and consistency to the whole? Yes, and that principle was, THE LOVE OF PEACE." It would be difficult, we think, to bestow a higher eulogium on any statesman. But the eulogium is far too high for the merits of Walpole. The great ruling principle of his public conduct was indeed a love of peace, but . . . the peace which Walpole sought was not the peace of the country, but the peace of his own administration. During the greater part of his public life, indeed, the two objects were inseparably connected. At length he was reduced to the necessity of choosing between them, of plunging the state into hostilities for which there was no just ground . . . or of facing a violent opposition in the country, in parliament, and even in the royal closet. No person was more thoroughly convinced than he of the absurdity of the cry against Spain. But his darling power was at stake, and his choice was soon made. He preferred an unjust war to a stormy session. It is impossible to say of a minister who acted thus that the love of peace was the one grand principle to which all his conduct is to be referred. The governing principle of his conduct was neither love of peace nor love of war, but love of power.

The praise to which he is fairly entitled is this, that he understood the true interest of his country better than any of his contemporaries and that he pursued that interest whenever it was not incompatible with the interest of his own intense and grasping ambition. It was only in matters of public moment that he shrank from agitation and had recourse to compromise. In his contests for personal influence there was no timidity, no flinching. He would have all or none. Every member of the government who would not submit to his ascendency was turned out or forced to resign. Liberal of everything else, he was avaricious of power. Cautious everywhere else, when power was at stake he had all the boldness of Richelieu or Chatham. He might easily have secured his authority if he could have been induced to divide it with others. But he would not part with one fragment of it to purchase defenders for all the rest. The effect of this policy was that he had able enemies and feeble allies. His most distinguished coadjutors left him one by one, and joined the ranks of the opposition. He faced the increasing array of his enemies with unbroken spirit, and thought it far better that they should attack his power than that they should share it. . . .

If the fate of Walpole's colleagues had been inseparably bound up with his, he probably would, even after the unfavorable elections of 1741, have been able to weather the storm. But as soon as it was understood that the attack was directed against him alone, and that, if he were sacrificed, his associates might expect advantageous and honorable terms, the ministerial ranks began to waver, and the murmur of *sauve qui peut* was heard. . . .

Never was a battle more manfully fought out than the last struggle of the old statesman. His clear judgment, his long experience, and his fearless spirit enabled him to maintain a defensive war through half the session. To the last his heart never failed him; and, when at last he yielded, he yielded not to the threats of his enemies, but to the entreaties of his dispirited and refractory followers. When he could no longer retain his power, he compounded for honor and security, and retired to his garden and his paintings, leaving to those who had overthrown him shame, discord, and ruin.

3. DESCENT OR ASCENSION?

The system perfected by Sir Robert Walpole was inherited by the Duke of Newcastle and Henry Pelham. The Rise of the Pelhams logically begins with the passing of the old regime, and John B. Owen has most satisfactorily weighed the meaning of Walpole's resignation to his contemporaries and successors. Owen's monograph is the first scholarly study of the Pelham brothers since Archdeacon William Coxe extended his labors over the Walpoles to encompass the Memoirs of . . . Henry Pelham *in 1829.*

JOHN B. OWEN*

What, then, were the fundamental reasons for Walpole's fall? Obviously the simplest and most comprehensive explanation is that his resignation was the natural consequence of his inability to command any longer a working majority in the House of Commons. . . . Walpole, by successively excluding from his administration all those who from time to time had dared to challenge his power, had gradually built up the most formidable opposition of the century, thereby committing the cardinal error of ranging against himself the weight of debating talent in both Houses. Carteret, Chesterfield, Marchmont, Pulteney, Hume Campbell, William Pitt, and a host of others represented an attacking force with which the administration benches were ill-equipped to cope. In the Commons in particular the advantage of superior oratory was decisive. Furnished with ample material by the manifest misconduct of the war, and aided by existing tensions within the ministry itself, the opposition succeeded in winning over sufficient of the independent members to reduce Walpole's majority below the minimum requisite for stable administration. Once his ability to maintain himself had thus become an open question, an ever-increasing number of administration supporters (including a significant proportion of the Court and Treasury party) were guilty of deliberate abstention. These defections, particularly evident during the hearing of election petitions, made it possible for the opposition to gain the upper hand. Walpole had undergone a similar experience in 1733, when his ill-starred excise bill had

---

* John B. Owen, *The Rise of the Pelhams* (London: Methuen & Co. Ltd., 1957), pp. 34–40.

provided a suitable focus for the efforts of his adversaries. But on that occasion the issue was specific, and a timely withdrawal of the offending measure had sufficed to overcome the crisis. In 1742, on the other hand, when Walpole's very political existence was at stake, there could be no compromise. So, for the first time, a minister who retained the full confidence and support of the king was forced to surrender his seals because he could no longer carry on his Majesty's business in the face of an antagonistic House of Commons. That the situation was unprecedented was shown by the tenacity with which Sir Robert clung to power, for he was seven times defeated in the lobbies before he accepted the inevitable. This fact is too often forgotten by historians who prefer to portray Walpole as a modern premier, accepting with constitutional propriety the implications of an adverse vote in the lower house. In 1742 a single defeat, even a series of defeats, did not by convention require the resignation of the existing administration. Walpole retired because it was made abundantly clear to him that no ministry of which he remained a member could hope to regain control of the Commons. An essentially personal attack was met at length by an essentially personal acceptance of defeat.

There were of course wider constitutional issues at stake, but these bore no relation to modern parliamentary practice. The theory of the constitution was still that all ministers held their offices of the king and were responsible to their royal master rather than to parliament. But if the appointment and dismissal of his servants was still acknowledged as an integral part of the royal prerogative, the choice of the sovereign since 1688 had been limited in practice by the necessity of having his measures carried through the Commons. Thus while the Glorious Revolution had preserved intact much of the appearance of royal government, it had implicitly denied something of its substance. Content with its practical assertion of the ultimate supremacy of parliament, it left to the tact and self-interest of subsequent monarchs the avoidance of any constitutional deadlocks that might arise from unwise insistence on the letter of the prerogative. In 1742 George II's reluctant acquiescence in his minister's resignation was a tacit recognition of the lesson of 1688. Nor was the significance of the occasion lost on the politicians of the day, as is shown in the following conversation between Egmont and Sir John Shelley.

I said . . . that to advise His Majesty to insist on his prerogative of choosing and dismissing his servants at this time, is not the part of a good subject, and it should be considered whether the prerogative ought to remain in the Crown, since the liberties of the people have been extended: that 'tis a solecism in our constitution to leave the same powers in the Crown which it had when more absolute, now that the subject has grown more powerful, for there will be eternal differences subsisting between the Crown and the people. The King will say, 'I won't or I will do this, and I insist on my prerogative,' but the Parliament will say, 'Sir, you have the prerogative indeed, but 'tis an abuse of your prerogative, and if insisted on, this matter in question will ruin us; therefore, if you are obstinate we will distress you, you shall have no supplies; you are ill-advised, and we will know who advised you so!'

He said, the King must think it hard to be forced from his prerogative, and thinks the question is brought to this point, whether he or the Prince shall place his servants about him.

I replied the question was not about placing, but displacing: if Sir Robert were out, His Majesty would still have the power of naming his successor. That whether it be the Prince or Parliament and nation, all complain that our affairs are brought to the brink of ruin, and all know who had the management of them: what they want is a change of measures, and they do not think the minister who had the conduct of all hitherto is proper to conduct them.

This was a shrewd appraisal of the essence of the situation, one which emphasizes an aspect too often overlooked. The opposition made no claim to determine whom the king *should* employ; it restricted itself to asserting that under certain conditions it could insist that there were some ministers whom he should *not* employ. This distinction was by no means purely academic. In a House of Commons that was for the most part independent, and in which the Court and Treasury party would, within reasonable limits, support any minister of the king's choice, the sovereign was left with considerable freedom of action. But an aging and obstinate George II, after being forced to part with Walpole, drew attention to the *limits* of his power by persisting in foolish and tactless attempts to form his ministries around Carteret and Bath, the two most notoriously unpopular politicians of the day. His failure, together with the consequent triumph of the Pelhams, seemed to give substance to the current Leicester House fiction of a "king in toils," who must be rescued from the clutches of an oligarchical cabal. But George II's difficulties, such as they were, were largely of his own making.

The events of 1741–42 then are of great importance in the evolution of ministerial responsibility, and illustrate strikingly the growing power of the House of Commons; but their significance must not be exaggerated. The transition from royal to parliamentary government, with which the 18th century was predominantly concerned, was a very gradual process. Toward the solution of the many difficulties bound up with that transition, the fall of Walpole made a contribution that was to some extent purely negative. While confining one aspect of the royal prerogative within limits consistent with the growing power of parliament, it gave no indication as to the most profitable way in which the king could operate within this more

restricted sphere. In other words, it emphasized the existence of the fundamental problem of maintaining harmony between the executive and legislative branches of the government, while offering nothing in the way of a
solution. So at least it seemed to contemporaries. Yet if the enforced resignation of Sir Robert is viewed in its proper perspective as against the
tremendous power he wielded at the height of his ministry, it takes on
an entirely new constitutional significance. Consideration of the essential
character of the position that Walpole had enjoyed for so long reveals the
strikingly positive contribution that his regime made towards the evolution
of parliamentary government, and at the same time suggests a more significant reason for his decline and fall.

The central problem left unsolved by the Revolution of 1688 was that of
preventing friction between the king and his parliament, between the
executive and the legislature. Ultimately the solution was to be found in
the modern practice of cabinet government, in choosing ministers from
the political party which enjoys the support of the majority in the House
of Commons. That the origins of the modern cabinet can be found in the
18th century is not to be denied, but in an age which preceded the development of the party system, and in which the king and civil service were
still an integral part of politics, no embryonic cabinet could hope, merely
by virtue of its membership, to command a majority in the lower house.
If the machinery of the constitution was to be kept functioning smoothly,
the necessary lubricant must be found elsewhere, and the weight of historical opinion still inclines toward "influence" as the dominant factor in
controlling the Commons during this critical transitional period. Consequently it is held that, by judicious exercise of Crown patronage, the king
and his ministers could "manage" sufficient of the members to enable them
to carry on the government without undue hindrance. Sir Lewis Namier
and a few other historians from time to time have suggested the obvious
weaknesses in this attractively simple theory and have exposed some of
the more prominent legends on which it is based. They have pointed out
that the 18th-century House of Commons was far more independent than
has generally been admitted, far more so in fact than its modern desced-
ant; that the distribution of patronage savored more of jobbery, even of
charity, than of parliamentary corruption. Yet, despite all this, the old
notions still persist, perhaps because although the efficacy of influence
has been challenged, there has been little attempt to explain how under
18th-century conditions, harmony *was* maintained between king and parliament. It is here that the ministry of Walpole reveals something of
prime importance. . . . His fall is in itself sufficient illustration of the fact
that influence was quite inadequate as a means of parliamentary control.

If further proof is needed, the rise of Chatham, the passage of Dunning's resolution, the overthrow of North, and the very reform of parliament by itself all bear ample testimony to this effect. Yet for 21 years Walpole had managed to maintain himself in power. If his strength did not stem solely from the coffers of the king whence did it derive?

Sir Robert has always been painted as a great parliamentarian, who by acknowledging the newly risen power of the Commons, and by establishing himself as its leader, made himself something more than a mere minister of the Crown. It is impossible to deny the justice of this picture, yet it must not be allowed to obscure the equally important fact that he was also a great "king's man." This one-sided emphasis on the parliamentary aspect of his office is perhaps the natural consequence of underestimating the power of the Crown under the first two Hanoverians. Engaged in the popular but unprofitable task of writing history by looking over their shoulders, many historians have projected the present-day relationship of king to parliament back into the early 18th century, and have consequently produced a badly balanced portrait of the chief ministers of the times. There were in Walpole's age not one but two main sources of political power. While the House of Commons was taking its first hesitant steps toward ultimate predominance, the king was still a very real force in politics. He who would rise to preeminence as a minister must have the confidence of both. Acting on this assumption, Sir Robert carved out for himself a new position and "successfully adapted the 17th-century constitution to the requirements of the 18th century on lines which, when the time came, enabled the whole political machine to change smoothly and easily into the gear of full responsible government." By establishing himself as a link between these two sources of power, he made himself indispensable to both, and at the same time provided the best guarantee of preventing friction between them. As "Minister for the King in the House of Commons" or "Minister for the House of Commons in the Closet," he could explain the views and wishes of each to the other and suggest a *media via* whenever conflict threatened. It was this that accounted for his predominance over his associates and entitled him to be acknowledged as the first of England's premiers. The administrations of the day were overwhelmingly aristocratic bodies, and for the greater part of his ministry Walpole was the sole commoner in his cabinet; so too was Henry Pelham during his term of office at the head of the Treasury. In these circumstances the so-called minister for the House of Commons inevitably arose above his associates. Forced in the House to defend the administration on all aspects of policy he had of necessity to become more than a mere departmental head. Hence that accretion of power that enabled him to become in a true sense a "prime" minister. Therein lay the secret of Walpole's greatness and the fundamental reason for his fall, which may more properly be regarded as dating from 1739 than from 1742. Before 1739 he was essential *to* the king because he was essential *in* the House of Commons. But by acquiescing against his will in the declaration of war against Spain, he virtually abdicated the dominant position he himself had created. Compelled to support a war in which he did not believe, he could no longer function as an effective link between the king and the Commons, both of whom were wholeheartedly in favor of hostilities. The last two years of his ministry were therefore in the nature of an epilogue; yet, although he had lost his *raison d'être*, neither he nor his contemporaries realized the significance of what had happened. How could they, when they failed to perceive the potency of the new office which he had evolved? So he lingered on until in time the weakness of his position inevitably manifested itself in the House of Commons, ultimately encompassing his formal retirement. When in February, 1742, he was forced to surrender the appearance as well as the substance of power, nothing was done to resurrect the office which he had allowed by default to fall into abeyance. No one saw that the reason for the prevalent political conflict was the divorce of power from responsibility. It was believed rather that wrong measures alone were at the root of the trouble, and that consequently all would be healed by a more vigorous prosecution of the war. The nonfulfillment of these hopes became increasingly evident during that period of ministerial and parliamentary strife which characterized the whole of the administration of Carteret and the opening years of the ministry of Henry Pelham. Not until after February, 1746, was Pelham able at last to grasp the inner essence as well as the outer trappings of Walpole's power; and only then did stable government return. Indeed throughout the 18th century, harmony between king and Commons was ensured only when there was a minister for the House of Commons who enjoyed the confidence of both. So it had been with Walpole; so it was to be with Pelham, Lord North, and the two Pitts. But when the dominant influence was held by a peer, the ministries were brief, unstable, and constantly striving to preserve their existence. Thus the country alternated between political calm and political confusion, for contemporaries were slow to realize the advantages of the new office, and the normal reaction to a long and successful ministry by a commoner was a determination that similar "usurpation" of power should at all costs be avoided.

4. THE CONSTRUCTIVE STATESMAN

The London Times Literary Supplement is noted for the cogency and honesty of its anonymous reviews of current literature. Its leading articles maintain the proud tradition of scholarly anonymity, but their vigorous assertions of controversial interpretations often encourage conjecture as to the authors' identities. John B. Owen (The Rise of the Pelhams, p. 38) has suggested that the author of the following essay is "from internal evidence obviously Romney Sedgwick," the editor of the definitive edition of Lord Hervey's Memoirs.

LONDON TIMES LITERARY SUPPLEMENT[*]

Sir Robert Walpole 1676–1745:
The Minister for the House of Commons

Sir Robert Walpole—whose name appears from the phonetic spelling of his contemporaries to have been pronounced "Warpoole"—is often said to have been prime minister for 21 uninterrupted years, a tenure of power unparalleled in the whole course of English history. The point is an arguable one, and in any case Walpole has a far stronger claim to the attention of posterity. Today, 200 years after his death on March 18, 1745, he stands out as a great empirical statesman who successfully adapted the 17th-century constitution to the requirements of the 18th century on lines which, when the time came, enabled the whole political machine to change smoothly and easily into the gear of full responsible parliamentary government.

Walpole's contribution to the machinery of the constitution was the creation of a "minister for the House of Commons," who fulfilled the dual function of "minister with the king in the House of Commons," and "minister for the House of Commons in the closet." At that time the king was still the effective head of the government; ministers regarded and referred to him as their "master" and themselves as his "servants"; the "closet," where the most important of them worked with him, was a higher political level than the cabinet; the government of the day and their supporters

---

[*] "Sir Robert Walpole 1676–1745: The Minister for the House of Commons," London *Times Literary Supplement,* March 24, 1945, pp. 133–134.

were known as the "court"; and the symbol and sign of real ministerial power was "habitual, frequent, familiar access" to the king. By creating a minister who, in Pitt's words, "went directly" between the king and the House of Commons, Walpole supplied a link, hitherto missing, between the two great centers of political power.

Walpole introduced this important innovation by the simple expedient of electing to remain in the House of Commons when, in 1721, he entered on his long period of office as head of the Treasury. Till then all first-class ministers had invariably been peers, or if, like Harley and St. John, they had been promoted to the highest political posts while members of the House of Commons, they had taken the earliest opportunity of transferring themselves to the House of Lords. Ministerial representatives in the House of Commons had been confined to underlings, who could not speak with authority, and whose station tended to approximate to that of the "official members" of a colonial assembly. Largely owing to this state of affairs the relations between the House of Commons and the government, when Walpole served his political apprenticeship, were characterized by an almost chronic condition of friction; the House of Commons still was frequently unworkable; and the political system generally displayed all the familiar symptoms associated with the divorce of power from responsibility.

Walpole's farsighted decision to remain in the House of Commons and to act as a link between the sovereign and the Commons had important effects upon his own functions and status. In the first instance he appears to have attempted to confine himself to his own province, leaving foreign affairs to his colleague and brother-in-law Townshend. Hervey describes clearly how circumstances, in the form of the Treaty of Hanover, negotiated by George I and Townshend at Hanover in 1725, showed Walpole that his position was untenable:

Till the making of this Treaty Sir Robert Walpole never meddled at all with foreign affairs; they were left entirely to Lord Townshend, whilst Sir Robert's province was confined solely to Parliamentary and domestic concerns. But when Sir Robert found the clamour against this Treaty so great at home, and the difficulties so many in which it entangled us abroad, he began to think it necessary to take some cognizance of what gave him immediately more trouble than all his own affairs put together. For though Lord Townshend only was the transactor of these peace and war negotiations, yet the labouring oar in their consequences always fell on Sir Robert; it was he was forced to stand the attacks of Parliamentary inquiry into the prudence of making these treaties; it was he was to provide the means necessary to support them; on him only fell the censure of entering into them, and on him lay all the difficulty of getting out of them.

The result of this episode was not only, as Walpole himself summed it up, the change of the name of the firm from "Townshend and Walpole" to "Walpole and Townshend," but the establishment of the principle that the minister for the House of Commons must be in effect prime minister.

The primacy of the minister for the House of Commons was reinforced by the emergence of a new political factor, of which Walpole himself had been the originator. This was an organized opposition, with the heir apparent at its head, aiming at forcing itself into office by parliamentary means. The existence of such a threat automatically increased the authority of the minister responsible for dealing with it in the same way as the state of war increases the authority of the services. From the point of view of the king the parliamentary struggle turned into a personal contest between himself and the Prince of Wales, invested with all the emotional bitterness of a family quarrel, and threatening the father with the supreme indignity of being taken prisoner by the son. In such circumstances all considerations tended to give way to the paramount necessity of supporting the minister whom the king regarded as his champion and protector against a fate almost worse than death. As Walpole himself once said:

When I tell them [the King and Queen] if they will arm me with power I will conquer and humble their son I receive such a flow of grace and good words that I could dictate nothing stronger.

Thus what Lord Morley describes as the "capacity of the modern Prime Minister in an emergency to take upon himself a power not inferior to that of a dictator" can be traced to the exigencies of those "old unhappy far-off things and battles long ago."

In contrast to prime ministers such as Godolphin, Sunderland, and later Newcastle, whose position was entirely derived from their personal credit with the sovereign, Walpole's primacy arose naturally out of the situation in which he was placed. Their status as prime minister rested on the precarious foundation of royal favor; his was firmly rooted in his parliamentary duties. The weakness of their position is illustrated by the following pathetic plaint from the Duke of Newcastle, who represented a deliberate and disastrous attempt to revive the pre-Walpole system of government:

His Majesty's direction to me to confine myself to my Treasury, "You will have enough to do to set that right; you have been attacked and objected to for meddling in everything. You know there is no such thing as First Minister in England and therefore should not seem to be so" ... how contrary this is to what we apprehended to be his Majesty's first intentions, when the King said

312 INTERPRETING EUROPEAN HISTORY

to me himself "I have made you as it were First Minister; you will be informed of everything."

It would have been impossible for George II to have taken this line with Walpole or Pelham, nor would he have wished to do so. Their claim to be informed of everything rested not on any royal mandate but on the fact that they were required to defend in the House of Commons all the actions of the government and that it would have been impossible for them to do so if they had "confined themselves to their Treasuries."

The association of the position of prime minister with the Treasury, to which Newcastle's complaint draws attention, did not arise from any special importance attached to public finance. The explanation, as Lord Hardwicke once told George II, was that:

The head of the Treasury was indeed an employment of great business, very extensive, which always went beyond the bare management of the revenue; that it extended through both Houses of Parliament, the members of which were naturally to look thither; that there must be some principal person to receive applications, to hear the wants and the wishes and the requests of mankind, with the reasons of them, in order to lay them before His Majesty for his determination.

In other words, the Treasury controlled the bulk of public patronage which was distributed to members of parliament and through them to their relations and constituents. In the absence of any sort of party machine and of any real party distinctions—for in Walpole's time the struggle for power lay between one set of Whigs and another—the power to confer or withhold these favors acted as a sort of substitute for party discipline. In fact the Treasury, under this system, played the part of a modern party machine, a state of affairs which is embodied in a vestigial form in the fact that to this day the government Whips are Lords of the Treasury.

The working of this system in Walpole's time is illustrated by the diary of the first Earl of Egmont, a member of the first parliament of George II. Egmont was a rich, respectable, public-spirited, and independent man, but he was perpetually pestering Walpole for places for relations, pensions for their widows, favors for his constituents, and incidentally a step in the peerage for himself. Indeed he seems to have felt that as a man of large property as well as a member of parliament he had a special right to expect favors, since his worldly position was a guarantee against any suggestion that he would allow his political independence to be influenced by them. . . .

The individual attention which Walpole in the midst of his other strenuous avocations gave to the solicitations of this particular member of parliament indicates the enormous amount of time which in the aggregate he must have spent on this peculiarly unpleasant and ungrateful part of his duties. It perhaps also throws some light on his well-known habit of giving priority in opening his mail to letters from his gamekeeper—whatever else they might contain, at any rate it would not be applications for places.

In addition to public patronage, the Treasury carried with it a further source of power—the secret service money. It was supposed by historians till very recently that this money was largely devoted to corrupting members of parliament by the simple process of administering to them pecuniary bribes for their votes. This legend has recently been dispelled by Professor Namier's analysis of the only surviving secret service accounts, those belonging to the Duke of Newcastle, who, on resigning from the Treasury, took advantage of the youth and inexperience of George III and kept them, instead of returning them to the king to be burned in accordance with the established practice. These books show that during Newcastle's tenure of office secret service expenditure averaged about £40,000 a year, and that of this sum only about £18,000 a year was spent in the House of Commons, of which about £10,000 was accounted for by pensions to members of parliament and the remaining £8,000 by expenditure on elections and constituencies. The expenditure on pensions turns out to be merely an extension of the open practice of bestowing places on members of parliament. That on elections and constituencies is in effect an anticipation of the modern party fund. In neither case, as Professor Namier points out, was there any question of purchasing a parliamentary majority. Rather, the secret service money represented a convenient supplementary source of rewards and favors for parliamentary supporters who under the 18th-century political system considered that they had a right to some return for, or contribution to, the cost of getting themselves elected. There is no reason to suppose that Walpole's accounts, if they were available, would disclose a different story. His total secret service expenditure, it is true, was very much larger than his successor's; in the reign of George II it averaged nearly twice as much as Newcastle's, and even more than Henry Pelham's, thus bearing out George II's verdict to Newcastle that

he [Walpole] managed the money matters very ill; he did not indeed give money abroad, but he gave it away liberally at home; he was a great man, he understood the country, but with regard to the money matters your brother [Pelham] does that, understands that, much better.

In 18th-century terminology, the "power of the Treasury, the secret service, the House of Commons" went to make up "the plenitude of power" which Walpole enjoyed as first minister. In modern language, he combined the positions of prime minister, leader of the House of Commons, and party manager; the first attribute arising from the last two, of which the second was the more important. For, when all is said, there can be no doubt that Walpole's success in curing the disorders which afflicted the body politic when he entered parliament lay in his role of minister for the House of Commons in the closet, and minister for the king in the House of Commons; responsible for interpreting the one to the other, for preventing or smoothing over any causes of friction between the legislature and the executive, and generally for satisfying and reconciling the two indispensable requisites for orderly government under 18th-century conditions—namely, that the government should be agreeable to the majority of the House of Commons and also acceptable to the king. For this purpose it was necessary that he should be a courtier as well as a politician, equally at home in the palace and in parliament; now persuading the king to make concessions to meet the wishes of those whom George II was accustomed to describe as "your scoundrels of the House of Commons"; now displaying, according to his enemies, "such a passion for the House of Commons, because he shined so well in the debates, that he dressed himself out every morning to appear there as if he were to see his mistress."

Walpole's system of government was proof against all attempts to upset it. In his own day he was bitterly assailed for having made himself "Sole Minister," a "kind of magistrate odious to the English constitution, who draws everything into the vortex of his own power"; and after the death of his successor, Henry Pelham, George II actually agreed to the abolition of the position of minister for the House of Commons and appointed Newcastle "as it were First Minister" on the somewhat unsatisfactory terms already described. The decision gave rise to an immediate outcry; those who had been loudest in their denunciation of Walpole's system now vehemently insisted on the "general principle that there must be a Minister with the King in the House of Commons"; and Hardwicke, who himself had advised the step, recognized with belated sagacity that a mistake had been made and that

the precedents of my Lord Godolphin's and my Lord Sunderland's time have been overruled by the long habits of seeing Sir Robert Walpole and Mr. Pelham there [*i.e.*, in the House of Commons] which go back as far as the memory of most people now sitting there, or indeed now in business, reaches.

The mistake took some time to rectify. Indeed the political history of the first decade of the next reign resolves itself into a series of attempts by George III to extricate himself from its consequences, and to return to the system of governing through a minister for the House of Commons. It was only after Fox, Grenville, and Pitt had been tried and found wanting that at long last the king found a minister possessing the requisite qualities for working such a system, and the era of weak and short-lived administrations ends with the appointment of North to the position of Walpole and Pelham. From this aspect the first quarter of a century of George III's reign may be compared to George II's read backward, with Bute as its Newcastle, North as its Pelham, and the younger Pitt as its Walpole. With Pitt the "Sole Minister" becomes the prime minister, a recognized and integral part of the constitution, and Walpole's system is made respectable, though the cynical old Whig statesman, who gave away money so liberally for political purposes, would have opened his eyes at the prices which his virtuous young successor was apparently prepared to pay for the purpose of securing a parliamentary majority at the general election of 1784.

Walpole died at the great house which he had built for himself on his ancestral estate of Houghton. He was buried at the neighboring parish church without monument or inscription. His best epitaph is contained in the simple words of George II: "He was a great man, he understood the country."

5. GOOD SIR ROBERT

Professor J. H. Plumb, of Christ's College, Cambridge, has published two volumes of a projected three-volume biography of Sir Robert Walpole: The Making of a Statesman *(1956) and* The King's Minister *(1961). His meticulous research and realistic interpretations have established him as the leading authority on his subject. While adhering to the "life-and-times" tradition of biography, Plumb has also reached a wide audience through such popular media as* History Today. *The following essay foreshadowed the conclusions of his definitive study and opened a new era of Walpolean studies.*

J. H. PLUMB[*]

Over the high table at King's College, Cambridge, hanging in the place of honor, is a splendid portrait of Sir Robert Walpole. There he is—short,

---

[*] J. H. Plumb, "Sir Robert Walpole," *History Today,* Vol. I (October, 1951), pp. 9–14, 16.

fat, coarse featured, jovial, resplendent in the Garter of which he was so proud. But he is not without dignity, nor even without a certain mystery; for his eyes, alert and guarded, hint that his character was not so obvious as, perhaps, he wished it to seem. The same remark may be made of Walpole's career. The lover of peace who carefully avoided sleeping dogs, the cynic who knew the price of men, the creator of parties, of cabinet government, and of the office of prime minister—these nursery and school-room myths vanish before the harsh reality: his long pursuit of power; the desperate, calculated risks; his vast appetite for detail; all of which made him for 20 years the colossus of English political life. By his own superhuman endeavors he held in check the aggressive appetites of English merchants who saw in war an opportunity for commercial plunder, men who afterward found their voice and inspiration in Chatham, to whom they raised the Guildhall monument, with its proud boast that he was the first minister to make trade flourish by war. But Walpole, hardheaded, obstinate, secure in power, would have none of it. He was too conscious of the great burden of debt, created by the long wars of William and Anne, which pressed like *peine forte et dure* on the owners of land. Above all else, Walpole wished to ease the land tax; and to achieve this object peace was essential. As for trade, he thought that efficient taxation, improved administration, and common-sense policy were the only real necessaries for the growth and development of English commerce.

In essentials, Walpole's policy was extremely simple—peace which would bring its own prosperity. Few prime ministers have had a policy so simple or so consistently held; but the pursuit of it demanded all his extraordinary qualities as a statesman. This was due to the exceptional intricacy of 18th-century politics, where there were no parties in a modern sense and no political programs. Broad issues about church and state might divide men, and make some die-hard Whigs and some die-hard Tories; but for the majority of politicians the issues were not so simple. Personal factors were more important; loyalty to their family connection or territorial group, personal ambition with its temptations of power, changed men from Tories to Whigs and back again with such bewildering speed that 18th-century politics have a cynical air of unreality.

The root of the trouble lay, as Hume understood, in the House of Commons. The vital factor was this: the king chose his ministers: they were his servants, and had to find their majority in the House of Commons, whereas today the leader of an organized party with a majority presents his ministers to the king. It is true that, even in the 18th century, the king's ministers usually had the support of a majority of members of parliament on the very broadest issues; but, once it became a question of detail—whether Irish yarn should be taxed, or London should have a second bridge—local loyalties, or personal views and idiosyncrasies, might easily predominate. Hence in the 18th-century parliament, there was always a considerable element of uncertainty and the danger of political anarchy. As Hume wisely observed, governments were forced to appeal to individual self-interest to secure constant support for a detailed policy. Coherence of government was maintained by an elaborate system of patronage. Every office in church or state, to which the Crown had the power to appoint, began to be used for political ends.

As a young man, Walpole had witnessed the first great expansion of the patronage system by Harley. It had taught him that in political circles there was a wolfish appetite for places, partly because of their financial reward, even more, perhaps, because of the social prestige which they carried. And it taught him, also, that any minister who intended to exploit the vast patronage of the Crown must have the complete and loyal support of the king. For, if there were two or three ministers who could give places, the insecurity of politics was merely removed from the Commons to the court. Hence Walpole's early determination to be sole, supreme minister, to brook no rivals at court, and to prefer as his colleagues, men of small ability but great loyalty, to able but less reliable men, such as Carteret, Pulteney, or Townshend. But neither the absolute support of the Crown, nor the most detailed exploitation of the patronage system, could give Walpole the complete political security for which he longed. It gave him stability no doubt, but not security. To maintain his ascendancy, he added a mastery of the detail of the nation's business that, maybe, only Burleigh has equaled. The nation was still small enough for one man—a man of fantastic industry and efficiency—to comprehend its affairs at a level of detail that made him the unrivaled expert on all questions relating to its welfare. He always knew more about everything than his rivals or his colleagues. This vast competence bred authority and confidence, and his contemporaries hesitated long before they opposed his policy. Always convincing, usually right, the fountain of profit, the channel of promotion, Walpole was irresistible at court and dominant in the Commons. Perhaps no other prime minister has enjoyed so much power for so long over both men and measures.

Walpole served a lengthy apprenticeship. Treasurer of the Navy, and later Secretary of War, in his early thirties he obtained a thorough grounding in financial administration during Godolphin's brilliant period of office as Lord High Treasurer. Accused of corruption on a trumped-up charge, condemned and sent to the Tower, he tasted the rancor and bitterness of 18th-century political struggles. Naturally enough, he developed a detestation of Tories, particularly Bolingbroke, which was to last his life. Back in power after the Hanoverian succession, he quickly showed his financial genius by consolidating all the various funds of the national debt, many of them bearing different interest rates, into one; he also instituted the sinking fund, a device to repay the debt, which lifted the dark fear of bankruptcy that the burden of debt had created. Indeed, the cloud more than lifted: a reckless financial optimism resulted which ended in the South Sea Bubble disaster. Walpole, luckily, was in no way responsible. He had gambled not on South Sea stocks, but on his own political future, by resigning offices, with his brother-in-law, Lord Townshend, in 1717, and entering into furious opposition against Sunderland and Stanhope, the other Whig leaders. Restored to office, he saw that the South Sea Bubble had given him his opportunity. With utter disregard of popular rage and the public insults hurled at him, Walpole handled parliament so skillfully that the court, which had been deeply implicated in the scandal, was successfully screened, the ministry preserved, the Tory opposition frustrated. His victory was political, not economic; for Walpole's financial arrangements are of little importance. In 1721, he emerged as the dominant political figure. But he still had a rival—Townshend.

It took nine years to resolve the struggle. Townshend was a rash man, who liked a vigorous, active, aggressive foreign policy. At one time he cheerfully envisaged England taking over half of the Austrian Netherlands, and becoming once again a European power. To back his policy, he was willing to enter into an alliance with any monarch with troops for hire; and he did not count the cost. Walpole, on the other hand, as Chancellor of the Exchequer, was obliged to think in terms of hard cash. Each year the financial burden mounted; and the landed gentry paid. Yet foreign policy was Townshend's business, not Walpole's. It was an extremely delicate situation, and Walpole got round it by a political maneuver of great dexterity which had a lasting effect on English constitutional development. It was essential that opposition to Townshend's policy should not come from Walpole alone; at the same time discussion in the cabinet, which at that period was very large and included the Archbishop of Canterbury and others, might divide it into two warring factions and split the government. So Walpole began to make more formal the informal meetings of the four or six chief ministers of state, which were especially active when the king, with Townshend, was in Hanover. They were easy for Walpole to manage; he could lobby them privately, and be certain of their views before the meeting. Thus Townshend was isolated and finally driven from office. But Walpole kept this small, efficient cabinet going, since it enabled him to retain a firm grasp of the details of foreign affairs. From this small cabinet our modern cabinet is derived; and Townshend's behavior was accepted as the only correct procedure. If a minister of this inner ring differed violently on policy with the others, it was felt that he ought to resign; and from this belief was gradually evolved the theory of cabinet responsibility. But, of course, Walpole had no idea that he was encouraging important constitutional developments. For him it was a means of getting his way, a convenient and ingenious maneuver by which he secured the fullest extension of his power for the sake of his peace policy.

But peace was difficult to secure. Many of his contemporaries genuinely thought that Walpole's policy in foreign affairs was inimical to England's interests, and wished to see a much more truculent and less compromising attitude to both France and Spain, which they regarded as serious obstacles to our commercial growth. Other politicians joined with them, including some whigs, such as Pulteney, whom Walpole would not have at any price, in the hope that a united front of opposition would pull Walpole down. They attacked him on every issue, including his policy of taxation by excise, which had done a great deal to promote the expansion of English commerce. But Walpole ignored torrents of personal abuse, violent public agitation, gave the growling dogs a sound kick when he had the chance, and persisted obstinately in his foreign policy and financial reforms, until he was faced with a threat of a split at court in the ranks of his own supporters. Then he saw the danger signal. He at once abandoned excise and, later, reluctantly declared war on Spain, telling the Duke of Newcastle bitterly that it was *his* war, and that he wished him joy of it. In such circumstances a modern prime minister would have resigned immediately; but Walpole did not regard himself as a prime minister, nor did he apply to himself the principles inherent in Townshend's resignation. Walpole regarded himself as the king's first servant; and, while he could carry on the king's business with the king's approval, he was prepared to stay in power and, if necessary, throw his own principles overboard. He continued to transact his master's business till in 1742, only resigning when it was made absolutely clear to him that he could no longer do so.

Walpole's career is extremely difficult to assess. He had none of Chatham's uncanny power of intuitively sensing the future destiny of England and, by his unrivaled rhetoric, inspiring the country to strive to attain it. It was a future of imperial grandeur, but also of endless war and indebtedness which Walpole would have deplored. He had none of the moral

stature of a Gladstone. Though he did not invent corruption or the exploitation of the self-interest of avaricious politicians, which were well on the
way by the time he entered politics, he was more ruthless in his use of
patronage, and more obvious, than his predecessors, and brought to the
question involved his infinite capacity for detail. Tidewaiters' places at
Berwick-on-Tweed, the promotion of an ensign in a regiment of foot, a
scholarship for a Wykehamist going on to New College, the foundation
of a school in the Bermudas—all applications were studied, docketed, filed,
and made to pay their dividends in terms of political allegiance. Knowing
well the importance of family connections, he did not hesitate to endow
his Norfolk cousinage with the best of places in the very center of government. This was common knowledge and bandied about in the press; and
it is undeniable that his brazen use of places brought the institutions of
government into disrepute and helped to foster the middle-class radicalism
of the later 18th century. Such is the case against him. Yet, although one
must discount his contribution to constitutional development—for that was
largely fortuitous and arose out of his methods, not his intentions—there
is much to his credit. His reorganization of taxation and of financial administration gave English government funds, throughout the 18th century,
a buoyancy and strength that no other European country could rival. It
drew to us the Dutch capital which enabled us to win a vast commercial
empire; and this made possible the industrial revolution. His policy of
peace, prosperity, stability, security, moreover, was surely in every way
admirable, and well worth the occasional injuries inflicted on our national
pride. Walpole's instinctive attitude to politics was much nearer to the
common aspirations of mankind than the majority of our prime ministers.
His vision of a secure, orderly, prosperous world, in which the ordinary
human story could be lived out according to its own strange necessities,
is one that must still command respect. Hence his bitterness toward those
who would casually jeopardize peace for the sake of Gibraltar or for the
alleged Spanish ill-treatment of Captain Jenkins, a mere smuggler-mer-
chant. Hence, in Walpole's mouth, the term "patriot" was to become a
term of abuse; for this was the patriotism of self-seeking greed and not
of solid human commonsense. Walpole's view was too sophisticated, too
urbane, to prevail. And yet, although the scales were weighted against
him, he secured a longer period of peace than England had enjoyed since
the reign of Elizabeth or was to enjoy until the 19th century; and in that,
possibly, lies his greatest achievement.

It was only achieved thanks to his inhuman energy and his quite exceptional insight into political tactics. We like to think of the 18th century
as a leisured world; but Walpole worked as hard as, or harder than, any

modern minister. At the Treasury before eight in the morning, prepared to conduct his first interviews, during the sessions of parliament he was almost continuously in the House. On his way to Houghton, we hear of him up at six o'clock at Newmarket, in order to deal with his letters. Wherever he goes, bundles of paper follow him; and, even if he makes time for hunting or drinking or his mistress, work goes on remorselessly. Treasury procedure, taxation yields, foreign despatches, electioneering, regimental promotion, the tribulations of dissenters or colonists, the difficulties of Eton College over a public house belonging to the Crown, everything great or small received his detailed attention.

This knowledge, coupled with his formidable powers of argument, made him difficult to dislodge. And yet, he always had time to spare. He would devote hours to the king and queen, to ensure their absolute support. No minister can have been easier of access; for his papers are full of letters of thanks for the trouble he has taken over cousins and younger sons up from the country in search of a career. He appears to have seen them all personally. Walpole's wide human contacts, coupled with patience and foresight, gave him an unrivaled knowledge of the shifting personal aspect of politics, from which he derived his superb certainty of decision in times of crisis. He seemed always to know whom he could disgrace with impunity, whom he must flatter and cajole back into alliance. No prime minister ever weathered so skillfully, or so often, the danger of a breakup of his ministry. Again and again the political world confidently expected his fall; but until 1742 he confidently rode through all storms. With his rare combination of detailed knowledge and subtlety in human relations, backed by a prodigious memory and an obstinate faith in his attitude to life, he knew exactly what he wanted—power for himself, to bring peace and prosperity to his country. After Walpole's defeat, England embarked on a race for wealth through aggressive war which was to last for nearly a century of tribulation and heroism, and at length called into being the industrial revolution, destined to destroy forever the world which he had struggled to maintain. Time has not served him well. His use of patronage and corruption, his worldliness and cynicism, are remembered in our textbooks; but his capacity, his wisdom, his aspirations are frequently neglected. Even more neglected is another aspect of his personality. None of our British prime ministers can compare with Sir Robert Walpole in appreciation of the fine arts. He personally supervised the building of Houghton, the design of the superb furniture by Kent, and the magnificent collection of pictures afterward sold to Catherine of Russia. To questions of taste he brought the same confident certainty of judgment that made him a political master.

Burdette C. Poland, Professor of History at Pomona College, was born in Philadelphia in 1926. He was graduated from Swarthmore College, studied at the University of Grenoble in France, and received his M.A. and Ph.D. degrees from Princeton University. He formerly taught history at Denison University and the University of Nebraska. He is the author of *French Protestantism and the French Revolution: A Study of Church and State, Thought and Religion, 1685–1815* (Princeton, N.J., 1952). He is a member of the American Historical Society and of the Society for French Historical Studies.

CHAPTER ELEVEN

BURDETTE C. POLAND

Pomona College

Political Reform in the Age of Reason

"HAPPINESS," DECLAIMED St. Just to the French National Convention in 1794, "is a new idea in Europe." Since he was speaking at a moment of crisis during the height of the Terror, we can perhaps forgive his over-looking the well-intentioned governors and zealous servants of God who had concerned themselves with the happiness and welfare of their fellow men throughout the ages. But in one sense there is a certain truth to what St. Just was saying. The European experience since the 18th century has differed from the preceding period in the degree to which people outside what we today call "the establishment" have concerned them-selves with schemes for the amelioration of life. Increasing numbers of people have believed that many or all of society's ills can be righted. They have remorselessly criticized the existing order, demanded change, and recommended reforms; they have often found receptive audiences and, when reforms failed to materialize or failed to produce the promised re-sults, they have helped create the climate of opinion which sometimes led to revolution. The modern age has been a period of reform and revolution, of confidence in the ability of man to create a better life and of the right of man to have and to enjoy that life.

The trail to this age of reform was blazed by the philosophes. They were encouraged to embark upon it by the lessons they read in the Scien-tific Revolution of the 17th century. In the scientific discoveries culminat-ing in the Newtonian synthesis, Western man found convincing proof for

a belief he formerly had held largely on faith: that there is a basic, under-
lying order and harmony to nature, that the universe is governed by law.
The idea itself was an old one, entertained by Stoics and Christians alike.
But it now seemed confirmed in an undeniable fashion. Moreover, the
Stoic and Christian had hoped at best for little more than a blurred com-
prehension of the laws of the universe. The startling revelation of the
Scientific Revolution was the demonstration that these laws are knowable
to man, subject to discovery and to mathematical expression. As Alexander
Pope would put it: "Nature and Nature's laws lay hid in night. God said,
'Let Newton be!' and all was light." All nature's secrets could be laid
bare, it seemed, if man would only have the courage to challenge accepted
belief and to go wherever reason led him. "If a man will begin with certainties, he shall end in doubts," wrote Francis Bacon, "but if he will be
content to begin in doubts he shall end in certainties."

Nature was found to be orderly and harmonious; the laws which governed it were knowable to man. But man, too, is a part of the natural
order. It therefore seemed appropriate to ask whether God had intended a
harmony in social affairs comparable to what had been discovered in the
natural realm, and whether man could devise a science of man and of
society which would reveal that intended harmony and through its revelation bring it within the grasp of man. Locke's *Essay on Human Understanding* suggested that we can indeed develop a science of man—as Pope
again would put it, that "the proper study of mankind is man"—and that
our knowledge of man is apt to be more certain than our knowledge of
the physical world around us. Yet it was one thing to hope that man could
be understood; it was still another to hope that he could be changed,
and changed for the better. But this was precisely the growing tendency
of 17th-century thought: a tendency to be impatient with any suggestion
that man is bound by habit, custom, or tradition, or worse still by the consequences of Adam's sin. Locke was prominent among such men, contending that man at birth is neither good nor bad; that he has the capacity to
become either or both, and that what he becomes is largely determined by
his environment. Improve the environment and man would be improved
with it. In short, there seemed to be good reason to believe that man
could not only come to know the harmony of the physical world in which
he lived but that he also had the ability to put himself in harmony with
it. That is, he had the capacity to judge what is right and the ability to
do it. He is a second Adam, possessed of free will. In the light of such
belief, the only apparent obstacle to the amelioration of man's lot was
ignorance and fanaticism.

Such beliefs and expectations found their most fertile soil in France, where the monarchy created by Louis XIV was rapidly decaying. Repeated but abortive attempts to stop that decay generated a sense of frustration which encouraged widespread criticism and suggestions for change. It was the historic task of the philosophe to attempt to devise a science of society and of man in order to find solutions for the manifold problems of the old regime. This was a noble enterprise, but at the hands of posterity the philosophe has been treated harshly. Scarcely anyone has deigned to honor him with the title his name suggests: philosopher. Instead, he is dismissed as a mere popularizer and polemicist of borrowed ideas. But if he was not a philosopher, did he succeed in his chosen role as a social scientist? Here, too, he has fared ill. The criticism which the philosophe leveled at the old regime helped establish, to a very significant degree, the ideological underpinnings of the revolution which followed. To many, nothing seemed more obvious than that the philosophes had "caused" the revolution, that the revolution constituted nothing less than a desperate attempt to realize overnight the utopian society they had prophesied. This Promethean attempt had failed, and its failure dramatized the falsity of the principles upon which the philosophes had worked. This notion is as old as the Revolution itself. The tragic Louis XVI, in prison awaiting the trial that would lead to his execution, upon seeing several books by Voltaire and Rousseau, is reported to have declared: "Ah! these two men have ruined France." The charge has been repeated ever since, by conservatives who dislike the republican tradition in French political life, and even by liberals who are perplexed by the tortured experience of France in liberal institutions and who have sought to lay bare the causes for that experience.

Actually, there are two aspects to the charge. First, the philosophes are accused of having prepared the Revolution intellectually by destroying public confidence in the old order and by encouraging hopes for a better society. This they certainly helped to do, and it would seem sterile to deny it. It is the other aspect of the charge which concerns us here. In addition to alienating society from its leaders and institutions, in addition to encouraging dreams of a better life, they are also accused of having been unfair in their criticism of the old order and totally unrealistic in their projections of the future. In the words of the *Shorter Oxford English Dictionary*, under the definition of Enlightenment, they were guilty of "shallow and pretentious intellectualism, unreasonable contempt for authority and tradition." They are denied, in other words, any claim to having been social scientists. Instead they are dismissed as inexperienced, irresponsible, dogmatic theoreticians who became intoxicated with their own rhetoric. More recently, however, the philosophes have found champions in a number of historians who have carefully reassessed their works and in so doing have sought to rehabilitate them as realistic critics and reformers. The following selections will illustrate some of the conflicting interpretations which have developed around this issue.

1. THE ENLIGHTENMENT: SIMPLISTIC OMNISCIENCE

The most severe indictments against the philosophes are often to be found not in works on the Enlightenment itself, but rather in studies of the Revolution, the authors of which have turned to the philosophes as one of the causal agents of the Revolution. This is evident among the earliest histories of the Revolution, but it received its classic expression in the work of Hippolyte Taine and has been echoed ever since by conservative historians such as Bainville, Gaxotte, and Madelin. Alexis de Tocqueville was less hostile than they to the liberal tradition in France, but he, too, pointed an accusing finger at the philosophes when he tried to explain why the Revolution led France into chaos rather than paradise. Most of the arguments advanced by these writers are ably summarized by the late George H. Sabine, professor of philosophy at Cornell University, in his chapter dealing with the Enlightenment in A History of Political Theory.

GEORGE H. SABINE*

The Changed Environment

Autocracy had done its work so thoroughly that no effective reform in France could attach itself to the idea of reviving the traditional constitution. The ancient ideal of a fundamental law, which 16th-century France had shared with all Europe and which had still vitality enough to hold an almost equal footing with sovereignty in Bodin's philosophy, had lost

---

* From George H. Sabine, *A History of Political Theory*, Copyright 1937, 1950, © 1961, by Holt, Rinehart and Winston, Inc. Used by permission.

all concrete meaning in the monarchy of Louis XIV. In England it was little more than a difference of terminology if a Leveller called his "birthright" the right of a man or the right of an Englishman; in either case it meant something concrete in the tradition of the common law. The rights of Frenchmen—unless one meant the privileges of the nobility—would have been a practically meaningless phrase. In consequence, the rights of man, and there was nothing else that a French liberal could appeal to, were necessarily more abstract, more detached from usage and concrete applicability, more open to speculative interpretation. In importing Locke into France, the French must omit precisely the most characteristic—at all events the most English—quality of Locke's political rationalism. They could not import . . . the gradual transition of ideas and institutions which made it possible for Locke to attach his philosophy to a tradition continuous with St. Thomas and the Middle Ages, nor could they tie back the new philosophy to any French thinker of the 16th century. The historical and with it the relatively conservative quality of the English Revolution —in fact as well as in idea—was bound to be lost. The effect of this upon French political philosophy was profound. Reason was placed in stark opposition to custom and fact as it had never been in Locke. Probably no English politician would ever have said, as a speaker said before the National Convention,

In dealing with matters so weighty I have sought the truth in the natural order of things and nowhere else. I have desired, so to speak, to preserve the virginity of my thought.

The a priori, dogmatic, and hence radical quality of French political thought, in contrast with its English model, was heightened also by the circumstances under which it was produced. Though a doctrine of liberty it was written under a despotism, mostly by men with no experience of government and no possibility of such experience. Outside the ranks of the civil service no one in France had experience, and bureaucrats (allowing for the exception of Turgot) produced little political philosophy. The autocracy had made government a mystery conducted in secret, never divulging, even if it knew, the information, financial or other, on which an intelligent judgment of policy might be formed. Criticism and discussion, in public assemblies or in the press, were out of the question. Local government, always the school of English politics, had been completely subjected to central control, with the normal accompaniments of delay, friction, and red tape. Neither was there in France any such body of common ideas, tested in continual application, as the English common law. Before the Napoleonic Code France had some 360 systems of local private law, left standing by the merely administrative unification of the monarchy. Of necessity French political philosophy in the 18th century, far more than English, was a literary philosophy, in a sense a bookish though not a scholarly philosophy, written for the salons and the educated bourgeoisie, the only public to which an author could address himself. It abounds in formulas and sweeping generalizations; it strives after brilliant effects; and it moves largely in an atmosphere of vague but familiar ideas. It is often effective propaganda, more frequently negative than positive, but relatively seldom responsible. It is only fair to add that one knows today as little as in the 18th century what criticism of existing French government might have been really constructive.

There were social causes as well as political that gave to French political philosophy a tone of bitterness that had no counterpart in Locke. French society was a tissue of privilege which made the cleavage between classes more conscious and more irritating, if not more real, than in England. . . . In French political writing there was a class consciousness and a sense of exploitation such as had appeared only sporadically in English political writing. And in fact the French Revolution was a social revolution as the English Revolution was not; it compressed into three or four years an expropriation of church lands, crown lands, and lands of *émigré* nobles comparable to that spread through the reigns of Henry VII and Henry VIII. It is hardly an exaggeration to say that Locke's philosophy in France before the Revolution was an attack on vested interests and in England after the Reformation a defense of them.

The foregoing divergences refer to the category of space but equally important ones refer to that of time. The fact that Locke in England belonged to the 17th century while Locke in France belonged to the 18th was itself a significant difference. In the days of Grotius and Descartes, and even in the days of Locke, the appeal to reason had been a high intellectual adventure, a new exploration on the frontiers of philosophy and science, and a deliverance from authority. In the 18th century it ran the risk of becoming a cliché. The farther it got from its source, the more assured it became, the more dogmatic, and the more commonplace. For despite the reverence expended on enlightenment, a good deal of what passed for rational ethics or rational politics was an obvious kind of prudential moralizing that was not intellectually penetrating and does not now seem morally stirring. . . . Yet thousands of Frenchmen, and of Englishmen and Germans too, read such books with passionate interest. They made known to a new and larger public what a series of great philosophers and scientists, from Descartes and Galileo to Locke and Newton, had created. It is inevitable that by comparison the 18th century now suffers heavily. A genius of any age is always worth reading, but nothing is so dead as popular philosophy that has ceased to be popular.

There is, however, another and a more important side to this. The assurance of the 18th century and its confidence in reason was not bred of familiarity alone but was partly the effect of solid achievement. Until the publication of Newton's *Principia* in 1687, modern science was on trial; a few philosophers had believed passionately in it but no one knew that it would work. After Newton everyone knew, even though he had only the vaguest conception of the new engine. The idea of the new science affected men's imaginations far more than the actuality affected technology. For the reason of Newton seemed to have pierced to the very heart of nature, to have disclosed "that wisdom which we see equally displayed in the exquisite structure and just motions of the greatest and subtilest parts." Nothing was beyond the power of reason; Bacon's saying that knowledge is power had come true and for the first time in history men could cooperate with the benevolent intentions which even atheists like Holbach still attributed to the harmony of nature. Nothing characterizes social thought in the 18th century so completely as belief in the possibility of happiness and progress under the guidance of reason. Much of this—the belief in the harmony of nature, for example—was sheer confusion in no way warranted by the new science. But on the whole the belief that man's fate was in the keeping of his intelligence was an honorable faith, more humane than the religion of authority that preceded it or the religion of sentimentality that followed it. In the large it did not overestimate the power of scientific reason to control nature, but whether that power extends to human relationships, no one knows today any more than the philosophers knew then. Their superficiality lay in a shocking exaggeration of the simplicity of the problem. . . .

The philosophy briefly described in this chapter . . . was important rather for the extent of the public which it influenced than for the novelty or the profundity of the ideas which it disseminated. It belonged more to the métier of popularization than of discovery. The 18th century has rightly been called the age of encyclopedias, an age in which Europe consolidated the gains made by the more original genius of the preceding century. This was true even of a figure as striking as Montesquieu. Its political philosophy remained essentially that of natural rights, inhering in individual personalities and setting the standards of what law and government may rightfully do and the limits beyond which they may not rightfully go. In the nature of the case such rights must be set up as axioms, the products of rational intuition, incapable of proof and still less defensible by empirical generalization. At the worst this was a better dogmatism than that of authority from which it released the 17th century, but the appeal to self-evidence was none the less dogmatism. Neither in science nor social studies could it withstand a wide and steady application of empirical methods.

There was a steady though not a completely conscious change in this respect throughout the 18th century: social philosophy was empirical as neither Hobbes nor Locke had been. It prosecuted the study of social history as the 17th century had never done; it explored the customs and the manners of outlandish folk as no rationalist would have thought worthwhile; it followed the processes of manufacture and the mechanic arts, of trade and finance and taxation, in a manner shocking to the pundits of the higher learning. Yet this empiricism had, so to speak, all the bias of rationalism; it had the foible of omniscience and the itch for simplicity. It appealed to fact but it insisted that facts should speak a predetermined language. Even the new ethics of utility and the new economics, which were the chief additions made to social theory, were logically incoherent for precisely this reason. They professed to rest on an empirical theory of human motives but they assumed a harmony of nature for which no scientific proof could ever have been given. Thus the popular thought of the 18th century reiterated a philosophy which in effect it only half believed and professed a method which it only half practiced. The practical importance of this popular philosophy was very great. It spread through all Europe the belief in science; it fostered the hope that intelligence might make men measurably the masters of their social and political fate; is passionately defended ideals of liberty, opportunity, and humane living, even though it did so mainly in the interest of a single social class. Beyond measure it did not apotheosize its prejudices. But intellectually it was superficial and partly for this reason it fell a prey to an appeal to sentiment, begun by Rousseau, which on the whole lacked its solid virtues.

2. MONTESQUIEU: SOCIAL SCIENTIST OR CHARLATAN?

One of the chief failings of the philosophes was that they tried to uitilize the method of mathematics and physics in the realm of social investigation —that is, they produced abstract systems based upon a priori, deductive thought—and that they concerned themselves primarily with what was common to all men and societies and tended to ignore the complex variations. Montesquieu alone has escaped this charge. In the words of Professor Sabine, of all the philosophes "he had perhaps the clearest conception of the complexities of a social philosophy ... [and] he alone undertook what purported to be an empirical study of society. ..." One of the best examples of Montesquieu's empiricism is to be found in his theory of the influence of climate on society. The theory first suggested itself to him through the works of such writers as Galen, Chardin, and the abbé Dubos. Traveling to Italy in 1728–29, he investigated the possible influence of climate upon the inhabitants of that land. The theory developed steadily in his mind from that time on and found its full expression in his Spirit of the Laws *published in 1748. In the following selection, Professor Shackleton describes this empirical aspect of Montesquieu's work and the importance Montesquieu attached to climate relative to other factors. Eighteenth-century readers of Montesquieu were greatly impressed by the theory and many thought it his most important contribution to political thought. The modern reader must ask himself how sophisticated this empiricism and the conclusions Montesquieu derived from it would appear to a modern political scientist.*

ROBERT SHACKLETON[*]

The development of Montesquieu's thought in relation to climate shows itself as being clearly inductive. Starting with an examination of the specific problem of Roman air, enlarging his ideas by reading, by observation, and by experiment, he arrives in the end at his general theory of climatic influence.

[*] Robert Shackleton, *Montesquieu: A Critical Biography*, 1961, pp. 309–13, 316–19, by permission of the Clarendon Press, Oxford.

The president begins his exposition of the influence of climate with an examination of the effect of heat and cold on man's body. The fibers of the human frame are contracted by cold air and expanded by hot air. When they are contracted, their elasticity or *ressort* increases; for this reason, and because the blood then flows more easily to the heart, the strength of the body becomes greater. Men, then, are stronger in cold climates.... The nerves, on the other hand, end in little bundles on the skin. According as the skin is tense or relaxed, so are the ends of the nerves less or more open to external stimuli. The skin is tense in cold climates, relaxed in hot ones. External stimuli therefore are more readily responded to in hot climates than in cold. Sensations are more numerous then, in hot climates, and imagination, taste, sensitivity, and vivacity, which depend on a multitude of sensations, are found in greater abundance where the sun shines more brightly.

For what he had said, Montesquieu has experimental justification. He takes the tongue of a sheep, examines it under a microscope, and discovers little pyramids on its surface. He regards these pyramids as being, in all probability, the principal organs of taste. He then freezes the tongue, and finds that the pyramids are no longer visible. They have retreated into the tissues of the tongue, and it is only as the tongue gradually regains the temperature of the air that the pyramids begin to reappear.

After this digression, Montesquieu returns to his enumeration of the psychological results of heat and cold.

Dans les pays froids, on aura peu de sensibilité pour les plaisirs; elle sera plus grande dans les pays tempérés; dans les pays chauds, elle sera extrême.

[In cold countries, people have little feeling for pleasure; it will be found to be greater in temperate countries; in hot lands, it is extreme.]

He has seen operas performed in Italy and in England. The same pieces, with the same actors, produce the most widely differing effects. The calmness of the one nation and the transport of the other can scarcely be believed. Pain, likewise, is variously felt in varied climates: "il faut écorcher un Moscovite pour lui donner du sentiment." [A Muscovite must be skinned alive before he will feel anything.] The love of one sex for the other is far more intense in the South, where the seat of pleasure is the harem. The more vigorous natives of the North have for their delectation hunting, travel, war, and drinking; they have few vices; they are honest and open. But as one approaches the lands of the South, one seems to be moving away from morality itself.

What immediate consequences follow from the principle thus enunciated? Some peoples, notably the inhabitants of India, need the offices of a good legislator more than others. The intellectually indolent—to wit, the races of the Orient—are slow to change their ways; hence the same laws and institutions exist in their lands as existed a thousand years ago. In these same lands speculation, rather than action, will be the habit of the people; hence monasticism will flourish. The number of dervishes in Asia increases with the heat of the climate, and this same phenomenon—it is recalled that monks, in the *Lettres persanes,* are called dervishes—is to be found in Europe. Alcohol is drunk with more impunity in the North, where coagulation of the blood is less to be feared; in the South, therefore, the legislator Mahomet has been compelled to forbid the consumption of wine. In England, the climate engenders weariness and disgust with everything, even life itself; it is therefore not expedient that the citizens should be able to vent their hostility to the government against a single man: it is better that laws rather than men should govern. Thus the government of England is what it ought to be. In the hottest of countries, where courage is almost unknown, another stimulus has to take its place in urging men to do hard and painful things; the fear of punishment is that alternative; and therefore climate is one of the many causes of slavery. In hot climates, since the early maturity of women cause them to marry while still infants, wives are in a position of clear subordination to their husbands; and since it costs less to maintain them than in cooler areas, a man can more easily afford more than one: hence polygamy. Courage is the characteristic of the North, to the point that even within a single country remarkable differences are seen:

> Les peuples du nord de la Corée sont plus courageux que ceux du midi.
> [The people of northern Korea are more courageous than those of the South.]

It follows that northern races are more frequently free, and southern races often enslaved. Asia, according to the accounts of travelers, which Montesquieu elaborately examines, has virtually no temperate zone, whereas Europe's is very extensive. In Asia, therefore, races of widely different characteristics find themselves contiguous. The warlike and the weak are adjacent, and this contrast weakens the continent as a whole, and promotes war and servitude. In Europe, the more even balance of races is an element of strength and encourages liberty. The vast empires of conquest in Asia can be governed only despotically. In the smaller states of Europe freedom can flourish.

These elements compose Montesquieu's theory of climate. It is not a rigorous and systematic doctrine. Certain effects on men's minds are in part caused by the climate, and as men's minds influence the forms of government under which they live, so climate, vicariously, influences those forms of government. This is a moderate and limited doctrine. It is only a part, and even a small part, of the doctrine of *L'Esprit des lois;* and the first impression one ought to retain of the theory of climate in Montesquieu's work is of the narrowness of the limits it occupies.

The first impression in the mind of the 20th-century reader, however, may well be that of the naïveté of the doctrine; and that impression, if one is to judge by absolute scientific standards, is justified. But if one wishes to understand Montesquieu properly one must judge him in relation to the standards of his own day, and the theories of climate current in the 17th and 18th centuries often took odd forms. It was thought that the high temperatures of the South and East stimulated black bile and therefore strengthened the imagination, fostering in particular religious inspiration and literary genius. Hence new religions and literary *genres* were deemed to arise in the East. This view, going back to Cardano in 16th-century Italy, was expressed by Huet in modest form, and was not wholly dissented from by Fontenelle. Others held that in cold climates the pores contract, the internal heat of the body cannot escape, and it is necessary to cool it: hence the notorious drunkenness of northern races. For such views as these Montesquieu has no use, and he marks a great advance on their exponents. He makes an effort to reject the a priori in relation both to the facts of climatic conditions and to the mode of influence. The seriousness of his attempts to discover experimentally the effect of heat and cold is surpassed only by the zeal with which he studies the accounts of travelers. He does not simply make assertions: he seeks evidence. . . .

The assembly of causes is one of the most important ideas of *L'Esprit des lois,* and it is an idea which had for long been germinating in Montesquieu's mind. In the fragment *De la politique,* which was a part of the *Traité des devoirs* of 1725, he had affirmed that in each society there is a common character or universal soul, whose mode of thinking is the result of an infinite sequence of causes which are multiplied through the ages. In the *Considérations sur les Romains* he alluded again to this common character, calling it now the *esprit général,* and insisting that power is based on it and must not offend it.

There are three places in which the factors of the *esprit général* are enumerated. There is first a passage in the *Pensées* dating from 1731–33, which lists five factors: religion, maxims of government, laws, *les mœurs,* and *les manières.* A later passage, written between 1733 and 1738 and not susceptible of closer dating, discards maxims of government in order to make way for climate, which now enters the *esprit général.* The third definition of the *esprit général* is penned after the subject has been further explored in the *Essai sur les causes*. It is found in the fourth chapter of Book XIX of *L'Esprit des lois*. This chapter, dating in the manuscript from 1740–43, is perhaps the most significant chapter of the whole work. It is also one of the shortest and it must be quoted in full:

> Plusieurs choses gouvernement les hommes: le climat, la religion, les lois, les maximes du gouvernement, les exemples des choses passées, les mœurs, les manières; d'ou il se forme un esprit général qui en résulte.
>
> A mesure que, dans chaque nation, une de ces causes agit avec plus de force, les autres lui cèdent d'autant. La nature et le climat dominent presque seuls sur les sauvages; les manières gouvernement les Chinois; les lois tyrannisent le Japon; les mœurs donnaient autrefois le ton dans Lacédémone; les maximes du gouvernement et les mœurs anciennes le donnaient dans Rome.
>
> [Mankind is governed by several factors: climate, religion, laws, traditions, precedents, customs, habits; from these a general spirit comes into being for each society.
>
> In each nation, to the degree that one of these factors acts with greater force, the others give way before it. Among savages, nature and climate are virtually supreme; the Chinese are governed by habits; the Japanese are tyrannized by laws; the Spartans were fashioned by their customs; the Romans by their traditions and their ancient customs.]

It is quite wrong, in view of this passage and its antecedents in the author's works, to say that Montesquieu recognizes but one cause in political societies. The fate of nations rests on a balance or equilibrium of these seven causes, on which the legislator must base his laws and the historian his analyses. Only one of these causes, climate, is physical. How, in Montesquieu's view, is the balance struck between them? Does he believe in the paramountcy of climate? . . .

What of the primitive condition of mankind? If one examines the *esprit général*, stripping off in turn like leaves from an artichoke those components which are the result of human activity, one sees laws, maxims, *mœurs*, and *manières* disappear. Religion itself is largely an artifact for Montesquieu, and the natural law which inspires the other, basic part of it, is not the first natural law in chronological order. And when human activity is first starting, there can be no *exemples des choses passées*.

There remains climate: "le premier de tous les empires [it is the first and most powerful of all empires]." In the earliest societies, the least civilized communities, the physical cause is prepotent: "la nature et le climat dominent presque seuls sur les sauvages [nature and climate are virtually supreme among savages]."

As society develops subsequently, religion is embraced, laws are made, precedents accumulate, *mœurs* and *manières* develop, maxims are pronounced. The further any society is from the moment of its original institution, the more important are the nonphysical factors in the *esprit général*.

The political role of physical causes is thus seen to be quite different from that of moral causes. . . . The duty of the legislator, Montesquieu has declared, is to oppose the force of the climate. It is also his duty, however, to act in accordance with the *esprit général*, and of the *esprit général* climate is a part. This means that the good legislator must shift the emphasis, within the framework of the *esprit général*, from physical factors to moral factors. He must rely less than his predecessors on climate, and more on manners, morals, laws, religion, and the appeal to past usage.

Not only is it the duty of the good legislator so to act. Legislators as a whole do so act. With the passage of time the sole empire of climate becomes more remote, and as the moral factors necessarily increase in number, the role of climate is necessarily a dwindling role. Tradition, way of life, customs, religion, and opinion—above all opinion—are constantly gaining in importance as determining factors in society. They may not always be morally valuable, but they are more desirable than climatic influence and their growing predominance over climate is progress.

This conclusion is implicit in Montesquieu's doctrine of the *esprit général*. He does not make any intuitive generalization like the famous one of Turgot:

La masse totale de genre humain, par des alternatives de calme et d'agitations, de biens et de maux, marche toujours, quoiqu'à pas lents, à une perfection plus grande.

[The totality of the human race—through calms and storms, good and ill winds in turn—steadily progresses, however slowly, toward an ever greater perfection.]

Montesquieu's theory is more tentative and more empirical. It is based on an attempt to synthesize the results of detailed study of scientific and historical fact. His documentation is incomplete. His synthesis is imperfect. He has omitted economic factors. Nevertheless, he has enunciated, not less than Turgot, a theory of progress, and far better than Turgot or any other contemporary, he has been able, in Gibbon's words, to conciliate the rights of liberty and of nature.

3. THEMES NOBLE, ROYAL, AND DESPOTIC

Je suis tombé par terre:
C'est la faute à Voltaire;
Le nez dans le ruisseau:
C'est la faute à Rousseau.

"I have fallen on my face: it's all Voltaire's fault! My nose is in the gutter: it's all Rousseau's fault!" This epigram would suggest that France had been led to her ruin, corrupted by Voltaire's "chaos of clear ideas," blinded by Rousseau's utopian schemes. Voltaire devoted his life to smashing idols; his criticisms were irresistibly charming, but at the same time devoid of any practical content. So runs the charge. Professor Gay, on the other hand, believes that Voltaire was a serious commentator of the French political scene. Although Voltaire never turned his hand to a work on political theory, in one way or another he gave his support to a political program which, properly executed, might have spared France the Revolution. Professor Gay also contends that it is a mistake to think of Voltaire as a champion of enlightened despotism, as so many do. A distinction must be drawn between enlightened despotism and what Professor Gay calls "constitutional absolutism." The latter had solid roots in French history. Can supporters of such a program be fairly accused of "unreasonable contempt for tradition?"

PETER GAY[*]

There are two ways of being unpolitical: to think that politics can do everything, and to think that politics can do nothing. The first leads to utopianism and fanaticism, the second to epicureanism and apathy; yet, despite their opposite effects, both are symptoms of the same disease, a failure of realistic vision. The makers of the legend have freely attributed both symptoms to Voltaire—cannot a flighty poet easily move from fanaticism to apathy? He has been charged with overestimating the efficacy of politics, believing that all unhappiness can be cured and all social problems solved, and at the same time wanting to dissolve politics into ethics, wish-

[*] From Peter Gay, *Voltaire's Politics. The Poet as Realist* (Princeton, N.J.: Princeton University Press, 1959), pp. 13–18, 22–23, 88–89, 315, 328–30, 333. Reprinted by permission of the Princeton University Press.

ing to achieve impossible goals by the mere application of reason without the use of force.

This legend does violence to the truth. Voltaire accepted limitations on political action; he agreed with the Machiavellians that private and public spheres are separate and that political power has imperatives of its own. But he rejected a philosophy that frees political actions from criticism and permits statesmen to act ruthlessly, faithlessly, brutally, with the excuse that power is demonic and that necessity knows no law. Far from seeking to make politics a panacea or from dissolving it in ethics, Voltaire sought to humanize it.

This position on power has close affinities to the liberal and the democratic traditions. The liberal, Franz Neumann has written, is deeply concerned with "the erection of fences around political power ... the dissolution of power into legal relationships, the elimination of the element of personal rule, and the substitution of the rule of law in which all relationships are to become purposive-rational, that is, predictable and calculable." The democrat, on the other hand, has "a positive attitude toward political power which appears essentially as a rational instrument to be used for desired and desirable ends." In Voltaire's political thought both elements, the control of power and the rational uses of power, are constantly at play; there is a continual tension between the need for effective action and the desirability of freedom.

This tension appears most sharply in Voltaire's treatment of the rule of law. Like most proponents of the rule of law since the Greeks, Voltaire was deeply devoted to it as an ideal: he alludes to it early and late, in his correspondence as in his political writings. Countries that possess it are to be envied and to be imitated: "Liberty consists of depending on the laws alone. On this basis, every man is free today in Sweden, England, Holland, Switzerland, Geneva, Hamburg.... A citizen of Amsterdam is a man; a citizen several degrees of longitude from there is a beast of burden." Freedom, and indeed civilization itself, depend upon the rule of law: "The only civilized country (bien policé) is the one in which vengeance is in the hands of the laws alone."

Voltaire fully grasped the psychological significance of the rule of law: it is a rational guide in an irrational world; it helps men to be certain in the midst of uncertainty by permitting them to predict the consequences of their actions. In England, under the rule of law, "Everyone knows what he has, what his duty is, and what he can do. Everything is subject to the law, starting from the crown and the church." Yet in absolute states, such as France, the chief executive also claimed to be the chief legislator with no effective restrictions on his powers. Here the rule of law either did not apply at all, or applied only through the self-restraint of the ruler. In this vexing situation—vexing, because Voltaire was anything but an opponent of absolutism—Voltaire had recourse to the traditional distinction between absolutism and arbitrariness, and to the traditional but rather unsatisfactory French theory of constitutional absolutism, a theory that solved the conflict between power and law largely on the level of rhetoric. Yet rhetoric or reality, Voltaire treated the rule of law as a standard that judged all existing governments. . . .

We must look for it and fight for it; the rule of law can be won or preserved only through political action. It is true that Voltaire said more than once that he was not interested in politics, but we need only to read him —his letters and his *Dictionnaire philosophique,* his plays and his tales, his occasional works and his histories—to know that this is a typical Voltairean disclaimer, designed to protect himself rather than to communicate to others, to lull authorities into believing that he is not active, and to warn his friends that he does not wish it known that he *is* active. His empiricism made him hostile to political theorizing, but throughout his life he intervened in political controversies; he meddled whether he was asked to or not, and even, as sometimes happened, when he was earnestly begged to mind his own business. He always said demurely that he was only cultivating his garden, but privately he defined his garden as Europe. . . .

His constant involvement with practical politics, obvious to Voltaire's contemporaries, has been obscured for his later commentators by the general and abstract tone of his writings. But this tone does not reflect his true attitude; it is a mask for the censors. The only way to penetrate this mask is to read Voltaire's writings in the light of the circumstances that called them forth. Ideas have meaning, logic, significance of their own, apart from time and place. But a political pamphleteer like Voltaire, unwilling and perhaps unable to compose a theoretical treatise on politics, called into action by public controversy and private aspiration, diverted from a candid statement of his position by his attempts to persuade a large audience and to evade a suspicious censorship—such a writer demands the examination of the environment that created and nourished his political ideas. A single example may suffice: in late May or early June, 1750, Voltaire published *La voix du sage et du peuple,* a political pamphlet that has been much quoted since. It is filled with generalizations in favor of absolutism, undivided sovereignty, and a politically feeble clergy. *La voix du sage* is a concrete controversial work, supporting the tax program of Controller General Machault, and opposing the resistance to this program by the Assembly of the Clergy. But Voltaire does not once mention Machault, the tax program, the Assembly; still these are the reasons for the pamphlet and they lurk behind every paragraph. It is only when we read *La voix du sage* in this way that we understand Voltaire's politics. It is only when we grasp Voltaire's passion for polemics, his deep sense of reality, his distrust of deductive schemes, that we grasp the extent of Tocqueville's misconception and the injustice of the Voltaire legend. Voltaire's politics was not "abstract, literary politics." It was literary, but only in the sense that his pamphlets are well written; it was abstract, but only to those who do not catch his allusions. Voltaire was indeed a *littérateur,* but he was a *littérateur engagé.* . . .

To the Augustinian philosophy of man, which Voltaire rejected as dismal and self-abasing, he opposed a Stoic philosophy of autonomy, responsibility, and dignity. "Dare to think for yourself," he wrote; and "We should say to every individual: 'Remember your dignity as a man.'"

Despite their sufferings, men can hold up their heads because they are capable of reasonable activity. "Man is born for action," wrote Voltaire in his first polemic against Pascal. "Not to be occupied and not to exist are the same thing for man." He preached the gospel of work early and late: "Let us work without arguing," he wrote in *Candide,* "that is the only way to make life endurable." And near the end of his long life, when he was 83, he told d'Argental: "We must battle nature and fortune until the last moment, and never despair of anything until we are good and dead." His writings—thousands of letters, scores of plays, voluminous histories, innumerable occasional pieces—show that he practiced what he preached; he worked even harder than the other philosophes, who were notorious for their indefatigable activity. . . . But while he was feverishly active, Voltaire was not an unhappy man. *Le monde comme il va,* less ferociously pessimistic than his other tales, expresses his philosophy most accurately: the world is a mixture of beauty and ugliness, refinement and grossness, loyalty and treachery, success and failure, and "if all is not good, all is passable." As a practical man, at home in his world, Voltaire possessed a sober confidence that the spread of philosophy would reduce the sufferings of some men, and console others.

Such a moderate philosophy is the philosophy of a political man. Indeed, Voltaire's political program, radical as it is, does not seek perfection. Voltaire explicitly separated himself from the utopianism of a Saint-Pierre or a Fénelon; he deplored poverty, hated war, campaigned against torture, but he admitted that poverty was necessary, war inevitable, and torture, in exceptional circumstances, useful. His expectations were more modest than his wishes. . . .

There was nothing new in deploring the selfishness, stupidity, cruelty of the governors and the sufferings of the governed. What was new in French politics was the conviction that the sickness of the state could be cured. As philosophes, freemasons, and worldly aristocrats spread the secular spirit among the educated, they awakened confidence in human will, hope for man's mastery of his environment, desire for political action. More and more people saw a great gap between the performance of the French government and the needs of the French public; and they believed that they had the means of closing this gap. Voltaire never tired of exhorting the public to action, of berating it for being too modest in its expectations, too timid in its demands, too conservative in its hopes: "I repeat . . . we do not want enough," he wrote at the end of his stay at Cirey.

Men who believe that their wishes can be translated into reality look for a party that will realize their hopes. Voltaire did not hesitate; in France the only possible agent of reform, the only party that the philosophes could support, was the crown: "The cause of the king is the cause of the philosophes." And, if Louis XV could only be made to see it, the cause of the philosophes was the cause of the king: ". . . the philosophic spirit that has penetrated practically all classes of society except the masses has done much to enhance the rights of sovereigns."

This unequivocal support of the French monarchy has often been taken as evidence of Voltaire's supposed doctrinaire predilection for enlightened despotism. In fact, Voltaire's royalism was a modern version of the *thèse royale,* a political position that dates from the 15th century, and was popular among administrators and practical politicians in Voltaire's own time. Voltaire's royalism was the result not of detachment from practical affairs and addiction to geometrical speculation but of involvement in French politics and an intimate knowledge of French history. . . .

Advocates of the *thèse royale* from Bodin to d'Argenson subjected the crown to the unwritten fundamental laws of France and assumed, further, that the king would obey the decrees he had made. This legal tradition was perhaps illogical in that it mixes elements from two positions usually treated as incompatible, constitutionalism and absolutism. But logical or not, it was this "constitutional absolutism" rather than naked despotism on which 18th-century royalists, including Voltaire, rested their case against the parliaments. . . .

As a proponent of constitutional absolutism for France, Voltaire rejected the widespread assertion that Maupeou's *coup d'état* established despotism in France. It led toward absolutism, but absolutism need not, indeed must not, be arbitrary. It is not only in his play *Les lois de Minos,* which the angry duchesse de Choiseul thought had been written to glorify

Maupeou, that Voltaire distinguished between the legitimate and the illegitimate exercise of royal authority. The distinction appears as early as
1731 in the *Histoire de Charles XII* and 1734 in the *Lettres philosophiques,*
and as late as 1777, in his drama *Agathocle.* The tyrant of Syracuse, Agath-
ocles, hands his throne to his son who in turn renounces power and gives
it to the people to whom it rightfully belongs. In a dramatic speech in
the last scene, the new, just tyrant descends from the throne:

> Peuples, j'use un moment de mon autorité:
> Je règne ... votre roi vous rend la liberté.
> (Il descend du trône.)
> [Good people, for but a moment I make use of my authority:
> I reign ... and your king restores you to your liberty.
> (He descends from the throne.)]

We should not dismiss this drama of self-abnegation as the utopian
dream of a senile poet: Voltaire had never been an indiscriminate royalist.
In his major histories, he had supported the king's cause in France, but
he never hesitated to criticize those—like Louis XI, Richelieu, and even
Louis XIV—who advanced that cause at the expense of the rule of law.
Long before the abbé Sieyès became famous for asserting the claims
of the third estate, Voltaire wrote that the third estate was the nation itself, and praised Louis XII for the edict of 1499—"forever memorable"—
which ordered people "always to follow the law, despite the orders contrary to law which importunity could wring from the monarch."

Voltaire's constitutional absolutism is patently open to a serious objection: it fails to provide institutions to determine whether the king is
observing the rule of law, and to resist him if he should disobey it. "Enlightened despotism," as I have repeatedly said, is not an apt phrase to
characterize Voltaire's political program, even for France. But his royalism seems to leave him almost defenseless against despotism, enlightened
or unenlightened.

It is improbable that Voltaire would have admitted the force of this
objection. He was willing to use Maupeou, but his version of good government was not the same as the chancellor's. Maupeou sought absolute
centralized power for the sake of reform, unhampered by competing institutions or by criticism. Voltaire too wanted to employ royal power as
the engine of reform in France, but as a radical man of letters, with a
firm faith in education, he wanted to check and guide that power by the
force of public opinion. That opinion was not embodied in formal institutions as it was in England, a country lucky enough to have a real parliament and rudimentary political parties. But public opinion could exercise
influence, and as the enlightenment of the middle classes grew, that in-

fluence too would grow. Voltaire's persistent demand for free speech in all matters, including religion and politics, envisaged a rational administration, governing through fixed rules and cooperating with a free and informed public. ...

In the 18th century, Frenchmen could take one of three major political positions: the *thèse nobiliaire*, the *thèse royale*, or Rousseau's democratic theory. But Rousseau's position was utopian and, in any event, had never been intended for France, and the *thèse nobiliaire* was no more than an ideology for special interests. What remained was the *thèse royale*, and all his life Voltaire had placed his trust in it. "Neither Louis XV or Louis XVI," Franz Neumann wrote in his brilliant essay on Montesquieu, "could possibly arouse the hope that a monarch could and would have the courage to cut himself loose from all ties with the aristocracy, to wipe out all privileges, to create economic freedom, to put the finances on a sound basis, to establish a reorganization of the administration, clean out the drones, and throw himself into the arms of the masses of the people. ... Turgot's short-lived administration proved the Utopian character of the *thèse royale*."

The beginning of this statement seems too harsh: for years the only realistic political position in France was Voltaire's. But its conclusion is just: with the dismissal of Turgot the *thèse royale* collapsed, and all positions became equally unrealistic. When Voltaire returned to Paris early in 1778, there was much prosperity and much gaiety, but some kind of revolution was now inevitable.

4. ROUSSEAU AS A REALIST

There is a timelessness to Rousseau's writings which is totally lacking in the other political works of 18th-century France. So much of what the philosophes wrote was colored by the special conditions of that period and that country that it is of little relevance today. Alone among them, Rousseau is still commonly read and studied. Yet, at the same time, many critics feel that Rousseau epitomizes the worst faults of the philosophes: he seems the most utopian, the least consistent, and, in terms of long-range influence, the most incendiary of them. It is often stated, but too often forgotten, that Rousseau, while preaching unattainable ideals and the right of revolution, could be quite practical when he addressed himself to specific problems. An example of his caution and realism is provided by his treatment of the problem of reform in the expiring kingdom of Poland. In the passage which follows, Kingsley Martin sketches out the manner of advice Rousseau offered the Poles.

KINGSLEY MARTIN[*]

When Rousseau turned to the complex question of the art of government the result was surprising. Few writers in the 18th century had studied and grasped *L'Esprit des Lois* to such effect. The whole trend of Montesquieu's thought, with its Whig assumption that change is permissible only as a result of careful adjustment to historic tradition and unchangeable environment, with its stress on the relativity of good and evil, and its consequent acceptance of compromise—this whole method of thought seemed the antithesis of Rousseau's abstract philosophy and revolutionary Protestantism. Yet so imbued with Montesquieu's caution had Rousseau become that even in his *Social Contract* he applies his principles with an unexpected timidity. Rousseau was revolutionary only in theory, and when he was called upon to suggest practical reforms Burke himself could scarcely have considered his proposals extravagant.

In his political writings two strands lie side by side: on one page we are dealing with absolutes and on the next making compromises and exceptions which seemed to undermine his most cherished principles. What are we to say of a philosopher who opens his treatise by declaring that "the terms of the contract . . . are everywhere the same and everywhere tacitly admitted and recognized," and then proceeds to tell us that there are "unfriendly and barren lands" where all political society is impossible; that "liberty not being the fruit of all climates is not within the reach of all peoples," that Montesquieu was right in thinking that considerations of territory and climate sometimes justify a monarchy, that democracy suits only States that are small and poor and that no one can say "what sort of government is absolutely the best"? In the same way, when Rousseau, who had opened *The Social Contract* by saying, "If I were a Prince or a Legislator, I should not waste time in saying what wants doing; I should do it or hold my peace," was actually offered the opportunity of becoming a legislator, the main burden of his advice was to move cautiously and to practice moderation.

[*] From Kingsley Martin, *The Rise of French Liberal Thought* (New York: New York University Press, 1954), pp. 208–12.

In *The Social Contract* he had admitted that the ideal conditions for which he sought were no longer attainable anywhere, and certainly not in most European countries. For "legislation is made difficult less by what it is necessary to build up than by what has to be destroyed; and what makes success so rare is the impossibility of finding natural simplicity together with social requirements. All these conditions are indeed rarely found united, and therefore few States have good constitutions." . . .

In 1769 the Polish Convention resolved to ask the French philosophes to make suggestions for a new constitution for Poland. In the next year Polish liberty was destroyed by the neighboring despots, whose philosophic principles did not prevent them from dividing among themselves the territory of an independent people. Voltaire enthusiastically approved of this example of enlightenment. Rousseau and Mably, however, had already made suggestions for the reorganization of a free Poland. Rousseau decided at once that the situation and traditions of Poland made anything like an ideal constitution out of the question. Montesquieu himself could not have been more statesmanlike. The most important thing was that Poland should be animated by the spirit of liberty, that every citizen should think only of his country, her independence and moral greatness. But the spirit of liberty was dangerous: "High-souled and holy liberty! If these poor men could only know thee, if they could only learn the price at which thou art won and guarded; if they could only be taught how far sterner are thy laws than the hard yoke of the tyrant; they would shrink from thee a hundred times more than from slavery, they would fly from thee in terror as from a burden made to crush them." Thus the Poles, and especially the serfs, should be moderate both in obtaining and using their liberty. "In thinking of what you would wish to acquire, do not forget what you may lose. Correct, if you can, the abuses of your Constitution, but never despise a Constitution which has made you what you are." Nevertheless, since "repose and liberty are incompatible . . . I will not say you ought to leave things as they are, but I will say that you must touch them with the greatest caution."

In accordance with these principles, Rousseau outlined a scheme of reforms. Poland, again, was too large for the democratic severity of ancient Sparta: "Your vast provinces will never admit the stern administration of a small State." Rousseau suggested, therefore, that the monarchy should become really elective; that taxation should be equitably administered and levied upon landed property; that the power should continue to reside in the aristocratic Senate. He offered the third estate no part in government and was opposed to anything more drastic than a

very gradual scheme for freeing serfs, who might so easily misuse liberty
when it was given them. He put his trust for the future of Poland in two
things: education and the development of the principles of federalism.
The education he recommended closely followed the precepts of *Émile:*
it was not to proceed from books, not to aim at intellect, but to be a
training for a useful life, rooted in virtue and inspired by patriotism.
"Your citizens must learn to guide their tastes and opinions so that by
inclination, by passion and by necessity they will be patriots." True patriotism and public spirit seemed to Rousseau to go only with a small state,
where everyone could actively share in the duties of government. He
pointed out to the Polish people that almost all the small states prospered
because they were small, while "all the large nations, crushed by their
own immensity, either grow like you into anarchy or sink beneath the
petty oppressors whom their kings are compelled to give them." Poland,
therefore, could hope to avoid the worst evils, though not to obtain the
perfect society, by resolving herself into a confederation consisting of
Lithuania, Great and Little Poland. Each of the three would have its own
government, but would be united by a "legislative bond" and "subordinated to the Republic as a whole." "In one word, set yourselves to
extend and perfect the system of federal government: the only one which
unites the advantages of the large and the small State, and, for that very
reason, the only one which is suited to your needs. If you disregard this
advice I doubt whether your enterprise will ever come to good."

5. ROUSSEAU: THERAPIST FOR A SICK
SOCIETY

*Rousseau has been described as a philosophe and an antiphilosophe;
an extreme rationalist and the first of the Romanticists; the advocate of an
anarchic individualism and the apostle of the modern, collectivistic, to-
talitarian state; a precursor of socialism and a spokesman of typically
bourgeois values. Professor Cobban is among those scholars who believe
that such contradictions are more apparent than real. The following
selection shows him in pursuit of the underlying unity Rousseau claimed
for his own work. At the same time it throws light on what Rousseau really
meant by "a return to Nature," and in a way which speaks well for the
sophistication of Rousseau's political thought.*

ALFRED COBBAN: JEAN-JACQUES ROUSSEAU AND THE MODERN POLITICAL MIND*

1. "Back to Nature" as a Basis for Political Theory

If ever a writer had a single inspiring idea it was Rousseau. His primary interest was ethical. As has often been observed, he was brought by ethics to politics. The apparent impossibility of achieving his ideal for human life and conduct in the existing condition of society convinced him of the necessity for thinking out afresh their political foundations. In order therefore to appreciate the inspiration of his political writings and understand their underlying unity, we must discover what more general principle is hidden behind his political thought. The first principle to which we might be disposed to refer is the rule of law. But this is rather a political than an ethical principle, and Rousseau does not uphold it for its own sake, but because only by accepting the sovereignty of the law can man in the civil state free himself from the oppression of tyrants and the encroachments of his fellow citizens. One might suggest next that his ideal is freedom. Yet in the *Contrat social* we find the primitive idea of freedom greatly restricted, and in fact natural liberty, as he recognizes, cannot exist once men have agreed to live together in a state. If we reflect on the careful moral training of *Émile*, the patriarchal regime of the *Nouvelle Héloïse,* the civic discipline of the *Contrat social,* the patriotic sacrifices demanded in the *Corsica* and the *Poland,* we can hardly accept the idea of liberty as by itself a sufficient explanation of his political system. Indeed we may say that the note which is sounded throughout Rousseau is the very opposite of unrestrained freedom. His revulsion against tyranny does not lead him to the glorification of anarchy, but rather to the idea of a self-imposed, voluntarily accepted discipline, which brings us back to the political ideal of the rule of law.

For a principle which applies to the fundamental bases of individual psychology we have to turn to another element in his writings, the idea of nature, a contrary but not hostile strand, which with the idea of law may be said to form the warp and the woof of the fabric of his thought. Burke's criticism of the metaphysical politicians, that "they are so taken up with the rights of man that they have totally forgotten his nature," is precisely that which is least applicable to Rousseau, who in fact is not particu-

* From Alfred Cobban, *Rousseau and the Modern State* (Hamden, Conn.: Archon Books, 1961), pp. 214–21, 224–28. By permission from George Allen & Unwin Ltd., London.

larly concerned with the rights of man, but is obsessed with the idea of following nature, included in which of course is human nature. The ideal
roughly summarized as the return to nature, provided, as is universally
recognized, his original inspiration, and is certainly his most persistently
reiterated principle. There was no novelty here: the idea of nature is the
keynote of all 18th-century thought. Only, of course, the term changed
its meaning in the latter part of the century and for its transformation
from a dead mechanical conception into a vital principle Rousseau more
than any other was responsible. He it was who rescued the idea of nature
from the jargon of the schools and made it the ethical, political, and artistic inspiration of a whole generation.

The idea of nature is inevitably less prominent in Rousseau's political
than in his other writings, and for this reason some students of Rousseau
have been disposed to put the one group in opposition to the other and
even to assume the existence of an irreconcilable contradiction. But
though in the civil state man has necessarily turned his back on the absolute freedom of the state of nature, the change in his condition is not
otherwise equivalent to a change in human nature; and one might present
Rousseau's main problem as that of finding institutions which would
reconcile the psychological needs of the individual born for the state of
nature, with the "unnatural" demands of social life. In achieving this
adjustment, his method was, as far as possible, to adapt society to the
nature of man, instead of forcing the individual into the mold determined
by artificial institutions—institutions, that is, arbitrarily imposed and derived not from the nature of things but partly from abstract theories and
partly from selfish, sectional interests.

We can see at once why as a result of his interpretation of the idea of
nature Rousseau's ideas seemed to go deeper than those of the philosophes.
They directed their campaign for the reform of social institutions very
successfully against the aberrations resulting from the self-interest of the
privileged classes, clergy and *noblesse,* but in laying down constructive
bases of a new social policy they were less successful, partly because of
the limitations of their interpretation of human nature. On the whole their
psychological theory was still that of Locke, which in some respects, indeed, had been made narrower. Man interested them only as a rational
and utilitarian animal. . . .

But for Rousseau, with the birth of *amour propre*—that sentiment
which only allows us to be happy insofar as we are in one way or another
better off than our neighbors—the degeneration of natural man, his breaking away from the rule of nature, has commenced; because from this
comes inequality—not the natural inequality of the stronger over the

weaker, but the artificial and functionless inequality resulting from self-pride. On this account social institutions are set up, creating artificial advantages of wealth and birth, which are perpetuated and intensified from generation to generation. Society once established on a false principle, the evil manifests itself in every phase of its activity. Pride and emulation become its motive forces. Instead of a life lived in peace and harmony we find a constant struggle of individuals, each attempting to get the better of his neighbors. The object of life becomes the acquisition and display of wealth and power, and the attempt always to outstrip one's fellows in ostentation is the ruin of all good taste. Simple comfort becomes a sign of social inferiority. Honest morals and natural courtesy are sacrificed to an artificial and meaningless code of politeness. The life of the country is despised and the situation of a worthless lackey or a penniless courtier preferred to that of the peasant or the country gentleman. And as society becomes more and more complicated and artificial, all natural pleasure is lost, and the ultimate result of the dominance of *amour propre* is the absolute reverse of that maximization of happiness which is the end of utilitarianism.

We must admit then that Rousseau is a utilitarian with a difference. His application of the principle of utility varies from that of the philosophes because he has a different idea of what constitutes human happiness, in other words, to return to the point from which we started, a different conception of human nature. His argument against utilitarianism as a complete explanation of political life is, to put it briefly, that men, corrupted by self-pride and evil institutions, do not obey its principles. "Presque tous les hommes," he writes to the elder Mirabeau, "connaissent leurs vrais intérêts, et ne les suivent pas mieux pour cela."

The return to nature thus involved a rejection of both the psychological ideas of the philosophes and the prevailing code of social behavior. One motive to which has been attributed Rousseau's criticism of society and its institutions is the feeling that all social ties confine and pervert the natural man, but this is the view only of his more pessimistic or paradoxical moments. Certainly he finds a hidden opposition between the constitution of man and that of the societies in which he lives. His deeply rooted personal conviction that human psychology is not well adapted to find contentment in the complicated civilization of the great state and under conditions of life that can truly be called unnatural has not become less patently true since he wrote. But no one who believed that society was in the nature of things destined to be corrupt could have written the *Contrat social*, or the latter part of the *Nouvelle Héloïse*. To have denied at least the bare possibility of some approximation to the ideal society of which he dreamed would have driven him to despair. What he says of the evil effects of society on the natural man, for instance in the Émile, we must take most often as a criticism of the society of his own day. "Back to nature" does not necessarily mean the abolition of all social life, nor does it mean a return to the life of the savage prowling shelterless about the woods and living on acorns—Rousseau was too fond of bourgeois comfort for that. "Comment savez-vous," he wrote indignantly, "que j'irais vivre dans les bois si ma santé me le permettait, plutôt que parmi mes concitoyens, pour lesquels vous connaissez ma tendresse? ... Le sage même, s'il en est, n'ira pas aujourd'hui chercher le bonheur au fond d'un désert [How do you know that I would go live in the forests if my health permitted, rather than among my fellow citizens, my fondness for whom is well known to you? ... Even the wise man, if there were one, would no longer seek happiness in the depths of a wilderness]." If the misanthropical strain grew stronger in him in his last years, that is to be attributed to his mental troubles and the persecution which drove a sensitive and unstable mind across the borders of sanity, rather to any philosophical condemnation of the principle of social life. On the other hand it does not seem to us correct to go to the other extreme and link Rousseau's return to nature with the idea of perfectibility instead of primitivism: the idea of progress is one which we certainly cannot attribute to him.

There is, in the last resort, only one way of interpreting the idea of nature, this basic principle of Rousseau's thought. The actual objective existence of the state of nature concerns him not at all; he finds its reality in the mind of man, for its essential principles are "gravés en nous en caractères ineffaçables [engraved within us in indelible letters]." When he invokes the return to nature he implies on the one hand that there is a certain permanent set of instincts or tendencies which can be called human nature, and which are capable of harmonious development, and on the other hand that human nature is constructed for a certain kind of environment, comprising in the main a simple agricultural existence. There is further implied the judgment that the development of human nature in its appropriate environment and unperverted by evil institutions is by the nature of things good. Thus the conception of natural man provides Rousseau with an ideal, a standard by which to measure social and political institutions. ...

But Rousseau ... is under no delusions as to the political nature of man. He is aware that man is a fond, foolish creature, governed mostly by delusions, that the wisest legislators have recognized the limitations of the material in which they worked and have therefore tried to implant the love of the *patrie* and a knowledge of the duties of citizenship by the emotional appeal in early years, when the cold arguments of the abstract reason have no sway. It is one of his most valuable qualities as a political thinker that while admitting the irrationality of man Rousseau still upholds the ideal of reason in politics. Or, to put it the other way round, that the abstract, rational nature of his fundamental argument in the *Contrat social* does not prevent him from acknowledging the necessary emotional elements in political life. On the whole it is true to say that in the age of utility and reason the emotional ingredients in politics were neglected. For their rehabilitation Rousseau certainly deserves, more even than Hume or Burke, the credit or the blame. The human understanding, he claims, owes much to the passions, without the aid of which nothing that is really great can be attained. It is an error, he says, to attempt to discriminate between those passions which can be permitted and those which must be forbidden. All are good when one has the mastery over them, and bad when they enslave us. . . .

However abstract or intellectualist his method may seem in the *Contrat social* Rousseau never ceases to be aware of the basic necessity of establishing satisfactorily the emotional foundations of political society. As early as the *Économie politique* he had drawn the conclusion that the man without passions would certainly be a very bad citizen: while the essay on the constitution of Poland is one long appeal for the bringing in of the motive force of passion to save the state. Back to nature, insofar as it meant "back to human nature," was by no means an unprofitable starting point for a new school of political thought, nor was the new spirit it introduced unneeded. That Rousseau should himself have been able to produce a complete and final explanation of the psychological foundations of politics was hardly to be expected. It is rather to be wondered at that he was able to comprehend so much of "human nature in politics" as he did.

By indicating the contrast between man's primitive nature and his highly complicated civilized environment Rousseau diagnosed one of the greatest maladies of modern Western civilization. His own solution was not, as is often alleged, to give up the problem as insoluble, and abandon the hope of reconciliation, even though, as we have seen, he detested that side of civilization manifested in the life of the great cities and states and yearned after the restoration of simpler ways of living. Although society be corrupt, says Rousseau in more optimistic mood, yet a man may live even under the government of a despot comparatively free from individual molestation, and the evil he sees round him will make him love the good. "O Émile! où est l'homme de bien qui ne doit rien à son pays? Quel qu'il soit, il lui doit ce qu'il y a de plus précieux pour l'homme, la moralité de ses actions et l'amour de la vertu [Oh Emile! where is there a good man who owes nothing to his country? Whoever he is, he is indebted to it for that which is most precious to man, his moral behavior and his love of virtue]." He hoped, by the educational methods he described in the *Émile*, by the political institutions for which he provided the theoretical basis in the *Contrat social*, by the economic principles scattered through his works, but especially to be found in the Project for Corsica, and by the civic and national ideals emphasized in the *Lettres de la Montagne* and the *Gouvernement de Pologne*, to create a form of society in which the man of the state of nature should find himself altered certainly but not nullified, and in place of his lost independence should gain a greater freedom. It is thus, and with this principle firmly in mind, that Rousseau effects the transition from the state of nature to political society, and throughout his political writings its operation is to be traced, giving them at bottom that unity which they are sometimes accused of lacking.

Chester V. Easum, Emeritus Professor of History, University of Wisconsin, was born in Clayton, Ill., in 1894 and did his undergraduate work at Knox College, which honored him with a degree of Doctor of Laws in 1961. He attended Oxford University as a Rhodes Scholar and was awarded B.A. and M.A. degrees there. He received his Ph.D. from the University of Wisconsin where he was a member of the department of history until retirement in 1964. He was a Cultural Attaché of the American Embassy in Germany, where a number of his lectures were published in German. His books include *The Americanization of Carl Schurz; Prince Henry of Prussia, Brother of Frederick the Great;* and *Half-Century of Conflict.* He is a member of the American Historical Association and of Phi Kappa Phi and Phi Beta Kappa.

CHAPTER TWELVE

University of Wisconsin

Frederick (II) the Great of Prussia:

Enlightened and Benevolent Despot

KING FREDERICK II of Prussia, already known during his lifetime as Frederick the Great, has had numerous biographers, and every general work on 18th-century Prussian, German, European, or world history gives him space. He was the last of the great kings in the period immediately preceding the French Revolution, a historical phenomenon comparable in significance to Washington (his contemporary), Napoleon, or Bismarck. Among his biographers, the one who came closest to hero worship was probably Thomas Carlyle, the one farthest from it, Norwood Young. Marriott and Robertson, in their *Evolution of Prussia* published in 1915, were remarkably objective. Of contemporary historians, Emeritus Professor Gerhard Ritter of the University of Freiburg im Breisgau, German-born Professor Hajo Holborn of Yale, and the late Walter L. Dorn in his monumental *Competition for Empire* are among the most scholarly.

Frederick's ancestry was illustrious. He was a great-grandson of Frederick William the Great Elector, who brought Brandenburg out of the Thirty Years' War ready to consolidate and to expand, grandson of the first of the Hohenzollern to bear the name of king, son of the royal drill sergeant who made of Prussia a state capable of maintaining the formidable army which he (Frederick) used to such effect. On his mother's side he was related to the Hanoverians of northern Germany and Britain. Frederick was an exceptionally promising young king; but in his early youth as crown prince he had been a problem to his father.

In writing of his father and grandfather, Frederick once drew a distinction between being great in small things and small in great things. It was his grandfather, Frederick I, who had secured recognition of the Hohenzollern as kings in Prussia, not merely in Brandenburg, the nucleus of his estates. It was he who, with his gracious queen Sophia Carlotta, had sought to make of their rather crude frontier capital, Berlin, an Athens of the North. To their son Frederick William I such fripperies were a waste of good German money which would be better spent on the army. He was the royal drill sergeant, penurious in all his expenditures except those for the army, aggressively—even boorishly—German in his tastes, meticulous in attention to the most minute details of dress as of the management of government business and of office routine. He associated masculinity with manliness. A prince born to labor and to command should, he thought, be early trained for both and should look like a soldier.

Frail of physique and showing poor muscular coordination as a boy, Frederick was a great disappointment to his father from the beginning. Soon his marked preference for French cuisine and styles, language and literature raised doubts in the King's mind as to whether he would ever be fit to be king. His persistent playing of the flute, his penchant for composing music for it and for small orchestra, and his rather inept attempts at writing French poetry exasperated his Philistine father still further. His younger brother Augustus Wilhelm pleased their father much more. The crisis of the tragedy of the king's misguided effort to make of the crown prince a man after his own image was reached when young Frederick made a futile and badly bungled attempt to run away to England. (There had been talk of his eventually marrying a daughter of a Hanoverian cousin who was later to be King George II of England, while his sister Wilhelmina, later of Bayreuth, married the Prince of Wales.)

The King of Prussia treated the juvenile escapade as military desertion, had the prince imprisoned and tried by a court martial, ordered that he be held up to a window to watch the execution of his principal accomplice Lieutenant Katte, and seemed intent upon somehow getting him out of the way for the succession of the second son Augustus Wilhelm. Frederick managed to cheat his father by fainting rather than watching the execution, but he had to pretend to submit and thereafter chose to dissemble. The effect on his character was imponderable; but clearly all the softness was hammered out of him. Only the toughness of spirit and character, the bitter cynicism and the active intellect remained; but these were enough to make him potentially great; his extraordinary sense of duty as a benevolent despot and his indomitable will drove him on to greatness.

1. THE MYTHICAL FIGURE

As head of the family and as a hated (and often unkind and unwise) disciplinarian, Frederick was disrespectfully called "Old Fritz" by his younger brothers before his Silesian wars began. From 1757 he was commonly so called by his soldiers. From 1763, as a father figure as well as army commander and king, he was a symbol of Prussia to his people, not universally beloved but by many actually revered, although there were those who would be glad when he was gone. To many foreigners, he had become almost a mythical figure.

One of the earliest English-language biographers of Frederick II was the British historian Thomas Carlyle. In his multiple-volume biography he gave full rein to his almost unbounded admiration of the Prussian monarch and to his own impressionistic, rather flowery, and often exclamatory style.

THOMAS CARLYLE[*]

About fourscore years ago, there used to be seen sauntering on the terraces of Sans Souci, for a short time in the afternoon, or you might have met him elsewhere at an earlier hour, riding or driving in a rapid business manner on the open roads or through the scraggy woods and avenues of that intricate amphibious Potsdam region, a highly interesting lean little old man, of alert though slightly stooping figure; whose name among strangers was King *Friedrich the Second,* or Frederick the Great of Prussia, and at home among the common people, who much loved and esteemed him, was *Vater Fritz*—Father Fred—a name of familiarity which had not bred contempt in that instance. He is a king every inch of him, though without the trappings of a king. Presents himself in a Spartan simplicity of vesture: no crown but an old military cocked hat—generally old, or trampled and kneaded into absolute *softness,* if new; no sceptre but one like Agamemnon's, a walking stick cut from the woods, which serves also as a riding stick (with which he hits the horse "between the ears," say authors); and for royal robes, a mere soldier's blue coat with red facings,

---

[*] Thomas Carlyle, *History of Friedrich II of Prussia, called The Great* (Boston, 1885), Vol. I, pp. 3–5.

coat likely to be old, and sure to have a good deal of Spanish snuff on the breast of it; rest of the apparel dim, unobtrusive in color or cut, ending in high over-knee military boots, which may be brushed (and, I hope, kept soft with an underhand suspicion of oil), but are not permitted to be blackened or varnished; Day and Martin with their soot pots forbidden to approach.

The man is not of godlike physiognomy, any more than of imposing stature or costume: close-shut mouth with thin lips, prominent jaws and nose, receding brow, by no means of Olympian height; head, however, is of long form, and has superlative gray eyes in it. Not what is called a beautiful man; nor yet, by all appearance, what is called a happy. On the contrary, the face bears evidence of many sorrows, as they are termed, of much hard labor done in this world; and seems to anticipate nothing but more still coming. Quiet stoicism, capable enough of what joy there were, but not expecting any worth mention; great unconscious and some conscious pride, well tempered with a cheery mockery of humor, are written on that old face, which carries its chin well forward, in spite of the slight stoop about the neck; snuffy nose rather flung into the air, under its old cocked hat, like an old snuffy lion on the watch; and such a pair of eyes as no man or lion or lynx of that century bore elsewhere, according to all the testimony we have. "Those eyes," says Mirabeau, "which, at the bidding of his great soul, fascinated you with seduction or with terror (*portaient, au gré de son âme héroïque, la séduction ou la terreur*)." Most excellent potent brilliant eyes, swift-darting as the stars, steadfast as the sun; gray, we said, of the azure-gray color; large enough, not of glaring size; the habitual expression of them vigilance and penetrating sense, rapidity resting on depth. Which is an excellent combination; and gives us the notion of a lambent outer radiance springing from some great inner sea of light and fire in the man. The voice, if he speak to you, is of similar physiognomy: clear, melodious and sonorous; all tones are in it.

2. THE YOUNG KING AT WORK

The neighboring monarchs had not long to speculate after Frederick's succession on how he would behave as king. He soon seized Silesia from Austria and hung on to it despite all that the Archduchess Maria Theresa (who was also Queen of Hungary) and her allies could do to dislodge him.

*Of the young king in the short period of uneasy peace which followed,
1746–56, Carlyle wrote:*

THOMAS CARLYLE: SANS SOUCI*

Friedrich has now climbed the heights, and sees himself on the upper
tableland of victory and success; his desperate life-and-death struggles
triumphantly ended. What may be ahead, nobody knows; but here is fair
outlook that his enemies and Austria itself have had enough of him. No
wringing of his Silesia from this "bad Man." Not to be overset, this one,
by never such exertions; oversets *us*, on the contrary, plunges us heels-
over-head into the ditch, so often as we like to apply to him; nothing but
heavy beatings, disastrous breaking of crowns, to be had on trying there!
"Five Victories!" as Voltaire keeps counting on his fingers, with upturned
eyes—Mollwitz, Chotusitz, Striegau, Sohr, Kesseldorf (the last done by
Anhalt; but omitting Hennersdorf, and that sudden slitting of the big
Saxon-Austrian Projects into a cloud of feathers, as fine a feat as any)—
"Five Victories!" counts Voltaire; calling on everybody (or everybody but
Friedrich himself, who is easily sated with that kind of thing) to admire.
In the world are many opinions about Friedrich. In Austria, for instance,
what an opinion; sinister, gloomy in the extreme: or in England, which derives from Austria, only with additional dimness, and with gloomy new
provocations of its own before long! Many opinions about Friedrich, all
dim enough: but this, that he is a very demon for fighting, and the stout-
est king walking the earth just now, may well be a universal one. A man
better not be meddled with, if he will be at peace, as he professes to wish
being.

Friedrich accordingly is not meddled with, or not openly meddled with;
and has, for the 10 or 11 years coming, a time of perfect external peace.
He himself is decided "not to fight with a cat," if he can get the peace
kept; and for about eight years hopes confidently that this, by good management, will continue possible; till, in the last three years, electric symptoms did again disclose themselves, and such hope more and more died
away. It is well known there lay in the fates a third Silesian war for him,
worse than both the others; which is now the main segment of his history
still lying ahead for us, were this halcyon period done. Halcyon period
counts from Christmas day, Dresden, 1745—"from this day, Peace to the
end of my life!" had been Friedrich's fond hope. But on the 9th day of

---

* Thomas Carlyle, *History of Friedrich II of Prussia, called The Great* (Boston,
1855), Vol. III, pp. 27–28.

September, 1756, Friedrich was again entering Dresden (Saxony some 12 days before); and the crowning struggle of his life was, beyond all expectation, found to be still lying ahead for him, awfully dubious for seven years thereafter!

3. THE TRAINING OF A PRINCE

As long as he could hope that Frederick would grow to be more like himself, the maniacally possessive father loved him after his own fashion. He always commanded his son first to love him, then obey—but always to obey.

The English marriage project, the attempted flight, the trial, and the prince's survival—however scarred—are here described by Professor Hajo Holborn.

Professor Holborn was born and educated in Germany and had become a teacher of modern European history there before the fall of the Weimar Republic. Finding the atmosphere of the approaching so-called Third Reich as uncongenial as it would soon have become dangerous to one of his political views and character, he emigrated to the United States where he soon won an established place for himself as a professor of modern European history at Yale University and as a naturalized citizen of the United States. He has written voluminously, both in general and in particular.

HAJO HOLBORN[*]

The project caused a turmoil of feelings at the court of Prussia. It had the blessings of the queen, who liked these matches and, in addition, enjoyed plotting. The young prince and princess suddenly saw the dawn of the day which would allow them to leave their surroundings, which had become stifling through the oppression of a tyrannical father. The King himself was brooding over the political implications of such marriages, but from the outset was worried lest the importation of a princess from the sinfully elegant London court would further ruin his Fritz. He agreed to the marriage of his daughter, but the English insisted on a double wedding. Negotiations were suspended, when an event occurred which

---

[*] Hajo Holborn, *A History of Modern Germany, 1648–1840* (New York: Alfred A. Knopf, Inc., 1964), pp. 205–6. © Copyright 1964 by Hajo Holborn. Reprinted by permission of Alfred A. Knopf, Inc.

ended the project. The crown prince decided to go to England. Supplied
with money from there, he prepared his flight while he was accompanying
his father on a visit to Heidelberg. A frightened page told the king, who
lost all self-control.

Frederick, who was 18, had, from early years, shown an independent
mind and great aversion to the outlook and manners of his father's court.
His tutor, a Reformed Frenchman, was a man of broad education and
liberal religious views. Frederick took to books and philosophical arguments with a natural delight, and French philosophy satisfied him more
than the religion of his father. Music and reading seemed to him better
nourishment than military drill and hunting. But he had to cover up his
inclinations and opinions before his father, and the relations between
them grew unnatural and even hostile. The King became alarmed at this
resistance in his own family, especially since he craved the love of his
son. When he discovered the contraction of debts and even an early
interest in the opposite sex, angry scenes took place. The discovery of the
planned escape to England aroused Frederick William's full fury. He
treated Frederick as a deserting officer, had him imprisoned, and did everything to break his will and self-respect. The most abominable penalty
which he inflicted was Frederick's forced attendance at the execution of
his friend and accomplice in the intended flight.

In the midst of all these acts of insanity, Frederick showed great stoic
qualities. He feigned repentance over the past and adapted his opinions
to those of his father, whose ire finally relaxed. Frederick was then compelled to learn the business of provincial administration at the war-and-
domain chamber in Küstrin. After he had made the greatest concession
to his pitiless father and married a nondescript Brunswick princess, he
was given a regiment and small household of his own away from Berlin,
in Rheinsberg. Here he spent the years before his accession to the throne
using his leisure hours for his beloved literary, musical, and artistic interests and also pondering what use he would make of Prussian power
once his hour had come. But he kept these ideas strictly to himself. The
struggle with his father had taught him not to trust others with his inner-
most thoughts. It had destroyed the last remnants of religion, except for
a deistic faith, and given him a cold view of human nature in general.
On the other hand, his experiences had not destroyed his belief in himself. As he began to understand the operations of the monarchy in both
the civilian and military field, Frederick discovered what a mighty instrument it might become in the hands of a ruler of spirit and courage. This
gave him respect for the task, while making him a most critical observer
of the clumsy foreign policy of Frederick William I.

4. FREDERICK AS CROWN PRINCE

Professors J. A. R. Marriott and C. Grant Robertson indicate the effect of Frederick's experience as crown prince on his character as king.

Professors Marriott and Robertson were lecturers in history at Oxford University before and during the World War I. Soon after the end of that war Professor Robinson published a biography of Bismarck, on which he must have been long at work, notable for its perceptiveness and objectivity, and which for many years was generally regarded as the finest in its field. In their Evolution of Prussia *they permit their personal predilections for British parliamentary and other political institutions and procedures occasionally to become apparent but do not permit these predilections to push them to the point of writing consciously biased history. Their detachment seems in fact more noticeable than their prejudices or natural pro-British tendencies.*

J. A. R. MARRIOTT AND C. GRANT ROBERTSON[*]

At Küstrin and then at Rheinsberg (1736–40) Frederick learned the Prussian machine and the necessity of work; but he could also make leisure and he spent it, sometimes in dissipation ("I am for enjoyment, afterwards I despise it"), but always in reading, scribbling French poetry, in history, French literature, theatricals, music, corresponding with Voltaire and other luminaries, and in much thinking. His *Anti-Machiavel,* a refutation of Machiavelli's *Prince,* was an academic and youthful exercise, on which his life and career as king are the most telling commentary. What he might have been under another father and in a cleaner and richer air we can only guess. That he retained his spirits, his confidence in himself, his intellectual buoyancy and social charm is an astonishing proof of the quality of fibre in his mind and body. In 1740 what he retained and had acquired were due to himself—for what he had lost and the perverted conviction that perhaps it was no loss, Frederick William I was responsible. His heart had withered up. Intellectual intimates, men whose knowledge or force of brain appealed to his head, ideas and the exchange of ideas, music, books, the service of soldiers, administrators, engineers—these he

* From J. A. R. Marriott and C. Grant Robertson, *Evolution of Prussia* (Oxford: Clarendon Press, 1917), pp. 116–17, 125–26. Reprinted by permission of the Clarendon Press, Oxford.

valued and was to know in abundance, but of charity, generosity, faith in the humanity that joy and sorrow can enrich he felt no need. He never had a friend, either man or woman. Friendship as a bond of human souls was unnecessary—a temptation to weakness. Duty, which became his watchword, was work without love or pity, the categorical imperative of a universal reason, not the daughter of God. Religion, Protestant or Catholic, was like court ceremonies, a waste of time, the invention of priests, a dupery for women, an instrument to be manipulated by the ruler for purposes of state. In the famous formula of his toleration—every one in this kingdom shall go to heaven in his own way—there rings beneath the principle of political expediency the veiled contempt of the crowned sceptic. If there was a heaven, let the fools or drones of humanity find it without hindrance; for the wise and strong—for the ruler above all—there was more rational work. . . .

The amount of work and the range of his activities were prodigious, and only accomplished by the sternest ideal of his duties as king, by an austere self-mastery which inevitably hardened all that was hard in soul and body, and by a mechanical apportionment of a long day that left no room for rest. He desired to be and he made himself the brain of his kingdom. It was his function to think, it was for his servants and subjects to act and carry out his thought. Frederick combined, as perhaps Napoleon alone of modern rulers combined, the duties of a supreme commander in chief, foreign minister, treasurer, and head of the civil administration. His was the executive will, but his was also the reflective brain concerned with principles as much as with execution and detail. But his thinking was not confined to the more obvious branches of an organized and coordinated state life. In expert knowledge of every department or province he was the director of the specialized staff; he knew his dominions from end to end; his cold and critical blue eyes penetrated every secret and every corner; peasant and burgher, the woman in the fields, merchant or artisan, landrat or councillor of a provincial chamber, pastor or monk, the soldier in the ranks, junker or general, had seen the figure in the worn blue uniform stained with snuff, knew the musical voice, trembled at that icy displeasure or contemptuous reprimand, much more rarely heard the brief assent which signified a dry approval. The privileged of the circle of Sans Souci saw another Frederick, witty, gay, profane, brilliant, a critic of life polished to a glittering adamant. But for all and for everything, whether it was a village pound, a new canal, a new way of planting beetroot, an opera house for Berlin, a prima ballerina, the new oblique order in minor or major tactics, Maria Theresia's feminine bigotry, Kaunitz's latest foppery, an amour of the Tzarina Elizabeth, or Voltaire's latest work, Frederick was the Grand Intelligence. How the

King worked and made others work, all his subjects knew—but he was always the king, and for Prussia and finally for Europe enlightened absolutism came to be identified with the personality of this royal master.

5. THE FAILURE TO TRAIN A SUCCESSOR

About the training of his own successors Frederick seemed to have learned very little. He wrote and said repeatedly that no one should presume to think of ruling a state without first forming within himself the highest resolves that he would spare himself none of the preparation, none of the pain and drudgery, none of the unceasing toil that the business of governing required of him. With his own three younger brothers, however, for whom he became head of the family in loco parentis when their father died, he was little wiser or more understanding than his father had been with him. Finding the heir apparent, his nephew Frederick William (II), lacking, he gave up hope of making anything of him.

J. A. R. MARRIOTT AND C. GRANT ROBERTSON[*]

It is the most regrettable and the most astonishing of his limitations that he took no steps to provide a successor to his brain as well as to his crown and authority: still more regrettable that from 1763 onward the principles, reorganization, and working of the autocracy prevented any such brain coming into existence. He left his Prussia, to which he had devoted 46 years of such toil and sacrifice as few monarchs in any age can show, at the mercy of an heir whose character had not been disciplined nor his mind educated, who had not even an adequate technical knowledge of the absolutist regime in the army and the state which he inherited —a ruler dependent on officials who had been taught the supreme duty of never thinking for themselves. Instead of a brain he left a series of political testaments with no guarantee that any one would obey them. Even the illiterate Frederick William I had done better than this, for he had insisted that his heir should know his work from top to bottom. Yet Frederick was under no illusions about the perfection of the Prussian machine or its capacity to run by itself. His criticism of the shortcomings of his officers, both in the army and the civil service, increased in volume

* From J. A. R. Marriott and C. Grant Robertson, *Evolution of Prussia* (Oxford: Clarendon Press, 1917), pp. 145–47. Reprinted by permission of the Clarendon Press, Oxford.

and bitterness as he aged. His orders and his memoranda were a perpetual indictment of their shortcomings in mind and in the performance of their duties. But like so many rulers to whom power is everything, and whose will to rule increases as the physical forces ebb, Frederick feared a rival authority in the state far more than he feared death.

6. THE RELUCTANT REBEL PRINCE

As in the eyes of the overawed Carlyle Frederick could do no wrong, in those of the iconoclastic Norwood Young, a younger contemporary of Marriott and Robertson, he could do nothing right unless by blundering into a situation that left him no alternative. The seizure of Silesia was a brazen act of aggression and conquest to be justified, if at all, only by success. That was a very near thing. In the course of the war he deserted his allies and rejoined them without admitting that acts of bad faith required, especially in a monarch, any other justification than reason of state. Some of his battles, as at Mollwitz, were won for him by generals chosen and soldiers trained by his father. The most disastrous defeats in the Seven Years' War, as at Kunersdorf, as well as victories such as those at Rossbach and Leuthen, were experienced under his personal command but won largely by subordinates such as the dashing cavalry leader Seydlitz and the King's cautious and methodical younger brother Henry. Like Hitler, he handcuffed his generals at a distance and committed them to destruction by leaving them no freedom to act at their own discretion. To Young he was a coward concerned only for his own personal safety or reputation, never a hero, never the enlightened despot that most historians have called him, but prone, as in the Miller Arnold case, to interfere impulsively and injudiciously with the orderly administration of justice by his responsible officials, and frequently to boast of it as if proud of it. (See Readings 13 and 10 below.)

Here Young gives a circumstantial though rather unsympathetic account of Frederick's attempted flight from Prussia.

NORWOOD YOUNG*

On July 15 the royal party left Potsdam, traveling south as far as Augsburg, and then west. At Feuchtwang they dined with the Dowager Mar-

---

* Norwood Young, *Life of Frederick the Great* (London: Constable, 1919), pp. 28–29, 30–31, 32–33.

gravine of Anspach. Frederick had the misfortune to drop his fork on the floor, and was immediately subjected to violent insults by the King. The former taunts were repeated. "If my father had treated me as I treat you," said Frederick William, "I should have made my escape a thousand times over, but you have no courage and are a coward. . . ."

At Wesel the King sent for his son. He demanded his reason for attempting to desert. "Because you do not treat me as your son, but like a slave." "You are a cowardly deserter, you have no honour." "I have as much as you," answered Frederick; "I have only done what, as you have told me a hundred times, you would have done in my place." The King is said thereupon to have drawn his sword with the intention of killing his son, but General Mosel, who was present, interposed his own person until the King had recovered from the mad impulse.

Frederick was sent to Küstrin, 60 miles east of Berlin. He was kept in solitary confinement, in a prisoner's cell containing the absolute minimum of furniture. His uniform was taken away, and a brown prison dress substituted; his food was limited to a cost of sixpence for dinner and fourpence for supper; it was cut small for him, as he was not allowed a knife. He was not permitted to leave the room on any pretext; three times a day an attendant entered, remaining not more than four minutes on each occasion; two captains were to be present to see that no words passed, no remarks of any kind being permitted; no books were allowed, nor writing materials. The conditions were very severe for a young man not yet aged 19. After some days, in the hope of being allowed a little communication with human life, he asked to take the Communion, but the request was refused, and complete silence settled once more upon him.

Katte had not deserted, but he had contemplated doing so, and he had given the crown prince active assistance in the preliminaries of his scheme. The sentence of the court was imprisonment for life. With regard to the crown prince, the court declared itself incompetent to decide. The members avoided the word desertion, speaking of an intention to "retire," or to "absent himself," and evidently did not consider the prince merited any very severe punishment.

The King's vengeance was turned against Katte, through whom he could touch his son. He overruled the sentence of the court-martial and ordered Katte to be beheaded.

The King received intercessions on behalf of the crown prince from the courts of England, Holland, Sweden, and Russia, and, more important than all, an autograph letter of intercession from the hand of the emperor himself. These representations were inspired by motives of humanity.

The life of the crown prince was of no value to any one of these powers. The emperor, indeed, had reason to regard the young man as anything but a friend, and his minister, Bartenstein, protested against the imperial intercession on behalf of a prince whose leanings were anti-Austrian. The return that Frederick made for the emperor's friendly interference was, as we shall see, a treacherous attack at the first opportunity. But it is an exaggeration to assert, as some have done, that the emperor saved Frederick's life. Frederick William I was forced by public opinion, by consideration of his popularity both at home and abroad, to abandon his cruel impulse. He pretended that he had done so only out of deference for his emperor.

Frederick had achieved his aim. He had protested, by the only means in his power, against being beaten like a slave. His father never struck him again. But he had still to undergo a long ordeal of severe discipline. His punishment had scarcely begun.

7. THE CALL OF DUTY

The first duty of a citizen, Frederick wrote, was to serve his fatherland. For the king, the first servant of the state, this obligation was the most imperative of all obligations. He was one of the hardest working of all kings. "My mind and body must heed the call of duty," he wrote in 1776. "It is not necessary that I live but it is necessary that I do my duty." (Gerhard Ritter, Friedrich der Grosse, 82.) From his performance of that duty to the state as he conceived it he permitted literally nothing ever to deter him.

NORWOOD YOUNG*

In describing himself as "the first servant of the State," Frederick was copying a phrase used by his father and expressing a policy which had already been announced by the Great Elector and by Louis XIV. It is true that he made more display of the sentiment than they had done; that he insisted upon the duties and responsibilities of a king; that he never spared himself; and that many princes, comparing the industrious apprentice in Prussia with the idle apprentice in France, reduced their

---

* Norwood Young, *Life of Frederick the Great* (London: Constable, 1919), pp. 414, 415.

expenditure in personal indulgence, paid their debts, and endeavored to promote the welfare of their people. It is equally true that whenever the interests of his people came in conflict with his own, Frederick considered himself only. In war, for example, he thought more of his reputation than of beating the enemy, declining risks for himself which he forced other commanders to face, with disastrous results. He used his people, regardless of their welfare, for the purpose of obtaining a personal "glory" from which they could derive no advantage. Then, he spoke of himself as the *avocat du pauvre,* and *chef des gueux,* but he put a tax on food for the express reason that it was the only one that could not be evaded, leaving it to his successor, Frederick William II, to relieve the distresses of the poor. The tax was for army and treasure, to be used to enhance the reputation of the King. Frederick deplored in moving terms the institution of slavery, but he took the part of the landed aristocracy against their dependents. The caste system, which made a rise to a superior station impossible, was rigidly enforced by the King. He professed a desire for the spread of enlightenment, but "did little for the spiritual life of his people," believing mankind to be wicked and foolish and incapable of improvement. He welcomed Maupertuis and other men of science, for his own delectation. His Academy of Science he treated as an appanage of the court; he would not permit any criticism of its decisions. His religious toleration was a Hohenzollern tradition, originating in a desire for immigrants. It was imperfect; Catholics and Jews had not the rights nor the freedom of Protestants. Though he became the ablest commander of his day, Frederick's military reputation was in excess of his deserts, owing to misrepresentations made by himself or by others on his behalf. The odds against him, both in potential resources and on the day of battle, were much less than he pretended. The famous "oblique attack" was used once only; even the spirit of attack was not sustained throughout his career, giving way in the end to Fabian tactics. Frederick acquired a character for iron determination, but during his wars he lived in a chronic state of "premature despair" (Voltaire's expression) and indulged freely in tears; after defeat at Kunersdorf he resigned the command; on the battlefield he gave several exhibitions of cowardice. When matters were going against him he bewailed the cruelty of war, but he ordered the refusal of quarter, treated prisoners and wounded with inhumanity, bombarded cathedrals and cut down fruit trees; and earned from his contemporaries the name of the "Attila of the North." Throughout his career he pretended that every aggression and every harsh act was forced upon him by necessity; he had to retaliate against his enemies for what they had already done, or was obliged to anticipate what they were about to do. In his writings he expressed principles of conduct, with regard to military plans and civilian policy, which in practice he ignored. Hypocrisy and fraud were outstanding features in the character of Frederick the Great.

8. THE UNHAPPY KING

In a study of the often tempestuous relations between Frederick and his gifted brother Henry, Professor Chester V. Easum of the University of Wisconsin found himself more sympathetic toward the king than Prince Henry usually was—and sometimes than he himself was toward the tempersome prince.

Professor Easum, now emeritus, is a specialist in the field of German history.

CHESTER V. EASUM[*]

One of many rather tragic aspects of the personal life of the great Frederick was that he had himself never known happiness. He had, to be sure, learned as a boy to form with his favorite sister Wilhelmina the same secretive and spiteful sort of partnership against his own father that his younger brothers later formed against him. He had learned intrigue and duplicity early enough, at the knees of a mother constantly guilty of the cardinal sin of setting the minds of her children against their father. He had had most of the softness hammered out of him by the blacksmith methods of his father, Frederick William I, in a determined and surprisingly successful though ill-directed effort to make a man of him, fit to be king in Prussia. He had perhaps come closer to knowing happiness during his halcyon period as crown prince at Rheinsberg—*Frederico tranquillitatem colenti*—than at any other period in his life, however little his well-meaning, long-suffering, and in many ways admirable wife may have helped him in his search for it. But he had not learned either how to find happiness for himself or how to command it for others. Always lonely, often hungry for human affection, yearning for the warmth of close and confidential friendship even when surrounded by the most brilliant galaxy of wits, he was doomed to go his way alone.

---

[*] Chester V. Easum, *Prince Henry of Prussia, Brother of Frederick the Great* (Madison: University of Wisconsin Press, 1942).

To say that he was a wicked man for whose many sins loneliness was only too light a punishment, or that one who lives for himself alone must expect to live by himself, alone, is to make a very easy and superficial generalization about the king, but to show no real understanding of the unrelieved loneliness of the man. To say that the spiritual desert in which he dwelt in such glittering but deadly isolation was of his own making is equally easy; but such a statement is either something more or something less than the truth, for it implies that he chose to make and to inhabit such a desert; and he did not so choose. . . .

Conversation with his friends gave him pleasure; the valor of his comrades-in-arms won his gratitude; faithful service of any sort earned his respect and occasionally a curt expression of approval, perhaps even a reward. But he outlived his most valued friends, soldiers, and servitors, or found them somehow wanting and sent them away. He lost interest in his visitors from other lands and saw them no more. Elizabeth Christina was his queen but not his wife; she shared neither his thoughts nor his retreat at Sans Souci. The more he saw of men, he said, the more respect he had for his dogs, which set no price on their love or their loyalty. So dogs enjoyed great license at Sans Souci, where no man dared venture uninvited or overstay his welcome. Thus the legend grew that the lonely king despised people as he said he did, that he loved no one and was loved by none.

9. REASON OF STATE

During a halcyon period at Rheinsberg, which his father had given him as a place of residence after his marriage, Crown Prince Frederick had an opportunity to live more nearly as he pleased than ever before or after. He had escaped from the constant scrutiny and tutelage of his father, and was not yet subject to the equally incessant and tyrannical demands which his position as king of Prussia and his concept of his duty to his state and people (or was it the mere love of the exercise of his intelligence and his extraordinary talents?) would immediately put upon him when his father died.

There, in a rather dreary area a few miles northeastward from Berlin, he developed a modest residence, decorated in the rococo style and taste of the day, with a study in a rounded tower overlooking a small lake.

There he maintained a small orchestra to play his favorite music and some of his own composition, which would be played again and win acclaim on its merits in the middle of the 20th century. He loved to play the flute with his own orchestra. He also read extensively, entertained, conducted a voluminous correspondence, wrote his Anti-Machiavel *and let people speculate as to what all this indicated as to the kind of king he would be when he should come to it. It seems fair to assume that, being of an inquisitive and speculative nature, he thought in those quiet days some long, long thoughts. He was already however more of a rationalist and a realist than a dreamer, more a man of action than a theoretician; and even his intellectual and artistic interests seem to have been more immediately concerned with history and the French life, literature, and culture of his own day than with long-range plans for the future, except for a ripening resolution that Prussia should no longer play second fiddle to Austria in Central European affairs.*

After his conquest and reconquest of Silesia, Frederick gave Rheinsberg to his brother Henry, who used it much as he had done. He had by then built for himself and (he hoped) his brooding spirit a more stately mansion, a lovely little gem of a country residence in an area elaborately parked, landscaped, and terraced—Sans Souci. There, he often told himself, and only there, would he eventually be "without care." There throughout the remainder of his life he sought solitude and found too much of it, musing in a more beautiful and commodious library-study looking out, this one, over glassed-in terraces where his gardeners grew some grapes for him and tried hard to cultivate many more exotic fruits. He could also see from his study window the well-tended little cemetery where his favorite horses and dogs were buried and where he often directed that he be buried with them in his turn.

CHESTER V. EASUM

In all his early wars for the conquest and retention of Silesia, Frederick earned an unenviable reputation for unreliability and bad faith in the making and breaking of treaties, and for cynicism and casuistry in self-justification. In his *Political Testament* of 1752 he wrote for the guidance of his successors—although his immediate successor Frederick William II came to the throne only in 1786:

Pursue a prudent financial policy, so that you will have money when you need it; make alliances only with those whose interests coincide with yours; never conclude treaties concerning far-off [future] events. Always wait for events, then make your decision and act accordingly. Beware of building on the number and loyalty of your allies. Reckon really only on yourself, then you will never be disappointed. Look upon your allies and your treaties only as emergency aids. A multiplicity of treaties brings more harm than help. Make only few, but always at the right moment, and make sure of all advantages for yourself while risking as little as possible. . . .

In the foreword written in 1775 for his *History of My Time* (*Oeuvres Posthumes*, I, 11) Frederick elaborated on this casuistry:

Posterity may perhaps be surprised to find in these *Memoirs* accounts of treaties made and broken. Although these examples are common, that would not justify the author of this work had he not other better reasons to excuse his conduct.

The interest of the state must serve as the law of Sovereigns. The cases for the breaking of alliances are these:

1. Where the ally has failed to fulfill his engagements.
2. Where the ally is thinking of deceiving you and where you have no resource left but to forestall him.
3. Superior force bears down upon you and makes it necessary for you to break your treaties.
4. Finally insufficiency of means to continue the war.

By I know not what fatality these unhappy financial circumstances have their influence upon everything. Princes are the slaves of their means. The interest of the state is their law, this law is inviolable. If the prince is obligated to sacrifice even his own person for the good of his subjects, by so much the more reason must he sacrifice for them liaisons the continuation of which has become prejudicial. Examples of such broken treaties are common. It is not our intention to justify them all, I dare however to posit that there are some such, that necessity, sagacity, prudence, or the good of the peoples oblige [one] to break them, there being no other way open to their Sovereigns to evade their ruin. . . .

The [broken] word of an individual injures only one person, that of Sovereigns entails calamities for whole nations. This reduces itself to the question: Is it better that the people perish, or that the Prince break his treaty? What sort of imbecile would debate how to decide this question?

The reader will have noted in the above writings of Frederick II, dating from the early years of his long reign, certain parallels of his thinking with Bismarck's. Both referred to reason of state (*raison d'état, Staatsraison*) as the supreme law of states and of statesmen in national affairs, discounting private morality and personal predilections of all sorts. In comments not altogether unlike those of President Washington warning his countrymen not only against permanent alliances but against continuing headlong emotional attachments or aversions to other peoples, Frederick criticized Charles XII of Sweden for continuing to hate his old enemies after he had changed alliances.

Frederick also wrote of the necessity of sacrificing the individual, even the prince himself, to "the law of Princes." For this and many other reasons there was a spate of publication during the Nazi period designed to capitalize on and use for propaganda purposes the legendary Frederick, even in support of the slogan *Gemeinnutz vor Eigennutz* (Community before individual interest). Frederick it was who had hung on and held out in the Seven Years' War when a man of weaker will would have counted the odds and gone under. He it was who had tried to hearten his brother Augustus Wilhelm in 1757 by telling him to ask not how strong the enemy was, but only where! Valor! Perseverance! Obstinacy! Tenacity! (Gustav B. Bolz and Max Kutschmann. *The Heroism of Perseverance* [*Das Heldentum der Beharrlichkeit*], Reichsführer Hauptamt, Berlin, 1944).

To anticipate an attack by making one does not make one an aggressor, Frederick had argued in 1757. "His Majesty is abandoning his accustomed moderation (*gewohnte Mässigung*) only because it ceases to be a virtue when he has to defend his Fatherland and his crown" (Reichsführer Hauptamt, *Friedrich der Einzige*, Berlin, 1944, 23). Hitler's "patience" was also exhausted, he said many times during his first 10 years as chancellor. It was Frederick in 1756, however, not Hitler in 1938, who wrote and was quoted by the Reichsführer's Principal Office in 1944:

His Majesty declares that the freedom of the German Reich shall be buried only with that of Prussia. He calls Heaven to witness that he has exhausted all appropriate means to save his states and all Germany from the scourge of the threatening war, now is forced however to take up arms to break up a conspiracy against his possessions and his crown. In vain has he trod every path to a friendly solution (*Beilegung*) [of the question], indeed has laid the decision between war and peace in the hands of the Empress [Maria Theresa].

The alliance of Austria, France, and Russia against which Frederick was soon compelled to defend himself was actually completed and confirmed after rather than before his invasion of Saxony. His three younger brothers and brother-in-law Ferdinand of Brunswick quickly convinced one another that he had started the war gratuitously and exposed his country to it and to certain defeat and destruction quite needlessly and only for his own vainglory. Ferdinand of Brunswick and Frederick's second younger brother Henry nonetheless served him efficiently and well, although none of them ever loved or trusted him. The Prince of Prussia, Augustus Wilhelm, died in disgrace after failing dismally as a commander in extremely trying circumstances after Frederick's disastrous defeat at Kolin in 1757. Personal relations between the royal brothers were permanently embittered.

The 1933 Nazi publication *Friedrich der Einzige* above cited includes a version of the *Foreword* of Frederick's 1742 *History of My Time* not

printed in the standard 1775 French version of that work printed in the
Posthumous Works in 1788. It states as a "fundamental law of government" of the smallest as well as the largest states the impelling urge to
expand (*Drang zur Vergrösserung*) which by the time of its Nazi repub-
lication Hitler was using as justification of his demand for *Lebensraum*
(living space). Mussolini had for 10 years by then called it evidence of
youth and vigor in a people and a state; and Professor Ludwig Dehio of
Berlin and Marburg, never a Nazi but a philosophical nationalist, would
write 10 years after the conclusion of Hitler's war (*Deutschland und die
Weltpolitik im 20. Jahrhundert* [Munich, 1955] translated as *Germany
and World Politics in the Twentieth Century* [London, 1959]) that it was
a part of the law of nature that younger and more vigorous peoples and
states should seek to expand at the expense of the old and the effete.

This passion [to expand] [the Nazi publication of 1933 quoted Frederick
as having written in 1742] is in every temporal power just as deeply rooted as
the thought of world mastery in the Vatican.

The princes do not rein in this passion however until they see their means
exhausted; these are the firm-standing laws of European politics to which
every statesman must bow. Were a prince less mindful of his own advantage
than his neighbors, they would grow ever stronger, and he more virtuous to be
sure—but weaker.

One remembers the statement attributed to Bismarck that in a pond
full of pike Prussia could not afford to go on being a carp.

What then determines success in this world competition of ambition in
which so many seek to destroy one another with the same weapons and to get
around one another with the same tricks? One thing and one only, the far-
seeing keenness of vision and the art of bringing one's plans to fruition by more
than one way. . . .

The history of every state, every kingdom, every republic shows agreements
and alliances as quickly broken as made, peace treaties at once again violated
and concluded anew. The only difference is that the policy of the little states
is more apprehensive than that of the great powers.

The description fits Hitler's treaty-breaking record of the 1930's about
as well as Frederick's of the 1740's.

10. ADMINISTRATION OF JUSTICE

CHESTER V. EASUM

What the British prohibited as "cruel and unusual punishments" were forbidden by Frederick II from the beginning of his reign; and to the end of it he was proud of the rarity of capital punishments even for major crimes of violence in Prussia; only 14 to 15 per year, he said in 1784. People were neither all devils nor all angels, he wrote in 1750 in an essay on lawgiving to be read in the Berlin *Akademie* (Koser, *Geschichte Friedrichs des Grossen*, II, 60–63). A soldier had been fined 200 thaler for concealing some tobacco. The King would not confirm such a judgment against a man who was paid "only eight groschen every five days." Where could he find the money for such a fine?

The King in a way shares the guilt of any crime left unpunished, wrote Frederick in his *Political Testament* of 1752. "One must have no mercy on the [official] forgetful of his duty; the voice of the widows and orphans cries out for vengeance, and it is the business of the prince to hold the officials up to their duty and to proceed sternly against those who abuse his authority and the public confidence under the guise of right and justice."

The King clearly stated in the same *Testament* that he was resolved never to interfere with the orderly course of justice in the courts; for there the law must speak and the ruler remain silent, being himself as much subject to the law as anyone, although it was his further duty to see that it was enforced without discrimination. The general code for the administration of justice drawn up by *Grand Chancellor* v. *Cocceji* under authority and direction of the King was at least a step in the direction of cheaper and much speedier settlement of cases. Security in possession of property by no matter whom was recognized by the *Testament* of 1752 and by the v. *Cocceji* code as fundamental and inviolable. It figured prominently in the suit of the miller Arnold, which became a *cause célèbre* in 1779.

Arnold operated a mill on land leased from a nobleman, Graf Schmettau. A local official, *Landrat* v. *Gersdorf,* diverted water from the millstream to fill a carp pond. Arnold could not or did not pay his rent, and was threatened with the forced sale of his mill. He brought suit, and lost in the first trial; but the case came to the attention of the king. Frederick dealt with it peremptorily on the ground that to deprive a miller of water he needed for his mill would be tantamount to taking a peasant's cart and plow, depriving him of means of earning his livelihood and putting water rights above human rights and justice. He reversed the judgment and ordered restitution, dismissed the presiding judge and district commissioner, and imprisoned two more judges who tried on appeal to uphold the earlier judgment of the court.

Let the judges know, said the King in a personal scolding delivered on the spot (and therefore quoted in slightly varying versions) that in the eyes of the law the meanest peasant or even a beggar was just as much a man as the king himself, [*ebensowohl ein Mensch ist, wie selbst der König*] and that all must experience the same justice, as before justice all were equal [*alle Leute gleich sind*]. It mattered not whether action was brought by a prince against a peasant or by a peasant against a prince. Justice must be rendered without respect of person. Courts would be inspected by royal judges on tour; and offending officials, who deserved double punishment, would find themselves doing business with the king. (Bolz and Kutschmann, *Friedrich der Einzige*, published 1933, 275–77.)

Norwood Young took a more jaundiced view of the miller Arnold case (366, 367), sharply charging the King with arbitrary and illegal interference with orderly process, and for the severity of his treatment of his own officials, and pointed out that soon after Frederick's death the judgment was reversed by his successor. That successor was one in whom Frederick had had no confidence and of whom he would never have been proud.

11. RELIGIOUS TOLERATION

CHESTER V. EASUM

The stated policy of religious toleration for which Frederick II was justly famous was genuine. So long as persons of all beliefs, including Jews and [he said] even Turks, obeyed the law and did not disturb the peace by trying to impose upon one another, he did not even wish to control church policy or religious observance or belief. This disinclination arose only partly from his own acknowledged agnosticism and indifference. It was for him as for his ancestors and successors a policy dictated ever since the Protestant Revolt by the fact that among his subjects were Protestants both Lutheran and Calvinist, and Catholics in increased numbers after the inclusion of Silesia. Jews could be used; and others would have been welcome if they brought with them useful skills or other assets. He thought therefore that he should not attempt to control all these in all aspects of their lives; he knew that he could not; so he did not try.

As crown prince he had written in his *Anti-Machiavel* in 1739 that religious wars, especially civil wars of this nature, were the results of imprudence on the part of rulers who foolishly favored one sect over another or who restricted the freedom of worship. This could fan smoldering brands into great conflagrations. One should leave the conscience free, be always king and never play the priest. Foreign religious wars especially were the peak of injustice and absurdity. The crusading urge was gone, he hoped, never to return.

After taking Silesia with its predominantly Catholic population, Frederick found it advisable first to assert the royal authority; so he interfered in the selection of a bishop of Breslau. With characteristic cynicism he wrote to Bishop Zinzendorff who was soon to retire: "The Holy Ghost and I have agreed that the Prelate Schaffgotsch shall be elected Coadjutor of Breslau [and presumptive successor to Zinzendorff], and that those of your cathedral chapter who object shall be considered souls sold to the Court of Vienna and the devil, who as obstructors of the Holy Will are deserving of the utmost degrees of damnation."

Zinzendorff replied in kind that this great understanding between the Holy Spirit and the King surprised him. He had not known that they were acquainted; but he hoped that God would enlighten the spirits of the pope and the cathedral chapter. The King got his man appointed. (Koser, *Geschichte Friedrichs des Grossen*, II, 135–38.)

The King was not always so cynical. In the same year 1743, in an essay on religion in Brandenburg, he wrote: "False zeal in religion is a tyranny which depopulates the land; tolerance is a tender mother who uplifts it and makes it flourish." (Preuss, *Friedrich der Grosse*, I, 138.) In an essay on the obligations of rulers, he wrote in 1777 that there should be no compulsion in worship; it was self-defeating, and not merely wrong but useless.

The King's best-known and most widely quoted statement that in Prussia everyone must be free to seek salvation or "go to Heaven" in his own way was also made in 1743, and was meant. A complaint was made on behalf of the children of Protestant soldiers in a garrison town that priests in a Catholic school to which it was found convenient to send them were taking advantage of the opportunity to proselyte. The original draft of this classical document was hastily scrawled on the spur of the moment in the King's own hand and in his inimitably careless German on the margin of the formal report which had been handed him. All religions must be tolerated, and the Fiscal must merely see to it that none imposed upon another, [das(s) keine den andern abrug (Abbruch?) Tuhe], for here must each [seek to] be saved in his own way. [den(n) hier mus(s) ein jeder nach seiner Fasson (façon) Selich (selig) werden]. (Preuss, Friedrich der Grosse, I, 138.)

12. OLD FRITZ

CHESTER V. EASUM*

The King was in fact concentrating so closely [in 1757] upon the first steps to be taken that he had not yet realized what a long way he had still to go, and he was somewhat oversanguine about it. With unutterable relief he had turned his back upon the war, and confidently he faced the future. Blind to any but his own conception of the paramount interest of the state, and refusing to look too long at the obstacles along any path he chose to take in its service, he suddenly announced his decision to re-establish the debased currency of his realm: "Our money will all be put on a better basis in the month of June; I shall pay off all the state debts between now and then; after that, I can die when I please. . . ."

It was, after all, quite in keeping with his character and with his place in the life of his people that the First Servant of the state should be the last to return from the war. Working—not tirelessly, but unremittingly— in his headquarters in Leipzig, with his thoughts running ever forward to meet and wrestle with the problems of reconstruction, never backward over the trials or the triumphs of the immediate past, Frederick the battler was already revealing himself as Frederick the builder. The hard-bitten old Haudegen whose image was and is familiar to all the world was giving way already to the Vater des Volkes, the patriarchal figure of the hard-working patriot-king that was to become even more familiar and dear to the minds of millions of Germans than that of the victor of Rossbach and Leuthen. . . .

---

* Chester V. Easum, Prince Henry of Prussia, Brother of Frederick the Great (Madison: University of Wisconsin Press, 1942), p. 231 ff.

"I do not personally regret that peace should be made on the terms already known to you," he wrote Henry. "If the state had acquired some new province or other, that would no doubt have been a good thing; but, as that did not depend upon me but upon fortune, that idea does not in any way disturb my tranquillity. *If I repair properly the ravages of the war, I shall have been good for something; and to that my ambition limits itself.*" [The italics are the author's.]

The one categorical imperative which Frederick invariably recognized and never denied or sought to evade was his sense of duty. "It is my duty in this situation...," he wrote again, "to work. If ever in my life I can do the state some service it is now, by raising it again from destruction and, if it is still possible, by correcting abuses and effecting reform where necessary. The task is vast and manifold, but if Heaven accords me a few more days of life, I shall complete it; if not, I shall mark out a course which others may follow if they see fit...."

Yielding again to his old temptation to consider already accomplished anything he had once planned and ordered, Frederick promised that changes would at once become apparent. Unused army stores would be released to relieve the food shortage and to depress the extortionate distress prices then being charged for foodstuffs. All conceivable government aid would be immediately available for the rehabilitation of agriculture and the rebuilding of the towns and villages. Within two years not a trace of the war would be visible.

Blandly ignoring the effects of the depreciation of the currency (except as he announced his intention to put it back at once upon a better footing), he was still as proud as ever of his refusal to levy new taxes, and scornful of any monarch who would do so in time of distress. "What a man!" he commented when reporting that one of the first acts of the king of Poland and elector of Saxony, upon regaining possession of the electorate, had been to levy new imposts....

March 30 was the date eventually set for Frederick's homecoming from Silesia, where all the intervals in a series of triumphal entries and receptions had been filled in by the examination of reports, accounts, and estimates of the quantities of seed and building material and of the sums of money needed for the first steps toward reconstruction. He had written to the queen that he would have supper that evening with the family, but he had neither ordered nor forbidden a public reception. Because he had ordered none, he seems to have anticipated none; but for once the burghers of Berlin thought they should act on their own initiative and arrange a triumphal entry for the returning monarch.

All day the populace was out in the streets, buzzing with excitement. All afternoon soldiers and townspeople watched the route by which the king was expected to reenter the city, waiting for an opportunity to cheer him as he passed. As he still had not appeared when darkness approached, torches were handed out so that he might be lighted through the crowd and that the effect of the triumphal arches and other decorations would not be lost; but Lehndorff says that thousands of people returned to their homes "angry and embittered."

Those who stayed out faithfully to the last were doomed to an even greater disappointment. Toward nine o'clock the king finally appeared at the Frankfort gate, but in no mood or condition to play the part of the returning hero. He had traveled that day approximately 75 (English) miles over very bad roads. A halt at the battlefield of Kunersdorf had consumed some time and had not cheered his spirit much. All day long, wherever he stopped at a relay post to change horses, he had been surrounded by crowds of his subjects praying for miracles, and bedeviled by officials asking for favors either for themselves or for their districts. And at the end of the ride he was expected to change from his traveling coach to a great gilded one, specially provided by his faithful Berliners, and parade the torchlighted streets of his war-impoverished capital like the Roman conqueror of a new province!

The next day he did it, to please them; but that night he could not. Phantom hosts of the dead from Kunersdorf and Torgau would have paraded between him and the cheering populace, and the torches would have lighted up once more in his memory the smoldering ruins of Küstrin and Dresden.

So he only let them greet him at the gate; then as the cavalcade made its way into the city with the triumphal chariot in its midst, the king in his service-battered old traveling carriage dropped off the rear end of the parade and made his way as quickly as possible, by obscure cross streets and bypaths, to a side entrance of his palace, where he slipped inside unobserved.

He gained thus a little time to refresh and compose himself before going to meet the members of his family and the distinguished representatives of civil and military officialdom, of the nobility, and of the diplomatic corps who had been waiting all afternoon and evening in the anterooms of the palace to receive him. When he did at last appear he singled out Prince Henry for his first and most effusive greeting—which was presumably not difficult to do, as everyone, the prince included, was expecting him to do that....

It was nearly midnight when he arose from the table and, after standing apart for a little while with his sister and Princess Henry, dismissed the weary family gathering by withdrawing to his own rooms—alone.

Alone, in privacy and in silence, but not in peace! Closer than the ghosts of the men of Kunersdorf and Torgau that had ridden the roads with him for years, closer than the princes, generals, and diplomats in his anteroom, more real to him than the surviving members of his family at that specter-haunted homecoming supper table, there had crowded around him unbidden, all evening, the faces and the spirits of those inseparable from the memory of his war-killed past. Old Schwerin, shot down as he defied the Austrians to stop him at Prague. Marshal Keith, who died as he dared them to drive him from his place at Hochkirch. General Goltz, of whom he had said: "I never had a more faithful friend." Prince William, who failed him, and for whose unhappy end he knew his other brothers still blamed him. Margrave Charles, whose death had made providentially available the lands and revenues with which Prince Henry was rewarded for his victory at Freiberg. Wilhelmina, his best-loved sister, who had written from her deathbed that he must not spare Baireuth to his own hurt or at Prussia's cost. His mother, who after every battle had rejoiced first over the survival of her sons and only then asked whether a victory had been won—and for whom he mourned afresh as Prince Henry had done on his first return after her death. All these and many more were gone; but his memories of them so filled the atmosphere around him that those who had replaced them seemed somehow guilty of trespass. "But for the buildings," he wrote soon thereafter to his sister of Sweden, "I am as much a stranger here as if I were in London." Never in his life had he known such loneliness as then—with all Europe agape at his achievements, all Prussia waiting to acclaim him on his tours of inspection, and all Berlin outside his palace windows to welcome him home from the war.

13. THE MIRACLE OF THE
HOUSE OF BRANDENBURG

Sir Andrew Mitchell, who represented the king of Britain at the Prussian court—usually Frederick's army headquarters—through most of the Seven Years' War, wrote once that he had often seen the King of Prussia great in triumph and prosperity but never greater than in adversity. Adversity reached its worst with his disastrous defeat at Kunersdorf, south-

east of Berlin, August 12, 1759. The Russians were threatening Berlin from the east and northeast and the Austrians from the southeast, while the principal Prussian armies were presumably tied down in Saxony, Lusatia, and Silesia. Frederick remarked that the defenders who failed in the northeast were "afraid."

CHESTER V. EASUM*

It would probably be unfair to say that Frederick himself was afraid, but a spirit of hopelessness was more and more noticeably weighing him down since the failure of his attempt in June to induce George II to invite their enemies to a peace conference. He was still fighting, but desperately, with his head down and his eyes closed. It was in that dangerous mood that, instead of sending his coolheaded brother to dispose of the Russians as he had said he intended to do, he suddenly decided to go himself. Henry might stop the Russians, but that would not answer the purpose. They must be destroyed; and for that sort of work—in spite of Zorndorf—Frederick would rather trust himself than anyone else.

To exchange roles without loss of precious time, the brothers had to exchange armies as well. . . .

Although these changes were made with all possible secrecy and speed, they gave Loudon his opportunity. As the victorious Russians approached the Oder in the direction of Frankfort he slipped away with an Austrian corps to join them. Frederick was not far behind, but could neither intercept nor overtake him. Marching night after night over sandy roads and resting but little in the heat of the August days, both the King and his men were badly worn down by fatigue, always one of the soldier's deadliest enemies, and were therefore already near the breaking point when they brought their human foe to bay at last in a strong position at Kunersdorf, a village a little to the east of Frankfort on the Oder, on August 12.

The Russian position could best be approached from the south or the east. Frederick chose to approach it from the east so that his enemy must fight with his back to the Oder and with his way of escape practically cut off by the swamps along the right bank of the river. He crossed at Oetscher, below Frankfort, leaving General Wunsch there with a detachment to guard the army's baggage and to make sure that the Russians could not escape over the bridges there. With the rest, which by that time included Finck and his corps from Lusatia and Wedell and the remnant

* Chester V. Easum, *Prince Henry of Prussia, Brother of Frederick the Great* (Madison: University of Wisconsin Press, 1942), pp. 101–6.

of the army recently defeated at Kai, he set out again, as at Zorndorf, on an exhausting move around his enemy's position. It was nearly noon the next day before his first regiments had dragged themselves and their guns through the pine woods to the positions from which they were to attack. They had then been on their feet for nine hours and were suffering from hunger and thirst and the burning heat. It was a man-killing march, and only the prelude to a murderous battle. The King complained of the inferior quality of those troops, and they were not the men of Prague or of the Zorndorf campaign of 1758. Yet none but good soldiers would have fought at all after such exertions and privations.

In their initial frontal attack the Prussian grenadiers secured a foothold on the Mühlberg, near Kunersdorf village on the left flank of the Russian position; but there they were stopped. The King had planned to use only a portion of his force in the principal attack, holding back the remainder as a reserve with which to follow up a victory or insure an orderly retreat if defeated; but before the afternoon was over he had used up all the men he could find, first in a desperate bid for victory and at last in a stubborn attempt to fight off defeat. Both he and his generals exposed themselves to danger with a reckless daring that approached foolhardiness; in the later stages of the battle he seemed to be actually trying to get himself killed. By late afternoon his reserve was gone, and with it his hope of victory; by sunset he had no army left. In the night he found shelter across the Oder in the village of Reitwein; the other fugitives straggled back to Oetscher, seeking the protection of Wunsch's fortunate troops, who had not had to fight that day. Wunsch, who had been left there to prevent the escape of the Russians, had to close the bridges to prevent the further flight of his demoralized compatriots. The next day, August 13, they were in better order; they recrossed the river without enemy interference and destroyed the bridges. Fortunately for Prussia, the Russian commander Saltykov was neither a Frederick nor a Napoleon, so did nothing "the next day" or the day thereafter.

If he had been pursued, Frederick might have pulled himself together instinctively to resist attack. Left unmolested, he collapsed. He had pushed himself far beyond the limits of his physical endurance; his nerves, which had clouded his judgment and darkened his outlook for a month, gave way at last under the strain, and for once even his courage deserted him. Those were the darkest days of his life. After all his grandiloquent declarations that he would conquer or die, he found himself still alive and unwounded but overwhelmingly defeated, with his weapon broken off short in his hand. In despair he flung it from him and decided to die. He would wait two days, while Prince Henry was notified of his new responsibilities as regent and commander in chief; then he would destroy himself. In the night of August 12–13 he wrote to his minister, Count Finckenstein:

I attacked the enemy today at eleven. We pushed them back to the Jewish churchyard near Frankfort. All my troops were engaged and did wonders, but the cemetery cost us a prodigious number. Our troops were thrown into confusion; I rallied them three times; at length I thought I was myself about to be taken prisoner, and had to abandon the field of battle. My clothes were riddled by bullets, and I had two horses killed under me; it is my misfortune that I am still alive. Our loss is very considerable; of an army of 48,000 men I have not three thousand. At this moment, while I write, all are in flight and I am no longer master of my men. You in Berlin will do well to think of your safety.

It is a cruel reverse, I shall not survive it. The consequences of the affair will be worse than the affair itself. I have no resources left and, to tell you the truth, I consider that all is lost; I shall not survive the ruin of my country.

Farewell forever. Federic.

Next day he turned over to General Finck the command of the army then reassembling on the west bank of the Oder. To minimize so far as possible the immediate moral effect of the change, he told the general that he was making it only because of a serious attack of illness, and only until he should recuperate. He told the general in so many words that the army was "no longer in a condition to fight the Russians," but suggested that an attack on the Austrians under Hadik might delay, if it could not prevent, an attack on Berlin. Finck must "report on everything" to Prince Henry, whom the King said he had made *Generalissimus* of the army, and take orders only from him. The army must swear allegiance to the King's nephew, Frederick William.

On the third day after Kunersdorf, August 15, the King's secretary Coeper secretly asked Finckenstein, "for the good of the state and of the king," to come to headquarters and try to hearten their ruler, who he said was still "in a state of discouragement infinitely painful to all who had the honor to approach him." Coeper himself did not think the situation quite so desperate as Frederick seemed to consider it, and clearly hated to see his master acting as if the end of the world had come.

Coeper's solicitude was really superfluous, and Finckenstein was not needed. On the fourth day, August 16, the king had recovered and resumed the active command which he had never in fact completely given up. To his great surprise his enemies were giving him time to reorganize his troops, to bring guns and munitions for them from the Berlin arsenals, to get a grip once more on his own habitual steadfastness and resolution; and time was life itself.

So he staggered to his feet. With reviving strength and courage returned also the will to live. The tempting thought of self-destruction gave way once more to his sense of duty; and perhaps unconsciously he announced his spiritual recovery. "At the moment when I told you of our misfortune," he wrote Henry, "everything appeared desperate; that is not [to say] that the danger is not still very great, but count [upon it] that, so long as my eyes are open, I shall sustain the state as it is my duty [to do]."

How profound had been the darkness through which he had just passed was revealed by his concluding words: "Picture to yourself all that my soul has suffered in this cruel crisis, and you will easily judge that the torment of the damned does not approach it. Happy are the dead! They have escaped from their sorrows and are free from trouble. Federic."

But the worst was past. By September 1, still alive and encouraged by the prompt and helpful activity of his brother and the continued comparative inactivity of his enemies, he was able almost to begin to believe in his good fortune. Slightly incredulous even yet, but himself again, he wrote to the prince from Waldow: "I have your note of the 25th, and I proclaim to you the miracle of the house of Brandenburg: during the whole time since the enemy crossed the Oder, when by risking a battle he could have ended the war, he has marched from Müllrose to Liebe-rose."[1]

14. DEATH OF A KING

As the King's physical infirmities increased during the summer months of 1786 he was more and more alone. Mirabeau was shuttling between Berlin-Potsdam and Rheinsberg, the rural residence of the King's brother Henry, and sending back to France a series of letters, largely gossip, clever but unfriendly and unreliable, subsequently published as a "secret history of the Court of Berlin." All were agog with expectancy, mixed with some eager impatience, to see what the new regime would be like; for Frederick would be king until he died.

CHESTER V. EASUM[*]

Although his legs were so frightfully swollen that they seemed about to burst, Frederick had for weeks been unable to lie in his bed because

---

[1] Norwood Young (pp. 291–93) would see in all this only alternating cowardice and stubbornness on Frederick's part, and said he abdicated because he feared his own men and people.

[*] Chester V. Easum, *Prince Henry of Prussia, Brother of Frederick the Great* (Madison: University of Wisconsin Press, 1942), pp. 333, 334.

he could not breathe there. At best he could sleep but fitfully, half reclining in a chair. . . . Early in the morning of August 17 he died in the arms of the orderly who knelt beside his chair. No member of his family was present. None of them had been summoned, and only Henry had sought the permission without which no one was expected to come. Old Fritz started his last journey, as he had started so many, before dawn and alone but for the presence of a body servant in soldier's uniform.

He had been king, and a soldier, to the end. If he had been interviewed just before his departure and could have answered with his usual lucidity, Frederick the king and soldier would have asked no more odds of death than he had asked of life; and Frederick the philosopher would have accepted no sympathy offered on the ground that he was about to die alone. All men are lonely in dying, if not in death, he would probably have said. Only Frederick the man would have confessed to years of unhappiness over his loneliness in life.

John Hall Stewart, Henry E. Bourne Professor of History at Western Reserve University, was born near Springfield, Ontario, Canada, in 1904. A graduate of the University of Toronto, he received his M.A. and Ph.D. degrees from Cornell University. He is the author of *France, 1715–1815: A Guide to Materials in Cleveland* (Cleveland, 1942), *A Documentary Survey of the French Revolution* (New York, 1951), and a chapter in *Carl Becker's Heavenly City Revisited,* ed. by R. O. Rockwood (Ithaca, N.Y., 1958); co-translator (with James Friguglietti) of the second part of Georges Lefebvre's *La Révolution française;* and compiler of portions of *The American Historical Association's Guide to Historical Literature,* ed. by George F. Howe and others (New York, 1961). He has contributed articles and book reviews to various historical journals and has served on Fulbright committees and committees of the American Historical Asociation and the Society for French Historical Studies, of which last-named society he is a past president. Member of the American Historical Association and of Phi Beta Kappa and a Fellow of the Royal Society of Antiquaries of Ireland, in 1962 Professor Stewart was decorated by the French government with the medal of Officier dans l'Ordre des Palmes académiques.

CHAPTER THIRTEEN

JOHN HALL STEWART

Western Reserve University

Danton and Robespierre[*]

A. THE FRENCH REVOLUTION AND ITS INTERPRETERS

IN THE 10 years following 1789, France, the leading arbiter of European culture and international politics, experienced a fundamental institutional change. This metamorphosis, the egalitarian and libertarian principles of which were to have a profound influence upon the civilized world, is known as the French Revolution.

Although the causes of the French Revolution remain a subject of debate, it is safe to say that the movement stemmed from several main sources. These included a widespread revolutionary trend throughout the 18th century, dissatisfaction (on the part of a considerable section of the French populace) with things as they were at home (the Old Regime), stimulation of this dissatisfaction by numerous ideologies (the Enlightenment—see Chapter 11 of this book), a decline and ultimate breakdown of the French political and fiscal structure, a crisis (1787–89), and ineffectual attempts to meet the exigencies of the moment.

The Revolution which took place during the ensuing decade was marked by several general features. Like most revolutions, it developed gradually from moderate reform by legislation to extreme change by fiat, followed by a somewhat conservative reaction, and ultimately ending in a dictatorship (Napoleon Bonaparte). It became involved in foreign

---

[*] NOTE: The writer is indebted to Dr. Samuel Bernstein, author of the last excerpt cited in this problem, for reading the Introduction and for making valuable suggestions, particularly in connection with Section B.

wars, which continued for a quarter century. It was largely the work of a minority. Although the "people" participated from time to time, particularly in the violence (much of which occurred in the cities), the Revolution was engineered by a very small portion of the populace, chiefly the "bourgeoisie." From the outset it was faced with opposition from counterrevolutionaries, with financial difficulties, and with disputes concerning the direction of the Revolution, what form it should take, and who should be its principal beneficiaries.

The changes effected by the Revolution were made mainly by elected "legislative" bodies (working through committees) and by political clubs and similar organizations (acting as pressure groups). Some knowledge of the former is essential to any understanding of the course of the Revolution. Here it is sufficient to examine only four of them. First there was the Estates General, revived in 1789 after a lapse of 175 years, acting as a consultative agency, then transforming itself (extralegally) into a National Constituent Assembly. This assembly, which lasted until September, 1791, provided France with its first written constitution (the Constitution of 1791), and produced the bulk of the enduring legislation of the entire Revolution.

The new constitution established a limited monarchy with a one-chamber legislature, the Legislative Assembly. This third body, entirely new in personnel, lasted until September, 1792. By that time, political complications and foreign war had produced another crisis, which resulted in the fall of the monarchy and thus necessitated a constitutional reorganization. Arrangements were made for the election of a National Convention to effect this reorganization, and this fourth assembly lasted until October, 1795. Like the National Constituent Assembly, the Convention worked at drafting a constitution and acted as a temporary legislature. It transformed France from a monarchy into a republic, it prosecuted the foreign war, and it tried to cope with counterrevolution. During its first year, much of its time was occupied with "party" conflicts, especially between two groups known as Girondins and Jacobins. By June, 1793, the more extreme element, the Jacobins, had gained control of the Convention, and for more than a year this faction applied a form of emergency government (begun during the spring of 1793) known as the Reign of Terror. By July, 1794, the main justification for the Terror no longer existed, and the Jacobins were overthrown. The last phase of the Convention (the Thermidorian Reaction) came into being, and the constitution was finally completed and put into effect. By 1795 most of the early revolutionary momentum was gone. Factional disputes followed until Bonaparte the adventurer took charge in 1799.

Knowledge of the French Revolution has come to us largely from historians. Just as contemporaries differed over the "goodness" or the "badness" of the movement, so these historians (especially the French ones) have differed (and still differ) in their interpretations of it (see Rudé's *Interpretations* in section D, below). Many of them have used it to justify, or to attack, the political, social, economic, and other trends of their own time. A galaxy of writers has portrayed the Revolution in many ways (see the item by McManners in section D, below); and today it is still one of the most discussed and rewritten of historical topics. Nor is the work limited to trends. It involves people as well, especially the people who led the Revolution.

B. LEADERS OF THE REVOLUTION; THE DANTON-ROBESPIERRE CONTROVERSY

Although much recent historical writing stresses trends, movements, and forces, there is no escaping the fact that these phenomena are largely the result of the efforts of *people,* particularly those *exceptional* people who emerge as leaders in periods of great crisis such as the French Revolution. As already indicated, the Revolution passed through several stages, each of which provided opportunities for talented men who otherwise might have remained politically obscure, for example, Sieyes, Bailly, Mirabeau, Barnave, Brissot, Vergniaud, Pétion, and Condorcet during the monarchical phase, Danton, Barère, Marat, Hébert, Saint-Just, and Robespierre under the republic. Apart from their inherent qualities, these leaders owed their positions of prominence to their capacity for gaining popular support for a party or faction which wished to determine the course of the Revolution. Inevitably contests for power developed, contests involving both personalities and policies. The conflict which has provoked the most discussion and inspired a vast literature is the one to which the present problem is devoted—Danton versus Robespierre.

Jacques-Georges Danton (1759–94) came of a "petty bourgeois" family in a small northern provincial town. A lawyer by training, he spent most of his professional career in Paris, where, early in the Revolution, he became involved in municipal politics. Unsuccessful as a candidate for the Legislative Assembly, he became a local prosecutor, and was active as a democratic leader in the summer disturbances of 1792. (Subsequently he was blamed for much of the bloodshed of these months.) Minister of Justice, then a member of the Convention and of its Committee of Public Safety, his onetime friendship with Robespierre turned to enmity. In April, 1794, he became a victim of his adversary.

INTERPRETING EUROPEAN HISTORY

Maximilien Robespierre (1768–94) also came from a northern provincial town. Following a family tradition, he, too, entered the practice of law. In 1789 he was elected to the Estates General, and gained considerable recognition during the Constituent Assembly. Active in the Paris Jacobin Club during the Legislative Assembly, he returned to national political life as a member of the Convention, and he succeeded Danton on the Committee of Public Safety. With the overthrow of the Girondins in 1793 he became the central figure in the ensuing Reign of Terror, only to succumb to the system that he represented. In July, 1794, he followed Danton to the scaffold.

As the excerpts quoted hereinafter indicate, these two men were opposites in both character and behavior, yet each made important contributions to the Revolution. The same might be said of many other revolutionary leaders. Why, then, did a special controversy develop around Danton and Robespierre?

Differences of opinion concerning Danton and Robespierre were manifested by historians during the first three quarters of the 19th century, but, so far as the present chapter is concerned, the serious controversy over them may be said to date from about 1870, with the establishment of the Third Republic in France. To supporters of this new republic, Danton symbolized the great patriot statesman, a democrat after their own hearts, while Robespierre appeared as a petty, radical dictator. Particularly was this true of Alphonse Aulard, who, in a variety of writings, exalted Danton and disparaged Robespierre. Aulard's outstanding protégé, Albert Mathiez, however, came to think otherwise. Concerned with social questions and socialism, to Mathiez Robespierre became the virtuous champion of the people, the hero, with Danton as the venal villian of the piece. Ultimately this and other differences of historical interpretation pushed master and pupil farther apart. Finally, Mathiez and his followers withdrew from Aulard's French Revolution Society (with its journal La Révolution française) and set up their own Society for Robespierrist Studies (with its own journal Annales révolutionnaires). For years Aulard and Mathiez were not even on speaking terms.

Strange though this type of behavior may seem to the less emotional historians of today, it was not uncommon a half century ago, especially in Europe. As might be expected, "schools" of Aulard (pro-Danton) and Mathiez (pro-Robespierre) disciples developed, each concerned with proving that Danton was either a great democratic statesman or a vile scoundrel, or that Robespierre was the personification of patriotism and virtue or a bloodthirsty monster. Dr. Bernstein's article at the end of this chapter traces the course of the controversy and the manner in which it seems now to be somewhat rationalized. Here we are concerned primarily with the way in which this controversy may be used as a problem in conflicting historical interpretations.

C. THE DANTON-ROBESPIERRE CONTROVERSY AS A PROBLEM IN CONFLICTING HISTORICAL INTERPRETATIONS

In view of what has been said, it should be apparent that the Danton-Robespierre controversy constitutes an excellent problem in conflicting historical interpretations—if only because it poses so many questions. Have writers approached the men and the controversy on the basis of foregone conclusions or preconceived hypotheses, or have they simply tried to describe and evaluate verifiable data? Have all of them had access to adequate evidence? To what extent have they been influenced by circumstances over which they apparently had no control—their times, their national origins, their political leanings? Should they have been aware of these influences; and if so, should they not have tried to offset them? Are their conclusions about Danton and Robespierre justified; and if not, are they irreconcilable? Is it possible to obtain any fair and just estimate of these men and their achievements? And, of course, how many more questions of this type may be asked?

At least some of the answers to the foregoing questions (and others that may be contrived) may be found in the illustrative excerpts that follow. These passages have been chosen for several reasons. For many years Carlyle provided the chief point of view for the English-speaking world on both Danton and Robespierre. Aulard and Mathiez precipitated the modern controversy over the two men, Madelin added to it, and Thompson presented something of a corrective based upon recent scholarship. And Bernstein has demonstrated how interpretations may be reassessed in the light of new evidence after the heat of argument has subsided. The items by Aulard, Mathiez, Madelin, and Thompson have been taken, not from their special studies of Danton and Robespierre (as might have appeared logical), but rather from their general histories of the Revolution which seem to provide a much better perspective.

Since this introduction is, of necessity, sketchy, and since many portions of the material quoted may require the type of explanation usually given in footnotes but not given here, students are referred to the following section D on FURTHER READING. And all readers are advised to consult two illuminating articles in the British periodical *History Today*: "Robespierre," by George Rudé (April, 1958); and "Georges-Jacques Danton," by Maurice Hutt (July, 1959).

D. FURTHER READING ON THE FRENCH REVOLUTION, DANTON, AND ROBESPIERRE

In addition to the studies by Carlyle, Aulard, Mathiez, Madelin, Thompson, and Bernstein, from which excerpts are used in this problem, the following works are recommended.

Antecedents of the Revolution

LOUGH, JOHN. *An Introduction to Eighteenth Century France.* London, 1960.
TOCQUEVILLE, ALEXIS DE. *The Old Regime and the French Revolution.* Trans. JOHN BONNER. New York, 1856; also available in several recent translations.
COBBAN, ALFRED. *Historians and the Causes of the French Revolution.* Historical Association pamphlets. London, 1958.
IDZERDA, STANLEY J. *The Background of the French Revolution.* Washington, D.C., 1959. Service Center for Teachers of History, publication No. 21.

The Advent of the Revolution

LEFEBVRE, GEORGES. *The Coming of the French Revolution.* Trans. ROBERT R. PALMER. Princeton, N.J., 1947. Repr. in Vintage Books, 1957.

The Revolution: General

GERSHOY, LEO. *The Era of the French Revolution, 1789–1799: Ten Years That Shook the World.* Princeton, N.J.: Anvil Books, 1957.
SYDENHAM, M. J. *The French Revolution.* New York, 1965.
GODECHOT, JACQUES. *France and the Atlantic Revolution of the Eighteenth Century, 1770–1799.* Trans. HERBERT H. ROWEN. New York, 1965.
BRINTON, CRANE. *A Decade of Revolution, 1789–1799.* New York, 1934. Repr. with rev. bibliography, 1959; also Harper Torch Books.
LEFEBVRE, GEORGES. *The French Revolution.* Trans. two volumes, the first by ELIZABETH MOSS EVANSON, the second by JOHN HALL STEWART AND JAMES FRIGUGLIETTI. New York, 1962, 1964.

The Revolution: Special

THOMPSON, JAMES M. *Leaders of the French Revolution.* New York, 1929. Repr. 1962.
HAMPSON, NORMAN. *A Social History of the French Revolution.* Toronto, 1963.
ROBIQUET, JEAN. *Daily Life in the French Revolution.* Trans. JAMES KIRKUP. New York, 1965.
PALMER, ROBERT R. *The Age of the Democratic Revolution: A Political History of Europe and America, 1760–1800.* 2 vols. Princeton, N.J., 1959, 1964.

Danton

MADELIN, LOUIS. *Danton.* Trans. LADY MARY LOYD. New York, 1921.
WENDELL, HERMANN. *Danton.* Trans. New Haven, Conn., 1935.

Robespierre

EAGAN, JAMES M. *Maximilien Robespierre: Nationalist Dictator.* New York, 1938.

KORNGOLD, RALPH. *Robespierre, First Modern Dictator.* London, 1937.

SIEBURG, FRIEDRICH. *Robespierre the Incorruptible.* Trans. JOHN DILKE. New York, 1938.

THOMPSON, JAMES M. *Robespierre and the French Revolution.* Teach Yourself History Series. London, 1952 and New York, 1953.

——. *Robespierre.* 2 vols. Oxford, 1935.

WARD, REGINALD S. *Maximilien Robespierre; a Study in Deterioration.* London, 1934.

The Historians

COBBAN, ALFRED. "Carlyle's French Revolution," *History*, Vol. 48, No. 164 (October, 1963), pp. 306–16.

GODFREY, JAMES L. "Alphonse Aulard 1849–1928," in SCHMITT, BERNADOTTE E. (ed.), *Some Historians of Modern Europe*, pp. 45–65. Chicago, 1942.

ACOMB, FRANCES. "Albert Mathiez (1874–1932)," in SCHMITT, *op. cit. supra*, pp. 306–24.

GOODWIN, ALBERT. "The Reverend James Matthew Thompson," *Proceedings of the British Academy*, Vol. 43 (1957), pp. 271–91.

McMANNERS, REV. J. "The Historiography of the French Revolution," being chap. 22 of Vol. 8 of *The New Cambridge Modern History*, pp. 618–52. Cambridge, 1965.

RUDÉ, GEORGE. *Interpretations of the French Revolution.* Historical Association pamphlet. London, 1961.

Primary Sources

HIGGINS, EARL L. *The French Revolution as Told by Contemporaries.* Boston, 1938.

STEWART, JOHN HALL. *A Documentary Survey of the French Revolution.* New York, 1951.

THOMPSON, JAMES M. *English Witnesses of the French Revolution.* Oxford, 1938.

1. ON DANTON AND ROBESPIERRE

Tempestuous in style, inaccurate in fact and interpretation, and based on inadequate research, nonetheless, The French Revolution, a History by Carlyle, Scottish litterateur, has been and still is widely read. First published in London in 1837, it has reappeared in many editions, one of the most useful of which was edited by C. R. L. Fletcher in three volumes (1902). The page references below are from the Fletcher edition in case any reader wishes to review the quotations in their larger context.

THOMAS CARLYLE (1795-1881)*

Danton in 1789

The huge, brawny figure, through whose black brows, and rude flattened face, there looks a waste energy as of Hercules not yet furibund—he is an esurient, unprovided Advocate; Danton by name: him mark. . . .

. . . the brawny, not yet furibund figure, we say, is Jacques Danton; a name that shall be "tolerably known in the Revolution." He is President of the electoral Cordeliers District at Paris, or is about to be it; and shall open his lungs of brass.

Danton in September, 1792

Brawny Danton is in the breach, as of stormed Cities and Nations; amid the sweep of Tenth-of-August cannon, the rustle of Prussian gallows-ropes, the smiting of September sabres; destruction all round him, and the rushing-down of worlds: Minister of Justice is his name; but Titan of the Forlorn Hope, and *Enfant Perdu* of the Revolution, is his quality,—and the man acts according to that. . . . Deep fear, is it not, as of its own accord, falling on our enemies? The Titan of the Forlorn Hope, he is not the man that would swiftest of all prevent its so falling. Forward, thou lost Titan of an *Enfant Perdu;* thou must dare, and again dare, and without end dare; there is nothing left for thee but that! . . . The Cause alone is great; and shall live, and not perish.—So, on the whole, here too is a Swallower of Formulas; of still wider gulp than Mirabeau: this Danton, Mirabeau of the Sansculottes.

Danton and "The Fatherland in Danger"

Little will it avail whether our Septemberers be punished or go unpunished; if Pitt and Cobourg are coming in, with one punishment for

---

* Thomas Carlyle, *The French Revolution, A History,* C. R. L. Fletcher (ed.) (3 vols.; New York: G. P. Putnam's Sons, 1902), Vol. I, pp. 172–73, 177–78, 273; Vol. II, pp. 106–7, 146, 199, 323; Vol. III, pp. 24–25, 175, 182, 191–94.

all; nothing now between Paris itself and the Tyrants but a doubtful Dumouriez, and hosts in loose-flowing loud retreat! —Danton the Titan rises in this hour, as always in the hour of need. Great is his voice, reverberating from the domes: Citizen-Representatives, shall we not, in such crisis of Fate, lay aside discords? Reputation: O what is the reputation of this man or of that? ... "Let my name be blighted; let France be free!" It is necessary now again that France rise, in swift vengeance, with her million right hands, with her heart as of one man. Instantaneous recruitment in Paris; let every Section of Paris furnish its thousands; every Section of France! Ninety-six Commissioners of us, two for each Section of the forty-eight, they must go forthwith, and tell Paris what the Country needs of her. Let Eighty more of us be sent, posthaste, over France; to spread the fire-cross, to call forth the might of men. Let the Eighty also be on the road, before this sitting rise. Let them go, and think what their errand is. Speedy Camp of Fifty-thousand between Paris and the North Frontier; for Paris will pour forth her volunteers! Shoulder to shoulder; one stong universal death-defiant rising and rushing; we shall hurl back these Sons of Night again; and France, in spite of the world, be free!— So sounds the Titan's voice: into all Section-Houses; into all French hearts. Sections sit in Permanence, for recruitment, enrolment, that very night. Convention Commissioners, on swift wheels, are carrying the fire-cross from Town to Town, till all France blaze.

Danton the Man

So passes, like a gigantic mass, of valour, ostentation, fury, affection, and wild revolutionary force and manhood, this Danton, to his unknown home. ... He had many sins; but one worst sin he had not, that of Cant. No hollow Formalist, deceptive and self-deceptive, *ghastly* to the natural sense, was this; but a very Man: with all his dross he was a Man; fiery-real, from the great fire-bosom of Nature herself. He saved France from Brunswick; he walked straight his own wild road, whither it led him. He may live for some generations in the memory of men.

Robespierre in the Estates General

... if Mirabeau is the greatest, who of these Six Hundred may be the meanest? Shall we say, that anxious, slight, ineffectual-looking man, under thirty, in spectacles; his eyes (were the glasses off) troubled, careful; with upturned face, snuffing dimly the uncertain future times; complexion of a multiplex atrabiliar colour, the final shade of which may be the pale sea-

green. That greenish coloured (*verdâtre*) individual is an Advocate of
Arras; his name is *Maximilien Robespierre*. . . . With a strict painful mind,
an understanding small but clear and ready, he grew in favour with official
persons, who could foresee in him an excellent man of business, happily
quite free from genius. The Bishop, therefore, taking counsel, appoints
him Judge of his diocese; and he faithfully does justice to the people: till
behold, one day, a culprit comes whose crime merits hanging; and the
strict-minded Max must abdicate, for his conscience will not permit the
dooming of any son of Adam to die. A strict-minded, strait-laced man! A
man unfit for Revolutions? Whose small soul, transparent wholesome-
looking as small ale, could by no chance ferment into virulent alegar—the
mother of ever new alegar; till all France were grown acetous virulent?
We shall see.

Robespierre in the Constituent Assembly

There likewise sits seagreen Robespierre; throwing in his light weight,
with decision, not yet with effect. A thin lean Puritan and Precisian, he
would make away with formulas; yet lives, moves, and has his being
wholly in formulas, of another sort. . . . Yet men of insight discern that
the Seagreen may by chance go far: "This man," observes Mirabeau,
"will do somewhat; he believes every word he says."

Robespierre and the Flight of the King

Perhaps, we may say, the most terrified man in Paris or France is—
who thinks the Reader?—seagreen Robespierre. Double paleness, with
the shadow of gibbets and halters, overcasts the seagreen features: it is
too clear to him that there is to be "a Saint Bartholomew of patriots,"
that in four-and-twenty hours he will not be in life. These horrid anticipations of the soul he is heard uttering. . . .

Robespierre in 1791

Incorruptible Robespierre retired for a little to native Arras: seven
short weeks of quiet; the last appointed him in this world. Public Accuser
in the Paris Department, acknowledged high-priest of the Jacobins; the
glass of incorruptible thin Patriotism, for his narrow emphasis is loved
of all the narrow—this man seems to be rising, somewhither? He sells his
small heritage at Arras; accompanied by a Brother and a Sister, he returns,

scheming out with resolute timidity a small sure destiny for himself and them, to his old lodging, at the Cabinet-maker's in the Rue St. Honoré:—O resolute-tremulous incorruptible seagreen man, towards *what* a destiny!

Robespierre at the Jacobin Club

. . . the Chief Priest and Speaker . . . is Robespierre, the long-winded incorruptible. What spirit of Patriotism dwelt in men in those times, this one fact, it seems to us, will evince: that fifteen hundred human creatures, not bound to it, sat quiet under the oratory of Robespierre; nay, listened nightly, hour after hour, applausive; and gaped as for the word of life. More insupportable individual, one would say, seldom opened his mouth in any Tribune. Acrid, implacable-impotent; dull-drawling, barren as the Harmattan-wind. He pleads, in endless earnest-shallow speech, against immediate War, against Woolen Caps or *Bonnets Rouges,* against many things; and is the Trismegistus and Dalai-Lama of Patriot men. . . .

Robespierre and the Worship of the Supreme Being

This day, if it please Heaven, we are to have . . . a New Religion.

Catholicism being burned out, and Reason-worship guillotined, was there not need of one? Incorruptible Robespierre, not unlike the Ancients, as Legislator of a free people, will now also be Priest and Prophet. . . .

Mahomet Robespierre, in sky-blue coat and black breeches, frizzled and powdered to perfection, bearing in his hand a bouquet of flowers and wheat-ears, issues proudly from the Convention Hall; . . .

The seagreen Pontiff takes a torch . . . ; mouths some other froth-rant of vocables, which happily one cannot hear; strides resolutely forward, in sight of expectant France; sets his torch to Atheism and Company, which are but made of pasteboard steeped in turpentine. They burn up rapidly; and, from within, there rises "by machinery," an incombustible Statue of Wisdom, which, by ill hap, gets besmoked a little; . . .

Mumbo jumbo of the African woods to me seems venerable beside this new Deity of Robespierre; for this is a *conscious* Mumbo-Jumbo, and *knows* that he is machinery. O seagreen Prophet, unhappiest of windbags blown nigh to bursting, what distracted chimera among realities art thou growing to! . . .

Mumbo is Mumbo, and Robespierre is his Prophet. A conspicuous man this Robespierre. . . . He enjoys the admiration of many, the worship of some; and is well worth the wonder of one and all.

Danton and Robespierre, 1794

A Danton, a Robespierre, chief products of a victorious Revolution, are now arrived in immediate front of one another; must ascertain how they will live together, rule together. One conceives easily the deep mutual incompatibility that divided these two: with what terror of feminine hatred the poor seagreen Formula looked at the monstrous colossal Reality, and grew greener to behold him;—the Reality, again, struggling, to think no ill of a chief-product of the Revolution; yet feeling at bottom that such chief-product was little other than a chief windbag, blown large by Popular air; not a man, with the heart of a man, but a poor spasmodic incorruptible pedant, with a logic-formula instead of heart; of Jesuit or Methodist-Parson nature; full of sincere-cant, incorruptibility, of virulence, poltroonery; barren as the eastwind! Two such chief-products are too much for one Revolution.

2. ON DANTON

From 1885 until his retirement in 1922 Aulard was the first incumbent of the chair of the history of the French Revolution at the University of Paris. He was a pioneer in the publishing of documentary materials, the author of many monographs, articles, and reviews, and, for nearly 40 years, editor of the historical journal La Révolution française. *The leader in his field for more than a generation, he will undoubtedly remain one of the greatest French Revolution scholars of all time.*

In 1901 Aulard published an extensive survey of the Revolution, a volume which subsequently appeared in a four-volume English translation (unfortunately, not a very good one) by Bernard Miall.

FRANCOIS VICTOR ALPHONSE AULARD (1849-1928)*

Danton's Character and Policies

Both in character and ideals, Danton formed a striking contrast to Robespierre.

* F. V. A. Aulard, *The French Revolution, a Political History,* trans. Bernard Miall (New York: Charles Scribner's Sons, 1910), Vol. 3, pp. 88–91. By permission of the publisher.

The foundation of Robespierre's character was a belief in the neo-Christianity of Rousseau, the religion of the *Vicaire Savoyard,* and his supreme but so far secret aim was to make this religion the religion of France. Danton does not seem to have believed in the doctrine of the immortality of the soul; one of those dogmas essential to society according to his rival. An atheist rather . . . . He was no philosopher. He did not, like Robespierre, dream of changing the soul of the nation. Leave the people their priests, but see that the latter do not do too much mischief in the State; spread education; trust to time; and, while waiting, since the mass of the nation is Catholic, do not wound the religious sentiment, even by the separation of Church and State, which, good in itself, would be premature in 1792 and 1793.

Politically Danton had no system, except to let conduct be ruled by reason, or rather reason enlightened by history. He was a democrat, but proposed no programme for organizing the democracy, except the spread of public education. He never outstripped opinion. He was a republican of the morrow. Since the Republic exists, let us accept it; let us make use of it to save the country and the Revolution. His method is to act from day to day, resolving, in an empirical manner, the immediate difficulties as they present themselves.

First we will expel the Parisians; afterward we shall see. . . .

At home he was in favour of preventing discord at any price; by concessions, by false appearances at need, by an alliance of the well-meaning men of all parties, with a view to forming a solid and homogeneous government, which should produce on Europe and the anti-revolutionary factions the impression that the republicans were agreed among themselves; to sacrifice everything, even the truth at times, to the propagation and triumph of this impression; to oppose individual passions with the idea of the native land; not a vague and mystical fatherland, but the actual, tangible France: this was Danton's policy. Hatred and vengeance he ignores. Publicly calumniated, he does not waste time in defending himself. He sacrifices his reputation and his honour; he allows men to call him "the drinker of blood." He believes in the omnipotence of material things, and of gold. Not venal, he seems so, and that he seems so is a matter of indifference to him.

His sober, lucid eloquence invites to immediate action; he does not leave his hearers for a moment uncertain as to what they must do, and the means of doing it. A man of action and a fighter, his advice is rapid and precise; not based upon principles, but yet conforming as closely as possible to the spirit of the Revolution.

Danton's policy is precisely what in our days is known as "opportunism," if that word be understood in a favourable sense. Danton springs from Mirabeau, as Gambetta springs from Danton.

He was not so popular as Marat or Robespierre. His language, stark, abrupt, and simple, and by no means academical, may perhaps have been admired by a few fastidious people; but it lacked the ornateness that pleased the people. The Faubourg Saint-Antoine kept the memory of Robespierre and Marat for many long years, by oral tradition; it soon forgot Danton. Yet he was, in his hour, the great national figure; the head of the national defences, the herald of patriotism. His period of greatest eminence was September, 1792. It rested solely with himself, although his eloquence was not a kind to stir the unlettered masses, to win for himself a lasting and widespread popularity, both in Paris and in the departments. But he did not stop to concern himself in the matter; out of sincerity, simplicity, and indifference, he fell into a kind of apathy; there was a lack of sequence in his activities.

3. ON ROBESPIERRE

Mathiez was Aulard's most outstanding pupil. The story of the differences that developed between them has already been told in the introduction to this problem. Although generally thought of in terms of economic and social history, Mathiez was, like his master, essentially a political historian, with a special interest in religion and in the conflicts of political groups and their leaders.

Mathiez's synthesis of the Revolution appeared in three volumes between 1922 and 1927, and it was supplemented by a study of the Thermidorian Reaction (1929) and a posthumous work, edited by Jacques Godechot, on the early Directory (1934). The first three volumes were published in a one-volume English translation as The French Revolution. *It is from this translation that the excerpts below are quoted.*

ALBERT MATHIEZ (1874-1932)*

Robespierre in the Jacobin Club, 1789

The inflexible Robespierre was listened to ... because he was the champion of the people and because his eloquence, instinct with sincerity,

---

* Albert Mathiez, *The French Revolution*, trans. Catherine Alison Phillips (New York: Alfred A. Knopf, 1928), pp. 78, 143, 145, 171, 211, 317, 318, 349, 350, 409, 410, 488, 509, 510. Quoted by permission of the publisher.

was capable of lifting the debate to a higher plane and unmasking trickery.

Robespierre's Distrust of the Girondins

In his eyes, Girondins ... with their exaggerated language and empty assertions, were dangerous rhetoricians. He was aware of their aristocratic tastes and close connexion with the commercial world and remained upon his guard. Since he had attacked the distinction between active and passive citizens, the property qualifications for electors and those eligible for election, the restrictions of the right of holding meetings, of presenting petitions, and of forming associations, and the exclusive privilege of the middle classes of bearing arms; since he had outspokenly pronounced against reinstating the perjured King in his functions and had demanded the summoning of a convention to give France a new constitution, since he was almost the only member of the Constituent Assembly who had remained at the Jacobins, and had prevented their dissolution by a brave resistance to the repression of the Feuillants, he had become the unchallenged leader of the democratic party. His rigorous probity and repugnance for anything resembling intrigue were well known and his ascendancy over the populace and the lower middle classes was unlimited.

Robespierre and the King

Robespierre believed that no reconciliation was possible between the perjured King and the Revolution. He sought salvation in an internal crisis which should overthrow the treacherous monarchy, and desired to use the Constitution itself as a legal weapon to provide this crisis.

Robespierre and the Revolutionary Tribunal

The extraordinary tribunal was formed of judges and a jury elected by the Parisian sections. Robespierre refused the position of president, in a letter stating that, since most of the political prisoners were his personal enemies, he could not be both judge and a party in the case. Perhaps there were also other reasons for his refusal which he did not mention. The Gironde had already started violently attacking this man, whom they mistrusted and regarded as the real leader of the Commune. In a poster headed "The Dangers of Victory," probably inspired by Roland, which was pasted up all over Paris, he was represented as a "violently jealous man," who wished to "make Pétion unpopular, put himself in his place, and proceed amid ruins to the tribunate, which was the constant object of his insensate desires." By refusing the presidency of the tribunal... Robespierre pointed the contrast between his disinterestedness and the accusation, fabricated by the Girondins, of aiming at a dictatorship.

Robespierre and the Montagnards

For a long time past Robespierre had been the unchallenged leader of the Montagnard party. During the Constituent Assembly he had consistently espoused the cause of the weak and unfortunate. He was the first to protest with indefatigable fervour against the property qualification for the suffrage, and it had at last collapsed under his continued blows; he had protested against martial law and demanded the arming of the people;... he had wanted to impose restrictions on inheritance, and as convinced a communist as Babeuf based his hopes upon him.... He complained... that those who had benefited by the Revolution despised the poor, and he attacked the middle-class oligarchy with cold fury; but he expressly repudiated communism. He alluded to the agrarian law as an "absurd scarecrow set up for the stupid by the depraved"... Robespierre never varied in this respect. He always regarded communism as an impossible and insensate dream. He desired to set limits to the rights of property and prevent its abuse, but he never dreamt of abolishing it.

Robespierre Against the Upper Classes

Robespierre, who was no visionary, but had a strong sense of reality and followed the slightest manifestations of public opinion with close attention, had realized from the very beginning that the Gironde could be defeated only by giving the sansculottes a direct interest in its overthrow. At the end of April he read out a declaration of rights, first at the Jacobins and afterwards at the Convention, which subordinated property to the interest of society and thus provided a theoretical justification for the policy of requisitioning beloved of the Enragés. He never ceased inciting the mass of the workers against the "culottes dorées (golden knee-breeches)," as he called them, who were endeavouring to gain control of the sections.... And he advised the sections to follow the precedent of the department of Hérault and raise a revolutionary army at the expense of the rich, to hold ill-disposed persons in check.... in order to facilitate the accomplishment of their civic duties by the labouring class he further proposed that those in needy circumstances should be compensated for the time spent at the assemblies of their section....

The social policy expounded by Robespierre with such remarkable precision was indeed a class policy. During the Constituent and Legislative Assemblies the sansculottes had placed their strength at the service of the revolutionary middle classes against the old regime for nothing, but the time for this idealistic fervour had gone by. The sansculottes had seen landowners growing rich by the purchase of national property or the sale of their commodities and goods at exorbitant prices, and had profited by the lesson. They were no longer ready to be exploited, and considered that the Revolution should feed those who had brought it about and were maintaining it.

Robespierre was merely echoing the voice of the people....

Robespierre in Power

The advent of Robespierre to power opens up a new era. He brought to the committee not only his rare personal qualities, his coolness and courage, his acute insight, his formidable eloquence, his remarkable faculty of organization, and his entire disinterestedness, but more besides. Since the days of the Constituent Assembly, Robespierre had been the most popular of the revolutionaries among the artisans and humble classes, whose entire confidence he possessed. He was the unchallenged leader of the sansculottes, especially since the death of Marat. He did not enter the committee alone. He had behind him most of the militants, all those who formed the permanent nucleus of the clubs, all those who had irrevocably thrown in their lot with the Revolution, all those who had no alternative save to conquer or to die.

The maintenance of Bouchotte in office meant that the democratization of the army general staffs was to continue. The entry of his protector Robespierre into the Government meant that in every part of the administration, whether civil or military, the sansculottes would be supported and their opponents silenced; that those in control of the Republic would no longer play a double game with the people, but would listen to their complaints, take pity upon their misery, and associate them with the effort to save the nation.

The policy which Robespierre was about to inaugurate was at once national and democratic. As a preliminary test he was faced in Paris itself with a struggle against the extremists of the left, allied with the extremists of the right. He had to join battle with them in the midst of increasing scarcity, while news of disaster upon disaster was arriving from the frontiers. The fact that he did not despair, that he accepted power at such a moment, that he bore such a crushing burden without faltering, and that he succeeded in raising the Republic from the abyss, ought to be sufficient to establish his renown.

Robespierre and Foreign Policy

In a great speech before the Convention on the 27th Brumaire, Robespierre endeavoured to reassure neutrals—Americans, Danes, and Turks, as well as Swiss—with regard to the intentions of revolutionary France. The latter, he said, cherished no dreams of subjugating the whole world. She only desired to defend her liberty and the independence of small nations. It was the Coalition powers alone who were animated by a spirit of conquest! Such a speech, which was greeted by applause from the Convention, must have seemed alarming to the foreign exiles and their Hébertist protectors, who saw salvation only in a fight to the finish, leading up to a universal republic.

Robespierre Head of the Government

Robespierre had become the real head of the Government in the eyes of all revolutionary France. His popularity, which had always been considerable, had increased out of all proportion since the fall of the factions which he had attacked to their faces. But Robespierre, whose whole character was instinct with impassioned sincerity, did not always spare the self-esteem of his colleagues in the Government. Severe to himself, he was equally so to others. Reservations and criticisms were more frequent upon his lips than compliments. Since he had been so cruelly deceived in his friends, he now refused to make any until he was sure of his ground; he rarely gave his confidence and maintained towards most people a cold and distant reserve which might have been mistaken for calculation or ambition. He felt himself to be misunderstood, and suffered from it. By a weakness which shows plainly that his character was not an overbearing one, he often vindicated himself and replied to the secret criticism which he suspected, and by so speaking of himself, laid himself open to the accusation of ambition, which was a torture to him.

Since this facile but terrible accusation of ambition had been formulated by the Girondins and repeated by the Hébertists, it had never ceased to be current among those who had cause, or imagined themselves to have cause, to complain of this influential man, whose power they still further exaggerated. . . .

The Fall of Robespierre

What tragic irony! Robespierre and his party went to their deaths largely for having tried to use the Terror as the instrument of a fresh upheaval affecting property. With them the levelling Republic, without rich or poor, which they had dreamt of establishing by the laws of Ventôse, received its death blow. . . .

Born of the war and its sufferings, cast in the mould of terrorism in opposition to its own basic principle, the Republic, owing to the force of circumstances, was fundamentally no more than an accident, in spite of its prodigious achievement. Resting on an increasingly narrow basis, it was misunderstood by the very persons whom it desired to associate with its existence. It had required all the fervent mysticism of its creators, and their superhuman energy, to make it last until victory was secured abroad. Twenty centuries of monarchy and slavery are not wiped out in a few months. The strictest laws are powerless to change human nature and the social order at a single stroke. Robespierre, Couthon, and Saint-Just, who desired to prolong the dictatorship in order to lay the foundation of civil institutions and overthrow the rule of wealth, were well aware of this. They could have succeeded only if the full dictatorship had been in their hands alone. But Robespierre's uncompromising character, which made him break with his colleagues in the Government at the very moment when they were making concessions to him, was enough to bring about the collapse of a structure existing in a legal vacuum. . . .

4. ON DANTON

Although today Madelin is apt to be thought of chiefly in connection with his many volumes on Napoleon I, a generation ago he was ranked among the leading writers on the French Revolution. Conservative, inclined to follow the antirevolutionary pattern established by H. A. Taine (but in a more moderate vein), his one-volume history of the Revolution, published in 1911, gained a wide following, partly because of its dramatic prose. Translated into English in 1916 as The French Revolution *it was widely used in university classes.*

LOUIS MADELIN (1871-1956)*

Danton's Character and Policies

Hitherto this Danton had been considered a rather vulgar agitator of the Clubs and Faubourgs; fierce, dangerous, not very serious compared

* Louis Madelin, *The French Revolution* (London: William Heinemann, Ltd., 1916), pp. 275–77, 283–84. By permission of the publisher.

with the grandiloquent Vergniaud or Robespierre. Yet in our eyes he towers high above them.

He was the son of a procurator in Champagne, and not at all the *parvenu* he has been described as being: a brilliant scholar and student of the greatest authors ...; then so remarkable a lawyer that before 1789, Barentin, the Keeper of the Seals, would have taken him into his own office: but this, foreseeing the advent of the "avalanche," he refused. ... He may have been an agent of the Duc d'Orleans: he certainly tried the Masonic lodges, and then, finding they suited him better, turned to the most advanced of the Clubs where, for the past three years, he had been busily engaged in working revolutionary opinion up to fever pitch. He had been at the bottom of every fresh movement and had now been carried by the wave into the chair hitherto occupied by d'Aguesseau.

He hardly sat himself down in it: from this chair he "bounded" upwards to the dictatorship. Before he did so, with a gesture at once brutal and childish, he broke off with his thumb the gilded fleur-de-lys of the clock in his cabinet which marked the hour of his advent to power. The man's whole impulsive nature is shown in that action: he broke off the hand! Robespierre would have had it taken off and put away.

Impulsive he was, and violent, passionate, audacious rather than persevering, loving life, wearing it and himself out, boasting more of his vices than of his virtues, ambitious, but not deeply calculating, noisy and powerful as an orator, but nothing of a rhetorician, and always ready to shed tears of blood over the disasters his own speech had let loose.

Everything about him accentuated the excessive violence of his language—most of all his face, the face of a "Mirabeau of the mob," with something in it of the bulldog and something of the lion.

"He was a man," says Sorel. Michelet took him to be "a sublime actor": what a mistake! He was horribly sincere: everything came from the depths of his heart—pity, rage, love, ferocity. He had no venom, was easily touched, quick to forget injuries done him by others, often driven to despair by those he wrought himself; rancour and calculation were alike foreign to him. He loved money, but we have no absolute proof that he ever made it dishonestly himself, though he allowed those about him to do so; for indeed, he never set up to be "incorruptible."

He had a great brain and a warm heart: he adored the Revolution and the Fatherland with the same deep-seated devotion: he was a Frenchman to the very marrow of his bones: when the day came the call of his country in danger stirred the very depths of his soul. This fact makes the man, so repulsive in some particulars, a great man in our eyes. He was a volcano, but above the horrible flood of lava played the purest flame.

One other feature to conclude: he was lazy. He was capable of every kind of audacity, and prone to the extremes of indolence. His action was always violent and spasmodic: he knew nothing of slow labour and patient hatreds. Robespierre would have reprobated the weakness that led him to pardon an enemy before that enemy was dead. . . .

He was not overburdened with theories: he would have preferred to see the widest toleration everywhere. . . . His dream was to see France united in the face of the threatening German: the Republic, to him, was a government that should mean unity, not division. He found it very hard in 1793 to endure the rancour of the Girondins, and in 1794 to believe in the hatred of Robespierre. In August, 1792, he began to dream of a great movement which was to raise the whole nation against the foe. Idle as he was, his patriotism was to keep him absorbed for weeks and weeks in a huge and urgent labour—the total reorganization of a country that had fallen a prey to the most unexampled confusion.

Taking him all in all this Danton was a great power. . . . Danton's apologists affirm that, seeing the populace preparing to descend upon the prisons, he tried to lure it to the Champ-de-Mars, there to turn the men who would fain have cut their fellow Frenchmen's throats into soldiers of the Republic. Danton certainly nursed no murderous dreams himself, but he was not blind; he knew well that murder was being plotted, and that at the first news of any reverse in Lorraine, the massacre would begin; and, before the news had spread in Paris, he himself had been informed of the capitulation of Verdun. That neither he, nor Roland, nor Servan, nor Pétion should have had the prisons safely guarded may have been the result in Roland's case, or in Servan's, of a most lamentable carelessness: in that of Danton, it can only have been caused by his deliberate complicity. But the elections to the Convention were just coming on: those in Paris were in the hands of the Commune, and Danton was a candidate. The Commune was determined on the massacre as a method of inspiring terror: Danton was determined to be blind. Carnage, indeed, was by no means repugnant to his fierce nature: he would have given orders for the bloodshed, if he had thought it necessary: he allowed it to go forward, believing it to be inevitable: the crime lies heavy on the memory of a man who, in spite of all, was not, as we have seen, an utter monster. Far from preventing the massacres, Danton facilitated the work: he attracted the genuine patriots to the Champ-de-Mars, and left the prisons at the mercy of the dregs of the population. To suppose that he did not see this clearly would be to take him for a fool. There was little of the fool about him. . . .

This man's curious nature is a perpetual puzzle to the historian. We find no difficulty in following Robespierre, his adversary, along his slow and calculating course, but we are constantly led astray by the impulsive quality of Danton's character. His dream, now, was all of peace and union. . . . like Mirabeau, he was perpetually carried away by his own temperament—that of the parliamentary orator—now quite in contradiction with his ideas as a statesman.

5. ON ROBESPIERRE

Although his early life was spent as an Anglican cleric, some of whose theological writings were highly controversial, Thompson ultimately taught history at Magdalen College, Oxford, and became the most distinguished British scholar of his time in the era of the French Revolution. Outstanding among his many works were The French Revolution *and a definitive, two-volume life of Robespierre. His books are eminently readable as well as scholarly.*

JAMES MATTHEW THOMPSON (1878-1956)*

Robespierre, Man and Politician

Maximilien Robespierre had appeared among the deputies of 1789 as the angular and aggressive spokesman of an extravagant liberalism. He was poor, discontented, and suspicious of ridicule; but he was consumed by a little man's ambition to play a big part. He forced himself to the front by the assiduous cultivation of second-class talents. His solemn air, his carefully composed speeches, his mastery of revolutionary technique, the bourgeois respectability of his conduct, and the touch of aristocracy (always irresistible to the bourgeoisie) that he gave to his dress and manners, made him the idol of middle-class Jacobinism. Tradesmen and artisans relied on his persistent championship of their rights. Their womenfolk found his speeches as comforting as sermons. His limited outlook and mediocre mind mirrored the thrifty virtues which had built up their small businesses. His vague and rhetorical platitudes hung like illuminated texts in their tidy parlours. They did not foresee that self-flattery and the need of power would turn his liberalism into a dogma,

* J. M. Thompson, *The French Revolution* (New York: Oxford University Press, 1945), pp. 257, 279, 424, 425, 459, 485, 541, 543, 544. By permission of Basil Blackwell, Publisher.

his cult of virtue into an Inquisition, and his shrinking from violence into the regime of the Terror. A cold, enigmatic, unattractive man, he repeated within the limits of his small study and of his narrow soul the full-blooded experiments of the revolution, and extracted nothing from them but gall and wormwood.

Robespierre and the War

Robespierre's shrewd leadership . . . , his imperviousness to any bribe except flattery, and his flair for high-sounding democratic sentiments, had won him the enthusiastic support of a class hitherto overlooked, but soon (as he saw) to control the Revolution—the lower middle class (*petite bourgeoisie*). These decent self-respecting folk resented, even more than the so-called working class, the monopolizing of wealth and power by people a little above them in the social scale. They disliked a constitution that gave them nothing but an ineffective franchise. They were ready to impute the worst motives to soldiers and politicians who sent their sons to be killed in an unnecessary and unnational war.

To this audience Robespierre declared, amidst applause, that Brissot's war was "not a war of liberation, leading to freedom, but a war waged by a despot against foreign princes, *émigrés*, and priests." The king, he said, hoped to use the war to restore the old regime; Brissot hoped to use it to set up a bourgeois republic; Lafayette hoped to use it to enslave the country under a military dictatorship. In any case, he maintained, neither the army nor the government was prepared for war; it could only lead to disaster.

Robespierre and the Committee of Public Safety

Robespierre himself was added to the committee as its most experienced parliamentarian, its most acceptable orator, and (had he been left outside) its most dangerous critic. He interested himself, more perhaps than his colleagues liked, in the affairs of every department. His belief in the spoken word, and his readiness to dogmatize any part of the Jacobin faith, marked him out as the natural *rapporteur* of the committee. . . . Robespierre was the best known and most admired Jacobin in the country. He was easily credited with a supremacy which he did not possess, and with designs upon a dictatorship which he was the last man to entertain. Yet as a minister without portfolio, with access to every department of government, he had more opportunity than the rest to look ahead, and to think out a common policy.

The note-book (*carnet*) that contains his rough memoranda for the last three months of 1793 ... is very suggestive of Robespierre's key position on the committee. It contains more than one hint of ideas which took shape in the ordering of the committee's work, the remodelling of the Revolutionary Tribunal, the cult of the Supreme Being, the law of the 22nd *prairial*, and the *bureau de police générale*. Nor can there be much doubt that Robespierre's special interest lay in those activities of the committee which caused most public apprehension, and which labelled its regime the Government of the Terror. In Opposition a devotee of absolute liberty, in Government Robespierre became a convinced disciplinarian. In his youth he had been an opponent of capital punishment. ... Now, at thirty-five he believed in the guillotine as the sovereign method for purging vice from the body politic; though he was always hoping, as terrorists have always hoped, that he had reached the point of transition from compulsion to persuasion, and that the next execution would be the last.

Robespierre, International Statesman

Robespierre's reputation as an international statesman rested on his speeches of November 17th and January 28th [1793, 1794]. They are full of boasting and abuse; but they contain no policy, unless it be the declaration that England, not Austria, is the real enemy, and that France must keep on good terms with countries such as Switzerland and the United States, from which it draws supplies of meat and corn. Since England is the arch-enemy, France becomes the champion of small nationalities. England, politically rotten, may be expected to perish at any moment by internal revolution: had not Paine been telling his French friends this ever since the spring of '91? The Jacobins have only to display their republican virtues, and they will win the support of the neutral states. France, Robespierre proudly asserts, is necessary to the universe. Without France, liberty would cease from off the earth.

Robespierre, the Incorruptible

It was Robespierre's pride that he was inaccessible to bribery and indifferent to gain. There were others of the Jacobin leaders who, when they died, left little or nothing behind them. But incorruptibility was not a common virtue.

Robespierre's Ideas

Robespierre had defined the Jacobin Utopia as "the peaceful enjoyment of liberty and equality, and the reign of eternal justice," embodied in a state in which "every soul grows greater by the constant sharing of republican sentiments." Instead of an "easygoing, frivolous, and discontented people" he would create "one that is happy, powerful, and stout-hearted." He would replace the vices and follies of the monarchy by the "virtues and the amazing achievements of the Republic."

To reach this result, Robespierre could see no means but compulsion. . . . It was no accident that the Law of the 22nd *Prairial* appeared within two days of a great festival by which Robespierre hoped to dedicate France to a religious profession of virtue and patriotism. . . .

The rule of superstition, Robespierre thought, was almost destroyed; philosophy had banished priestcraft; and the only dogmas still present in the human mind were those that supported moral ideas. . . . Soon the gospel of reason and liberty would overrun the world. . . . He looked beyond the republic of '92 to a regime of moral patriotism, in which a regenerated religion and a cult expressed in patriotic images would play their part. . . .

The Republic would proclaim its official belief in the essential dogmas of enlightened Theism. The French people would learn, in the regular and dignified worship of the Supreme Being, to forget the superstitions of Catholicism, and to ignore the differences between constitutional and refractory priesthoods. Catholics, Protestants, and free-thinkers would worship side by side. Europe would acknowledge that the Revolution had achieved the reformation, not only of the Gregorian calendar and of the accepted system of weights and measures, but also of the Christian church.

6. "THE DANTON-ROBESPIERRE CONTROVERSY TODAY"

The one living writer of the six whose works are used in this problem, Dr. Bernstein is the author of numerous books, most of which deal with socialists and socialism in France. For many years he was editor of the quarterly journal Science and Society *in New York. The item which follows (in abridged form and minus all but 2 of 41 footnotes) appeared, under the title cited above, in that periodical in the Summer, 1959 issue. Originally presented at a session of the Society for French Historical Studies in Cleveland, Ohio, in April, 1959, the article represents the only significant attempt in English to revalue the controversy more than a half century after the final break between Aulard and Mathiez.*

SAMUEL BERNSTEIN[*]

The reputations of Robespierre and Danton have seesawed since the French Revolution. The story of their ups and downs, as a historian once had it, runs as follows: Had a contemporary of the Revolution been asked to mention the most popular political personality of his day, he would have named Robespierre. Had the same question been posed to an average Frenchman during the reigns of Charles X and Louis Philippe, he would have given the same answer. So would the republicans of 1848. Opinion, after 1852, would have been divided among Hébert, Danton and Robespierre. After the establishment of the Third Republic, the choice would have been Danton. Bringing the story nearer to our own time, . . . we venture to say that Robespierre would be preferred. . . .

. . . we can but state the reasons for the emergence of Danton, after 1870, as the great patriot and statesman of the Revolution. In the first place, the memory of Robespierre had been overshadowed during the Second Empire, thanks to Michelet and Quinet. In the second place, a line of special pleaders had pedestaled Danton as the towering figure of the Revolution. In the third place, as Georges Lefebvre pointed out, Danton best symbolized the standards of the founders of the Third Republic.

Of Danton's panegyrists under the Third Republic Aulard was the most authoritative. . . . Aulard . . . disparaged Robespierre and exalted Danton. The first in Aulard's estimate, was a representative of the past, a mystic and cruel pontiff who had subordinated politics to religion; the second, tolerant, a truly modern man, an empiricist in politics and an heir of the eighteenth-century scientific spirit.

With further research, Aulard revised his estimates of the two men. According to his new version, Danton, the statesman and practical politician, was not without faults, such as indolence and weak character. His

* Samuel Bernstein, "The Danton-Robespierre Controversy Today," *Science and Society*, Vol. 23, No. 3 (Summer, 1959), pp. 221–32. Reprinted by permission of the publishers.

part in the Revolution was prominent, but not preponderant. Nor did he have a monopoly of patriotism and prudence. . . .

Aulard's demotion of Danton from the abode of positivist saints made him more acceptable to the positivist oriented political opportunists of the Third Republic. In their quest for a legitimate genealogy they hailed Aulard's heresy as heuristic. Neither Robespierre, nor Marat, nor Hébert, could be admitted to their roster of ancestors. Of the top men in the Revolution Danton alone was a worthy antecedent of the republican leaders at the highest level. He was neither incorruptible, nor an innovator in matters of property, nor an anti-annexationist, neither a die-hard nor a dogmatist. He was moreover an early champion of opportunism and of republican unity. . . .

Aulard in time modified his view of Robespierre. The leading Jacobin continued to be the high priest. Still, the religion he had set up was a means of worshiping the *patrie;* and he enjoyed immense popularity after the feast of the Supreme Being. These facts Aulard took into account when he wrote his famous history of the Revolution. Without diluting his loyalty to Danton, he conceded a measure of high statesmanship to Robespierre.

Whether or not Aulard's concessions induced his pupil, Albert Mathiez, to look more closely at the record cannot be answered. Certain it is that the teacher, in the course of advising the young man on his theses, discovered differences emerging between them. . . .

The disagreements started in the area of religious history. Aulard held that the revolutionary cults were but expedients of defense. Mathiez argued that, instead of having been devised to meet an emergency, they were part of a grand policy designed to regenerate the nation. . . .

. . . conflicting political and social outlooks drew teacher and pupil further apart. The one was a radical socialist, that is a radical minus socialism; the second drew closer to the socialist persuasion. . . .

It was a tribute to the teacher that, while he was disinclined to share the conclusions of his pupil's theses, he praised highly their originality and rigid documentation. . . . But discrepant interpretations of the Revolution and clashing outlooks pulled them apart.

The story of their final break is too well known to be detailed here. All we need recall is that seceders from the "Société de l'histoire de la révolution française" founded in 1907 the "Société des études robespierristes," and its journal, *Annales révolutionnaires*. In its first volume appeared Mathiez's review of Aulard's book against Taine. . . .[1]

---

[1] *Taine, historien de la révolution française* (Paris, 1907).

416   INTERPRETING EUROPEAN HISTORY

His book presented the following counts against Taine: He was a conservative snob; his erudition was deceptive, amounting to a piling up of facts; his history had gaps and errors; his method inspired distrust, for his archival evidence was far less than he claimed; and finally, he ignored the pamphlet literature.

Mathiez's comments on Aulard's book were made with hammer-blows rather than with a well-honed edge. The reviewer claimed to have found in it the following fundamental defects: it was destitute of methodical order; it was congested with tiresome repetition; it was encumbered with pedanticism and chicane, which stripped the findings of persuasiveness; and it overlooked the causal connection between Taine's past experience and his theory of history....

Aulard's indictment of Taine's history falls short on the grounds Mathiez indicated. But the tone of the review was so out of keeping with academic canons of courtesy that it further ruffled feelings between the two camps of French revolutionary historiography.

Aulard never answered his critic, but reprinted in *La révolution française* Mathiez's laudatory article on him written three years earlier. Incensed by that, the younger man came back with more charges, even disputed the validity of Aulard's history of the Revolution, which he had considered impeccable. He seemed irritated by the disdainful indifference of the older man to the evidence he had been piling up on Danton and Robespierre.... Undoubtedly subjective factors amplified the strife. But beneath the foam of feeling lay deep differences. Mathiez, who was explosive at a low flash-point, set upon Aulard for his malevolent appraisal of Robespierre's religious policy, which suited the social patterns of conservatives and professional anticlericals. Actually, Mathiez contended, it was heavily taxed with errors and unproved assertions.

The gap betwen their basic sincerities was filled with bitter dissension in 1914, after historians had accused Aulard of having penciled documents in the National Archives. Mathiez came out with a peppery piece, "le scandale Aulard," then followed it up with two others. Again Aulard failed to reply, save to refer to the charge as the "farcical affair of the marginal pencil strokes," and to Mathiez's invective as "silly malice."

It is pointless to continue with the acrimony of the controversy. Seeing it in retrospect, we can only regret that the two great historians found no meeting ground.... Yet it is well to recall that both took their departure from the same body of evidence, namely, the political and religious history of the Revolution.

Why did their paths bifurcate? The answer, we think, may be found, not in the asperity of judgment, but in the big problems and brewing tempests of the respective periods they lived in, Aulard reached intellectual maturity in the post-Commune era, when parliamentary democracy waged a war of attrition against the right. Consequently his main concern was the religious policies and the monarchist-republican conflicts of the Revolution. From his field of vision, ideas were primary in setting men in motion, not the social and economic forces. . . .

The tempestuous surge of crucial issues equally shaped the intellectual development of Mathiez. His generation was preoccupied with such questions as the separation of church and state, the challenge of socialism and syndicalism and the unsavory collusion between politics and finance. Then followed World War I with its economic controls, and the rise of Bolshevik power, in which he espied many parallels with Jacobin power.

Two years before his death, Mathiez marked out the following stages of his revolutionary studies: clerical and anticlerical policies; Dantonist demagogy; financial corruption; plebeian poverty; and finally, social and economic problems.

Such seems to have been the sequence of his thought process. If in going from effects to causes he came to regard economics and class incompatibilities as the taproots of the revolutionary crisis, it was because they explained more than did politics and religion. His new directions notwithstanding, he never got over his early penchant for political history which he at times exhibted in disproportionate narrations of parliamentary and party disputes. His approach to social and economic problems was via politics. What made *le peuple* act as it did was a question that lay beyond his horizon. . . . This is but another way of saying that Mathiez was basically a political historian.

We are not implying that he was nearer to Aulard than he believed. Aulard stayed close to the political course of the Revolution; Mathiez went prospecting for its mainsprings in the social and economic records after the political and religious facts alone had failed to give him the answer. And both resurrected heroes who personified their respective values. . . . under the Third Republic Aulard and Mathiez came to represent two schools of historiography, the one moored to middle class standards, the other standing nearer to socialism.

Their portraits of the two revolutionists are well known. Aulard saw Danton as the symbol of what was genuinely French and human in the Revolution, as the foe of fanaticism and the disciple of the *philosophes* in action. With all his new documentation, Aulard's Robespierre remained a petty dimensioned cleric and dictator. Mathiez, on the other hand, garlanded him with glory, in fact made him the demiurge of the democratic cosmos. His rival, by contrast, was converted into a unprincipled politico, into a defeatist intriguing with foreign powers for a peaceful settlement in order to restore monarchy in France. Mathiez left unfinished his studies on Robespierre, but his case against Danton seemed complete.

It is appropriate at this point to evaluate his indictment of Danton. Rereading the testimony after a lapse of many years, we confess that some of it lacks cogency. But the evidence on Danton's venality is so unassailable that even his admirers have accepted it. They have continued to dwell on his Gallic nature, on his conciliatory spirit and broad humanity, but not on his probity after Mathiez's inquiry, which two subsequent investigators confirmed. How did Danton make his fortune? By selling his services to the court and foreign powers, Mathiez answered. But his case, it has been pointed out, would have been stronger had he sifted the evidence, according to its probability.

What is the worth of Mathiez's dossier? The most balanced estimate was given by Georges Lefebvre in the course of assessing the biographies of Danton by Herman Wendel and Louis Barthou.[2] Danton, Lefebvre argues, can neither be exalted nor debased; he was neither Wendel's exemplar of the will to power, nor Barthou's irreproachable statesman, nor Mathiez's calculating scoundrel. Any appraisal of him must take into account his temperament. He had a talent for improvisation and a vibrating sensitivity to popular applause. Though he had a strong appetite for life, he was given to depressions which reduced him to a state of atony. Principles meant as little to him as did moral discipline. His lack of vindictiveness, his generosity, and his behavior without regard to guiding rules made him a magnet for unscrupulous, self-seeking men.

Bearing in mind these traits of Danton's character, Lefebvre proceeds to assess Mathiez's dossier. He has no reservations on the charge of venality; and he thinks it probable that Danton shared the foreign gold earmarked for the saving of the King. The evidence on that, however, is indecisive. Even more so is the testimony on Prussian bribery, continues Lefebvre.... Did he misappropriate secret government funds or pillage Belgium when he was there as an official emissary? We shall never know, answers Lefebvre, for the records were destroyed. It is too simple, he contends, to ascribe Danton's shifts of policy either to corruption or to tough realism. Neither explanation takes his character into consideration.

---

[2] *Annales historiques de la Révolution française,* Vol. 9 (1932), pp. 385–424, 484–500; republished in his *Études sur la Révolution française* (Paris, 1954), pp. 25–66.

He was an empiricist without a piloting theory. Apart from all venality, says Lefebvre, he was impassioned with the *patrie* and the Revolution. To deny him that is to lose sight of the ascendancy he had over masses. No corrupt adventurer could long have that power over them without revealing himself.

Lefebvre furthermore refuses to admit Mathiez's contention that Danton's audacity was but a devious maneuver to be on the winning side. The argument disregards the man's faculty of mastering men without commanding them. Otherwise, reasons Lefebvre, the Girondins would not have invited him to the ministry after August 10, 1792. There is no proof that his resistance to the abandonment of Paris, after the French military defeats, was shrewd patriotism, or that his peace negotiations were part of a plan to stop the Revolution. That may be possible, but not criminal, Lefebvre replies. Peace without conquest after Valmy would have preserved the reforms of the Constituent Assembly and spared the nation years of war. All that can be said is that Danton's policy of conciliation failed, at home as well as abroad. And in time of war, especially in a war *à outrance,* any attempt to relax the war effort or to placate passions is equated with defeatism and treason.

Unfortunately, Danton was surrounded by sordid men whose corrupt practices were for Robespierre a sort of prism reflecting Danton's political record. His past deeds, it seemed to the Incorruptible, had derived from immoral motives and illicit designs. Studying Robespierre's notes on the Dantonists, Lefebvre came up with the acute observation that the purpose of Mathiez's research was to document what Robespierre had said. And Robespierre, according to Mathiez, always told the truth. Having once started on that line of thought, he seized on everything that could possibly add to his indictment of Danton.

Lefebvre's competent analysis of Mathiez's dossier did not reconcile Robespierrists and Dantonists. It served, however, to quiet the controversy after the death of its two principal antagonists.

Stripping the debate of verbal sparring, we can but admire the enduring benefits the two historians brought to French revolutionary historiography. Aulard, the founder of the school of scientific documentation in the sources of the Revolution, the editor of monumental collections of its records, the author of a masterly account of its political aspects, the great teacher who indelibly impressed his pupils with the primary value of *inédits;* Mathiez, indefatigably devoted to his students, inflaming their minds with his enthusiasm, blazing new paths of research and probing to bed-rock for the social and economic forces of men's actions. These are the permanent values the two historians added to the study of the French

Revolution. We may pass by some of their conclusions regarding its two great leaders. But we cannot set aside their high level techniques of historical investigations. These have been their legacy to us. . . .

Robert B. Holtman, Professor of History at Louisiana State University, was born in Kenosha, Wis. in 1914. His B.S., M.A., and Ph.D. degrees were awarded by the University of Wisconsin. He has contributed numerous articles to scholarly journals and is the author of *Napoleonic Propaganda* (Baton Rouge, La., 1950) and *The Napoleonic Revolution* (New York and Philadelphia, 1967). He is a member of the American Historical Association, is a past vice president of the Society for French Historical Studies, and has headed the European section of the Southern Historical Association.

CHAPTER FOURTEEN

ROBERT B. HOLTMAN

Louisiana State University

The War Guilt Question of 1803

WHEN NAPOLEON BONAPARTE came to power in November of 1799, France was involved in the War of the Second Coalition, fighting such formidable foes as Great Britain, Russia, Austria, and the Ottoman Empire. One of the reasons for his accession to power was a feeling that he, of all Frenchmen, would best be able to bring the war to a victorious conclusion.

This he succeeded in doing. The Treaty of Lunéville in February of 1801 left Great Britain as his only opponent; and even the British, who had been at war with France since early in 1793, were soon willing to come to terms. Although William Pitt the Younger had resigned as prime minister, he supported his successor, Viscount Addington, and Foreign Minister Lord Hawkesbury, whose efforts led to the signing of the Treaty of Amiens in March of 1802. For the next 14 months Bonaparte was at peace for the only time in the almost 15 years he was to be in power.

In May of 1803 the war between Great Britain and Napoleonic France was renewed, never to let up; other powers allied with the British on varying occasions. Among the later wars fought against Napoleon were those of the Third Coalition (1805) and the Fourth Coalition (1806–7); the Peninsular War (1808–13); an Austrian war (1809); and the Russian campaign of 1812, continued in the War of Liberation in Germany in 1813 and the invasion of France in 1814. The final campaign against Napoleon, during the Hundred Days, ended at Waterloo in 1815. It is noteworthy that not one of these wars was declared by Napoleon. Could the fault always have rested with his foes?

Since the fighting which started in 1803 greatly affected Napoleon's outlook and his governmental system, an examination of why the peace of Amiens failed is of prime interest to historians. Deciding on the aggressor can, however, be extremely difficult. The question of who was to blame for World War I is still not fully solved; it is even more difficult for the Napoleonic period, when international law was less highly developed, to answer the question of "war guilt."

Is the aggressor the country which fails to live up to the letter of the treaty? There cannot be a rule of law among nations if treaties may be violated with impunity. Most authors agree that England's refusal to evacuate Malta violated the treaty. (Édouard Driault, however, states that Britain was not obligated to do so because certain stipulations with respect to the evacuation were not met.) Or is the aggressor the government which is not content with the situation at the time of the treaty and so extends its power that the other side feels itself endangered? Is a country justified in going to war over issues involving honor and prestige as well as for survival? Just as we should feel displeased with a United States government which permitted our relative position to decline, so the British in 1802–3 did not want to see themselves surpassed by France. Is it helpful to ask which country is benefiting more from the peace, on the assumption that the other is more likely to end the peace?

In the excerpts which follow, different views of the history of this time are expressed. Albert Sorel, while blaming Great Britain, presents a "deterministic" view: that by the very nature of things, resumption of war between England and France was inevitable. Such a conception virtually negates the role which individuals play in the making of history. Driault would not at all accept this point of view; he feels that the issue of whether or not war would be renewed rested largely with Bonaparte. Earlier in the volume than the quoted excerpt, he particularly stresses the expansionist policy followed by Bonaparte and speaks of Bonaparte's "continual encroachments," his "provocations and usurpations." Driault also states that the annexation of Elba by Bonaparte was a violation of the Treaty of Amiens. Georges Lefebvre tends to place the blame on Bonaparte, but his final conclusion is not far different from that of Sorel. Harold C. Deutsch, who made a more detailed study of this particular phase of Napoleon's career than any of the other authors cited, leaves no doubt as to his conviction that Great Britain was primarily responsible. And our final author, Geoffrey Bruun, after citing numerous facts, states that the question is unresolved.

Three books not cited in the excerpts are worth noting. One is the biography of *Napoleon Bonaparte* by J. M. Thompson (New York, 1952) which concludes that Bonaparte was more conciliatory in the final negotiations, but that the goals of the two sides were incompatible. The real tragedy, Thompson says, lay in the terms of the treaty rather than in the breaking of it. Nevertheless, if England did violate the treaty, it cannot be excused on the ground that it had come to terms unwisely. A second is the biography *Napoleon* (New York, 1966), whose author, Felix Markham, feels that technically England was in the wrong, but that in the long run the final decision was Bonaparte's. In *Napoleon, For and Against* (New Haven, 1949), Pieter Geyl examines the writings of French historians on the Amiens issue as well as on others.

In addition to the question of "who," two other fundamental issues are involved. Was the party mainly responsible for the renewal of war "justified" in its actions? On what factors should a decision regarding this point be based?

This question leads us to the second issue, the "what," which is just as important and controversial as the "who." Again we find a difference of opinion, as to what developments really brought on a resumption of war. Here it is especially important not to seek or give a simplistic answer. Was it Napoleon's expansionism on the Continent and in the colonies —his establishment of control over Switzerland, for example, or his expedition to put down the native rising in Santo Domingo? Was it the scurrilous part of the British press, favored by the freedom under which it operated, or the asylum Britain gave to conspirators against Bonaparte's regime? Was it the Sebastiani report, a survey of conditions in the Near East designed solely for Bonaparte's information, but which stirred up a hornet's nest when he had it published because it criticized the English and stated that France could easily reconquer Egypt? Or was it Britain's attempt to rectify by a preventive war its error made in 1802? Was it Bonaparte's refusal to sign a commercial treaty which would have been advantageous to Britain? Was he in error in doing everything possible to build up French trade? Or was it Malta?

In view of the importance of this issue of Malta in the thinking of both sides and in the negotiations which preceded the rupture, and in view of the divergence of historical interpretation on Article X dealing with Malta, it is mandatory to know just what the treaty did say on this and related issues. Malta was to be returned to the Order of St. John[1] under the following stipulations: The Knights should return to Malta and elect a new grand master. [Nobody objected when the pope appointed a new

---

[1] A semireligious, semimilitary order founded during the Crusades. It owned Malta until 1798, when Bonaparte captured it on his way to Egypt. The British had later seized it.

one.] No Frenchman or Englishman was to be admitted to the Order. Paragraph four stated:

The forces of His Britannic Majesty will evacuate the island and its dependencies within three months of the exchange of ratifications ... provided that the Grand Master, or Commissioners fully authorized by the statutes of the Order, are in the aforesaid island to take possession of it, and that the force which is to be furnished by His Sicilian Majesty as hereafter stipulated, has arrived.

This garrison was to consist of 2,000 men, native to the Kingdom of the Two Sicilies, and was to remain on Malta for a year after its restoration to the Knights. The Order was to be permanently neutral, and Paragraph 6 stipulated that "The independence of Malta ... is put under the protection and guarantee of France, Great Britain, Austria, Spain, Russia, and Prussia," all of whom were invited in Paragraph 13 to accede to the stipulations. According to Article XI, France was to evacuate the Kingdom of Naples and the Papal States; England, in like manner, was to evacuate Porto-Ferrajo [on Elba] and all the ports and islands it occupied in the Mediterranean or Adriatic; and such evacuations were to take place within a month.

It is up to you to decide whether the various authors' statements about Malta are consistent with the terms of the treaty itself. Or whether each historian is consistent with his own material. For example, did all countries have to guarantee the independence of Malta before the evacuation clause became operative? Was it enough if five powers guaranteed Malta's independence even though the sixth failed to act? Did the evacuation clause stand alone, without reference to any guarantee?

Was England perhaps partly altruistic in defending the balance of power on the Continent? Is the assumption valid that the balance of power is inherently superior to other arrangements possible at that time? Should it have been extended to the sea?

In diplomatic history we are dealing with one of the most tangible forms of history, based largely on official documents. Yet it is easy to see that this problem raises more questions than we can expect to answer on the basis of a few excerpts. Perhaps its study leads us merely to agree with the conclusion of Thucydides over 2,000 years ago that "War is right against right." ...

A word about the excerpts. Since some of them span a good many pages, there may be an abrupt change of thought within an excerpt. They are arranged in chronological order. The first three are translations from the French by the editor; although the paragraphing has been changed slightly, the translations are as close to the original as is consistent with good English. In this way the reader may get some feel for the change in historical style, as well as becoming acquainted with different interpretations. The excerpts contain the names of numerous people. When it is not obvious from the context who a particular person is, a footnote identifies him.

1. ENGLAND GIVES AN ASSIST TO DESTINY

Albert Sorel was almost exclusively a diplomatic historian. His eight-volume masterpiece, L'Europe et la révolution française (1885–1904) was the first successful attempt to view the French Revolution in the broader framework of European history. It has understandably been extremely influential. Although the last four volumes, starting with the Directory and going to 1815, are inferior to the first four, suffering especially from a failure to use foreign archives, they are still valuable. Volume VI, La Trêve—Lunéville et Amiens (1800–1805), published in 1903, covers the time period in which we are interested for this problem. [The title for this excerpt was devised by the editor.]

ALBERT SOREL*

The general peace is concluded. It is the splendor of the Republic; but it is only a theatrical spectacle and a complete illusion....

Bonaparte tried... to keep the continent in the submission in which he had placed it and to use the freedom of movement he had given himself by seeking the advantages of peace in India and in America. He tried [it]; but it was precisely this effort to insist on the peace of Amiens in Europe and to develop it in France by commerce and industry, by expansion in the colonies, which made England decide to break it.... The Treaty of Amiens was, like many others, a precarious work, a clay building on shifting sand....

For it to last, Europe would have had to accept in it a character which none of the preceding treaties had presented.... It would have been necessary that this Europe... accept as a definitive establishment what

* From Albert Sorel, *L'Europe et la révolution française*, trans. R. B. Holtman, Vol. VI, pp. 202–7, 209–13, 253–6, 258, 260, 262, 264, 271, 278, 283–7, 290, 294, 296, 300.

it had fought as a monster, the Leviathan, in its plans and endeavors. It would have required France, still exalted from its Revolution, suddenly to stop short and calm the passions which for 10 years had been pushing it to spread out over Europe, and which precisely had brought it to this triumph. . . . Another Europe, another France, other peoples, other governments, would have been necessary; the history of this Europe would have had to turn out of the path it had been following since the 14th century, and the French Revolution flow backward on its course.

Let us add the man, finally, Bonaparte, whose person and character count in these conjunctures for as much as those of Pitt in England and Alexander in Russia, and who can no more be removed from the events which follow than from those which precede. Lovers of speculation, who explain his genius so easily, demand of this genius a work more prodigious than all those it has accomplished: not only to transform himself, but to modify the nature of things, to become a different man, in another Europe. . . .

He judged the circumstances for what they were, convinced that if he drew back a single step he would, at the same time, be invaded by Europe and renounced by France. His supremacy in Europe and his popularity in France seemed to him indissolubly bound. His genius did not lie in awaiting the events he feared. His skill lay in anticipating them. The policy of France in the Revolution which had raised him, which had made his glory and which remained his *raison d'être,* inexorably put him face to face with England. Thus, to keep the formidable peace, he was led to practice, as had Louis XIV, the invading peace. . . .

The manner in which the peace was welcomed at London left no illusion . . . the peace of Amiens had to bring England all the business advantages expected from it; if not, there would shortly be war. . . .

The treaty was going to be deliberated in parliament. It was necessary to find arguments to oppose to the critics, who, with growing violence, rose on every side. "The ministry," wrote Otto,[1] "thinks itself strong on all points except those which concern commerce. . . . Mr. Addington sees, as we do, that it would be absurd to think about a commercial treaty; but he ardently wants to draw nearer to us by partial and limited exchanges, by simple essays with a fixed time limit or revocable at will." But, on these commercial "preliminaries," no understanding was reached. . . .

There was no longer any talk of a treaty. The act of Amiens was qualified as a truce. . . . Addington expressed the regret which the aggrandize-

---

[1] Louis Guillaume Otto, at this time French ambassador to England, filled many diplomatic posts for Napoleon.

ments of France caused him; but it was not up to England to redress this evil. "For the moment, our duty is to husband our forces; let us reserve them for future opportunities, when we can resume the offensive with hope of success.... Let us not squander them without any chance of advantages." The treaty was ratified in these terms.

If it is true that Bonaparte did not believe in the permanence of the peace, no one had more interest than he in prolonging it as much as possible, at least to defer the rupture. He had to take possession of the acquired or restored colonies, consolidate his domination in Italy, wind up the affairs of Germany which were a complement of the treaty of Lunéville; to push forward and entrench himself so strongly on the continent that a new coalition would become, if not impossible, at least very difficult. He had to establish his government in France; he was in the process, under title of consul for life, of raising himself to the supreme power. National ratification would be obtained only by benefits; peace was the foremost of them.... There was talk only of maritime expeditions, for the "Isles," for Louisiana, for the Île de France, Madagascar, India. But everything had to be rebuilt, reorganized—the ships and the crews. Maritime war would have destroyed everything. Bonaparte thought he could gain the time to get ready.

Peace thus prolonged would contribute to the supremacy of France on the Continent, to the reestablishment of its industry and commerce. Hence Bonaparte's persistent refusal of any arrangement which would open the French market and that of its allied republics to English goods. The English demanded a commercial treaty because they thought it would enrich England and because it was for them the very object of the peace; Bonaparte refused it because he judged that it would impoverish France, suspend and stop its industrial renaissance....

"France," wrote an English historian, "remained dangerously strong, and it was not only the ardor of Bonaparte for conquest which cast a cloud over affairs, it was the rivalry of France and England, manifesting itself more violently than ever." How to expect, in these conditions, that England would evacuate Malta? What ministers would have dared abandon this dominant position in the Mediterranean and hand over to the French this sea whose key they held at Gibraltar? The struggle for the exploitation of the peace was more intense than the war itself. The struggle to open outlets for English products, thus to repress French commerce and crush the renascent French industry, was more bitter, also more popular, than the struggle against the Revolution. "England," reported Otto, "will be less restless when the gradual diminution of its profits has lessened its means to resume war."

That was Bonaparte's directing thought. How to expect, at that time, that he would strip himself of the means he had obtained to reduce the English to this point and to force them to give up the rivalry? He controlled them by Holland, Spain, Portugal, Germany, Italy, finally by Piedmont and Switzerland, which occupy the passes from France and Germany into Italy. He had promised the Emperor of Russia, whom he humored, to evacuate Rome and Naples. He did it... an added reason for him to demand the evacuation of Malta by the English, formally stipulated in the treaty. He had conformed to the treaty, let the English conform to it. For the rest, nothing had been promised, nothing written. Thus the whole debate came back to this island of Malta. The struggle for this little rock was going to become the symbol of secular rivalry....

The expedition to Santo Domingo turned into a disaster.... He [Bonaparte] no longer had any holds on England except through Europe; it was necessary for him to forestall the maneuvers of English and Russian policy, whose rapprochement was obvious. On September 11 he proclaimed the annexation of Piedmont, arranged and announced for over a year. The Batavians demanded the evacuation of their republic by French troops, the occupation having to cease when the war against England did.... Bonaparte answered that he would recall his troops only when the English had executed the Treaty of Amiens, and when he was sure that they were not intriguing at the Hague. He invited the Batavians to remain on guard, as he did, "against the dangers of every kind which the sudden departure of the French troops could bring."

This danger appeared in Switzerland. The French troops which had been occupying this republic withdrew in July. Immediately anarchy broke out; aristocrats and democrats, federalists and unionists, struggled for power, and the intrigues of the foreigners, Austrians, and especially English, resumed. Bonaparte could not tolerate them.... On September 30 he notified the Swiss of his mediation; Ney, with 30,000 men, was ready to enter the cantons. The Swiss submitted.

He concerned himself with the Mediterranean. He annexed Elba to France (August 26, 1802). He sent to Constantinople as ambassador the most turbulent, the most annoying of the malcontents and politicians of the army, Brune.... Then, Louisiana being henceforth forbidden, he came back to his favorite dream: Egypt. He sent there an officer whose intelligence and dexterity he appreciated, the Corsican Colonel Sebastiani.... General Decaen would receive an analogous mission for India.

Those were measures which neither England nor Russia intended to tolerate on the part of any French government, monarchy or republic, but especially republic....

The September 30 proclamation of Bonaparte to the Swiss furnished the pretext to call everything into question again: there would be discussion about the ambiguity of the preliminaries and the Treaty of Amiens. . . . In fact, at the time of the preliminaries they [the English] knew perfectly well the views of Bonaparte on Piedmont. . . . The truth is that they decided not to execute the Treaty of Amiens in the articles essential for them: India and Malta. . . .

He [Bonaparte] lay the blame on the English, on the provocations of their newspapers, on their refusal to expel George,[2] on the complicities they ascribed to their ministers, for the fury which he felt. At the same time, he armed very ostentatiously, for he was not able to arm fully, and he tried to instill fear by the rolling of cannons on the roads and the hammering of carpenters in the arsenals. . . .

This astonishing ultimatum [to revive the Western Empire] would have passed for the colossal blustering of some political bully if all the threats it contained had not been executed in less than five years and if they had not represented only a part of the great destruction of states which was beginning. Bonaparte concluded: *The whole Treaty of Amiens, nothing but the Treaty of Amiens,* that is to say, the evacuation of Malta, which is in the treaty; and no demand on Piedmont, the Italian Republic, Liguria, Etruria, Switzerland, which are not. To which Hawkesbury answered, when Otto communicated this terrible note to him on October 29, by this no less peremptory injunction: *The state of the continent as it was then* (at the time of the treaty), *and nothing but this state;* that is to say, no Piedmont nor Liguria annexed, nor Helvetia under protectorship; without a return to this state, England would keep Malta. . . .

But such was the fatalism which pushed France and England to renew their quarrel, as old as their history; the main deeds of Bonaparte, those which made peace most precious to him, were exactly the kind to precipitate war. . . .

Switzerland was the weak point of his argumentation, for if the treaty did not speak of it, the mediation was flagrantly later than the peace. The English did not fail to draw an argument from it. . . .

He [Bonaparte] took up one by one the grievances of England: Piedmont, Switzerland, they were trifles. They were in the natural order of things and easy to presume when negotiations were taking place at Amiens; the English should not have agreed then, or else have done what they had promised, namely at Malta. As for Egypt: "If I had felt the least inclination to seize it by force, I should have done so a month ago."

[2] George Cadoudal, a French royalist, a rebel against Bonaparte, and active in the conspiracy exploited by Bonaparte to become emperor.

After various delays, Bonaparte had decided to have Decaen leave. This general left Paris on February 16, and Brest March 6, with the small expedition destined to retake possession of the factories of India which the English were to restore. Bonaparte was therefore still thinking about the prolongation of the peace; he certainly was not getting ready to break it: to do so would have been to hand over to the English Decaen, his soldiers, and the squadron which took them. In the morning of March 11 he received the text of the royal message of the 8th. It meant war, and very soon. From the precipitation, the complexity of his actions in this morning of the 11th, it is clear that he was taken unaware. . . .

One reads in the royalist correspondence (April 4–12): "The news is of war. It is certain that Bonaparte does not want it; but it seems that England does." Bonaparte wrote to Melzi[3] on April 2: "I tell you, for yourself alone, that I do not think that this beginning of a quarrel will have any follow-up, and that I presume everything will be arranged according to the tenor of the treaty of Amiens. . . ."

Malta became the object of all Europe, the rock where the clouds accumulate and announce, according to the direction they take, good weather or storm. [Alexander] told Simon Vorontsov: "I must confess that on this occasion, at least in appearance, the English government has acted contrary to the letter of the treaty of Amiens, and that, juridically, it does not have the law in its favor, having obligated itself to the evacuation of Malta in terms already fulfilled or which can be when it so desires. . . ."

It would be necessary therefore, on land and on sea, to proceed to formidable armaments. . . . Millions would be needed, and the Treasury did not have any. . . . The cession of Louisiana, sold to the Yankees even before France had taken delivery of it, seemed an offense to the Spaniards, who had, as gentlemen, restored it to France . . . in exchange for Etruria.

"I find in Bonaparte," wrote Whitworth,[4] "a great desire to negotiate, and to avoid the rupture if possible." But the English cabinet attached conditions which London knew Bonaparte would never accept. . . .

It is therefore, on confession even of the partisans of the English, a preventive war, a war like that which they had made on Louis XV in 1755, and which Frederick had begun in 1756 against France and Austria. But, strong with these precedents which had brought them the peace of Paris in 1763, the true English peace; feeling themselves supported at Petersburg, at Berlin, at Vienna, at the Hague, even at Madrid, finally

---

[3] François Melzi d'Eril, vice president of the Italian Republic, of which Bonaparte was president.

[4] The English ambassador to France.

at Paris by almost the entire government of the Consul, by his family, by the army, by what they believed to be public opinion; seeing Bonaparte blamed, spied on, badly served if not yet betrayed in the true sense of the word; convinced that a setback would ruin him, that war would shake his power if it did not overthrow him; sure finally that this war would get for them the benefits which the peace denied them, the monopoly of trade and the supremacy of the seas—for all these reasons—the English pushed their demands, and, since they thought it easy, undertook to intimidate France, to humiliate and disconcert Bonaparte. . . .

But Bonaparte was at the end of his patience. The little maneuvers of the pacifically inclined seemed to him henceforth idle and compromising. . . .

On May 16 the king announced the rupture; he proclaimed an embargo, letters of marque. No consternation, or even uneasiness; it was a business transaction.

In reality, it was 700 years of English history continuing the struggle with 700 years of French history. The arms carried farther, the machines produced more quickly, the leaders of the state conceived more grandly, operated at a longer distance with larger masses of men; but the basis, the initial motive, the general aspect remained the same. William Pitt and Bonaparte were only the new names of these leaders of the seven-century war who were called William the Conqueror and Henry Plantagenet, the Black Prince and Duguesclin, Louis XIV and William of Orange, Chatham and La Fayette. The spirit of the French Revolution disturbing the Old World, the English temper conserving "established Europe;" the conquering proselytism of France, the commercial and mercantile expansion of England, were merely renewing, under a more impassioned form, this venerable rivalry.

2. THE RUPTURE (MARCH–MAY, 1803)

Driault, like Sorel a diplomatic historian, concentrated to a greater extent on the Napoleonic period. His most impressive work is a five-volume study of Napoléon et l'Europe (1910–27), *in which the volume cited here is the earliest. Although Driault clearly held Bonaparte responsible for the resumption of fighting, his overall attitude toward Napoleon was one of sympathetic understanding. He ascribed a much more important role to Bonaparte personally than did Sorel, whose out-*

look Driault thought belittled Napoleon. Driault felt that Napoleon had a deep and beneficial influence on Europe. His general thesis is that Napoleon wanted to be a new Charlemagne. With this idea, the last sentence of the excerpt agrees fully.

ÉDOUARD DRIAULT*

The essential clauses of the Treaty of Amiens dealt with Malta. Some attempts were made to apply them. The island was to be returned to the Knights of St. John, on some conditions it is useful to recall: the provisional establishment, for a year or more, of a Neapolitan garrison of 2,000 men, the nomination of a grand master, the guarantee and adhesion of the great powers, France, England, Austria, Russia, Spain, Prussia. Particularly, Paragraph 4 of Article X provided for the evacuation of the island by the English within six months of the arrival of the Neapolitan garrison....

On February 10, 1803, he [the pope] named as grand master the bailiff Tommasi, who lived at Messina and could quickly be at his post.... The British did not budge; they knew then of the Sebastiani report and did not lack other pretexts, or even good reasons, for keeping Malta.

In the Treaty of Amiens, the 13 paragraphs of Article X on Malta were an arsenal of pretexts not to evacuate the island.... Paragraphs 6 and 13 especially stipulated the guarantee of the six great powers; so long as the guarantee was not obtained, the British ministry considered it had the right to refuse restoration of the island to the Knights of St. John even if they had a grand master.... During the whole year which followed the Treaty of Amiens, the conditions which it placed on the evacuation of Malta were not met....

In the presence of new increases of French power, the idea of demanding compensations naturally sprang up among English statesmen.... The First Consul gave no thought to abstaining from any conquest so as to deny the British a pretext for keeping Malta, or even to profiting from the convenient principle of compensations by leaving them Malta in return for recognition of the new situation on the continent....

He had had inserted in the *Moniteur*: "England will have the treaty of Amiens, nothing but the treaty of Amiens." Unsupportable formula: if consequently he had occupied Portugal and Turkey, of which there was no question in the Treaty of Amiens, would England have had nothing to say about it? And Lord Hawkesbury answered Otto by another formula:

* From Édouard Driault, *La politique extérieure du premier consul, 1800–1803*, trans. R. B. Holtman, pp. 384, 387–88, 390, 393–99, 401–2, 404–10, 414–17. By permission of the Presses Universitaires de France.

"England wants the status of the continent as it was at the time of the peace of Amiens, and nothing but this status." The first formula claimed to bind only England to the conditions of the Treaty of Amiens; the second bound the two contracting powers to it together; it was literally more faithful to the treaty....

After the lively alert aroused by the affairs of Switzerland, calm had returned to the relations between France and England, and the year 1802 had ended in a political truce. The publication of the Sebastiani report at the end of January, then at the end of February the message of the First Consul to the Legislative Body, opened a new crisis, which, after three months of discussion, was to end in a final rupture and in 12 years of war. It is necessary to follow the stages of it with precision, since there are no events of greater importance in the whole history of Napoleonic politics. These negotiations can be thought of in two principal phases: that of March, 1803, where the two adversaries marked their respective positions, which seemed immediately irreconcilable; and that of May when the break was effected.

On March 8, in response to the message of the First Consul, the king of England addressed to Parliament another message in which, taking note of the great military preparations in the ports of France and Holland, he announced his intention to take precautionary measures; he declared ... that his government, however, would do everything to keep the peace.

The First Consul answered by a note, dictated by himself and corrected by his hand: There were no military preparations in the French or Dutch ports; it was a question at the very most of reinforcements destined for Santo Domingo....

At this time, the British government, to give satisfaction to Russia, even more than to execute the Treaty of Amiens, had Alexandria evacuated by its last troops.... The First Consul saw in it only weakness; he thought strongly about making England draw back further and removing once and for all its ability to oppose him.

Andréossy[1] received the order to demand officially the evacuation of Malta.... He made it positively understood that if the English did not evacuate the island of Malta and its dependencies, the First Consul would see himself forced to occupy Tarentum again, since "in the system of the Mediterranean, it is, to tell the truth, the equivalent of Malta, and since France had moreover evacuated it in the anticipation of a like conduct by the English with respect to Malta...."

The First Consul desired to base peace on the preponderance of

---

[1] Antoine-François Andréossi [or Andreossy], a general, succeeded Otto as ambassador to England.

France, established strongly enough to contain any attempt at disorder; the English wanted to base it on the balance of the great powers, the guarantee of their respective independence. How to reconcile such contrasts? . . .

Godoy,[2] the Prince of Peace, invited by the French ambassador, Beurnonville, to exert pressure on England to evacuate Malta, answered that avoidance of war depended only on the French government. . . . Russia, on its side . . . was already showing dispositions favorable to England. . . . Austria was not yet taking a stand, but its sentiments toward the First Consul were known. These circumstances inspired in the British ministry the answer it made to the demands of Bonaparte.

This answer, in a note of Lord Hawkesbury dated March 15, 1803, had capital importance. . . . It set forth once again the point of view of England on the subject of the evacuation of Malta; it recalled that this evacuation was bound to the execution of various stipulations which still remained in suspense. It added, on this subject:

The evacuation of Tarentum and of Brindisi has no relation with that of Malta; the French government had engaged itself to evacuate the kingdom of Naples by a treaty with the king of the Two Sicilies, prior to the Malta stipulation. . . .

It had been intended to conclude the treaty with respect to the state of things then existing; for the compensation then obtained by His Majesty has had to be calculated relative to the acquisitions of France at that time; and if the intervention of the French government in the general affairs of Europe since then, if its conduct toward Switzerland and Holland—whose independence it had guaranteed at the time of the conclusion of the treaty of peace—if the acquisitions which have been made by France in various places (notably in Italy) have extended its territory and increased its power, His Majesty would be justified, in accordance with the spirit of the treaty of peace, in claiming for these acquisitions equivalents which could serve as counterweight to the increase of the power of France. . . .

In short, the note opposed to the French policy of unlimited aggrandizement the European policy of compensations in the interest of equilibrium; it represented the political traditions of modern Europe. . . .

In truth, it is undeniable that England, in refusing to evacuate Malta, violated the letter of the Treaty of Amiens, although it could always point out the nonexecution of certain important stipulations. . . . The historical fact is that England could not not break the peace of Amiens, become by the policy of the First Consul fatal, mortal perhaps to its interests and its very existence. . . .

Bonaparte had two overwhelming reasons for not entering the path where England entreated him. He did not want to leave it Malta at any

---

[2] Manuel Godoy, Spanish statesman and royal favorite.

price, because from there it would always be able to bar the route to Egypt and to renew against every French armament some other battle of the Nile. . . . Furthermore, Bonaparte did not want to admit the principle of compensations which, once established, could be applied indiscriminately at every new increase of his power, and which was in basic contradiction with the essential hopes of his ambition. . . .

Will one not see in the sale of Louisiana, effected April 30, 1803, after some weeks of negotiation, a new proof that, from the first months of the year 1803, the First Consul was resolved on inexpiable war against the English, since he was already burning his bridges? . . .

On both sides, armaments were pushed with the greatest activity; war seemed inevitable. . . . Now he [Bonaparte] had a great interest in delaying the opening of hostilities. . . . But England had an exactly opposite interest, that of not letting things drag out, of not leaving to its enemy the advantages of a delay. . . . Especially, in continuing the negotiation, the First Consul gave himself the appearance of moderation and of pacific dispositions, and left to England the responsibility for the break. . . .

The royal message which on May 16, 1803, announced to the English chambers the break with France was welcomed by acclamation: in one year the peace had become so burdensome, so threatening for the future of England, that the news of the war was a veritable relief. . . .

Malta summed up for all the English the reasons of the war which was beginning: it was, so to speak, the symbol of the vital interests of England. . . .

It is suitable to seek the real responsibilities not in a unique and fragile diplomatic incident but in the comparison of the two policies. England was obliged to go to war by the continental and maritime enterprises of the First Consul. A year before, it had signed the peace because it was abandoned by its continental allies and because it had thought, with much wisdom, that it was prudent to await more favorable circumstances. In 1803 it declared war because the dispositions of the Continent were changed, because it knew that Austria, Prussia, and Russia would not indefinitely permit the aggrandizement of France, because it counted on them to stop and restrain Bonaparte on land while it assured itself the empire of the seas. . . .

France did not desire war; it did not applaud the rupture of the peace of Amiens. It felt that peace was necessary to consolidate its natural frontiers; to assimilate the new provinces which had been so easily annexed (and which, moreover, were never returned to their former holders); to accustom Europe to this territorial extension which it no longer contested, whatever may have been said about it; to keep the sympathies of the peoples who had been the invincible force of revolutionary France; to give the world the great example of moderation which is the finest and rarest virtue of the victorious; to remake its material fortune, compromised by the reversals of the last few years; to reunite on land and on sea, by industry and commerce, the admirable resources which its soil and its population constituted and which would have permitted it in a few years to dispute the domination of the oceans with England. Peace was for France the only means of conquering its rival, as war was for the latter the only means of not being conquered. And it was not a question of a dishonorable peace, of a peace at any price. . . .

England was fighting for the supremacy of the seas, which it considered, with some reason, as the condition of its political existence. France would have wished to keep its national existence in peace. But Bonaparte was the man of war; it had brought him to power; to it he entrusted his fortune, from it he demanded the Empire.

3. BONAPARTE'S ECONOMIC POLICY AND THE RUPTURE OF THE PEACE OF AMIENS

With the writings of Georges Lefebvre we for the first time deal with a historian basically hostile to Napoleon. Despite that fact, the author was professional enough to be judicious in his outlook. The study of the period of Napoleon (1935) which is here excerpted is the second volume Lefebvre wrote for the general history series, "Peuples et Civilisations"; the first (translated into English in two volumes) dealt with the French Revolution, the subject of his most important research and writing. For many years before his death in 1959, Lefebvre was considered the outstanding authority on the French Revolution. Particularly noteworthy are his studies of the French peasantry.

GEORGES LEFEBVRE[*]

That the Addington ministry was resolved seriously to try the experiment of peace and thought it of some duration is difficult to contest. . . .

---

[*] From Georges Lefebvre, *Napoléon*, trans. R. B. Holtman, pp. 146–58. By permission of Routledge and Kegan Paul and the Columbia University Press.

Yet the government counted some critics in its own majority: asserting that the peace was going to permit France to prepare a new assault on the British Empire, these Tories preached war to the knife, as had the Whigs a hundred years earlier. Part of the press sided with them, and the émigré Peltier helped them by vituperating against the Revolution and against the military dictatorship of Bonaparte. As between the two policies, businessmen hesitated. The peace wounded many interests: the war industries were coming to a halt; the monopoly on Baltic and German commerce, particularly that in colonial goods, was going to be lost; the restoration of the conquests meant a lessening of trade—for Dutch Guiana alone it was estimated at 10 million pounds; finally, after the peace was signed, prices fell so far that neutrals, principally the United States, also considered it a calamity.

It was, however, it was said, only a bad passing moment. The cries of alarm of the Tories did not fail to make an impression; but on the sea and in the colonies the danger did not seem imminent, and English opinion was not inclined to get stirred up regarding the continent. The real question was knowing whether Bonaparte would reopen France and the countries it controlled to British commerce, for no accord with the British was possible if business relations which they judged profitable were not established with them. In May, 1802, Hawkesbury repeated that in order to "interest as many people as possible in the peace," it was necessary to hasten to reestablish commercial exchanges. The key of the problem was therefore the economic policy of the First Consul. . . . Like Colbert, obliged in circumstances which are not without analogy to finance the enterprises of the Great King, Bonaparte found himself therefore converted to mercantilism: it was necessary for France to defend its metal by buying little and to procure some at the expense of the foreigner, either by increasing its export or by conquest. . . .

Of the Colbertist system, only tariff protection remained usable. A powerful number of interests recommended it. . . . Even before the peace of Amiens English contraband had been steadily denounced; when the war ended, it was still worse, and the cotton manufacturers especially announced that if there was a return to the treaty of 1786, the serious depression which had followed it would not fail to appear again. . . . Bonaparte had not withdrawn the prohibition against English goods pronounced by the Directory; moreover, on May 19, 1802, he had himself authorized to raise customs duties provisionally and had taxed colonial products, which were all English, at a minimum of 50 percent above the imports from French possessions.

Yet, at first he had not rejected the idea of concluding a commercial treaty with England. Coquebert de Montbret[1] and some commercial agents were sent there, and they received proposals to return to the treaty of 1786, with modifications and with permission for France to take temporary measures to husband its industry.... Between free competition and prohibition there was therefore room, with the consent of the English, for the reasonable protection which Chaptal [Minister of the Interior] proposed and which French industry needed. Between the unreasonable demands of its leaders and the national interest which required peace, it was up to Bonaparte to arbitrate, and he was the master of doing so. He finished, however, by rallying implicitly to prohibition.

It was because he did not want the peace to last. "A first consul," he had said to Thibaudeau, "does not resemble these kings by the grace of God who regard their States as a heritage... He needs dazzling actions and, as a result, war." Knowing the opinion of the nation, he would refrain from declaring it: "I have too much interest to leave the initiative to foreigners"; but, he added, "they will be the first to take up arms again." With such a frame of mind, he was inclined to encourage them to do so; in any case, the prohibition would permit preparing for hostilities by accumulating specie, until it became a weapon of war, as during the Revolution. More than ever, it was thought that the finances and economy of England, based on credit and on inflation, were vulnerable.... Without being deceived on the peril which threatened it, he let himself again be carried away to believing that France by itself could make them mortal.... There was no longer talk of a commercial treaty; ships were seized because items of British origin were found on them.... The English capitalists understood that the economic war would continue and became disgusted with a peace which yielded them nothing.

Colonial goods being one of the essential items of trade, it was natural that France retrieved as soon as possible the Antilles which were left to it.... If the English could scarcely find fault there, they became uneasy about Bonaparte's plans for Louisiana. An expedition was being prepared in the North Sea to take Victor there; the departure, fixed for March, 1803, was delayed. In the meantime, the Spaniards had closed the Mississippi to the Americans. As France was the ally of Spain and mistress of Holland, the Gulf of Mexico seemed to be at its disposal, and, as a result, the contraband with the Spanish Indies, where it was moreover possible that France would be granted a license to trade. All these prospects vanished without England's having to intervene. The Americans, who were already dreaming of taking Florida from Spain, did not want to hear any talk of French at New Orleans....

---

[1] Charles Étienne Coquebert de Montbret, a naturalist and physician, at this time named "Commissioner of Commercial Relations" by Bonaparte.

If it could not please the English to see France reconstitute a colonial empire for itself, perhaps they would not have renewed the war so soon to prevent it. Yet, it was necessary not to threaten them in their own possessions. That, however, is what Bonaparte did: he had in mind another great thought, aimed at the Mediterranean, that is to say, Egypt. The Treaty of Amiens had finally decided Turkey to sign a peace treaty with the French, June 26, 1802, and to open the Straits to them. Ruffin[2] immediately busied himself with reestablishing the consulates of the Levant. Pacts had also been concluded with the pasha of Tripoli in 1801 and with the bey of Tunis in 1802; in August, a fleet forced the dey of Algiers to imitate them. Already Constantinople was becoming uneasy about French intrigues in the Morea, at Janina, and among the Serbs; the Turkish government thought it was threatened with a partition. At the end of August Sebastiani left for Egypt, by way of Tripoli, and then visited Syria, trying everywhere to become intimate with the native chiefs. Cavaignac had been sent to Mascate and Decaen was destined for India with an important general staff, fit to serve as a cadre for sepoys. . . . From all that the English concluded that Bonaparte was meditating a new attack against Egypt and India, and that it was wise neither to let him finish his preparation nor especially to abandon Malta. To keep the island was to violate the Treaty of Amiens.

The continental policy of Bonaparte furnished the pretext for it. Despite the entreaties of Schimmelpenninck,[3] he refused to evacuate Holland, alleging that the conditions of peace were not fulfilled. He had abandoned the Neapolitan ports and the Papal States, but he annexed the island of Elba in August, 1802, Piedmont in September, and occupied Parma in October, after the death of the duke. In Switzerland, scarcely had the French left when Reding[4] roused the mountain cantons to revolt in the night of August 27–28 and convoked a diet at Schwyz. Zurich, Berne, Fribourg fell into his hands. The government . . . had no choice but to appeal to Bonaparte. On September 30 Bonaparte imposed his mediation and disarmament. Ney entered Switzerland; the diet, getting only fine words from the British and Austrians, dispersed, and Reding was arrested. An assembly met at Paris, on December 10; Bonaparte had it discuss his project with some senators and draw up the special constitutions of the cantons, which were annexed to it to constitute the Act of Mediation of February 19, 1803. . . . The following September 27 the Helvetic Confederation signed a 50-year treaty of defensive alliance with France and renewed the capitulations for the recruiting of four regiments of 4,000

---

[2] Pierre-Jean-Marie Ruffin, a French diplomat in Turkey.

[3] Rutger Jan Schimmelpenninck, Grand-Pensionary of the Batavian Republic.

[4] Aloys Reding, Swiss magistrate and general.

men each. But it had no army, and Bonaparte did not even permit it to create a general staff.

During this time, French influence was making giant steps in Germany by means of arranging the indemnities promised the princes formerly owning land on the left bank of the Rhine.... Bonaparte had agreed with Alexander to settle the affair in common. In fact, all the German princes, the king of Prussia at their head, negotiated at Paris and bribed Talleyrand, who received 10 to 15 millions, to assure themselves the finest possible share....

The dislocation of Germany could profit only France: all southern Germany had turned to it to oppose the Hapsburgs. Prussia had gained much, but not so much as it wanted, having refused Hanover and the French alliance so as not to embroil itself with England. With the peace, its domination of northern Germany had disappeared....

England, powerless, was a witness to these inversions; they were not contrary to the letter of the Treaty of Amiens, but England did not consider them consonant with its spirit. As it further knew that the fate of Switzerland was preoccupying Russia and Austria and that the latter was not consoled about having lost Germany as well as Italy, England was cheered at the same time as irritated: as Addington had foreseen, England was going to regain allies. Up to October, 1802, its relations with France had remained rather good.... The Italian annexations, and especially the intervention in Switzerland, which caused the same sensation as that of 1798, provoked the about-face. Hawkesbury expressed his "profound regret." "We want peace ... but we need the assistance of the French government." In his mind was defined precisely the idea that every aggrandizement of France demanded a compensation. The interest of France advised at least delay; it had only 43 ships of the line and was going to build another 23 which would be finished only in 1804.... Talleyrand ... threatened: "The first cannon shot can suddenly create the Gallic empire" and determine Bonaparte to "revive the empire of the West." As Hawkesbury did not insist and let the ambassadors, Andréossy and Whitworth, go to their posts, this apparent weakness merely excited the First Consul.

In reality, the submission of Hawkesbury was purely provisional. "It would be impossible in the present circumstances, even admitting that it was prudent," he wrote to Whitworth on November 25, 1802, "to engage the country in a war by invoking some one of the aggressions committed by France. Our policy must be to seek to make of these aggressions the basis of a defensive system for the future jointly with Russia and Austria." As early as October 27 he had, in fact, proposed an alliance to the former for the maintenance of the status quo in Europe. Occupied then in settling the affairs of Germany in concert with France, Alexander at first turned a deaf ear. But the eastern policy of Bonaparte ended in stirring him, too, and, like the Egyptian expedition of 1798, it drew Russia closer to England: if Malta could not come back to Russia, better that it be English than French. On February 8, 1803, Hawkesbury learned, therefore, that the Tsar wanted to see the evacuation postponed. . . . The next day Hawkesbury told Whitworth that England demanded some "reassuring explanations" before abandoning the island. . . .

For the moment, England was justified in not leaving Malta, for the agreed-on conditions were not fulfilled: Alexander had surrounded his guarantee with reservations which implied a revision of the treaty, and Prussia had imitated him. But Addington was now determined to keep the island, and henceforth prevailed in speeding up events. On March 15 he demanded it for 10 years, in compensation for the territorial gains of France, to which Talleyrand replied by offering to negotiate within the framework of the peace of Amiens. Meanwhile, Hawkesbury was informed on April 14 that Russia, while again declining an alliance, promised its aid if Turkey was attacked and renewed its advice with respect to Malta. On the 26th, Whitworth handed Paris an ultimatum.

The resolute attitude suddenly adopted by the English had disconcerted the entourage of the First Consul. Fouché supposedly said to him in the Senate: "You are yourself, as are we, a result of the Revolution, and war calls everything back into question." Bonaparte himself had been agitated by the uneasiness of Russia; on March 11 he had written to the Tsar to reassure him and to ask him to calm the English. He now requested his mediation and proposed to leave Malta to Great Britain for a year or two, after which it would be handed back to Russia. Addington answered that Russia would not accept, and Whitworth left Paris May 12.

In reality, Alexander had accepted the mediation; not only had Bonaparte's offer flattered him, but it would have suited him to occupy Malta to remove the Orient from England, as from France. To Vorontsov, who demanded explanations, Addington answered that he had not had time to consult the king. His stiff attitude, which contrasted so strongly with his past conduct, can be explained only by the intervention of the war party and, perhaps, of Pitt. It did not make a good impression, and the Whigs had the game in their hands in denouncing it; England still needed some time to be a match for the circumstances; but Bonaparte was so redoubtable that its restoration was much more rapid than during the Revolution.

The responsibility for the split has been passionately discussed. If the provocations of Bonaparte are incontestable, it is no less true that England had broken the treaty and taken the initiative of a preventive war as soon as it had been able to hope for the cooperation of Russia. It justified itself by concern for defending the European balance. But there was no question of extending the equilibrium to the ocean, the God of the Bible having created it in order for it to be English. Between Bonaparte and England, there was in reality only the conflict of two imperialisms.

4. THE COLLAPSE OF THE
AMIENS SETTLEMENT

One volume, although far from being all that he has written, made the historical reputation of Harold C. Deutsch, at present chairman of the department of history at the University of Minnesota. That volume, published in 1938, is the one under consideration here. The outgrowth of his doctoral dissertation, it is a sound piece of work based on thorough research. Since World War II Professor Deutsch has been primarily interested in more recent developments, particularly those affecting Western Europe. Among his postwar writings are Our Changing German Problems, Problems of Western Europe, America's Stake in Western Europe, The New Europe, the Common Market, and the United States.

HAROLD C. DEUTSCH*

The response in England to the news of the conclusion of the definitive treaty was far less favorable than the reception of the preliminaries had been. . . . Nowhere do we find a trace of genuine satisfaction or optimism, a disposition which augured ill for the future.

While the news of the conclusion of the definitive treaty hardly created much vocal enthusiasm in France, there can be no doubt but that it met with universal approbation. As for the First Consul, the peace was too great a personal triumph to provoke in him any reaction other than satisfaction. . . . Just how permanent he wished and expected the peace to be is of course another question. . . .

* Reprinted by permission of the publishers from Harold Charles Deutsch, *The Genesis of Napoleonic Imperialism,* Cambridge, Massachusetts: Harvard University Press, Copyright 1938, by the President and Fellows of Harvard College; renewed 1966 by Harold Charles Deutsch; pp. 36–37, 95–97, 100, 106, 111, 115–20, 122–23, 125, 127–30, 135, 139–41, 147.

The question of the responsibility for the rupture of the peace of Amiens has been the subject of endless discussions, the evidence, as in the case of all "war guilt" questions, being made to serve one point of view or another. Was the renewal of the conflict inevitable or not? To those who maintain that it was, the personal element involved is of minor significance. . . . Probably the larger number of historians, however, reject this deterministic viewpoint; to them the personality of Bonaparte is of much greater importance. This is the opinion even of such balanced critics as Driault, who feel compelled to admit that his great program of expansion after the return of general peace was chiefly responsible for its rupture. If France had remained within her natural limits of the Rhine and the Alps, say they, England would not have taken up arms again, for then she could never have had any prospect of finding allies on the Continent. While there is much to be said for this contention, the solution of the problem is hardly so simple. . . . One cannot hold the First Consul exclusively responsible for the aggressive features of the French policy in 1802. . . . The peace itself was like a proclamation of the freedom of France to do what she wished on the Continent. Britain had thereby allowed herself to be inveigled into a bargain which she later felt herself incapable of living up to, for the peace she had signed was the utter negation of every principle for which her traditions commanded her to fight to the bitter end. Not only was the balance of power on the Continent overthrown, but all the axioms of this doctrine were equally strained. In addition to this, the great French colonial empire, which the cherished peace of 1763 was thought to have abolished for all time, seemed on the point of being reestablished.

Yet . . . there would hardly have been sufficient feeling to bring about a rupture if there had not been another consideration which affected the island kingdom even more closely. The chief reason for the entrance of Britain into the war against France in 1793 had been the occupation of Belgium and the consequent opening of the Scheldt. Her motive was defensive in a commercial as well as a military sense, for she felt her continental trade threatened at one of its principal points of contact. . . . England was therefore inclined to accept a peace which sacrificed her influence on the Continent, but only if her old commercial relations were not thereby endangered. As soon as peace with the Republic seemed probable, the hope that it would be accompanied by a great expansion of trade with the Continent was frequently uttered. . . . It was confidently expected that France would show little reluctance about renewing the commercial treaty of 1786, which had been so very advantageous to England. . . . The First Consul on his part was perfectly aware that France herself would benefit by a reasonable arrangement, for in the uncertain state of things commerce could not flourish. . . .

The more general question as to how far Bonaparte worked for or welcomed the renewal of war is more difficult of analysis. It is quite probable that the First Consul was honestly convinced that a frank rapprochement with England was out of the question, and it is certainly true that only a complete change in his political system could have made any such possible. . . .

Bonaparte was determined to remain at peace with Great Britain for some years to come, though it is also evident that he would insist upon the maintenance of the Amiens settlement. . . .

Generally speaking, the relations between France and England at the time of the exchange of ambassadors were rather better than they had been since the signature of the definite peace. The pacific intentions of the First Consul are amply evidenced by the instructions given Andréossy, while the Addington ministry perceived that the only hope of its preservation lay in the maintenance of peace. . . .

On December 1 he [Whitworth] philosophizes on the position of the First Consul. . . . His conclusion: "It is not the wish of this Government to come to a rupture with Great Britain, but it will always avail itself of our security to carry its projects into effect." Much can be said for this point of view—Bonaparte was anxious to avoid war, but he was prone to take the utmost advantage of every opportunity which the negligence or lethargy of his opponents provided for him.

The most disastrous influence upon the course of the negotiations was the constant irritation of the First Consul by the attacks of the British press. A close examination of the sources can leave little doubt about the complete sincerity of his feelings. All of the First Consul's most intimate associates testify to his extreme sensitiveness to newspaper criticism. . . . On more than one occasion the temper or intractability of the First Consul can be ascribed to a particularly stinging newspaper article, rather than immoderation concerning the point under discussion. . . .

It is difficult to pronounce a definite judgment on the nature and purpose of this [Sebastiani's] fatal report. The idea that Bonaparte then wished to goad England to war is the most difficult explanation to accept, for it would have been the worst possible time for such an adventure. . . . The view that the report was intended as a warning to England if she should not fulfill her treaty engagements is based on much better ground. . . . In a sense the report may also have been intended as a warning to Russia, whose reluctance in accepting the guarantee of Malta provided the British with a ready excuse for postponing the evacuation of the island. Yet even these motives hardly provide sufficient explanation for an act which was far more apt to irritate than to admonish. The key to the problem lies in the ever reappearing factor of the English press outrages.... That the publication of the Sebastiani report was an unparalleled diplomatic blunder soon became evident. The reaction in London and throughout England was electrical....

Matters were, in fact, fast approaching a crisis. A factor of the greatest importance in stiffening the backs of the British was the rapidly changing attitude of Russia.... What particularly irritated Alexander was the realization that he had been completely outwitted in the question of the German indemnities, in which his assistance had so materially contributed to the establishment of French influence in South Germany.... Russia therefore turned more and more to England, in whose interest she was really acting in refusing to accept the guarantee of Malta....

At London Andréossy made despairing efforts to arrive at a modus vivendi on the score of questions which divided the two governments.... Bonaparte was given the impression that in England two definitely opposed parties, the one pacific, the other bellicose, stood arrayed against each other, when, as a matter of fact, his threats operated as a bond of union between the various political factions....

On March 8 came the reply to the threats of the First Consul which the British public had anxiously been awaiting. George III appeared before the Houses of Parliament and read his famous "Speech from the Throne," the tenor of which can be sufficiently judged from the first line: "His Majesty thinks it necessary to acquaint the House of Commons that as very considerable military preparations are carrying on in the ports of France and Holland, he has judged it expedient to adopt additional measures of precaution for the security of his dominions." It was recommended that the militia be called out and a levy of 10,000 additional men for the navy be ordered. These measures were actually adopted by parliament on the 11th, and that same night press gangs were scouring the streets and inns of London for sailors....

The argument of contemporaries and certain historians that this action was on a par with the Consular Exposé is unconvincing. While the First Consul had played with indirect threats, England here made a move which, according to diplomatic usage, was a preliminary step to war, basing it on a statement which was soon shown to be entirely false....

On March 13 occurred the famous scene in the Tuileries in which Bonaparte, contrary to all rules of diplomatic courtesy, made a violent attack upon the British ambassador....

Whitworth seems to have been convinced that this brusquerie was due entirely to a loss of temper, and rightly judges that Bonaparte was soon ashamed of it. . . . This was, in fact, the last occasion upon which the First Consul's amateurish precipitation aggravated the relations between France and England; from now on his conduct never ceased to be conciliatory.

But the reply to the overtures of which Andréossy had expected so much was another ultimatum repeating in essence what had been demanded before. . . . Britain was making a last-minute attempt to appear as the protector of the European equilibrium. . . .

England certainly saw all the powers in the light of pawns to be used against France; in how far was this attitude reciprocated? The answer provides the solution for the problem as to why Britain forced France again to take up arms after barely a year of peace. In times of peace England had no ready means of pressure upon France in continental affairs, for the Republic of 1810 was too strong to be restrained by the usual means of diplomacy. This was very well appreciated by Bonaparte, who had been making almost frantic efforts during the last month of negotiation to avoid a rupture. Yet no one was convinced more than he of the inevitable and fatalistic conflict between the two countries. He has been criticized for refusing to make a peace which provided a solid basis for future amity and cooperation, but who can say that this was possible? France as she was then . . . was straining every sacred principle of British policy. The lordship on land has never been able to live in peace with the lordship of the sea. . . .

Britain did not go to war to protect the Continent. This might have been the case in October or November, when, for a moment, public pressure had induced the ministry to take a stand which would have resulted in war if the First Consul had not acted so rapidly in the occupation of Switzerland. After that his expansive activity on the Continent had ceased, where, indeed, further "conquests in peace" were scarcely feasible. At the time of the rupture the colonial expansion of France was also no longer a cause of much apprehension to the British, for the affairs of Santo Domingo were in the worst state possible, while Louisiana had already been sold to the United States.

What, then, were the motives of the Addington ministry in going to war in the spring of 1803? After a close study of British politics of the period it is difficult to avoid the conclusion that the ministry was principally interested in its own preservation. . . .

The claim sometimes brought forward that Bonaparte desired the conflict with England in the hope that sooner or later a profitable continental war would become attached to it hardly merits refutation. . . . The only rational explanation, let us repeat, is that the rupture with England proved in every way inopportune to the head of the Republic. The Consulate was essentially a period of reconstruction; in two years of peace it had raised France to heights unknown in the annals of modern history. War could only tear down and disturb, and while it later became almost an integral part of the Napoleonic system, it was the conflict with England which gave its permanent military tone to the Empire.

5. THE BALANCE OF POWER DURING THE WARS

Geoffrey Bruun is co-author of one of the most successful college fresh-man history textbooks, and he has authored or co-authored three other texts. As a result he has been able, after a teaching career at New York University, to devote himself for the past several years to research and writing. In addition to a Berkshire series volume on The Enlightened Despots, *he has written biographies of Saint-Just and Clemenceau. He is a long-time student of the Napoleonic period; in 1938 he completed* Europe and the French Imperium, 1799–1814, *the volume on Napoleon in "The Rise of Modern Europe" series. Although his general outlook is somewhat critical of Napoleon, the following excerpt shows that he is not one-sided.*

GEOFFREY BRUUN*

The definitive treaty of Amiens (March 27, 1802) was negotiated by Joseph Bonaparte and the Marquis Cornwallis. It confirmed the prelimi-naries, stipulating further that the British would withdraw from Malta within three months after ratification and the island would be restored to the Knights of Malta under a guarantee of all the great powers. The rights and territories of the Ottoman Empire and of Portugal were to be respected save that France kept Portuguese Guiana. Prisoners of war were to be exchanged and there was henceforth to be peace and friendship between Great Britain and the French Republic.

In reality the peace of Amiens could hardly be considered more than a truce for it omitted the most critical questions that divided Britain and

* From *The New Cambridge Modern History,* Vol. IX, *War and Peace in an Age of Upheaval, 1793–1830* (Cambridge, Eng., 1965), ed. by C. W. Crawley, pp. 261–64. By permission of the publishers, the Cambridge University Press.

France. While admitting the right of the British to concern themselves with the affairs of some maritime states (Spain, Portugal, the Batavian Republic) Bonaparte refused to discuss with them the fate of the Belgian Provinces, Savoy, or Switzerland. In both London and Paris the prospect of peace after a decade of conflict excited joyful popular demonstrations, but in Britain the enthusiasm cooled rapidly. When the terms of the definitive treaty became known in the spring of 1802 the comments, in parliament and out, held a note of skepticism and disappointment that boded ill for the duration of the peace. Three developments that gathered momentum during 1802 hardened the British determination to resume hostilities.

One consequence of the peace that shocked and sobered British opinion was the revelation of Bonaparte's colonial ambitions. With Louisiana to control the mouth of the Mississippi and French Guiana expanded to the mouth of the Amazon, he could control the two greatest rivers of the Americas and held the potential bases for a Caribbean empire. France had obtained the Spanish half of Haiti in 1795, regained Louisiana in 1800, and Tobago at Amiens. In November, 1801, taking prompt advantage of the maritime truce, Bonaparte dispatched an expedition under General Leclerc to suppress the Negro insurrection in Haiti. Leclerc and most of his troops succumbed to yellow fever, and the ill-success of the Haitian project cooled Bonaparte's interest in New World conquests. But he pressed other ventures equally alarming to the British government. The recovery of the French posts in India provided him with an excuse to send troops and ships there, and the force that sailed appeared more formidable than the circumstances warranted. In April, 1802, a French expedition explored the southern coast of Australia, claiming it as *Terre Napoléon*. At the same time Bonaparte indicated that he had not abandoned his interest in the Ottoman Empire. . . .

For British manufacturers and merchants the suspension of hostilities provided more grievances than it alleviated. Their hope that peace would bring a renewal of the commercial treaty of 1786 was unrealistic. . . . Yet even a statesman as well informed as the Earl of Minto ventured to predict that "Our commerce will penetrate deep into France itself and flourish at Paris." Instead of expanding with the return of peace, however, British foreign trade declined. . . . When peace ended the naval blockade the ships of France and her client states renewed contacts with their restored colonies. That Bonaparte should seek to protect French manufacturers from the competition of the more advanced British factories was understandable, but it exasperated the British to find that high tariffs virtually excluded their wares from Holland, Spain, and Italy also. . . .

The disappointment felt in British business circles sharpened to apprehension as Bonaparte made it clear that the general peace would bring, not a cessation, but an acceleration of French expansion in Europe. In Talleyrand's judgment, Bonaparte's moves after Amiens revealed for the first time an immoderation that increased with each of his subsequent successes. . . . Following a secret understanding with Russia (October 10, 1801) he encouraged a radical reassignment of German territories. . . . Representatives of the German states, meeting in the Diet of Ratisbon, accepted the changes, and Austria, yielding under pressure, granted its consent (December 26, 1802).

The mounting dissatisfaction in London, and the chagrin and humiliation felt at Vienna, strained the newly established peace, but Bonaparte saw no reason to check his course. His achievement of a successful peace, and his conclusion of a Concordat with the papacy (promulgated on Easter Day, April 18, 1802), had raised his popularity in France to a new peak. A second plebiscite (August 2, 1802) made him consul for life; a third, two years later, was to make him emperor. Such success might well have corrupted the sanest of mortals. It helps to account for his peremptory attitude in 1803 and 1804, which hastened the collapse of the precarious peace.

Malicious and scandalous attacks by the British press on Bonaparte and his family provoked his ire, and the frosty reserve of Lord Whitworth, British ambassador to France, did little to soothe it. When Whitworth protested against the continued expansion of the French frontiers, Bonaparte dismissed Piedmont and Switzerland as "bagatelles." The British, he pointed out, had violated the treaty by refusing to evacuate Malta and Alexandria as stipulated. At a diplomatic reception, March 13, 1803, he upbraided Whitworth violently, declaring that the English wanted war; and on May 2 Whitworth asked for his passports. Despite the efforts of Talleyrand and Joseph Bonaparte, who sought to prolong the negotiations, Whitworth left Paris 10 days later and crossed the Channel on May 17. The following day the British government issued a declaration of war. It is still a matter of debate whether Bonaparte or the Addington cabinet should bear the heavier responsibility for the rupture.

If the British had delayed another year or longer they would almost certainly have been forced to resume hostilities under graver handicaps. With the Netherlands, Spain, and northern Italy subordinate to his wishes, Bonaparte planned to raise his naval forces to equality with those of England. Whether a prolongation of the peace would have enabled him to do so is questionable, but it seems clear that the resumption of war came sooner than he anticipated. On March 6, 1803, he allowed an expedition under General Decaen to sail for India from Brest, with instructions that did not seriously envisage renewed hostilities before September, 1804. Ten days later a swift ship followed to warn Decaen to seek Mauritius instead. The precipitate sale of Louisiana to the United States suggested a similar unanticipated urgency, for the negotiations were completed in three weeks (April 12–May 2, 1803). Whatever hopes Bonaparte may have nursed that he might come in time to match the British at sea, he could not ignore the fact that they held a two-to-one superiority in 1803, and this sufficed to strangle his colonial projects. Thenceforth, Bonaparte's sphere of operations was restricted to Europe, a limitation of portentous significance for world history. "Viewed from the standpoint of racial expansion," John Holland Rose concluded, "the renewal of war in 1803 is the greatest event of the century."

The conclusion that British recalcitrance disrupted Bonaparte's plans is strengthened by the fury of his retaliation. On May 22 he ordered that all Englishmen between 18 and 60 found in France should be arrested as prisoners of war. This savage reprisal against civilians flouted accepted practice, the more so as the British ambassadors to Turkey and Denmark were among the unfortunate victims. The arrest of Sir George Rumbold at Hamburg further violated the principle of diplomatic immunity and roused even the hesitant Frederick William III of Prussia to forward a vigorous protest to Paris.